T0367994

KNOWLEDGE MINING USING INTELLIGENT AGENTS

Advances in Computer Science and Engineering: Texts

Editor-in-Chief: Erol Gelenbe *(Imperial College)*
Advisory Editors: Manfred Broy *(Technische Universitaet Muenchen)*
Gérard Huet *(INRIA)*

Published

Vol. 1 Computer System Performance Modeling in Perspective:
A Tribute to the Work of Professor Kenneth C. Sevcik
edited by E. Gelenbe (Imperial College London, UK)

Vol. 2 Residue Number Systems: Theory and Implementation
by A. Omondi (Yonsei University, South Korea) and
B. Premkumar (Nanyang Technological University, Singapore)

Vol. 3: Fundamental Concepts in Computer Science
edited by E. Gelenbe (Imperial College Londo, UK) and
J.-P. Kahane (Université de Paris Sud - Orsay, France)

Vol. 4: Analysis and Synthesis of Computer Systems (2nd Edition)
by Erol Gelenbe (Imperial College, UK) and
Isi Mitrani (University of Newcastle upon Tyne, UK)

Vol. 5: Neural Nets and Chaotic Carriers (2nd Edition)
by Peter Whittle (University of Cambridge, UK)

Vol. 6: Knowledge Mining Using Intelligent Agents
edited by Satchidananda Dehuri (Fakir Mohan University, India) and
Sung-Bae Cho (Yonsei University, Korea)

Advances in Computer Science and Engineering: Texts   Vol. 6

KNOWLEDGE MINING
USING INTELLIGENT
AGENTS

editors

Satchidananda Dehuri
Fakir Mohan University, India

Sung-Bae Cho
Yonsei University, Korea

Imperial College Press

ICP

Published by

Imperial College Press
57 Shelton Street
Covent Garden
London WC2H 9HE

Distributed by

World Scientific Publishing Co. Pte. Ltd.
5 Toh Tuck Link, Singapore 596224
USA office: 27 Warren Street, Suite 401-402, Hackensack, NJ 07601
UK office: 57 Shelton Street, Covent Garden, London WC2H 9HE

British Library Cataloguing-in-Publication Data
A catalogue record for this book is available from the British Library.

KNOWLEDGE MINING USING INTELLIGENT AGENTS
Advances in Computer Science and Engineering: Texts – Vol. 6

ISBN-13 978-1-84816-386-7
ISBN-10 1-84816-386-X

Typeset by Stallion Press
Email: enquiries@stallionpress.com

Printed in Singapore.

PREFACE

The primary motivation for adopting intelligent agent in knowledge mining is to provide researcher, students and decision/policy makers with an insight of emerging techniques and their possible hybridization that can be used for dredging, capture, distributions and utilization of knowledge in the domain of interest e.g., business, engineering, and science. Knowledge mining using intelligent agents explores the concept of knowledge discovery processes and in turn enhances the decision making capability through the use of intelligent agents like ants, bird flocking, termites, honey bee, wasps, etc. This book blends two distinct disciplines–data mining and knowledge discovery process and intelligent agents based computing (swarm intelligence + computational Intelligence) – in order to provide readers with an integrated set of concepts and techniques for understanding a rather recent yet pivotal task of knowledge discovery and also make them understand about their practical utility in intrusion detection, software engineering, design of alloy steels, etc.

Several advances in computer science have been brought together under the title of knowledge discovery and data mining. Techniques range from simple pattern searching to advanced data visualization. Since our aim is to extract knowledge from various scientific domain using intelligent agents, our approach should be characterized as "knowledge mining".

In Chapter 1 we highlight the intelligent agents and their usage in various domain of interest with gamut of data to extract domain specific knowledge. Additionally, we will discuss the fundamental tasks of knowledge discovery in databases (KDD) and a few well developed mining methods based on intelligent agents.

Wu and Banzhaf in Chapter 2 discuss the use of evolutionary computation in knowledge discovery from databases by using intrusion detection systems as an example. The discussion centers around the role of evolutionary algorithms (EAs) in achieving the two high-level primary goals of data mining: prediction and description. In particular, classification and regression tasks for prediction and clustering tasks for description. The use of EAs for feature selection in the pre-processing step is also discussed. Another goal of this chapter was to show how basic elements in EAs, such as representations, selection schemes, evolutionary operators, and fitness functions have to be adapted to extract accurate and useful patterns from data in different data mining tasks.

Natural evolution is the process of optimizing the characteristics and architecture of the living beings on earth. Possibly evolving the optimal characteristics and architectures of the living beings are the most complex problems being optimized on earth since time immemorial. The evolutionary technique though it seems to be very slow is one of the most powerful tools for optimization, especially when all the existing traditional techniques fail. Chapter 3, contributed by Misra *et al.*, presents how these evolutionary techniques can be used to generate optimal architecture and characteristics of different machine learning techniques. Mainly the two different types of networks considered in this chapter for evolution are artificial neural network and polynomial network. Though lots of research has been conducted on evolution of artificial neural network, research on evolution of polynomial networks is still in its early stage. Hence, evolving these two networks and mining knowledge for classification problem is the main attracting feature of this chapter.

A multi-objective optimization approach is used by Chen *et al*, in Chapter 4 to address the alloy design problem, which concerns finding optimal processing parameters and the corresponding chemical compositions to achieve certain pre-defined mechanical properties of alloy steels. Neurofuzzy modelling has been used to establish the property prediction models for use in the multi-objective optimal design approach which is implemented using Particle Swarm Optimization (PSO). The intelligent agent like bird flocking, an inspiring source of PSO is used as the search algorithm, because its population-based approach fits well with the needs of multi-objective optimization. An evolutionary adaptive PSO algorithm is introduced to improve the performance of the standard PSO. Based on the established tensile strength and impact toughness prediction models, the proposed optimization algorithm has been successfully applied to the optimal design of heat-treated alloy steels. Experimental results show that the algorithm can locate the constrained optimal solutions quickly and provide a useful and effective knowledge for alloy steels design.

Dehuri and Tripathy present a hybrid adaptive particle swarm optimization (HAPSO)/Bayesian classifier to construct an intelligent and more compact intrusion detection system (IDS) in Chapter 5. An IDS plays a vital role of detecting various kinds of attacks in a computer system or network. The primary goal of the proposed method is to maximize detection accuracy with a simultaneous minimization of number attributes, which inherently reduces the complexity of the system. The proposed method can exhibit an improved capability to eliminate spurious features from huge amount of data aiding researchers in identifying those features that are solely responsible for achieving high detection accuracy. Experimental results demonstrate that the hybrid intelligent method can play a major role for detection of attacks intelligently.

Today networking of computing infrastructures across geographical boundaries has made it possible to perform various operations effectively irrespective of application domains. But, at the same time the growing misuse of this connectively in the form of network intrusions has jeopardized the security aspect of both the data that are transacted over the network and maintained in data stores. Research is in progress to detect such security threats and protect the data from misuse. A huge volume of data on intrusion is available which can be analyzed to understand different attack scenarios and devise appropriate counter-measures. The DARPA KDDcup'99 intrusion data set is a widely used data source which depicts many intrusion scenarios for analysis. This data set can be mined to acquire adequate knowledge about the nature of intrusions thereby one can develop strategies to deal with them. In Chapter 6 Panda and Patra discuss on the use of different knowledge mining techniques to elicit sufficient information that can be effectively used to build intrusion detection systems.

Fukuyama *et al.*, present a particle swarm optimization for multi-objective optimal operational planning of energy plants in Chapter 7. The optimal operational planning problem can be formulated as a mix-integer nonlinear optimization problem. An energy management system called FeTOP, which utilizes the presented method, is also introduced. FeTOP has been actually introduced and operated at three factories of one of the automobile companies in Japan and realized 10% energy reduction.

In Chapter 8, Jagadev *et al.*, discuss the feature selection problems of knowledge mining. Feature selection has been the focus of interest for quite some time and much work has been done. It is in demand in areas of application for high dimensional datasets with tens or hundreds of thousands of variables are available. This survey is a comprehensive overview of many existing methods from the 1970s to the present. The strengths and weaknesses of different methods are explained and methods are categorized according to generation procedures and evaluation functions. The future research directions of this chapter can attract many researchers who are novice to this area.

Chapter 9 presents a hybrid approach for solving classification problems of large data. Misra *et al.*, used three important neuro and evolutionary computing techniques such as polynomial neural network, fuzzy system, and Particle swarm optimization to design a classifier. The objective of designing such a classifier model is to overcome some of the drawbacks in the existing systems and to obtain a model that consumes less time in developing the classifier model, to give better classification accuracy, to select the optimal set of features required for designing the classifier and to discard less important and redundant features from consideration. Over and above the model remains comprehensive and easy to understand by the users.

Traditional software testing methods involve large amounts of manual tasks which are expensive in nature. Software testing effort can be significantly reduced by automating the testing process. A key component in any automatic software testing environment is the test data generator. As test data generation is treated as an optimization problem, Genetic algorithm has been used successfully to generate automatically an optimal set of test cases for the software under test. Chapter 10 describes a framework that automatically generates an optimal set of test cases to achieve path coverage of an arbitrary program.

We take this opportunity to thank all the contributors for agreeing to write for this book. We greatfully acknowledge the technical support of Mr. Harihar Kalia and financial support of BK21 project, Yonsei University, Seoul, South Korea.

S. Dehuri and S.-B. Cho

CONTENTS

Chapter 1

THEORETICAL FOUNDATIONS OF KNOWLEDGE MINING AND INTELLIGENT AGENT

S. DEHURI and S.-B. CHO

Department of Information and Communication Technology,
Fakir Mohan University, Vyasa Vihar Campus,
Balasore 756019, Orissa, India
satchi.lapa@gmail.com

Department of Computer Science,
Yonsei University, 262 Seongsanno, Seodaemun-gu,
Seoul 120-749, South Korea
sbcho@yonsei.ac.kr

Studying the behaviour of intelligent agents and deploy in various domain of interest with gamut of data to extract domain specific knowledge is recently attracting more and more number of researchers. In this chapter, we will summarize a few fundamental aspects of knowledge mining, the fundamental tasks of knowledge mining from databases (KMD) and a few well developed intelligent agents methodologies.

1.1. Knowledge and Agent

The definition of knowledge is a matter of on-going debate among philosophers in the field of epistemology. However, the following definition of knowledge can give a direction towards the goal of the chapter.

Definition: Knowledge is defined as i) an expertise, and skills acquired by a person through experience or education; the theoretical and practical understanding of a subject, ii) what is known in a particular field or in total; facts and information or iii) awareness or familiarity gained by experience of a fact or a situation.

The above definition is a classical and general one, which is not directly used in this chapter/book. Given the above notion we may state our definition of knowledge as viewed from the narrow perspective of knowledge mining from databases as used in this book. The purpose of this definition is to specify what an algorithm used in a KMD process may consider knowledge.

Definition: A pattern obtained from a KMD process and satisfied some user specified threshold is known as knowledge.

Note that this definition of knowledge is by no means absolute. As a matter of fact, it is purely user oriented and determined by whatever thresholds the user chooses. More detail is described in Section 1.2.

An agent is anything that can be viewed as perceiving its environment through sensors and acting upon that environment through effectors. A human agent has eyes, ears, and other organs for sensors, and hands, legs, mouth, and other body parts for effectors. A robotic agent substitutes cameras and infrared range finders for the sensors and various motors for the effectors. A software agent has encoded bit strings as its percepts and actions. Here the agents are special kinds of artificial agents created by analogy with social insects. Social insects (bees, wasps, ants, and termites) have lived on Earth for millions of years. Their behavior is primarily characterized by autonomy, distributed functioning and self-organizing capacities. Social insect colonies teach us that very simple organisms can form systems capable of performing highly complex tasks by dynamically interacting with each other. On the other hand, a great number of traditional models and algorithms are based on control and centralization. It is important to study both advantages and disadvantages of autonomy, distributed functioning and self-organizing capacities in relation to traditional engineering methods relying on control and centralization.

In Section 1.3 we will discuss various intelligent agents under the umbrella of evolutionary computation and swarm intelligence.

1.2. Knowledge Mining from Databases

In recent years, the rapid advances being made in computer technology have ensured that large sections of the world population have been able to gain easy access to computers on account of falling costs worldwide, and their use is now commonplace in all walks of life. Government agencies, scientific, business and commercial organizations are routinely using computers not just for computational purposes but also for storage, in massive databases, of the immense volume of data that they routinely generate, or require from other sources. The bar code scanners in commercial domains and sensors in scientific and industrial domains are an example of data collection technology, generates huge amounts of data. Large scale computer networking has ensured that such data has become accessible to more and more people around the globe.

It is not realistic to expect that all this data be carefully analyzed by human experts. As pointed out by Piatetsky-Shapiro,[1] the huge size of real world database systems creates both a need and an opportunity for an at lest partially automated form of knowledge mining from databases (KMD), or knowledge discovery from databases (KDD) and or data mining. Throughout the chapter, we use the term KMD or KDD interchangeably.

An Inter-disciplinary Nature of KMD: KMD is an inter-disciplinary subject formed by the intersection of many different areas. These areas can be divided into two broad categories, namely those related to knowledge mining techniques (or algorithms) and those related to data itself.

Two major KM-related areas are machine learning (ML),[2,3] a branch of AI, and statistics,[4,5] particularly statistical pattern recognition and exploratory data analysis. Other relevant KM-related areas are data visualization[6-8] and cognitive psychology.[9]

Turning to data related areas, the major topic relevant to KDD is database management systems (DBMS),[10] which address issues such as efficiency and scalability in the storage and handling of large amounts of data. Another important, relatively recent subject is data warehousing (DW),[11,12] which has a large intersection with DBMS.

KMD: As a Process: The KMD process is interactive and iterative, involving numeruous steps with many decisions being made by the user. Brachman & Anand[13] give a practical view of the KMD process emphasizing the interactive nature of the process. Here we broadly outline some of its basic steps:

(1) Developing an understanding of the application domain, the relevant prior knowledge, and the goals of the end-user.
(2) Creating a dataset: selecting a data set, or focusing on a subset of variables or data samples, on which discovery is to be performed.
(3) Data cleaning and preprocessing: basic operations such as the removal of noise or outliers if appropriate, collecting the necessary information to model or account for noise, deciding on strategies for handling

missing data fields, accounting for time sequence information and known changes.

(4) Data reduction and projection: finding useful features to represent the data depending on the goal of the task. Using dimensionality reduction or transformation methods to reduce the effective number of variables under consideration or to find invariant representations for the data.

(5) Choosing the data mining task: deciding whether the goal of the KMD process is classification, regression, clustering, etc.

(6) Choosing the data mining algorithms: selecting methods to be used for searching patterns in the data. This includes deciding which models and parameters may be appropriate (e.g., models for categorical data are different than models on vectors over the reals) and matching a particular data mining method with the overall criteria of the KMD process.

(7) Data mining: searching for patterns of interest in a particular representational form or a set of such representations: classification rules or decision trees, regression, clustering, and so forth. The user can significantly aid the data mining method by correctly performing the preceding steps.

(8) Interpreting mined patterns, possibly return to any of the steps 1–7 for further iteration.

(9) Consolidating discovered knowledge: incorporating this knowledge into the performance system, or simply documenting it and reporting it to interested parties. This also includes checking for and resolving potential conflicts with previously believed (or extracted) knowledge.

The KMD process can involve significant iteration and may contain loops between any two steps. Most of the literatures on KDD has focused on step 7–the data mining. However, the other steps are of considerable importance for the successful application of KDD in practice.[13]

1.2.1. *KMD tasks*

A number of KMD systems, developed to meet the requirements of many different application domains, has been proposed in the literature. As a result, one can identify several different KMD tasks, depending mainly on the application domain and on the interest of the user. In general each KMD task extracts a different kind of knowledge from a database, so that each task requires a different kind of KMD algorithm.

1.2.1.1. *Mining Association Rules*

The task of mining association rules was introduced by Agrawal *et al.*[14] In its original form this task is defined for a special kind of data, often called basket data, where a tuple consists of a set of binary attributes called items. Each tuple corresponds to a customer transaction, where a given item has value true or false depending on whether or not the corresponding customer bought the item in that transaction. This kind of data is usually collected through bar-code technology — the typical example is a grand-mart scanner.

An association rule is a relationship of the form $X \Rightarrow Y$, where X and Y are sets of items and $X \cap Y = \phi$. Each association rule is assigned a support factor Sup and a confidence factor $Conf$. Sup is defined as the ratio of the number of tuples satisfying both X and Y over the total number of tuples, i.e., $Sup = \frac{|X \cup Y|}{N}$, where N is the total number of tuples, and $|A|$ denotes the number of tuples containing all items in the set A. $Conf$ is defined as the ratio of the number of tuples satisfying both X and Y over the number of tuples satisfying X, i.e., $Conf = \frac{|X \cup Y|}{|X|}$. The task of discovering association rules consists of extracting from the database all rules with Sup and $Conf$ greater than or equal to a user specified Sup and $Conf$.

The discovery of association rules is usually performed in two steps. First, an algorithm determines all the sets of items having Sup greater than or equal to the Sup specified by the user. These sets are called frequent itemsets–sometimes called large itemsets. Second, for each frequent itemset, all possible candidate rule are generated and tested with respect to $Conf$. A candidate rule is generated by having some subset of the items in the frequent itemset to be the rule antecedent, and having the remaining items in the frequent itemset to be the rule consequent. Only candidate rules having $Conf$ greater than or equal to the $Conf$ specified by the user are output by the algorithm.

1.2.1.2. *Classification*

This is the most studied KDD task. In the classification task each tuple belongs to a class, among a pre-specified set of classes. The class of a tuple is indicated by the value of a user specified goal attribute. Tuples consists of a set of predicting attributes and a goal attribute. This later is a categorical (or discrete) attribute, i.e., it can take on a value out of a small set of discrete values, called classes or categories.

The aim of the classification task is to discover some kind of relationship between the predicting attributes and the goal one, so that the discovered knowledge can be used to predict the class (goal attribute value) of a new, unknown-class tuple.

1.2.1.3. *Clustering*

Clustering is a common descriptive task where one seeks to identify a finite set of categories or clusters to describe the data. This is typically done in such a way that tuples with similar attribute values are clustered into the same group. The categories may be mutually exclusive and exhaustive, or consist of a richer representation such as hierarchical or overlapping clusters.

1.2.1.4. *Dependency Modeling*

This task consists of finding a model which describes significant dependencies between variables. Dependency models exists at two levels: the structural level of the model specifies which variables are locally dependent on each other, whereas the quantitative level of the model specifies the strengths of the dependencies using some numerical scale.

These dependencies are often expressed as "IF-THEN" rules in the form "IF (antecedent is true) THEN (consequent is true)". In principle both the antecedent and the consequent of the rule could be any logical combination of attribute values. In practice, the antecedent is usually a conjunction of attribute values and the consequent is a single attribute value. Note that the system can discover rules with different attributes in the consequent. This is in contrast with classification rules, where the rules must have the same user-specified attribute in the consequent. For this reason this task is sometimes called generalized rule induction. Algorithms to discover dependency rule are presented in Mallen and Bramer.[15]

1.2.1.5. *Change and Deviation Detection*

This task focuses on discovering the most significant changes in the data from previously measured or normative values.[16–18]

1.2.1.6. *Regression*

Regression is learning a function which maps a data item to a real valued prediction variable. Conceptually, this task is similar to classification. The major difference is that in the regression task the attribute to be predicted is continuous i.e., it can take on any real valued number or any integer number in an arbitrarily large range rather than discrete.

1.2.1.7. *Summarization*

This involves methods for finding a compact description for a subset of data. A simple example would be tabulating the mean and standard deviations for all attributes. In other words, the aim of the summarization task is to produce a characteristic description of each class of tuples in the target dataset.[19] This kind of description somehow summarizes the attribute values of the tuples that belong to a given class. That is, each class description can be regarded as a conjunction of some properties shared by all (or most) tuples belonging to the corresponding class.

The discovered class descriptions can be expressed in the form of "IF-THEN" rules, interpreted as follows: "if a tuple belongs to the class indicated in the antecedent of the rule, then the tuple has all the properties mentioned in the consequent of the rule". It should be noticed that in summarization rules the class is specified in the antecedent ("if part") of the rule, while in classification rules the class is specified in the consequent ("then part") of the rule.

1.2.1.8. *Causation Modeling*

This task involves the discovery of relationships of cause and effect among attributes. Causal rules are also "if-then" rules, like dependence rules, but causal rules are intuitively stronger than dependence rules.

1.3. Intelligent Agents

1.3.1. *Evolutionary computing*

This section provides an overview of biologically inspired algorithm drawn from an evolutionary metaphor.[20,21] In biological evolution, species are positively or negatively selected depending on their relative success in surviving and reproducing in their current environment. Differential survival and variety generation during reproduction provide the engine for evolution. These concepts have metaphorically inspired a family of algorithms known as evolutionary computation. The algorithms like genetic algorithms, genetic programming, evolution strategies, differential evolution, etc. are coming under the umbrella of evolutionary computation.

Members of the evolutionary computation share a great deal in common with each other and are based on the principles of Darwinian evolution.[22] In particular, a population of individuals is evolved by reproduction and selection. Reproduction takes place by means of recombination, where a new individual is created by mixing the features of two existing individuals, and mutation, where a new individual is created by slightly modifying one existing individual. Applying reproduction increases the diversity of the population. Selection is to reduce the population diversity by eliminating certain individuals. To have this mechanism work, it is required that a quality measure, called fitness, of the individuals is given. If reproduction is applied to the best individuals and selection eliminates the worst individuals, then in the long run the population will consist of individuals having high fitness values–the population is evolving. An overview of the field can be found in Darwin.[23]

1.3.2. *Swarm intelligence*

Swarm intelligence is the branch of artificial intelligence based on the study of behavior of individuals in various decentralized systems.

Many phenomena in nature, society, and various technological systems are found in the complex interactions of various issues (biological, social, financial, economic, political, technical, ecological, organizational, engineering, etc.). The majority of these phenomena cannot be successfully analyzed by analytical models. For example, urban traffic congestion represents complex phenomenon that is difficult to precisely predict and which is sometimes counterintuitive. In the past decade, the concept of agent-based modeling has been developed and applied to problems that exhibit a complex behavioral pattern. Agent-based modeling is an approach based on the idea that a system is composed of decentralized individual "agents" and that each agent interacts with other agents according to localized knowledge. Through the aggregation of the individual interactions, the overall image of the system emerges. This approach is called the bottom up approach. The interacting agents might be individual travelers, drivers, economic or institutional entities, which have some objectives and decision power. Transportation activities take place at the intersection between supply and demand in a complex physical, economic, social and political setting. Local interactions between individual agents most frequently lead to the emergence of global behavior. Special kinds of artificial agents are the agents created by analogy with social insects. Social insects (bees, wasps, ants, and termites) have lived on Earth for millions of years. Their behavior in nature is, first and foremost, characterized by autonomy and distributed functioning and self-organizing. In the last couple of years, the researchers started studying the behavior of social insects in an attempt to use the swarm intelligence concept in order to develop various artificial systems.

Social insect colonies teach us that very simple organisms can form systems capable of performing highly complex tasks by dynamically interacting with each other. On the other hand, great number of traditional models and algorithms are based on control and centralization. It is important to study both advantages and disadvantages of autonomy, distributed functioning and self-organizing capacities in relation to traditional engineering methods relying on control and centralization.

Swarm behavior is one of the main characteristics of many species in the nature. Herds of land animals, fish schools and flocks of birds are created as a result of biological needs to stay together. It has been noticed that, in this way, animals can sometimes confuse potential predators (predator could, for example, perceive fish school as some bigger animal). At the same time individuals in herd, fish school, or flock of birds has a higher chance to survive, since predators usually attack only one individual. Herds of animals, fish schools, and flocks of birds are characterized by an aggregate motion. They react very fast to changes in the direction and speed of their neighbors.

Swarm behavior is also one of the main characteristics of social insects. Social insects (bees, wasps, ants, and termites) have lived on Earth for millions of years. It is well known that they are very successful in building nests and more complex dwellings in a societal context. They are also capable of organizing production. Social insects move around, have a communication and warning system, wage wars, and divide labor. The colonies of social insects are very flexible and can adapt well to the changing environment. This flexibility allows the colony of social insects to be robust and maintain its life in an organized manner despite considerable disturbances.[24] Communication between individual insects in a colony of social insects has been well recognized. The examples of such interactive behavior are bee dancing during the food procurement, ants pheromone secretion and performance of specific ants which signal the other insects to start performing the same actions. These communication systems between individual insects contribute to the formation of the "collective intelligence" of the social insect colonies. The term "Swarm intelligence", denoting this "collective intelligence" has come into use.[25]

The self-organization of the ants is based on relatively simple rules of individual insects behavior. The ants successful at finding food leave behind them a pheromone trail that other ants follow in order to reach the food. The appearance of the new ants at the pheromone trail reinforces the pheromone signal. This comprises typical autocatalytic behavior, i.e., the process that reinforces itself and thus converges fast. The "explosion" in such processes is regulated by a certain restraint mechanism. In the ant case, the pheromone trail evaporates with time. In this behavioral pattern, the decision of an ant to follow a certain path to the food depends on the behavior of his nestmates. At the same time, the ant in question will also increase the chance that the nestmates leaving the nest after him follow the same path. In other words, one ants movement is highly determined by the movement of previous ants.

Self-organization of bees is based on a few relatively simple rules of individual insects behavior. In spite of the existence of a large number of different social insect species, and variation in their behavioral patterns, it is possible to describe individual insects behavior as follows.

Each bee decides to reach the nectar source by following a nestmate who has already discovered a patch of flowers. Each hive has the so-called dance floor area in which the bees that have discovered nectar sources dance, in that way trying to convince their nestmates to follow them. If a bee decides to leave the hive to get nectar, she follows one of the bee dancers to one of the nectar areas. Upon arrival, the foraging bee takes a load of nectar and returns to the hive relinquishing the nectar to a food storer bee. After she relinquishes the food, the bee can (a) abandon the food source and become again an uncommitted follower, (b) continue to forage at the food source without recruiting nestmates, or (c) dance and thus recruit nestmates before returning to the food source. The bee opts for one of the above alternatives with a certain probability. Within the dance area the bee dancers "advertise" different food areas. The mechanisms by which the bee decides to follow a specific dancer are not well understood, but it is considered that the recruitment among bees is always a function of the quality of the food source. It is important to state here that the development of artificial systems does not entail the complete imitation of natural systems, but explores them in search of ideas and models. Similarly wasps and termites have their own strategies of solving the problems.

1.3.2.1. *Particle Swarm Optimization*

The metaheuristic Particle swarm optimization (PSO) was proposed by Kennedy and Eberhart.[26] Kennedy and Eberhart[26] were inspired by the behaviors of bird flocking. The basic idea of the PSO metaheuristic could be illustrated by using the example with a group of birds that search for a food within some area. The birds do not have any knowledge about the food location. Let us assume that the birds know in each iteration how distant the food is. Go after the bird that is closest to the food is the best strategy for the group. Kennedy and Eberhart[26,27] treated each single solution of the optimization problem as a "bird" that flies through the search space. They call each single solution a "particle". Each particle is characterized by the fitness value, current position in the space and the current velocity.[28] When flying through the solution space all particles try to follow the current optimal particles. Particles velocity directs particles flight. Particles fitness is calculated by the fitness function that should be optimized.

In the first step, the population of randomly generated solutions is created. In every other step the search for the optimal solution is performed by updating (improving) the generated solutions. Each particle memorizes the best fitness value it has achieved so far. This value is called *PB*. Each particle also memorizes the best fitness value obtained so far by any other particle. This value is called p^g. The velocity and the position of each particle are changed in each step. Each particle adjusts its flying by taking into account its own experience, as well as the experience of other particles. In this way, each particle is leaded towards p_{best} and g_{best} positions.

The position $X_i = \{x_{i1}, x_{i2}, \ldots, x_{iD}\}$ and the velocity $V_i = \{v_{i1}, v_{i2}, \ldots, v_{iD}\}$ of the ith particle are vectors. The position X_{k+1}^i of the ith particle in the $(k + 1)$st iteration is calculated in the following way:

$$X_{k+1}^i = X_k^i + V_{k+1}^i \, \Delta t, \qquad (1.1)$$

where V_{k+1}^i is the velocity of the ith particle in the $(k + 1)$st iteration and Δt is the unit time interval.

The velocity V_{k+1}^i equals:

$$V_{k+1}^i = w \cdot V_k^i + c_1 \cdot r_1 \cdot \frac{PB^i - X_k^i}{\Delta t} + c_2 \cdot r_2 \cdot \frac{P^g - X_k^i}{\Delta t}, \qquad (1.2)$$

where w is the inertia weight, r_1, r_2 are the random numbers (mutually independent) in the range $[0, 1]$, c_1, c_2 are the positive constants, PB^i is the best position of the ith particle achieved so far, and P^g is the best position of any particle achieved so far. The particles new velocity is based on its previous velocity and the distances of its current position from its best position and the groups best position. After updating velocity the particle flies toward a new position (defined by the above equation). Parameter w that represents particles inertia was proposed by Shi and Eberhart.[29] Parameters c_1 and c_2 represent the particles confidence in its own experience, as well as the experience of other particles. Venter and Sobieszczanski-Sobieski[30] used the following formulae to calculate particles velocity:

$$V_{k+1}^i = w \cdot V_k^i + c_1 \cdot r_1 \cdot \frac{PB^i - X_k^i}{\Delta t} + c_2 \cdot r_2 \cdot \frac{P_k^g - X_k^i}{\Delta t}, \qquad (1.3)$$

In other words, when calculating the particles velocity, Venter and Sobieszczanski-Sobieski[30] replaced the best position of any particle achieved so far P^g, by the best position of any particle achieved in the kth iteration P_k^g.

The PSO represents search process that contains stochastic components (random numbers r_1 and r_2). Small number of parameters that should be initialized also characterizes the PSO. In this way, it is relatively easy to perform a big number of numerical experiments. The number of particles is usually between 20 and 40. The parameters c_1 and c_2 were most frequently equal to 2. When performing the PSO, the analyst arbitrarily determines the number of iterations.

1.3.2.2. Ant Colony Optimization (ACO)

We have already mentioned that the ants successful at finding food leave behind them a pheromone trail that other ants follow in order to reach the food. In this way ants communicate among themselves, and they are capable to solve complex problems. It has been shown by the experiments that ants are capable to discover the shortest path between two points in the space. Ants that randomly chose the shorter path are the first who come to the food source. They are also the first who move back to the nest. Higher frequency of crossing the shorter path causes a higher pheromone on the shorter path. In other words, the shorter path receives the pheromone quicker. In this way, the probability of choosing the shorter path continuously increases, and very quickly practically all ants use the shorter path. The ant colony optimization represents metaheuristic capable to solve complex combinatorial optimization problems. There are several special cases of the ACO. The best known are the ant system,[31] ant colony system[32,33] and the maxmin ant system.[34]

When solving the Traveling Salesman Problem (TSP), artificial ants search the solution space, simulating real ants looking for food in the environment. The objective function values correspond to the quality of food sources. The time is discrete in the artificial ants environment. At the beginning of the search process (time $t = 0$), the ants are located in different towns. It is usual to denote by $\tau_{ij}(t)$ the intensity of the trail on edge(i, j) at time t. At time $t = 0$, the value of $\tau_{ij}(0)$ is equal to a small positive constant c. At time t each ant is moving from the current town to the next town. Reaching the next town at time $(t + 1)$, each ant is making the next move towards the next (unvisited) town. Being located in town i, ant k chooses the next town j to be visited at time t with the transition probability $p_{ij}^k(t)$ defined by the following equation:

$$
p_{ij}^k(t) = \begin{cases} \dfrac{[\tau_{ij}(t)]^\alpha \cdot [\eta_{ij}]^\beta}{\Sigma_{h \in \Omega_i^k(t)}[\tau_{ih}(t)]^\alpha \cdot [\eta_{ih}]^\beta} & j \in \Omega_i^k(t) \\ 0 & \text{otherwise} \end{cases}
\tag{1.4}
$$

where $\Omega_i^k(t)$ is the set of feasible nodes to be visited by ant k (the set of feasible nodes is updated for each ant after every move), d_{ij} is the Euclidean distance between node i and node j, $\eta_{ij} = \frac{1}{d_{ij}}$ is the "visibility", and α and β are parameters representing relative importance of the trail intensity and the visibility. The visibility is based on local information. The greater the importance the analyst is giving to visibility, the greater the probability that the closest towns will be selected. The greater the importance given to trail intensity on the link, the more highly desirable the link is since many ants have already passed that way. By iteration, one assumes n moves performed by n ants in the time interval $(t, t+1)$. Every ant will complete a traveling salesman tour after n iterations. The m iterations of the algorithm are called a "cycle". Dorigo *et al.*[31] proposed to update the trail intensity $\tau_{ij}(t)$ after each cycle in the following way:

$$
\tau_{ij}(t) \leftarrow \rho.\tau_{ij}(t) + \Delta\tau_{ij},
\tag{1.5}
$$

where ρ is the coefficient $(0 < \rho < 1)$ such that $(1-\rho)$ represents evaporation of the trail within every cycle. The total increase in trail intensity along link (i, j) after one completed cycle is equal to:

$$\Delta \tau_{ij}(t) = \sum_{k=1}^{n} \Delta \tau_{ij}^{k}(t) \qquad (1.6)$$

where $\Delta \tau_{ij}^{k}(t)$ is the quantity of pheromone laid on link(i, j) by the kth ant during the cycle.

The pheromone quantity $\Delta \tau_{ij}^{k}(t)$ is calculated as $\Delta \tau_{ij}^{k} = \frac{Q}{L_k(t)}$, if the kth ant walks along the link(i, j) in its tour during the cycle. Otherwise, the pheromone quantity equals: $\Delta \tau_{ij}^{k} = 0$, where Q is a constant; $L_k(t)$ is the tour length developed by the kth ant within the cycle. As we can see, artificial ants collaborate among themselves in order to discover high-quality solutions. This collaboration is expressed through pheromone deposition. In order to improve ant system Dorigo et al.[35] proposed ant colony optimization (ACO) that represents metaheuristic capable to discover high-quality solutions of various combinatorial optimization problems.

The transition probability $p_{ij}^{k}(t)$ is defined within the ant colony optimization by the following equation:

$$j = \begin{cases} \arg\max_{h \in \Omega_i^k(t)} \left\{ [\tau_{ih}(t)][\eta_{ih}]^{\beta} \right\} & q \leq q_0 \\ J & q \leq q_0 \end{cases} \qquad (1.7)$$

where q is the random number uniformly distributed in the interval $[0, 1]$, q_0 is the parameter $(0 \leq q_0 \leq 1)$, and J is the random choice based on the above relation; one assumes $\alpha = 1$ when using the equation (1.4).

In this way, when calculating transition probability, one uses pseudo-random-proportional rule (equation (1.8)) instead of random-proportional rule (equation (1.4)). The trail intensity is updated within the ACO by using local rules and global rules. Local rule orders each ant to deposit a specific quantity of pheromone on each arc that it has visited when creating the traveling salesman tour. This rule reads:

$$\tau_{ij}(t) \leftarrow (1 - \rho)\tau_{ij}(t) + \rho\tau_0, \qquad (1.8)$$

where ρ is the parameter $(0 < \rho < 1)$, and τ_0 is the amount of pheromone deposited by the ant on the link(i, j) when creating the traveling salesman tour. It has been shown that the best results are obtained when τ_0 is equal to the initial amount of pheromone c.

Global rule for the trail intensity update is triggered after all ants create traveling salesman routes. This rule reads:

$$\tau_{ij}(t) \leftarrow (1 - \alpha)\tau_{ij}(t) + \alpha\delta\tau_{ij}, \qquad (1.9)$$

where

$$\delta\tau_{ij} = \begin{cases} (L_{gb}(t)) & \text{if } (i,j) \in \text{to the best created traveling salesman tour} \\ 0 & \text{otherwise} \end{cases}$$

$$(1.10)$$

$L_{gb}(t)$ is the length of the best traveling salesman tour discovered from the beginning of the search process, and α is the parameter that regulates pheromone evaporation ($0 < \alpha < 1$). Global pheromone updating is projected to allocate a greater amount of pheromone to shorter traveling salesman tours.

1.3.2.3. *Artificial Bee Colony (ABC)*

The bee colony optimization (BCO) metaheuristic has been introduced fairly recently[36] as a new direction in the field of swarm intelligence. It has been applied in the cases of the Traveling salesman problem,[36] the ride-matching problem (RMP),[37] as well as the routing and wavelength assignment (RWA) in all-optical networks.[38]

Artificial bees represent agents, which collaboratively solve complex combinatorial optimization problem. Each artificial bee is located in the hive at the beginning of the search process, and from thereon makes a series of local moves, thus creating a partial solution. Bees incrementally add solution components to the current partial solution and communicate directly to generate feasible solution(s). The best discovered solution of such initial (first) iteration is saved and the process of incremental construction of solutions by the bees continues through subsequent iterations. The analyst-decision maker prescribes the total number of iterations.

Artificial bees perform two types of moves while flying through the solution space: forward pass or backward pass. Forward pass assumes a combination of individual exploration and collective past experiences to create various partial solutions, while backward pass represents return to the hive, where collective decision-making process takes place. We assume that bees exchange information and compare the quality of the partial solutions created, based on which every bee decides whether to abandon the created partial solution and become again uncommitted follower, continue to expand the same partial solution without recruiting the nestmates, or dance and thus recruit the nestmates before returning to the created partial solution. Thus, depending on its quality, each bee exerts a certain level of loyalty to the path leading to the previously discovered partial solution. During the second forward pass, bees expand previously created partial solutions, after which they return to the hive in a backward pass and engage in the decision-making process as before. Series of forward and backward passes continue until feasible solution(s) are created and the iteration ends. The ABC also solves combinatorial optimization problems in stages (see Fig. 1.1).

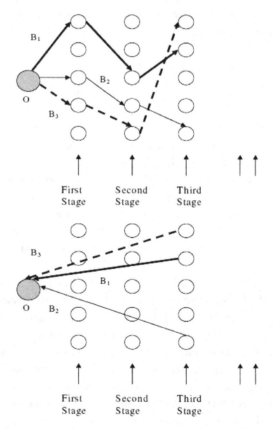

Fig. 1.1.   First forward and backward pass.

Each of the defined stages involves one optimizing variable. Let us denote by $ST = st_1, st_2, \ldots, st_m$ a finite set of pre-selected stages, where m is the number of stages. By B we denote the number of bees to participate in the search process, and by I the total number of iterations. The set of partial solutions at stage st_j is denoted by S_j $(j = 1, 2, \ldots, m)$. The following is pseudo-code of the bee colony optimization:

Bee colony optimization:

(1) Step 1: Initialization:- Determine the number of bees B, and the number of iterations I. Select the set of stages $ST = st_1, st_2, \ldots, st_m$. Find any feasible solution x of the problem. This solution is the initial best solution.

(2) Step 2: Set $i = 1$. Until $i = I$, repeat the following steps:

(3) Step 3: Set $j = 1$. Until $j = m$, repeat the following steps:
Forward pass: Allow bees to fly from the hive and to choose B partial solutions from the set of partial solutions S_j at stage st_j.
Backward pass: Send all bees back to the hive. Allow bees to exchange information about quality of the partial solutions created and to decide whether to abandon the created partial solution and become again uncommitted follower, continue to expand the same partial solution without recruiting the nestmates, or dance and thus recruit the nestmates before returning to the created partial solution. Set, $j = j+1$.

(4) Step 4: If the best solution x_i obtained during the ith iteration is better than the best-known solution, update the best known solution $(x = x_i)$.

(5) Step 5: set $i = i + 1$.

Alternatively, forward and backward passes could be performed until some other stopping condition (i.e., the maximum total number of forward/backward passes, or the maximum total number of forward/backward passes between two objective function value improvements) is satisfied. During the forward pass (Fig. 1.1) bees will visit a certain number of nodes, create a partial solution, and return to the hive (node O), where they will participate in the decision-making process, by comparing all generated partial solutions. Quality of the partial solutions generated will determine the bees loyalty to the previously discovered path and the decision to either abandon the generated path and become an uncommitted follower, continue to fly along discovered path without recruiting the nestmates or dance and thus recruit the nestmates before returning to the

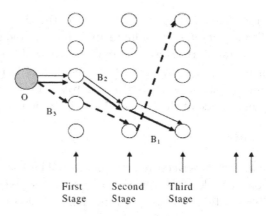

Fig. 1.2. Second forward pass.

discovered path. For example, bees B_1, B_2, and B_3 compared all generated partial solutions in the decision-making process, which resulted in bee B_1s decision to abandon previously generated path, and join bee B_2. While bees B_1 and B_2 fly together along the path generated by bee B_2, at the end of the path they will make individual decisions about the next node to be visited. Bee B_3 continues to fly along the discovered path without recruiting the nestmates (see Fig. 1.2). In this way, bees are performing a forward pass again.

During the second forward pass, bees will visit few more nodes, expand previously created partial solutions, and subsequently perform the backward pass to return to the hive (node O). Following the decision-making process in the hive, forward and backward passes continue and the iteration ends upon visiting all nodes. Various heuristic algorithms describing bees behavior and/or "reasoning" (such as algorithms describing ways in which bees decide to abandon the created partial solution, to continue to expand the same partial solution without recruiting the nestmates or to dance and thus recruit the nestmates before returning to the created partial solution) could be developed and tested within the proposed BCO metaheuristic.

1.3.2.4. *Artificial Wasp Colony (AWC)*

In both nature and marketing, complex design can emerge from distributed collective processes. In such cases the agents involved–whether they are social insects or humans–have limited knowledge of the global pattern they are developing. Of course, insects and humans differ significantly in what the individual agent can know about the overall design goals.

Wasp colony optimization (WCO)[39,40] mimics the behavior of social insect wasp and serves as a heuristic stochastic method for solving discrete optimization problem. Let us have a closure look on the behavior of wasp colony in nature. The wasp colony consists of queens (fertile females), workers (sterile female), and males. In late summer the queens and males mate; the male and workers die off and the fertilized queen over winters in a protected site. In the spring the queen collects materials from plant fibre and other cellulose material and mixes it with saliva to construct a typical paper type nest. Wasps are very protective of their nest and though they will use the nest for only one season the nest can contain as many as 10,000 to 30,000 individuals. Wasps are considered to be beneficial because they feed on a variety of other insects. Fig. 1.3 shows the different stages of a wasp colony. A young wasp colony (Polistes dominulus) is founding a new colony. The nest was made with wood fibers and saliva, and the eggs were laid and fertilized with sperm kept from the last year. Now the wasp is feeding and taking care of her heirs. In some weeks, new females will emerge and the colony will expand.

Theraulaz *et al.*[41] introduced the organizational characteristic of a wasp colony. In addition to the task of foraging and brooding, wasp colonies organize themselves in a hierarchy through interaction between the individuals. This hierarchy is an emergent social order resulting in a succession of wasps from the most dominant to the least dominant and is one of the inspirations of wasp colony optimization (WCO). In addition it mimics the assignment of resources to individual wasps based on their importance for the whole colony. For example, if the colony has to fight a war against an enemy colony, then the wasp soldiers will receive more food than others, because they are currently more important for the whole colony than other wasps.

1.3.2.5. *Artificial Termite Colony (ATC)*

During the construction of a nest, each termite places somewhere a soil pellet with a little of oral secretion containing attractive pheromone. This pheromone helps to coordinate the building process during its initial stages. Random fluctuations and heterogeneities may arise and become amplified by positive feedback, giving rise to the final structure (mound). Each time

Fig. 1.3.   Stages of wasp colony in nature.

one soil pellet is placed in a certain part of the space, more likely another soil pellet will be placed there, because all the previous pellets contribute with some pheromone and, thus, attract other termites. There are, however, some negative feedback processes to control this snowballing effect, for instance, the depletion of soil pellets or a limited number of termites available on the vicinity. It is also important to note that the pheromone seems to loose its biological activity or evaporate within a few minutes of deposition.[42]

A simple example of the hill building behavior of termites provides a strong analogy to the mechanisms of Termite. This example illustrates the four principles of self organization.[42] Consider a flat surface upon which termites and pebbles are distributed. The termites would like to build a hill from the pebbles, i.e., all of the pebbles should be collected into one place. Termites act independently of all other termites, and move only on the basis of an observed local pheromone gradient. Pheromone is a chemical excreted by the insect which evaporates and disperses over time. A termite is bound by these rules: 1) A termite moves randomly, but is biased towards the locally observed pheromone gradient. If no pheromone exists, a termite moves uniformly randomly in any direction. 2) Each termite may carry only one pebble at a time. 3) If a termite is not carrying a pebble and it encounters one, the termite will pick it up. 4) If a termite is carrying a pebble and it encounters one, the termite will put the pebble down. The pebble will be infused with a certain amount of pheromone. With these rules, a group of termites can collect dispersed pebbles into one place. The following paragraphs explain how the principles of swarm intelligence interplay in the hill building example.

Positive Feedback: Positive feedback often represents general guidelines for a particular behavior. In this example, a termites attraction towards the pheromone gradient biases it to adding to large piles. This is positive feedback. The larger the pile, the more pheromone it is likely to have, and thus a termite is more biased to move towards it and potentially add to the pile. The greater the bias to the hill, more termites are also likely to arrive faster, further increasing the pheromone content of the hill.

Negative Feedback: In order for the pheromone to diffuse over the environment, it evaporates. This evaporation consequently weakens the pheromone, lessening the resulting gradient. A diminished gradient will attract fewer termites as they will be less likely to move in its direction. While this may seem detrimental to the task of collecting all pebbles into one pile, it is in fact essential. As the task begins, several small piles will emerge very quickly. Those piles that are able to attract more termites will grow faster. As pheromone decays on lesser piles, termites will be less likely to visit them again, thus preventing them from growing. Negative feedback, in the form of pheromone decay, helps large piles grow by preventing small piles from continuing to attract termites. In general, negative feedback is used to remove old or poor solutions from the collective memory of the system. It is important that the decay rate of pheromone be well tuned to

the problem at hand. If pheromone decays too quickly then good solutions
will lose their appeal before they can be exploited. If the pheromone decays
too slowly, then bad solutions will remain in the system as viable options.

Randomness: The primary driving factor in this example is
randomness. Where piles start and how they end is entirely determined
by chance. Small fluctuations in the behavior of termites may have a
large influence in future events. Randomness is exploited to allow for new
solutions to arise, or to direct current solutions as they evolve to fit the
environment.

Multiple Interactions: It is essential that many individuals work
together at this task. If not enough termites exist, then the pheromone
would decay before any more pebbles could be added to a pile. Termites
would continue their random walk, without forming any significant piles.

Stigmergy: Stigmergy refers to indirect communications between
individuals, generally through their environment. Termites are directed to
the largest hill by the pheromone gradient. There is no need for termites
to directly communicate with each other or even to know of each others
existence. For this reason, termites are allowed to act independently of
other individuals, which greatly simplifies the necessary rules.

Considering the application of intelligent agents segregated in different
chapters of this book one should also expect much more applications in
various domain. We do believe that the method based on intelligent agents
hold a promise in application to knowledge mining, because this approach
is not just a specific computational tool but also a concept and a pattern
of thinking.

1.4. Summary

Let us conclude with some remarks on the character of these techniques
based on intelligent agents. As for the mining of data for knowledge the
following should be mentioned. All techniques are directly applicable to
machine learning tasks in general, and to knowledge mining problems in
particular. These techniques can be compared according to three criteria:
efficiency, effectivity and interpretability. As for efficiency, all the agent
based techniques (considered in this chapter) may require long run times,
ranging from a couple of minutes to a few hours. This however is not
necessarily a problem. Namely, the long running times are needed to find
a solution to a knowledge mining problem, but once a solution is detected,

applying such a solution in a new situation can be done fast. Concerning the issue of effectivity, we can generally state that all agent based techniques are equally good. However, this is problem dependent and one has to take the time/quality tradeoff into account. As far as interpretability is concerned, one can say that the simple techniques are generally the easiest to interpret.

References

1. G. Piatetsky-Shapiro. Knowledge discovery in real databases: A report on the ijcai-89 workshop, *AI Magazine.* **11**(5), 68–70, (1991).
2. P. Langley. *Elements of Machine Learning.* (Morgan Kaufmann, 1996).
3. J. W. Shavlik and T. G. Dietterich (Eds.). *Readings in Machine Learning.* (Morgan Kaufmann, San Mateo, CA, 1990).
4. J. F. E. IV and D. Pregibon. A statistical perspective on knowledge discovery in databases. In *Proc. 1st Int. Conference Knowledge Discovery and Data Mining (KDD-95)*, pp. 87–93, (1995).
5. J. F. E. IV and D. Pregibon. A statistical perspective on knowledge discovery in databases. In eds. U. M. Fayyad, G. Piatetsky-Shapiro, P. Smyth, and R. Uthuruusamy. *Advances in Knowledge Discovery and Data Mining*, pp. 83–113. AAAI/MIT Press, (1996).
6. H.-Y. Lee, H.-L. Ong, and L.-H. Quek. Exploiting visualization in knowledge discovery. In *Proc. 1st Int. Conference Knowledge Discovery and Data Mining (KDD-95)*, pp. 198–203, (1995).
7. E. Simoudis, B. Livezey, and R. Kerber. Integrating inductive and deductive reasoning for data mining. In eds. U. M. Fayyad, G. Piatetsky-Shapiro, P. Smyth, and R. Uthuruusamy. *Advances in Knowledge Discovery and Data Mining*, pp. 353–373. AAAI/MIT Press, (1996).
8. G. D. Tattersall and P. R. Limb. Visualization techniques for data mining, *BT Technol. Journal.* **12**(4), 23–31, (1994).
9. E. J. Wisniewski and D. L. Medin. The fiction and nonfiction of features. In eds. R. S. Michalski and G. Tecuci. *Machine Learning IV: A Multistrategy Approach*, pp. 63–84. Morgan Kaufmann, (1994).
10. C. J. Date. *An Introduction to Database System.* (Addison-Wesley, Reading, MA, 1995), 6th edition.
11. V. Poe. *Building a Data Warehouse for Decision Support.* (Prentice Hall, 1996).
12. W. H. Inmon. *Building the Data Warehouse.* (John Wiley and Sons, 1993).
13. R. J. Brachman and T. Anand. The process of knowledge discovery in databases: A human centered approach. In eds. U. M. Fayyad, G. Piatetsky-Shapiro, P. Smyth, and R. Uthuruusamy. *Advances in Knowledge Discovery and Data Mining*, pp. 37–57. AAAI/MIT Press, (1996).
14. R. Agrawal, T. Imielinski, and A. Swami. Mining association rules between sets of items in large databases. In *Proc. 1993 Int. Conference Management of Data (SIGMOD-93)*, pp. 207–216, (1993).

15. J. Mallen and M. Bramer. CUPID–an iterative knowledge discovery framework, *Expert Systems*. (1994).

16. W. Klosgen. Anonymization techniques for knowledge discovery in databases. In *Proc. 1st International Conference Knowledge Discovery & Data Mining*, pp. 186–191. AAAI/MIT Press, (1995).

17. W. Klosgen. Explora: a multipattern and multistrategy discovery assistant. In eds. U. M. Fayyad, G. Piatetsky-Shapiro, P. Smyth, and R. Uthuruusamy. *Advances in Knowledge Discovery and Data Mining*, pp. 249–271. AAAI/MIT Press, (1996).

18. I. Guyon, N. Matic, and V. Vapnik. Discovering informative patterns and data cleaning. In eds. U. M. Fayyad, G. Piatetsky-Shapiro, P. Smyth, and R. Uthuruusamy. *Advances in Knowledge Discovery and Data Mining*, pp. 181–203. AAAI/MIT Press, (1996).

19. G. Piatetsky-Shapiro. Discovery, analysis and presentation of strong rules. In eds. G. Piatetsky-Shapiro and W. J. Frawley. *Knowledge Discovery in Databases*, pp. 229–248. AAAI/MIT Press, (1991).

20. D. E. Goldberg. *Genetic Algorithms in Search, Optimization and Machine Learning*. (Addison-Wesley, Boston, 1993).

21. J. H. Holland. *Adaptation in Natural and Artificial Systems*. (University of Michigan Press, Michigan, 1975).

22. C. Darwin. *On the Origin of the Species by Means of Natural Selection, or the Preservation of Favoured Races in the Struggle for Life*. (Penguin Books, London, 1959).

23. K. D. Jong, D. B. Fogel, and H.-P. Schwefel. A history of evolutionary computation. In eds. T. Back, D. B. Fogel, and T. Michalewicz. *Evolutionary Computation 1: Basic Algorithms and Operators*, pp. 40–58. Institute of Physics Publishing, (2000).

24. E. Bonabeau, M. Dorigo, and G. Theraulaz. *Swarm Intelligence*. (Oxford University Press, Oxford, 1999).

25. G. Beni and J. Wang. Swarm intelligence. In *Proc. of the Seventh Annual Meeting of the Robotic Society of Japan*, pp. 425–428. RSJ Press, (1989).

26. J. Kennedy and R. C. Eberhart. Particle swarm optimization. In *Proc. of the IEEE International Conference on Neural Networks*, pp. 1942–1948, Piscataway, NJ, (1995).

27. J. Kennedy and R. C. Eberhart. The particle swarm: The social adaptation in information processing systems. In eds. D. Corne, M. Dorigo, and F. Glover. *New Ideas in Optimization*, pp. 379–388. McGraw-Hill, (1999).

28. J. Kennedy, R. C. Eberhart, and Y. Shi. *Swarm Intelligence*. (Morgan Kaufmann, San Francisco, 2001).

29. Y. Shi and R. C. Eberhart. Parametre selection in particle swarm optimization. In *Evolutionary Programming VII: Proc. of the Seventh Annual Conference on Evolutionary Programming*, pp. 591–600, New York, (1998).

30. G. Venter and J. Sobieszczanski-Sobieski. Particle swarm optimization, *AIAA Journal*. **41**, 1583–1589, (2003).

31. A. Colorni, M. Dorigo, and V. Maniezzo. Distributed optimization by ant colony. In eds. F. Varela and P. Bourgine. *Proceedings of the First European Conference on Artificial Life*, pp. 134–142. Elsevier, Paris, France, (1991).
32. M. Dorigo and L. M. Gambardella. Ant colony for the travelling salesman problem, *BioSystems*. **43**, 73–81, (1997).
33. M. Dorigo and L. M. Gambardella. Ant colony system: A cooperative learning approach to the travelling salesman problem, *IEEE Transactions on Evolutionary Computation*. **1**, 53–66, (1997).
34. T. Stutzle and H. Hoos. Max-min ant system, *Future Generation Computer Systems*. **16**, 889–914, (2000).
35. M. Dorigo, G. Di Caro, and L. M. Gamberdella. Ant algorithms for discrete optimization, *Artificial Life*. **5**, 137–172, (1999).
36. P. Lucic and D. Teodorovic. Computing with bees: attacking complex transportation engineering problems, *International Journal on Artificial Intelligence Tools*. **12**, 375–394, (2003).
37. D. Teodorovic and M. Dell'Orco. Bee colony optimization–a cooperative learning approach to complex transportation problems. In *Advanced OR and AI Methods in Transportation. Proc. of the 10th Meeting of the EURO Working Group on Transportation*, pp. 51–60, Poznan, Poland, (2005).
38. G. Markovic, D. Teodorovic, and V. Acimovic Raspopovic. Routing and wavelength assignment in all-optical networks based on the bee colony optimization, *AI Communications-European Journal of Artificial Intelligence*. **20**, 273–285, (2007).
39. M. Litte. Behavioral ecology of the social wasp, *Mischocyttarus Mexicanus Behav. Ecol. Sociobiol.* **2**, 229–246, (1977).
40. T. A. Runkler. Wasp swarm optimization of the c-means clustering model, *International Journal of Intelligent Systems*. **23**, 269–285, (2008).
41. G. Theraulaz, S. Gross, J. Gervert, and J. L. Deneubourg. Task differentiation in polistes wasp colonies: A model for self-organizing groups of robots. In eds. J. A. Meyer and S. W. Wilson. *Simulation of Adaptive Behavior: From Animals to Animats*, pp. 346–355. MIT Press, Cambridge, MA, (1991).
42. P.-J. Courtois and F. Heymans. A simulation of the construction process of a termite nest, *J. Theor. Biol.* **153**(4), 469–475, (1991).

Chapter 2

THE USE OF EVOLUTIONARY COMPUTATION IN KNOWLEDGE DISCOVERY: THE EXAMPLE OF INTRUSION DETECTION SYSTEMS

SHELLY X. WU* and WOLFGANG BANZHAF†

Computer Science Department, Memorial University,
St John's, Canada, A1B 3X5,
*xiaonan@mun.ca
†banzhaf@mun.ca

This chapter discusses the use of evolutionary computation in data mining and knowledge discovery by using intrusion detection systems as an example. The discussion centers around the role of EAs in achieving the two high-level primary goals of data mining: prediction and description. In particular, classification and regression tasks for prediction, and clustering tasks for description. The use of EAs for feature selection in the pre-processing step is also discussed. Another goal of this chapter was to show how basic elements in EAs, such as representations, selection schemes, evolutionary operators, and fitness functions have to be adapted to extract accurate and useful patterns from data in different data mining tasks.

2.1. Introduction

As a result of the popularization of the computer and the Internet, the amount of data collected from various realms of human activity continues to grow unabatedly. This creates great demand for new technology able to assist human beings in understanding potentially valuable knowledge hidden in huge, unprocessed data. Knowledge Discovery in Databases (KDD) is one of the emergent fields of technology that concerns itself with the development of theories and tools to extract interesting information from data with minimum human intervention. Data Mining (DM) as the core step in KDD studies specific algorithms for extracting patterns from data and their real-world applications.

This chapter discusses the use of evolutionary computation in data mining and knowledge discovery. We restrict our discussion to Intrusion Detection Systems (IDSs) as an application domain. IDSs are an indispensable component of security infrastructure used to detect cyber attacks and threats before they inflict widespread damage. We choose IDSs as an example, because it is a typical application for DM. Popular DM algorithms and techniques applied in this domain reflect the state of the art in DM research. In addition, intrusion detection is well-studied, though from a practical perspective still an unsolved problem. Some of its features, such as huge data volumes, highly unbalanced class distribution, the difficulty to realize decision boundaries between normal and abnormal behavior, and the requirement for adaptability to a changing environment, present a number of unique challenges for current DM research. Also, the findings obtained in intrusion detection research can be easily transformed to other similar domains, such as fraud detection in financial systems and telecommunication.

There are two high-level primary goals of data mining: prediction and description.[1] This chapter focuses on how evolutionary algorithms actively engage in achieving these two goals. In particular, we are interested in their roles in classification and regression tasks for prediction and clustering for description. We also discuss the use of EC for feature selection in the pre-processing step to KDD. When designing an evolutionary algorithm for any of these DM tasks, there are many options available for selection schemes, evolutionary operators, and fitness functions. Since these factors greatly affect the performance of an algorithm, we put effort into systematically summarizing and categorizing previous research work in this area. Our discussion also covers some new techniques designed especially to fit the needs of EC for knowledge acquisition. We hope this part of the discussion could serve as a good source of introduction to anyone who is interested in this area or as a quick reference for researchers who want to keep track of new developments.

The chapter is organized as follows. Section 2.2 presents a brief introduction to KDD, data mining, evolutionary computation, and IDSs. Section 2.3 discusses various roles EC can play in the KDD process. Sections 2.4 and 2.5 discuss how genetic operators and fitness functions have to be adapted for extracting accurate and useful patterns from data. Section 2.6 presents conclusions and outlook for future research.

2.2. Background

2.2.1. *Knowledge discovery and data mining*

KDD is the nontrivial process of identifying valid, novel, potentially useful, and ultimately understandable patterns in data.[1] The whole KDD process comprises three steps. The first step is called data pre-processing and includes data integration, data cleaning and data reduction. The purpose of this step is to prepare the target data set for the discovery task according to the application domains and customer requirements. Normally, data are collected from several different sources, such as different departments of an institution. Therefore, data integration will remove inconsistencies, redundancies and noise; data cleaning is responsible for detecting and correcting errors in the data, filling missing values if any, etc.; data reduction, also known as feature selection, removes features that are less well-correlated with the goal of the task. Once all preparation is complete, KDD is ready to proceed with its core step: data mining. DM consists of applying data analysis and discovery algorithms that, within acceptable computational efficiency boundaries, produce a particular enumeration of patterns (or models) over the data.[1] Patterns should be predictively accurate, comprehensible and interesting. The last step is post-processing. In this step, mined patterns are further refined and improved before actually becoming knowledge. Note that the KDD process is iterative. The output of a step can either go to the next step or can be sent back as feedback to any of the previous steps.

The relationship between KDD and DM is hopefully clear now: DM is a key step in the KDD process. Data mining applies specific algorithms on the target data set in order to search for patterns of interest. According to different goals of the KDD task, data mining algorithms can be grouped into five categories: classification, regression, clustering, association rules and sequential rules. Classification and regression both predict the value of a user-specified attribute based on the values of other attributes in the data set. The predicted attribute in classification has discrete value whereas it has continuous value in regression. Classification normally represents knowledge in decision trees and rules, while regression is a linear or non-linear combination of input attributes and of basic functions, such as sigmoids, splines, and polynomials. Clustering, association rules and sequential rules are used for common descriptive tasks. Clustering identifies groups of data such that the similarity of data in the same group is high

Table 2.1.   Confusion matrix.

	Prediction Result	
	Not C	C
Actual Result		
Not C	True Negative (TN)	False Positive (FP)
C	False Negative (FN)	True Positive (TP)

but is low between different groups; association rules reveal correlations between different attributes in a data set; sequential rules summarize frequent sequences or episodes in data.

Once an appropriate DM algorithm is adopted, one needs to divide the data set being mined into two subsets, the training set and the test set. Data mining algorithms are trained on the training set for construction of patterns. These patterns are then verified on the test set. The verified results are summarized in a confusion matrix such as the one shown in Table 2.1. C in the table denotes the value of a predicted attribute. Based on the confusion matrix, the following measures are used to quantify the performance of a data mining algorithm:

- True Negative Rate (TNR): $\frac{TN}{TN+FP}$, also known as Specificity.
- True Positive Rate (TPR): $\frac{TP}{TP+FN}$, also known as Detection Rate (DR) or Sensitivity.
- False Positive Rate (FPR): $\frac{FP}{TN+FP} = 1 -$ Specificity, also known as False Alarm Rate (FAR).
- False Negative Rate (FNR): $\frac{FN}{TP+FN} = 1 -$ Sensitivity.
- Accuracy: $\frac{TN+TP}{TN+TP+FN+FP}$.

2.2.2. *Evolutionary computation*

Evolutionary computation, inspired by natural selection and variation of Darwinian principles, is often viewed as an optimization process, as it favors the best solutions among a set of randomly varied ones. Nevertheless, EC is also useful for acquiring knowledge. The learning problem can be formulated as a search problem by considering it as a search for a good model inside the space of models. Such a space might consist of if-then rule sets or points representing cluster centers. Compared with traditional search techniques, evolutionary algorithms (EAs) are more efficient in that they involve search with a "population" of solutions, not a single solution which might have to backtrack. Because of other advantages such as adaptiveness, robustness, and flexibility, EC has been demonstrated to be an important tool for learning and extracting knowledge in data mining tasks.[2]

The EC family encompasses Genetic Algorithms (GAs),[3,4] Genetic Programming (GP),[5,6] Evolution Strategies[7,8] and Evolutionary Programming.[9] Although these different types of evolutionary methods were developed independently, the underlying idea of these algorithms is the same, as shown in Fig. 2.1.

Initially, a set of candidate solutions are randomly generated. In the terminology of EC, we call this set "population" and candidate solutions "individuals". The performance of every individual is evaluated according to an explicitly defined fitness metric. Given this fitness metric to be maximized, individuals with higher fitness are selected to enter the mating pool with a higher probability (refers to parent selection). Reproduction takes place in the mating pool. With probability p, two individuals recombine and produce one or two offspring. With probability q (often $q < p$), an individual mutates and produces another offspring. Based on their fitness, these offspring compete with their parents for a spot in the next generation (refers to survivor selection). This process is iterated until a solution is found or a preset limit of iterations is reached.

Evidently, selection and variation are two fundamental forces that push evolution forward. Fitter individuals have greater chances to survive due to the strong selective pressure, and will reproduce more varied offspring. Offspring generated by crossover and mutation is biased towards regions of the search space where good solutions have already been discovered. As a result, the fitness of a population increases over the generations.

In this chapter, GA and GP are of particular interest, because they are the two most popular evolutionary algorithms employed in data mining

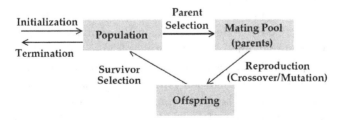

Fig. 2.1. The flow chart of a typical evolutionary algorithm.

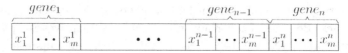

Fig. 2.2. A chromosome in a GA contains n genes, where n is the number of parameters
to be optimized. Each gene contains several nucleotides, which stores the specific value
of a parameter.

tasks. The main difference between them is the representation of solutions;
GP works on a superset of representations compared to GAs. GAs were
introduced by John H. Holland in the early 1960s[3] for solving machine
learning problems, so it represents candidate solutions as fixed length binary
strings (i.e., chromosomes), as shown in Fig. 2.2. A chromosome in a GA
contains n genes, where n is the number of parameters to be optimized.
Each gene contains several nucleotides which carry the binary encoding of
the specific value of a parameter. Over the years of development, other types
of encodings have been suggested, such as real values, categorical values, or
the combinations of them.

Genetic programming provides a framework for automatically creating
computer programs. Originally computer programs were confined to tree
structures, as illustrated in Fig. 2.3(a). Functions are located at the inner
nodes, while variables and constants are at leave nodes. The main limitation
of tree-based GP is the translation from tree structures to S-expressions
in LISP, and then to instructions understood by computers at the fitness
evaluation step. In order to boost the evolutionary process, Linear Genetic
Programming (LGP), another major approach to GP, evolves sequences
of instructions from an imperative programming language or from a
machine language.[10] As shown in Fig. 2.3(b), instructions operate on
one or two indexed variables (registers), or on constants from predefined
sets. Therefore, individuals are manipulated and executed directly without
passing an interpreter during fitness calculation. Other variants of GP
in the literature include Grammatical Evolution,[12] Cartesian Genetic
Programming (CGP),[13] Gene Expression Programming (GEP),[14] etc.

Figure 2.1 is only a conceptual framework that reflects the
Darwinian principle. In fact, when one starts to design an evolutionary
algorithm, specific representations, fitness functions, selection schemes and
evolutionary operators should be considered according to the application
domain and data mining task at hand. We will discuss this in the following
sections.

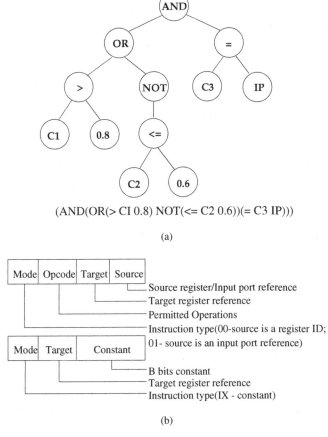

(AND(OR(> CI 0.8) NOT(<= C2 0.6))(= C3 IP)))

(a)

Mode	Opcode	Target	Source

Source register/Input port reference
Target register reference
Permitted Operations
Instruction type(00-source is a register ID;
01- source is an input port reference)

Mode	Target	Constant

B bits constant
Target register reference
Instruction type(IX - constant)

(b)

Fig. 2.3. Chromosome structures of Tree GP and Linear GP; (a) Tree GP Chromosome (b) Linear GP Chromosome.[11]

2.2.3. *Intrusion detection systems*

An intrusion detection system dynamically monitors the events taking place in a system, such as traffic on a network or activities on a host, and decides whether these events are symptomatic of an attack or constitute a legitimate use of the system.[15]

In general, IDSs fall into two categories according to the detection methods, namely misuse detection and anomaly detection. Misuse detection identifies intrusions by matching observed data with pre-defined signatures of intrusive behavior. So, well-known intrusions can be detected efficiently with a very low false positive rate. However, intrusions are usually polymorph, and evolve continuously. Misuse detection fails easily when facing unknown intrusions. Manually updating the intrusion signatures is generally infeasible because it is time consuming and laborious. A possible way is to automatically extract intrusive patterns from history data for future prediction. Anomaly detection is orthogonal to misuse detection. It hypothesizes that abnormal behavior is rare and different from normal behavior. Hence, it builds models for normal behavior and detects anomaly in observed data by noticing deviations from these models. Clearly, anomaly detection has the capability of detecting new types of intrusions, and only requires normal data when building the profiles. However, its major difficulty lies in discovering boundaries between normal and abnormal behavior, due to the scarcity of abnormal samples in the training phase.

The two detection methods perfectly match the two high-level primary goals of data mining: prediction and description. Therefore, classification and regression tasks for prediction are suitable for automatically constructing misuse models, while clusterings, association rules or sequential rules for description fit the need of establishing a profile for normal behavior.

2.3. The Role of Evolutionary Computation in KDD

Evolutionary algorithms actively engage in the three steps of the KDD process. In this section, we mainly concentrate on feature selection in the pre-processing step, and prediction and description tasks in data mining. In the post-processing step, an EA is often used for resolving contradictions when several patterns disagree with the output for a given data instance. An example can be found in Ref. 16.

2.3.1. *Feature selection*

One of the main obstacles for improving the performance of IDSs is the high dimensionality of data; for example, there are 41 features in the KDD99 data set.[17] High dimensional data means huge research spaces, hence requires expensive computation. However, the information in attributes sometimes overlaps, or is redundant. Feature selection by eliminating useless features can enhance the accuracy of the detection while speeding up the computation, thus improving the overall performance of an IDS. Feature selection studies fall into two categories based on whether or not they perform selection independently of learning algorithms. Independent selection is known as a filter approach; the opposite is called a wrapper approach.[18]

Research work conducted by Faraoun *et al.*[19] is an typical example of GA-based filter approach for feature selection. Individuals are vectors of integer numbers which represent the index of a selected feature. The fitness function computes the information gain of a given feature subset with regard to all the classes or a specific class. Hence, it guides the GA to search for the best feature subset that maximizes the information gain for all the classes, or for a given class.

In the wrapper approach, in contrast, the definition of a fitness function is no longer necessary. Instead, different classification models are called to measure the importance of a feature or feature subsets, such as a Decision Tree Model,[20] a Support Vector Machine,[21] a Naive Bayesian Network,[22] a *k*-Nearest Neighbor method.[23] The results returned from these external models are used as the fitness of an individual. Therefore, the goal of the GA is to maximize the predicted classification accuracy. This approach, while more computationally expensive, tends to provide better results than the simpler filter method.

Another commonly used GA representation for feature selection tasks is binary strings that represent the set of all existing features, with a value of 1 at the *i*th position if the *i*th feature is selected, and 0 otherwise.[20–22] If one changes the representation from binary strings to real vectors, the feature selection can be extended to feature ranking. The ranking value of each feature reflects the relative importance or relevance of the attribute to the classification task. A value in a real vector, indicating the ranking of an attribute on that position, ranges between 0 and 1, with 0 showing the attribute is not selected and 1 for the most important attribute.[21,23] Research work discussed in Refs. 24 and 25 also demonstrates the capability of LGP in feature ranking and selection. The evolved high-ranking programs are analyzed for the number of times each attribute appears in a way that it contributes to the fitness of the programs. The best feature subset is then output as the recommended feature set to be used in the actual input for classifiers.

2.3.2. *Classification*

Classification is probably the most studied data mining task. Every data sample in a data set used for classification contains two parts, namely a set of predictor attributes and a goal attribute. EC discovers a combination of conditions on predictor attributes that describes and distinguishes different values in the goal attribute. The goal attribute is also known as class label.

2.3.2.1. Representation

Classification rules are normally represented by IF-THEN rules with the following format:

$$\text{IF}(cond_1) \text{ AND} \cdots \text{AND } (cond_m) \text{ THEN } class = c_i$$

This type of rules contains two parts. The rule antecedent (the IF part) contains a conjecture of m conditions on predictor attributes (i.e., $cond_i$), and the rule consequent (the THEN part) contains a prediction about the value of a goal attribute (i.e., c_i). $cond_i$ is a predicate of the form $attri_i$ $operator$ $value_{ij}$, where $attri_i$ denotes the i-th attribute in the predictor attribute set, $value_{ij}$ means the j-th value of attribute i and $operator$ is a comparing operator (e.g., $=, \neq, >, \geq, <, \leq$ for continuous attribute, $=$ and $\neq$ for nominal or boolean attributes).

Encoding such complicated rule structure by GAs is not obvious, since GAs use fixed length binary strings for representation. Therefore, the rule format is normally simplified by only considering "$=$" as the operator. In this case, given n attributes, if referring to Fig. 2.2, there will be n genes in the chromosome, where the first $n - 1$ genes represent values of $n - 1$ attributes in the IF part, and the last gene represents the value of the goal attribute. Two ways are available to decide the number of nucleotides for each gene. Suppose a given attribute $attri_i$ can take k discrete values, then there will be k nucleotides for this gene. For example, if the value of attribute "$login\_time$" can be "morning", "noon", "afternoon", "evening", and "midnight", then the gene for this attribute has five bits. If the gene has the value "01001", then they would be representing a condition like (login_time = "noon" OR "midnight"). Obviously, such type of representation is able to encode more than one value for an attribute at the same time, but will suffer performance issues if an attribute has hundreds of values. Another way to decide the number of nucleotides is to use the equation $len = \lceil log_2^n \rceil$,[26,27] where n is the number of values of an attribute. So this time there will be three bits for attribute "login_time". The binary string "010" here means (login_time= "afternoon").

With the development of GAs, other encoding schemes were conceived and applied, such as hexadecimal strings,[28,29] real-number vectors[30,31] or a vector mixed with real numbers and characters.[32,33] Sometimes, a special symbol, called "don't care" ("#") symbol, is used as a wild card that allows any possible value in a gene, thus improving the generality of rules.[28-33] More complicated representations consider different kinds of logic operators between conditions.[27]

Compared to GAs, tree-based GP integrates more operators into the representation of classification rules, such as using various comparison operators (i.e., $=, \neq, >, \geq, <, \leq$) to connect leaf nodes, and logic operators such as "OR", "AND", "NOT" to connect conditions. Applying different operators to attributes will produce many different attribute combinations that will greatly increase the descriptive power of classification rules, which could not be considered by a traditional GA. An example is shown in Fig. 2.4(a). Because the execution of such a parse tree only outputs "True" or "False" when given an input data instance, and the class label cannot be encoded as a part of the representation, an extra step is needed to map a specific class label, such as "Intrusion", to an output, say "True". Obviously, such kind of representation is only suitable for binary classification. Another

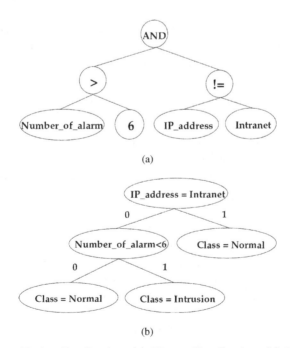

(a)

(b)

Fig. 2.4. Tree GP for Classification; (a) Binary Classification. (b) Multiple Class Classification.

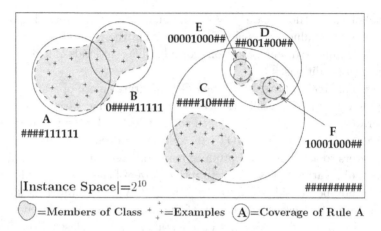

Fig. 2.5. Classification rules are represented as circles which cover the data points (denoted as "+") of unknown concepts (represented as shaded regions).[34]

representation option for tree-based GP is a decision tree, as illustrated in Fig. 2.4(b). Internal nodes are predicates of the form $(cond_i)$. In the leaf nodes we have a class assignment of the form $(class = c_i)$, where c_i is a category selected from the domain of the goal attribute. This type of representation is normally adopted by GP in multiple class classification.

2.3.2.2. Learning approaches

For most real-world applications, due to the high volume of data sets and the complicated relationship between predictor attributes and goal attributes, it is impossible to use only one if-then rule to classify all data instances accurately. Rather, a set of rules is needed, as depicted in Fig. 2.5. In this 2D example, classification rules are represented as circles which cover the data points (denoted as "+") of unknown concepts (represented as shaded regions). Now the task of the EA is to find the smallest rule set in which each rule covers as much data samples as possible from its class, and also generalizes well to unseen but similar data samples.

The learning approach for evolving a set of rules by EAs can broadly be categorized into the following three branches:

- Michigan Approach:[35] In the Michigan approach, each individual in the population represents an if-then rule, and is only a part of the solution for the problem under consideration. The complete solution is provided by the entire population. Crossover and mutation act on individual rules.

- Pittsburgh Approach:[36] In the Pittsburgh approach, each individual is a set of rules, representing a complete solution for the target problem. Crossover exchanges rules in two sets, and mutation creates new rules. Please refer to Tsang *et al.* and Tsang *et al.*[37,38] for examples.

- Iterative Rule Learning Approach:[39–41] Individuals are defined in the same way as in the Michigan approach. After a pre-defined number of generations the best classification rule is added to the set which keeps track of the best individuals found so far. The data covered by this rule are either removed from the training data set[39] or their probability of being selected again is decreased.[40,41] In the latter case, a weight is normally associated with every training instance with the same initial value. Weights of misclassified instances remain the same, while weights of correctly classified instances are decreased. Therefore, hard instances have a higher probability to be selected again.

The three approaches have pros and cons. The goal of an EA is not to find the best rule but the best set of rules, therefore the interactions between rules (i.e., changes in one rule affect other rules) must be considered. The Pittsburgh approach evaluates the quality of the whole rule set, therefore directly considering interactions. However, in the Michigan and Iterative Rule Learning approach, rules are evaluated separately, so the quality of the entire rule set is ignored. Furthermore, in order to maintain multiple distinct rules inside of the population, special techniques have to be used to prevent the population from converging to a single individual. Credit assignment and niching are then introduced. The iterative rule learning approach, because of the reduction of training instances, is more efficient at the fitness evaluation step.

2.3.2.3. *Rule discovery*

Research exploring the evolution of classification rules for intrusion detection is summarized in Table 2.2. The difference between binary classifiers and multi-classifiers is the representation.

For a GA, the consequent part of rules is usually omitted from the representation for binary classifiers, because the same class label applies to all rules. The contributions listed for GAs all employ the Michigan approach as their learning approach, but are based on various GA models. Research

Table 2.2.   Evolving classification rules by EC.

Type	Contributions
GA	
Binary Classifiers	Refs. 29, 32, 33, 26, 27, 28, 42
Multi-classifiers	Refs. 30, 31, 43, 44, 45, 46, 47, 48
Tree GP	
Binary Classifiers	Refs. 49, 50, 51
Multi-classifiers	Refs. 52, 53

work described in Refs. 28–31 and 43 uses classic GAs with niching to help cover all data instances with a minimum set of accurate rules. Mischiatti and Neri[32,33] use the REGAL to model normal network traffic. REGAL[54] is a distributed genetic algorithm-based system. It exhibits several novelties, such as a hybrid Pittsburgh and Michigan learning approach, a new selection operator allowing the population to asymptotically converge to multiple local optima, a new model of distribution and migration, etc. Dam and Shafi[44–48] report initial attempts to extend XCS, an evolutionary Learning Classifier System (LCS), to intrusion detection problems. Although XCSs have shown excellent performance on some data mining tasks, many enhancements, such as mutation and deletion operators, and a distance metric for unseen data in the testing phase, are still needed to tackle hard intrusion detection problems.[44]

Tree-based GP, on the other hand, uses different tree structures for binary and multi-class classification: the parse tree shown in Fig. 2.4(a) for binary classification,[49–51] and a decision tree as in Fig. 2.4(b) for multiple class classification.[52,53] Crosbie[49] and Folino *et al.*[52,53] improve the performance of a GP system by introducing cooperation between individuals. The former use autonomous agents, each being a GP-evolved program to detect intrusions from only one data source. The latter deploy their system in a distributed environment by using an island model.

Recently, there is a trend to evolve *fuzzy* classification rules, in effect a combination of fuzzy logic and evolutionary computation. Fuzzy logic, dealing with the vague and imprecise, is appropriate for intrusion detection for two reasons. First, intrusion detection problems involve many numeric attributes, and various derived statistical measures. Building models directly on numeric data causes substantial detection errors. For example, an intrusion that deviates only slightly from a model may not be detected or a small change in normal behavior may cause a false alarm.

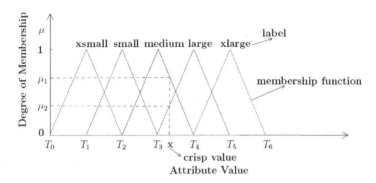

Fig. 2.6.   An example of fuzzy sets and membership functions.

Second, the security itself includes fuzziness, because the boundary between the normal and abnormal is not well defined.

Compared with classic if-then rules, fuzzy rules have the following form:

IF x_1 (!) = A_1 and $\cdots$ and x_n (!) = A_n THEN Class C_j with CF = CF_j

where x_i is a predictor attribute; A_i is a fuzzy set; C_j is the class label; CF_j is the degree of certainty of this fuzzy rule belonging to class C_j.

Technically, evolving fuzzy rules is identical as evolving classic if-then rules, but with two extra steps. The first step is to determine fuzzy sets and corresponding membership functions for continuous attributes before evolution. Fuzzy sets define the linguistic notions for an attribute, such as "small", "high", or "hot". The transition from "belonging to a set" to "not belonging to a set" is gradual, and is characterized by membership functions. Take Fig. 2.6 as an example, the fuzzy space for a continuous attribute, say $attri_i$ contains five fuzzy sets: xsmall, small, medium, large and xlarge. Each fuzzy set has a membership function with a triangular shape. This membership function maps the value of $attri_i$, x, to a fuzzy set with a continuous membership value between 0 and 1. Note that x can be mapped to members in different fuzzy sets at the same time, but with different membership degree. The functions mostly used include triangular,[26,27,40,41,55,56] trapezoidal,[57] sigmoid,[37,38] and Gaussian.[16] However, it is difficult to guarantee that a partition of fuzzy sets for each fuzzy variable is complete and well distinguishable. Therefore, genetic algorithms have been useful[16,37,38,58] in tuning membership functions.

The second step is to calculate the compatibility grade of each data instance with the fuzzy rules either in the fitness evaluation or detection

Table 2.3.   Fuzzy logic operators.

Logic Operator	Fuzzy Operator
p AND q	$\min\{\mu_p(x),\ \mu_q(y)\}$
p OR q	$\max\{\mu_p(x),\ \mu_q(y)\}$
NOT p	$1 - \mu_p(x)$

phase. To this end, the mapping between a logic operator and a fuzzy operator has to be defined, as shown in Table 2.3,[26,27,41] where p and q are fuzzy sets, x and y are continuous values of attributes and μ is the membership function associated with a fuzzy set. According to this table, the firing strength of a fuzzy rule can be calculated for a given data instance. Since an input value can belong to more than one fuzzy set, it is possible that a data sample will trigger more than one fuzzy rule with different class labels. Winner-takes-all[16] or majority vote[37,38] are two commonly used techniques to resolve the conflict. "Winner" refers to the rule with maximum CF_j.

2.3.3. *Regression*

Regression is a process of estimating the value of a continuous target attribute as a function of one or more predictor attributes, a set of parameters, and a set of arithmetic operators. In the context of intrusion detection or other similar domains, regression can be viewed as a special case of classification. That is, regression outputs an equation which transforms data in a high dimensional space into a specific value or a range of values in a low dimensional space according to different class labels, as shown in Fig. 2.7.

The simplest regression function is a linear regression function with the following format: $C(\chi) = \sum_{j=1}^{n}(w_j \times \chi_j)$, where n is the number of attributes, w_j is a weight[59] or coefficient[60] of attribute χ_j. A GA usually searches for the best set of weights or coefficient that map any data from the normal class to a value larger than δ ($C(\chi) > \delta$) and any data from the anomaly class to a value less than δ ($C(\chi) < \delta$). δ is a user defined threshold. Individuals in this case contain n genes, each standing for a weight or coefficient.

Compared with GAs, regression equations evolved by GP have more complex structures, normally employing nonlinear functions. Only arithmetic operators, such as "+", "−", "×", "÷", "log", etc., and

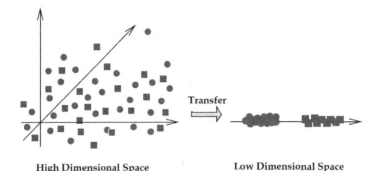

Fig. 2.7.   Regression outputs an equation which transforms data in a high dimensional space into a specific value or a range of values in a low dimensional space according to different class labels.

numeric values are allowed in the representations of tree-based GP or LGP. Categorical attributes have to be converted to a numeric value beforehand.

Abraham *et al.*[61–64] and Heywood *et al.*[11,65,66] are two major research groups working on LGP and its application in intrusion detection. Abraham *et al.* focused on investigating basic LGP and its variations, such as Multi-Expression Programming (MEP)[67] and Gene Expression Programming (GEP),[14] to detect network intrusion. Experiments, in comparing LGP, MEP, GEP and other machine learning algorithms, showed that LGP outperformed SVMs and ANNs in terms of detection accuracy at the expense of time;[64,68] MEP outperformed LGP on Normal, U2R and R2L classes and LGP outperformed MEP on Probe and DoS classes.[61–63] Song *et al.* implemented a page-based LGP with a two-layer subset selection scheme to address the binary classification problem. An individual is described in terms of a number of pages, where each page has the same number of instructions. Page size was dynamically adjusted when the fitness reached a "plateau" (i.e. fitness does not change for several generations). Since intrusion detection benchmarks are highly skewed, the authors pointed out that the definition of fitness should reflect the distribution of class types in the training set. Two dynamic fitness schemes, dynamic weighted penalty and lexicographic fitness, were introduced. The application of this algorithm to other problems related to intrusion detection can be found in Refs. 69 and 70.

The above mentioned transform functions evolved by GPs are only used for binary classification. Therefore, Faraoun *et al.*[71] and Lichodzijewski *et al.*[72] investigated the possibility of GP in multi-category classification.

Table 2.4.   Evolving regression functions by EC.

Type	Research Work
Binary Classifiers	
GA	Refs. 60, 59
LGP	Refs. 61, 62, 63, 73, 69, 70, 64, 65, 66, 11
Multi-classifiers	
Tree-based GP	Ref. 71
LGP	Ref. 72

Faraoun *et al.* implemented multi-classification in two steps. In the first step, a GP maps input data to a new one-dimensional space, and in the second step, another GP maps the output to different class labels; Lichodzijewski *et al.* proposed a bid-based approach for coevolving LGP classifiers. This approach coevolves a population of learners that decompose the instance space by the way of their aggregate bidding behavior.

Research work that investigates evolving regression functions for intrusion detection is summarized in Table 2.4.

2.3.4. *Clustering*

Clustering is a process of partitioning a given set of n instances into K groups based on some similarity metrics: instances in the same cluster have high similarity, while similarity is low between different clusters. The number of clusters and cluster centers are two factors that affect the performance of a clustering algorithm. For example, the well-known K-means clustering algorithm depends on the number of clusters as an input parameter.

Evolutionary algorithms are useful in clustering algorithms in three ways. First, genetic algorithms are used to search for the optimal number of clusters. For example, Lu *et al.*[74,75] proposed a clustering algorithm based on Gaussian mixture model (GMM). This model assumes that the entire data set can be seen as a mixture of several Gaussian distributions, each potentially being a cluster. The GA, therefore, is asked to search for all possible Gaussian distributions. Each individual is composed of a three-tuple vector $\langle \alpha, \mu, \theta \rangle$, where α is the mixing proportions, μ refers to the mean of data samples and θ stands for the variance of data samples. An entropy-based fitness function is defined to measure how well the evolved models approximate the real data distribution. The number of Gaussian distributions returned at the end of evolution will be the optimal number of clusters. A K-means clustering algorithm is run subsequently to locate the centers of clusters.

Another trend is to use a GA to optimize cluster centers. This type of algorithm consists of two stages, namely deciding preliminary cluster centers and genetic optimization.[76,77] To establish the initial clusters, simple clustering algorithms are used, such as the nearest neighbor method[76] or K-means algorithm.[77] This step groups very similar instances into a cluster and filters instances that are not adjacent to any other. In the second step, a genetic optimization process searches for the near optimal cluster centers. Preliminary clusters are used to set up the initial chromosomes. The main purpose of the first stage is to reduce the data set to a moderate size which is suitable for GAs to search in the second stage.

GAs are also used to search for cluster centers directly without knowing the number of clusters in advance, such as the unsupervised niche clustering approach proposed by Leon *et al.*[78] "Unsupervised" means that the cluster number is automatically determined by the GA. An individual represents a candidate cluster, which is determined by its center, an n-dimensional vector, with n being the dimension of the data sample, and a robust measure of its scale (or radius) δ^2. Niching maintains several distinct solutions in the population, which result in different cluster centers.

2.3.5. *Comparison between classification and regression*

In the context of IDSs, classification and regression are suitable for automatically constructing misuse models, but using different mechanisms. To gain a better understanding of the strength and weakness of each approach, we compared the algorithms of these two approaches based on the KDD99 test data set. The results are shown in Table 2.5. The first five rows in this table record the detection rates obtained by each algorithm on each class; the last two rows list the overall detection rate and false positive rate.

We can see from the table that EAs generally achieve better performance than the winning entry which had 50 × 10 decision trees. In particular, regression functions (column 7–9) have higher detection rates than classification rules (column 3–4); they especially improve detection rates on the "U2R" and "R2L". This is because of the limited description power provided by classification rules. In addition, rules are more or less a high level abstraction of data samples. They cannot separate data in two classes very well if the two classes overlap considerably. Classification rules

Table 2.5. Performance comparison of various EC approaches on the KDD99 test data set.

Type	Wining Entry	Classification				Regression		
	Decision Tree	GA (XCS)	GP	Fuzzy Sets		GP	LGP	Coevolution
	79	44	53	38	16	71	11	72
Normal	94.5	95.7	—	98.365	98.4	99.93	96.5	99.5
DoS	97.1	49.1	—	97.202	99.5	98.81	99.7	97
Probe	83.3	93	—	88.598	89.2	97.29	86.8	71.5
U2R	13.2	8.5	—	15.790	12.8	45.2	76.3	20.7
R2L	8.4	3.9	—	11.014	27.3	80.22	12.35	3.5
DR	90.9	—	91.017	92.767	95.3	98	94.4	—
FPR	0.45	—	0.434	—	1.6	0.07	3.5	—

again cannot outperform evolved fuzzy rules (column 5–6). Fuzzy rules obtain noticeable improvement on all classes, which clearly demonstrates that fuzzy sets are able to increase the robustness and adaption of IDSs. Transform functions and fuzzy rules achieve similar results, but fuzzy rules are easier to comprehend.

2.4. Evolutionary Operators and Niching

2.4.1. *Evolutionary operators*

In EC, during each successive generation, some individuals are selected with certain probabilities to go through crossover and mutation for the generation of offspring. Table 2.6 summarizes commonly used selection, crossover and mutation operators employed in intrusion detection tasks.

Some special evolutionary operators are introduced to satisfy the requirements of representations. For example, page-based LGP algorithms[11,65,66,69,70] restrict crossover to exchange of pages rather than instructions between individuals. Mutation operators take two forms: (i) the mutation operator selects two instructions with uniform probability and performs an XOR on the first instruction with the second one; (ii) the mutation operator selects two instructions in the same individual with uniform probability and then exchanges their positions. Hansen et al.[73] propose a homologous crossover in LGP that attempts to mimic natural evolution more closely. With homologous crossover, two programs are juxtaposed and crossover is accomplished by exchanging sets of contiguous instruction blocks having the same length and the same position between the two evolved programs.

Table 2.6.　Evolutionary operators employed in intrusion detection tasks.

Operators	Research Work
Selection	
Roulette wheel	Refs. 44, 71
Tournament	Refs. 80, 81, 73, 65
Elitist	Refs. 82, 31
Rank	Refs. 83, 42
Crossover	
Two-point	Refs. 44, 80, 71, 31, 50, 32, 33, 51
One-point	Refs. 43, 83, 78, 42, 84
Uniform	Refs. 82, 32, 33
Arithmetic	Ref. 82
Homologous	Refs. 73, 70, 69, 65, 66, 11
Mutation	
Bit-flip	Refs. 44, 80, 82, 78, 32, 33, 42, 84
Inorder mutation	Ref. 30
Gaussian	Ref. 82
One point	Refs. 71, 50, 51

Most researchers have confirmed the positive role mutation can play in a searching process. However, they hold different opinions about crossover in multimodal problems whose population contains niches. A mating restriction is considered when individuals in different niches are recombined. Recombining arbitrary pairs of individuals from different niches may lead to unfit or lethal offspring. For example, if crossover were conducted on the class label part, which means rules in different classes exchange their class labels, it would cause a normal data point to be anomalous or vice versa. Pillai *et al.*[30] applies mutation, but not crossover, to produce offspring; Dass[80] only applies mutation and crossover to the condition-part of rules; Leon *et al.*[78] introduces an additional restriction on the deterministic crowding selection for controlling the mating between members of different niches.

In addition to these three operators, other operators are conceived for improving detection rate, maintaining diversity or other purposes. Among them, seeding and deletion are two emerging operators that are adopted by many EC algorithms in intrusion detection applications.

• Seeding.[40,41,44,50,51,54–56] As discussed earlier, evolving classification rules can be regarded as a "set covering" problem. If some instances are not yet covered, seeding operators will dynamically generate new individuals to cover them. Normally, this method is used to initialize the first population.

- Deletion.[44] EC works with a limited population size. When newly generated individuals are inserted into the population, but the maximum population size is reached, some old individuals have to be removed from the population. In traditional EC with a global optimum target, the less fit individuals are preferably replaced. However, for multimodal problems, other criteria in addition to fitness, such as niches or data distribution, should be considered to avoid replacement errors. Dam *et al.*[44] considers class distribution in the deletion operator, especially for highly skewed data sets, to handle minority classes. For example, normal instances constitute approximately 75% of total records in the KDD99 data set. Rules which cover normal data points will have a higher fitness than rules from other classes, hence have a much lower chance to be deleted.
- Adding and Dropping. These two operators are variations of mutation. Dropping means to remove a condition from the representation, thus resulting in a generalized rule.[50,51] In contrast, adding conditions results in specialized rules.

2.4.2. *Niching*

Most EC applications have focused on optimization problems, which means that individuals in the population compete with others to reach a global optimum. Niching is an effective technique to preserve diversity in the population long enough to perform a reasonable exploration of the search space. However, pattern recognition or concept learning is actually a multimodal problem in the sense that multiple rules (see Fig. 2.5) or clusters[78] are required to cover the unknown knowledge space. In this case, niching can promote the formation and maintenance of stable subpopulations within a single population, which has been proven by Forrest *et al.*[85] Researchers in Refs. 28–31 and 43 suggested niching in basic GAs when evolving classification rules.

Within the context of intrusion detection, sharing,[28,86] crowding[29] and deterministic crowding (DC)[78] have been applied to encourage diversity. DC is an improved crowding algorithm, which nearly eliminates replacement errors of De Jong's crowding. As a result, DC is effective to discover multiple local optima compared to De Jong's method.[87] Unfortunately, there is no experimental result available in Sinclair *et al.*,[29] so we cannot verify the limitations of De Jong's crowding in intrusion detection problems. Hamming distance[28,29] or Euclidean distance[86] are used to measure the similarity between two individuals.

However, defining meaningful and accurate distance measures and selecting an appropriate niching radius are difficult. Computational complexity is also an issue for these algorithms. The shared fitness evaluation requires, in each generation, a number of steps proportional to M^2, with M being the cardinality of the population.[54] So, Giordana *et al.* introduce a new selection operator in REGAL, called *Universal Suffrage*, to achieve niching.[54] The individuals to be mated are not chosen directly from the current population, but instead indirectly through the selection of an equal number of data points. It is important to note that only individuals covering the same data points compete, and the data points (stochastically) "vote" for the best of them. In XCS, a niching mechanism is demonstrated via reward sharing. Simply, an individual shares received rewards with those who are similar to them in some way.

Lu *et al.*[50] implemented niching neither via fitness sharing nor via crowding, but via token competition.[88] The idea is as follows: a token is allocated to each record in the training data set. If a rule matches a record, its token will be seized by the rule. The priority of receiving the token is determined by the strength of rules. The number of tokens an individual acquires also helps to increase its fitness. In this way, the odds of two rules matching the same data are decreased, hence the diversity of the population is maintained.

2.5. Fitness Function

An appropriate fitness function is essential for EC as it correlates closely with the algorithm's goal, and guides the search process. IDSs are designed to identify intrusions as accurately as possible. Therefore, accuracy should be a major factor when design a fitness function. In Table 2.7, we categorize fitness functions from the research work we surveyed. The categorization is based on three terms: detection rate (DR), false positive rate (FPR) and conciseness.

The research contributions in the first row are all devoted to anomaly detection problems. Since no attack presents in the training phase, DR is not available. Fitness functions may vary in format, but all look for models

Table 2.7.   Fitness functions considering different factors {Con:Conciseness}.

Factors			Examples	References
DR	FPR	Con		
×	√	×	$\frac{H(C_i)}{H_{max}(C_i)}$	Refs. 83, 78, 75, 74
√	√	×	$\frac{\alpha}{A} - \frac{\beta}{B}$	Refs. 60, 81, 71, 70, 30, 29, 59, 77
			$w_1 \times support + w_2 \times confidence$	Refs. 43, 31, 50, 42, 51
			$1 - |\varphi_p - \varphi|$	Refs. 89, 49, 63, 28, 65
√	√	√	$w_1 \times sensitivity + w_2$ $\times specificity + w_3 \times length$	Ref. 27
			$(1 + Az) \times e^{-w}$	Refs. 80, 32, 33

which cover most of the normal data. In this example, $H(C_i)$ represents the entropy of data points who belong to cluster C_i, and $H_{max}(C_i)$ is the theoretical maximum entropy for cluster C_i.

Accuracy actually requires both DR and FPR, since ignoring either of them will cause misclassification errors. A good IDS should have a high DR and a low FPR. The first example in the second row directly interprets this principle. α stands for the number of correctly detected attacks, A the number of total attacks, β the number of false positives, and B the total number of normal connections. As we know, patterns are sometimes represented as if-then rules, so in the second example, the support-confidence framework is borrowed from association rules to determine the fitness of a rule. By changing weights w_1 and w_2, the fitness measure can be used for either simply identifying network intrusions or precisely classifying the type of intrusion.[31] The third example considers the absolute difference between the prediction of EC (φ_p) and the actual outcome (φ).

The third row considers another interesting property: conciseness. This is for two reasons: concise results are easy to understand, and avoid misclassification errors. The second reason is less obvious. Conciseness can be restated as the space a model, such as a rule, or a cluster, uses to cover a data set. If rule A and rule B have the same data coverage, but rule A is more concise than B, so A uses less space than B does when covering the same data set. Therefore, the extra space of B is more prone to cause misclassification errors. Apparently, the first example of this kind considers all three terms, where length correlates with conciseness. The second example of this type considers the number of counterexamples covered by a rule (w), and the ratio between the number of bits equal to one in the chromosome and the length of chromosome (z), which is the conciseness of a rule. A is a user-tunable parameter. The fitness function in Ref. 78, also prefers clusters with small radius if they cover the same data points.

2.6. Conclusions and Future Directions

This chapter discusses the use of evolutionary computation in data mining and knowledge discovery by using intrusion detection systems as an example. The discussion centers around the role of EAs in achieving the two high-level primary goals of data mining: prediction and description. In particular, classification and regression tasks for prediction, and clustering tasks for description. The use of EAs for feature selection in the pre-processing step is also discussed. Another goal of this chapter was to show how basic elements in EAs, such as representations, selection schemes, evolutionary operators, and fitness functions have to be adapted to extract accurate and useful patterns from data in different data mining tasks.

Although experiments reasserted the effectiveness and accuracy of EC in data mining algorithms, there are still challenges that lie ahead for researchers in this area. The first challenge is the huge volume of data that makes building effective evolutionary models difficult, especially in fitness evaluation. We can either resort to hardware specific approaches, such as to relocate the fitness evaluation step from CPU to GPU,[90] or to software approaches, such as various data sampling techniques,[11,66] divide-and-conquer algorithms,[40,41] distributed and parallel EAs.[53,54,56] The second challenge is handling imbalanced data distributions. Both Ref. 44 and Ref. 65 point out that individuals which have better performance on frequently occurring patterns would be more likely to survive, even if they perform worse than competing individuals on less frequent patterns. Therefore, when designing a data mining algorithm based on EAs, one should consider how to improve the accuracy on relatively rare patterns without compromising performance on more frequent patterns. Finally, acquiring knowledge from data is often regarded as a multimodal problem. In our perspective, it is even harder than normal multimodal problems, simply because adaptation and optimization occur on subsolutions (i.e., rules in a rule set such as the Michigan approach) at the same time. New evolutionary techniques or extensions in EAs are needed. We believe solving these challenges will further improve the performance of EC-based data mining algorithms.

Acknowledgment

Funding from NSERC under RGPIN 283304-07 is gratefully acknowledged.

References

1. U. Fayyad, G. Piatetsky-Shapiro, and P. Smyth. From data mining to knowledge discovery in databases: An overview, *Advances in Knowledge Discovery and Data Mining.* pp. 1–30, (1996).
2. A. A. Freitas. *Data Mining and Knowledge Discovery with Evolutionary Algorithms.* (Springer, New York, NJ, USA, 2002).
3. J. H. Holland. *Adaptation in Natural and Artificial Systems.* (University of Michigan Press, Ann Arbor, MI, USA, 1975).
4. D. E. Goldberg. *Genetic Algorithms in Search, Optimization, and Machine Learning.* (Addison-Wesley, Reading, MA, USA, 1989).
5. J. R. Koza. *Genetic Programming: On the Programming of Computers by means of Natural Evolution.* (MIT Press, Cambridge, MA, USA, 1992).
6. W. Banzhaf, P. Nordin, R. Keller, and F. Francone. *Genetic Programming — An Introduction.* (Morgan Kaufmann, San Francisco, CA, USA, 1998).
7. I. Rechenberg. *Evolutionsstrategie: Optimierung technischer Systeme und Prinzipien der biologischen Evolution.* (Frommann-Holzboog, Stuttgart, Germany, 1973).
8. H. P. Schwefel. *Numerical Optimization of Computer Models.* (John Wiley & Sons, New York, NJ, USA, 1981).
9. D. B. Fogel. *Evolutionary Computation: Toward a New Philosophy of Machine Intelligence.* (IEEE Press, Piscataway, NJ, USA, 1995).
10. M. Brameier and W. Banzhaf. *Linear Genetic Programming.* (Springer, New York, NJ, USA, 2007).
11. D. Song, M. I. Heywood, and A. N. Zincir-Heywood. Training genetic programming on half a million patterns: An example from anomaly detection, *IEEE Transactions on Evolutionary Computation.* **9**(3), 225–239, (2005).
12. M. O'Neill and C. Ryan. *Grammatical Evolution: Evolutionary Automatic Programming in an Arbitrary Languag.* (Springer, Berlin/Heidelberg, Germany, 2003).
13. J. F. Miller and P. Thomson. Cartesian genetic programming. In eds. R. Poli, W. Banzhaf, *et al. Proceedings of the 3rd European Conference on Genetic Programming, Edinburgh, Scotland, UK,* Vol. LNCS 1802/2000, pp. 121–132. Springer, Berlin/Heidelberg, Germany, (2000).
14. C. Ferreira. Gene expression programming: A new adaptive algorithm for solving problems, *Complex Systems.* **13**(2), 87–129, (2001).
15. H. Debar, M. Dacier, and A. Wespi. Towards a taxonomy of intrusion-detection systems, *Computer Networks.* **31**(8), 805–822, (1999).
16. A. N. Toosi and M. Kahani. A new approach to intrusion detection based on an evolutionary soft computing model using neuro-fuzzy classifiers, *Computer Communications.* **30**(10), 2201–2212, (2007).
17. The KDD99 Dataset. Retrieved Nov. 26, 2008, from http://kdd.ics.uci.edu/databases/kddcup99/task.html.
18. R. Kohavi and G. H. John. Wrappers for feature subset selection, *Artificial Intelligence.* **97**(1–2), 273–324, (1997).

19. K. Faraoun and A. Rabhi. Data dimensionality reduction based on genetic selection of feature subsets, *INFOCOMP Journal of Computer Science.* **6**, 36–46, (2007).
20. G. Stein, B. Chen, A. S. Wu, and K. A. Hua. Decision tree classifier for network intrusion detection with GA-based feature selection. In ed. V. A. Clincy, *Proceedings of the 43rd Annual ACM Southeast Regional Conference*, Vol. 2, pp. 136–141, Kennesaw, GA,USA, (2005). ACM Press, New York, NY, USA.
21. D. S. Kim, H.-N. Nguyen, and J. S. Park. Genetic algorithm to improve SVM based network intrusion detection system. In *19th International Conference on Advanced Information Networking and Applications (AINA '05)*, Vol. 2, pp. 155–158. IEEE Press, Piscataway, NJ, USA, (2005).
22. C. H. Lee, S. W. Shin, and J. W. Chung. Network intrusion detection through genetic feature selection. In *The 7th ACIS International Conference on Software Engineering, Artificial Intelligence, Networking, and Parallel/ Distributed Computing (SNPD '06)*, pp. 109–114, (2006).
23. M.-Y. Su. Feature weighting and selection for a real-time network intrusion detection system based on GA with KNN. In eds. C. C. Yang, H. Chen *et al.*, *Intelligence and Security Informatics*, Vol. LNCS 5075/2008, pp. 195–204. Springer, Berlin/Heidelberg, Germany, (2008).
24. S. Mukkamala and A. H. Sung. Significant feature selection using computational intelligent techniques for intrusion detection. In eds. S. Bandyopadhyay, U. Maulik, L. B. Holder, and D. J. Cook. *Advanced Methods for Knowledge Discovery from Complex Data*, number 2 in Advanced Information and Knowledge Processing, pp. 285–306. Springer, London, UK, (2005).
25. A. H. Sung and S. Mukkamala. The feature selection and intrusion detection problems. In ed. M. J. Maher. *Advances in Computer Science — ASIAN 2004*, Vol. LNCS 3321/2005, pp. 468–482. Springer, Berlin/Heidelberg, Germany, (2005).
26. J. Gómez and D. Dasgupta. Complete expression trees for evolving fuzzy classifier systems with genetic algorithms and application to network intrusion detection. In *Proceedings of the 21st International Conference of the North American Fuzzy Information Society (NAFIPS '02)*, pp. 469–474, New Orleans, LA, USA, (2002). IEEE Press, Piscataway, NJ, USA.
27. J. Gómez and D. Dasgupta. Evolving fuzzy classifiers for intrusion detection. In *Proceedings of the 2002 IEEE Workshop on Information Assurance*, West Point, NY, USA, (2002). IEEE Press, Piscataway, NJ, USA.
28. W. Li. Using genetic algorithm for network intrusion detection. In *Proceedings of United States Department of Energy Cyber Security Group 2004 Training Conference*, Kansas City, KS, USA, (2004).
29. C. Sinclair, L. Pierce, and S. Matzner. An application of machine learning to network intrusion detection. In *Proceedings of 15th Annual Computer Security Applications Conference (ACSAC '99)*, pp. 371–377, Phoenix, AZ, USA, (1999). IEEE Press, Piscataway, NJ, USA.

30. M. M. Pillai, J. H. Eloff, and H. S. Venter. An approach to implement a network intrusion detection system using genetic algorithms. In *Proceedings of the 2004 annual research conference of the South African institute of computer scientists and information technologists on IT research in developing countries*, Vol. 75, pp. 221–221, Stellenbosch, Western Cape, South Africa, (2004).

31. R. H. Gong, M. Zulkernine, and P. Abolmaesumi. A software implementation of a genetic algorithm based approach to network intrusion detection. In *The 6th International Conference on Software Engineering, Artificial Intelligence, Networking and Parallel/Distributed Computing, 2005 and the First ACIS International Workshop on Self-Assembling Wireless Networks (SNPD/SAWN '05)*, pp. 246–253. IEEE Press, Piscataway, NJ, USA, (2005).

32. M. Mischiatti and F. Neri. Applying local search and genetic evolution in concept learning systems to detect intrusion in computer networks. In eds. R. L. de Mántaras and E. Plaza. *Proceedings of the 11th European Conference on Machine Learning (ECML '00), Barcelona, Spain, 31 May–2 June, 2000*, Vol. LNCS 1810/2000. Springer, Berlin/Heidelberg, Germany, (2000).

33. F. Neri. Mining TCP/IP traffic for network intrusion detection by using a distributed genetic algorithm. In eds. R. L. de Mántaras and E. Plaza. *Proceedings of the 11th European Conference on Machine Learning (ECML '00), Barcelona, Spain, 31 May–2 June, 2000*, Vol. LNCS 1810/2000, pp. 313–322. Springer, Berlin/Heidelberg, Germany, (2000).

34. J. Horn and D. E. Goldberg. Natural niching for evolving cooperative classifiers. In eds. J. R. Koza, D. E. Goldberg, D. B. Fogel, and R. L. Riolo. *Proceedings of the 1st Annual Conference on Genetic Programming*, pp. 553–564. The MIT Press, Cambridge, MA, USA, (1996).

35. J. Holland and J. Reitman. Cognitive systems based on adaptive algorithms. In eds. D. Waterman and F. Hayes-Roth. *Pattern-Directed Inference Systems*. Academic Press, New York, NJ, USA, (1978).

36. S. Smith. *A learning system based on genetic adaptive algorithms.* PhD thesis, Department of Computer Science, University of Pittsburgh, USA, (1980).

37. C.-H. Tsang, S. Kwong, and H. Wang. Anomaly intrusion detection using multi-objective genetic fuzzy system and agent-based evolutionary computation framework. In *Proceedings of the 5th IEEE International Conference on Data Mining (ICDM '05)*, pp. 4–7. IEEE Press, Piscataway, NJ, USA, (2005).

38. C.-H. Tsang, S. Kwong, and H. Wang. Genetic-fuzzy rule mining approach and evaluation of feature selection techniques for anomaly intrusion detection, *Pattern Recognition.* **40**(9), 2373–2391, (2007).

39. Y. Chen, J. Zhou, and A. Abraham. Estimation of distribution algorithm for optimization of neural networks for intrusion detection system. In eds. L. Rutkowski, R. Tadeusiewicz, L. A. Zadeh, and J. Zurada. *The 8th International Conference on Artificial Intelligence and Soft Computing*

(ICAISC '06), Vol. LNCS 4029/2006, pp. 9–18. Springer, Berlin/Heidelberg, Germany, (2006).

40. M. S. Abadeh and J. Habibi. Computer intrusion detection using an iterative fuzzy rule learning approach. In *IEEE International Conference on Fuzzy Systems (FUZZ-IEEE '07)*, pp. 1–6, London, UK, (2007). IEEE Press, Piscataway, NJ, USA.

41. T. Özyer, R. Alhajj, and K. Barker. Intrusion detection by integrating boosting genetic fuzzy classifier and data mining criteria for rule pre-screening, *Journal of Network and Computer Applications.* **30**(1), 99–113, (2007).

42. D. Wilson and D. Kaur. Using grammatical evolution for evolving intrusion detection rules. In ed. G. R. Dattatreya. *Proceedings of the 5th WSEAS Int. Conf. on Circuits, Systems, Electronics, Control & Signal Processing*, pp. 42–47, Dallas, TX, USA, (2006).

43. Z. Bankovic, D. Stepanovic, S. Bojanica, and O. Nieto-Taladriz. Improving network security using genetic algorithm approach, *Computers & Electrical Engineering.* **33**(5–6), 438–451, (2007).

44. H. H. Dam, K. Shafi, and H. A. Abbass. Can evolutionary computation handle large dataset? In eds. S. Zhang and R. Jarvis. *AI 2005: Advances in Artificial Intelligence- 18th Australian Joint Conference on Artificial Intelligence, Sydney, Australia, 5-9 December, 2005*, Vol. LNCS 3809/2005, pp. 1092–1095. Springer, Berlin/Heidelberg, Germany, (2005).

45. K. Shafi, H.A.Abbass, and W. Zhu. An adaptive rule-based intrusion detection architecture. In *The Security Technology Conference, the 5th Homeland Security Summit*, pp. 345–355, Canberra, Australia, (2006).

46. K. Shafi, Kamran, H. A. Abbass, and W. Zhu. The role of early stopping and population size in XCS for intrusion detection. In eds. T.-D. Wang and *et al.*, *Simulated Evolution and Learning*, Vol. LNCS 4247/2006, pp. 50–57. Springer, Berlin/Heidelberg, Germany, (2006).

47. K. Shafi, H. Abbass, and W. Zhu. Real time signature extraction during adaptive rule discovery using UCS. In eds. D. Srinivasan and L. Wang. *Proceedings of the IEEE Congress on Evolutionary Computation (ICEC '07)*, pp. 2509–2516, Singapore, (2007). IEEE Press, Piscataway, NJ, USA.

48. K. Shafi, T. Kovacs, H. A. Abbass, and W. Zhu. Intrusion detection with evolutionary learning classifier systems, *Natural Computing.* (2007).

49. M. Crosbie and E. H. Spafford. Applying genetic programming to intrusion detection. In eds. E. V. Siegel and J. R. Koza. *Working Notes for the AAAI Symposium on Genetic Programming*, pp. 1–8, MIT, Cambridge, MA, USA, (1995). AAAI Press, Menlo Park, CA, USA.

50. W. Lu and I. Traore. Detecting new forms of network intrusion using genetic programming, *Computational Intelligence.* **20**(3), 475–494, (2004).

51. C. Yin, S. Tian, H. Huang, and J. He. Applying genetic programming to evolve learned rules for network anomaly detection. In eds. L. Wang, K. Chen and Y. S. Ong. *Advances in Natural Computation*, Vol. LNCS 3612/2005, pp. 323–331. Springer, Berlin/Heidelberg, Germany, (2005).

52. G. Folino, C. Pizzuti, and G. Spezzano. An evolutionary ensemble approach for distributed intrusion detection. In eds. P. Liardet, P. Collet, C. Fonlupt, E. Lutton and M. Schoenauer. *International Conference on Artificial Evolution (EA '05)*, Marseilles, France, (2005).

53. G. Folino, C. Pizzuti, and G. Spezzano. GP ensemble for distributed intrusion detection systems. In eds. S. Singh, M. Singh, C. Apté and P. Perner. *Pattern Recognition and Data Mining, Third International Conference on Advances in Pattern Recognition (ICAPR '05), Bath, UK, August 22-25, 2005, Proceedings, Part I*, Vol. LNCS 3686/2005, pp. 54–62. Springer, Berlin/Heidelberg, Germany, (2005).

54. A. Giordana, F. Neri, and L. Saitta. Search-intensive concept induction, *Evolutionary Computation*. 3(4), 375–416, (1995).

55. M. S. Abadeh, J. Habibi, Z. Barzegar, and M. Sergi. A parallel genetic local search algorithm for intrusion detection in computer networks, *Engineering Applications of Artificial Intelligence*. 20(8), 1058–1069, (2007).

56. M. S. Abadeh, J. Habibi, and C. Lucas. Intrusion detection using a fuzzy genetics-based learning algorithm, *Journal of Network and Computer Applications*. 30(1), 414–428, (2007).

57. X. S. Wu and W. Banzhaf. Combatting financial fraud: A coevolutionary anomaly detection approach. In eds. M. Keijzer and et al.. *Proceedings of the 10th Annual Conference on Genetic and Evolutionary Computation (GECCO '08)*, pp. 1673–1680, Atlanta, GA, USA, (2008). ACM Press, New York, NY, USA.

58. S. M. Bridges and R. B. Vaughn. Fuzzy data mining and genetic algorithms applied to intrusion detection. In *Proceedings of the 23rd National Information Systems Security Conference*, pp. 13–31, Baltimore, MA, USA, (2000).

59. T. Xia, G. Qu, S. Hariri, and M. Yousif. An efficient network intrusion detection method based on information theory and genetic algorithm. In eds. M. A. Diethelm and et al.. *The 24th IEEE International Conference on Performance, Computing, and Communications (IPCCC 2005)*, pp. 11–17, Phoenix, AZ, USA, (2005). IEEE Press, Piscataway, NJ, USA.

60. A. Chittur. Model generation for an intrusion detection system using genetic algorithms. Technical report, High School Honors Thesis, Ossining High School. In cooperation with Columbia Univ., (2002).

61. A. Abraham and C. Grosan. Evolving intrusion detection systems. In eds. N. Nedjah, A. Abraham, and L. de Macedo Mourelle. *Genetic Systems Programming*, Vol. 13, pp. 57–79. Springer, Berlin/Heidelberg, Germany, (2006).

62. A. Abraham, C. Grosan, and C. Martin-Vide. Evolutionary design of intrusion detection programs, *International Journal of Network Security*. 4(3), 328–339, (2007).

63. C. Grosan, A. Abraham, and S. Y. Han. MEPIDS: Multi-expression programming for intrusion detection system. In eds. J. Mira and J. Alvarez. *Artificial Intelligence and Knowledge Engineering Applications: A Bioinspired*

Approach, Vol. LNCS 3562/2005, pp. 163–172. Springer, Berlin/Heidelberg, Germany, (2005).
64. S. Mukkamala, A. H. Sung, and A. Abraham. Modeling intrusion detection systems using linear genetic programming approach. In eds. R. Orchard, C. Yang, and M. Ali. *The 17th International Conference on Industrial & Engineering Applications of Artificial Intelligence and Expert Systems, Innovations in Applied Artificial Intelligence*, Vol. LNCS 3029/2004, pp. 633–642. Springer, Berlin/Heidelberg, Germany, (2004).
65. D. Song. A linear genetic programming approach to intrusion detection. Master's thesis, Faculty of Computer Science, Dalhousie University, Canada, (2003).
66. D. Song, M. I. Heywood, and A. N. Zincir-Heywood. A linear genetic programming approach to intrusion detection. In eds. E. Cantú-Paz and et al.. *Proceedings of the 5th Annual Conference on Genetic and Evolutionary Computation (GECCO '03), Part II, Chicago, IL, USA, July, 2003*, Vol. LNCS 2724/2003, pp. 2325–2336. Springer, Berlin/Heidelberg, Germany, (2003).
67. M. Oltean. Multi expression programming. Technical report, Department of Computer Science, Babes-Bolyai University, Romania, (2006).
68. S. Mukkamala and A. H. Sung. A comparative study of techniques for intrusion detection. In *Proceedings of 15th IEEE International Conference on Tools with Artificial Intelligence*, pp. 570– 577. IEEE Press, Piscataway, NJ, USA, (2003).
69. P. LaRoche and A. N. Zincir-Heywood. 802.11 network intrusion detection using genetic programming. In ed. F. Rothlauf. *Proceedings of the 7th Annual Conference on Genetic and Evolutionary Computation (GECCO '05)*, pp. 170–171, Washington D.C., USA, (2005). ACM Press, New York, NY, USA.
70. P. LaRoche and A. N. Zincir-Heywood. Genetic programming based WiFi data link layer attack detection. In eds. J. Almhana, M. Barbeau, and A. Kamal. *Proceedings of the 4th Annual Communication Networks and Services Research Conference (CNSR '06)*, pp. 8–15. IEEE Press, Piscataway, NJ, USA, (2006).
71. K. Faraoun and A. Boukelif. Genetic programming approach for multi-category pattern classification applied to network intrusions detection, *International Journal Of Computational Intelligence And Applications.* **3**(1), 77–90, (2006).
72. P. Lichodzijewski and M. I. Heywood. Pareto-coevolutionary genetic programming for problem decomposition in multi-class classification. In ed. H. Lipson. *Proceedings of the 9th Annual Conference on Genetic and Evolutionary Computation (GECCO '07)*, pp. 464–471, London, UK, (2007). ACM Press, New York, NY, USA.
73. J. V. Hansen, P. B. Lowry, R. D. Meservy, and D. M. McDonald. Genetic programming for prevention of cyberterrorism through dynamic and evolving intrusion detection, *Decision Support System.* **43**(4), 1362–1374, (2007).

74. W. Lu. *An unsupervised anomaly detection framework for multiple-connection based network intrusions.* PhD thesis, Department of Electrical and Computer Engineering, University of Victoria, Canada, (2005).
75. W. Lu and I. Traore. An unsupervised anomaly detection framework for network intrusions. Technical report, Information Security and Object Technology (ISOT) Group, University of Victoria, Canada, (2005).
76. Y. Liu, K. Chen, X. Liao, and W. Zhang. A genetic clustering method for intrusion detection, *Pattern Recognition.* **37**, 927–942, (2004).
77. J. Zhao, J. Zhao, and J. Li. Intrusion detection based on clustering genetic algorithm. In *Proceedings of the 4th International Conference on Machine Learning and Cybernetics*, Vol. 6, pp. 3911–3914, Guangzhou, China, (2005). IEEE Press, Piscataway, NJ, USA.
78. E. Leon, O. Nasraoui, and J. Gomez. Anomaly detection based on unsupervised niche clustering with application to network intrusion detection. In *Proceedings of the IEEE Congress on Evolutionary Computation (ICEC '04)*, Vol. 1, pp. 502–508, Portland, OR, USA, (2004). IEEE Press, Piscataway, NJ, USA.
79. C. Elkan. Results of the KDD '99 classifier learning, *ACM SIGKDD Explorations Newsletter.* 1:ACM Press, New York, NY, USA, (2000).
80. M. Dass. LIDS: A learning intrusion detection system. Master of science, Department of Computer Science, The University of Georgia, USA, (2003).
81. P. A. Diaz-Gomez and D. F. Hougen. A genetic algorithm approach for doing misuse detection in audit trail files. In ed. L. O'Conner. *The 15th International Conference on Computing (CIC '06)*, pp. 329–338, Mexico City, Mexico, (2006). IEEE Press, Piscataway, NJ, USA.
82. A. Hofmann, C. Schmitz and B. Sick. Rule extraction from neural networks for intrusion detection in computer networks. In *IEEE International Conference on Systems, Man and Cybernetics*, Vol. 2, pp. 1259–1265, Washingtong, D.C., USA, (2003). IEEE Press, Piscataway, NJ, USA.
83. S. J. Han and S.-B. Cho. Evolutionary neural networks for anomaly detection based on the behavior of a program, *IEEE Transactions On Systems, Man, And Cybernetics, part B.* **36**(3), 559–570, (2006).
84. Q. Xu, W. Pei, L. Yang, and Q. Zhao. An intrusion detection approach based on understandable neural network trees, *International Journal of Computer Science and Network Security.* **6**(11), 229–234, (2006).
85. S. Forrest, R. Smith, B. Javornik, and A. Perelson. Using genetic algorithms to explore pattern recognition in the immune system, *Evolutionary Computation.* **1**(3), 191–211, (1993). MIT Press Cambridge, MA, USA.
86. H. G. Kayacik, A. N. Zincir-Heywood, and M. Heywood. Evolving successful stack overflow attacks for vulnerability testing. In *Proceedings of the 21st Annual Computer Security Applications Conference (ACSAC '05)*, pp. 8–15, Washington D.C., USA, (2005). IEEE Press, Piscataway, NJ, USA.
87. S. W. Mahfoud. Crossover interactions among niches. In *Proceedings of the IEEE Congress on Evolutionary Computation (ICEC '94)*, Vol. 1, pp. 188–193, Orlando, FL, USA, (1994). IEEE Press, Piscataway, NJ, USA.

88. K. S. Leung, Y. Leung, L. So, and K. F. Yam. Rule learning in expert systems using genetic algorithms: 1, concepts. In *Proceeding of the 2nd International Conference on Fuzzy Logic and Neural Networks*, Vol. 1, pp. 201–204, (1992).
89. B. Balajinath and S. V. Raghavan. Intrusion detection through learning behavior model, *Computer Communications*. **24**(12), 1202–1212, (2001).
90. S. Harding and W. Banzhaf. Fast genetic programming on GPUs. In eds. M. Ebner and *et al.*. *Proceedings of 10th European Conference on Genetic Programming, Valencia, Spain, April 2007*, Vol. LNCS 4445/2007, pp. 90–101. Springer, Berlin/Heidelberg, Germany, (2007).

Chapter 3

EVOLUTION OF NEURAL NETWORK AND POLYNOMIAL NETWORK

B. B. MISRA*, P. K. DASH[†] and G. PANDA[‡]

*Department of Information Technology,
Silicon Institute of Technology,
Bhubaneswar-751024, Orissa, India
misrabijan@gmail.com

[†]Multidisciplinary Research Cell,
SOA University,
Bhubaneswar-751030, Orissa, India
pkdash_india@yahoo.com

[‡]School of Electrical Sciences,
Indian Institute of Technology,
Bhubaneswar, Orissa, India
ganapati.panda@gmail.com

Natural evolution is the process of optimizing the characteristics and architecture of the living beings on earth. Possibly evolving the optimal characteristics and architectures of the living beings are the most complex problems being optimized on earth since time immemorial. The evolutionary technique, though seems to be very slow, is one of the most powerful tools for optimization, especially when all the existing traditional techniques fail. This chapter presents how these evolutionary techniques can be used to generate optimal architecture and characteristics of different machine learning techniques. Mainly two different types of networks considered in this chapter for evolution are Artificial Neural Network and Polynomial Network. Though research has been conducted on evolution of Artificial Neural Network, research on evolution of polynomial Networks is still in its early stage. Evolution of both the networks have been discussed in detail. Experimental results are presented for further clarification of the evolution process of such networks.

3.1. Introduction

Evolutionary computation (EC) involves the study of the computational techniques based on the principles of natural evolution. Evolution is responsible for the structural design of all living beings on earth. EC employs this powerful philosophy to find solutions to complex problems.

The first work on the use of evolution-inspired approaches to problem solving was attempted during late 1950s.[1-5] Independent and almost simultaneous research conducted by Rechenberg and Schwefel on evolution strategies,[6-9] by Holland on genetic algorithms,[10,11] and by Fogel on evolutionary programming[12,13] triggered the study and the application of evolutionary techniques.

The introduction of evolutionary techniques has inspired different subjects such as the optimal design of artificial neural network (ANN) and fuzzy systems to solve their problem using it. EC follows heuristic and stochastic principles based on populations made up of individuals with a specified behavior similar to the biological phenomenon. EC techniques are robust and efficient at exploring an entire solution space of the optimization problem.

The designing of ANN architecture for a specific problem come across a number of difficulties, such as finding optimal number of hidden layers, optimal number of neurons for each hidden layer, choosing the node transfer function for the neurons, learning rule, and the parameters for the algorithm. Again after deciding all these values finding the optimal connection weights between the nodes of different layers is also a highly complex task. Further these ANN design requirements depend on one another. This leaves little scope for a human designer to achieve optimal result by manually choosing them from the vast multidimensional search space using his personal expertise or by the trial and error method. A suitable alternative is to employ the evolutionary approach to resolve such complex problems. EC techniques have been successfully used to evolve weights, structure, and learning parameters of ANN in recent years.[14-16]

Though polynomial neural network (PNN) is similar to the feed forward neural network in architecture it is also a self organizing network.[17-22] Therefore the difficulties associated with ANN to obtain an optimal architecture are resolved in PNN. Normally the weights associated with the neurons/partial descriptions (PDs) are estimated with least square estimation (LSE) method. But there are certain complexities associated with the PNN which can be efficiently resolved using the evolutionary technique.

The input size is a constraint for PNN. If the input variables and data points are very large, PNN algorithm has a tendency to produce overly complex network. On the other hand, if a small number of input variables are available, PNN does not maintain good performance.

In addition to input variables, the type or order of polynomial used for the PDs plays an important role in construction of the network model and its performance. These parameters must be chosen in advance before the architecture of the PNN is constructed. In most cases, they are determined by trial and error method, leading to heavy computational load and low efficiency. Evolutionary techniques may be used to determine the number of input variables to be optimally chosen among many input variables for each node and to determine the appropriate type of polynomials for each PD.[23–27]

The rest of the chapter is organized as follows. Section 3.2 gives a brief overview of the evolving neural network. Section 3.3 discusses how swarm intelligence can be used for evolving neural network. Further, the application of swarm intelligence for evolving polynomial network is discussed in Section 3.4. This chapter is concluded at Section 3.5.

3.2. Evolving Neural Network

In evolving neural network (ENN) evolution is the fundamental form of adaptation in addition to learning.[28–30] Evolutionary algorithms (EA) has been used successfully to perform various tasks, such as connection weight training, architecture design, learning rule adaptation, input feature selection, connection weight initialization, rule extraction from ANN, etc. One important feature of ENN is its adaptability to a dynamic environment. Evolution and learning are the basic two forms of adaptation required in general for developing an evolving network. ENN adapts to the dynamic environment much more effectively and efficiently. ENN may be considered as a general framework for adaptive systems, where the system changes its architecture and learning rule without involvement of the designer/user.

Figure 3.1 illustrates a feed forward ANN architecture consisting of a set of processing elements called neurons or nodes performs a transfer function f_i of the form:

$$y_i = f_i \left(\sum_{i=1}^{n} w_{ij} x_j - \theta_i \right) \tag{3.1}$$

where y_i is the output of the node i, x_j is the jth input to the node, and w_{ij} is the connection weight between nodes i and j. Θ_i is the threshold (or bias)

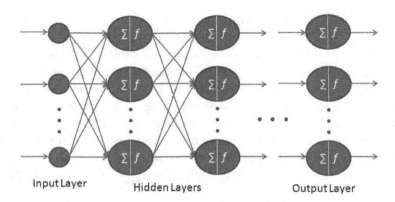

Fig. 3.1.   ANN architecture.

of the node. Usually, f_i is nonlinear, such as sigmoid, Gaussian function, etc. In general, the topological structure, i.e., the way the connections are made between the nodes of different layers and the transfer functions used determines the architecture of ANN. Learning in ANN can broadly be classified into three groups; supervised, unsupervised, and reinforcement learning. Supervised learning makes a direct comparison between the actual output of an ANN and the desired/target output. Generally we formulate it as the minimization of an error function such as the total mean square error (MSE) between the actual output and the desired output summed over all available data. To minimize the MSE, gradient descent-based backpropagation (BP)[31] algorithm is used to adjust connection weights in the ANN iteratively.

Reinforcement learning may be considered as a special case of supervised learning where the exact desired output is unknown; rather it is based on the information that the estimated output is correct or not. Unsupervised learning is mostly based on the correlations among input data; no information regarding correctness of the estimated output is available for learning. The mechanism to update the connection weights are known as the learning rule, examples of popular learning rules include the delta rule, the Hebbian rule, the anti-Hebbian rule, and the competitive learning rule.[32]

The ideas and principles of natural evolution have been used to develop the population based stochastic search evolution algorithms (EA), which includes evolution strategies (ES),[33,34] evolutionary programming (EP)[13,35,36] and genetic algorithms (GAs).[11,37] Population based search strategy is the common feature of all these algorithms. The candidates in a population compete and exchange information with each other in order to perform certain tasks; see Algorithm 3.1.

Algorithm 3.1. *A general framework of EAs*

(1) *Generate the initial population P(0) at random, and set gen=0;*
(2) *Repeat*

  (a) *Evaluate each individual in the population;*
  (b) *Select parents from P(gen) based on their fitness in P(gen);*
  (c) *Apply search operators to parents and produce offspring which form P(gen+1);*
  (d) *gen=gen+1;*

(3) *Until "termination criterion" is satisfied.*

Many complex problems containing several numbers of local optima uses EA, because it is less likely to be trapped in local minima than traditional gradient-based search algorithms. EA do not depend on gradient information and thus is quite suitable for problems where such information is not available or very costly to estimate. EA can deal with problems where no explicit and/or exact objective function is available. These features make EA much more robust than many other search algorithms. An introduction to various evolutionary algorithms has been given by Fogel[38] and Back et al.[39]

Generally we use evolution at three different levels: connection weights; architecture; and learning rules. Difficulties with the gradient based training methods can be alleviated by evolving the connection weights. Choosing an appropriate topology for the ANN architecture is a complex task, needs lots of hit and trail efforts of the designer. The evolution of architectures helps ANNs to adapt appropriate topologies without human intervention. The evolution of learning rules can be regarded as the automatic discovery of novel learning rules.

3.2.1. *The evolution of connection weights*

The weight training in ANNs is usually the minimization of an error function, such as the mean square error between target and actual outputs. Most training algorithms, such as BP and conjugate gradient algorithms,[32,40–42] are based on gradient descent. BP has drawbacks due to use of gradient descent[43] technique, which often gets trapped in a local minimum of the error function and is incapable of finding a global minimum if the error function is multimodal and/or non-differentiable.

ENN can be adapted to overcome the shortcomings of gradient descent based training by evolving the connection weights. The fitness of an ANN can be defined according to the needs; the fitness functions need not be differentiable or even continuous like gradient descent methods. Further since EAs do not depend on gradient information, EAs can handle large, complex, non-differentiable and multimodal spaces.[43-60] A typical cycle of the evolution of connection weights is shown in Algorithm 3.2.

Algorithm 3.2. *Evolution of connection weights*

(1) *Decode each individual into a set of connection weights and construct the corresponding ANN with the weights.*
(2) *Evaluate each ANN by computing its total mean square error between actual and target outputs. The fitness of each individual is determined by the error. The higher the error, the lower the fitness of the individual.*
(3) *Select parents for reproduction based on their fitness.*
(4) *Apply search operators, such as crossover and mutation to parents to generate offspring, which form the next generation.*

3.2.2. *The evolution of architecture*

In the previous discussion, it is assumed that architecture of ANN is predefined and fixed during the evolution of connection weights. Here the process of evolving the architecture of ANN will be discussed. The architecture of an ANN includes its topological structure, and the transfer function of each node in the ANN. Architecture design is crucial because the architecture has significant impact on a network's information processing capabilities.

Architecture design is a human expert's job till date. It depends heavily on the expert experience and a tedious trial-and-error process. There is no systematic way to design a near-optimal architecture of ANN for a given task automatically. Constructive and destructive algorithms attempt for the automatic design of architectures.[61-68] A constructive algorithm starts with a minimal network with minimal number of hidden layers, nodes with connections, and adds new layers, nodes, and connections when necessary during training. But a destructive algorithm starts with the maximal network and deletes unnecessary layers, nodes, and connections during training. However, such structural hill climbing methods are susceptible to trapping at structural local optima. They only investigate restricted topological subsets rather than the complete class of network architectures.[69]

Design of the optimal architecture for an ANN is considered to be a search problem in the architecture space where each point represents an architecture. Given an optimality criteria, e.g., lowest training error, lowest network complexity, etc., the performance level of all architectures form a discrete surface in the space. The optimal architecture design is as good as finding the highest point on this surface. The characteristics of such a surface has been indicated by Miller *et al.*[70] which make EAs a better candidate for searching the surface than those constructive and destructive algorithms mentioned above. These characteristics are:

(1) The surface is infinitely large since the number of possible nodes and connections is unbounded;
(2) The surface is non-differentiable since changes in the number of nodes or connections are discrete and can have a discontinuous effect on ENNs performance;
(3) The surface is complex and noisy since the mapping from an architecture to its performance is indirect, strongly epistatic, and dependent on the evaluation method used;
(4) The surface is deceptive since similar architectures may have quite different performance;
(5) The surface is multimodal since different architectures may have similar performance.

Two major phases of the evolution of architectures are the genotype representation and the EA used. With direct encoding, all the details, i.e., every connection and node of an architecture, can be represented in the chromosome. Whereas with indirect encoding, only the most important parameters of an architecture, such as the number of hidden layers and hidden nodes in each layer, are encoded. Other details are left for the training process to decide. The evolution of architectures can progress according to Algorithm 3.3. Lot of research on evolving ANN architectures has been carried out in recent years,[69–79] maximum of the research has been on the evolution of ANN topological structures.

Algorithm 3.3. *Evolution of architecture*

(1) *Decode each individual into an architecture.*

(2) *Train each ANN with the decoded architecture by the learning rule starting from different sets of random initial connection weights and learning rule parameters.*

(3) *Compute the fitness of each individual according to the above training result and other performance criteria such as the complexity of the architecture.*

(4) *Select parents from the population based on their fitness.*

(5) *Apply search operators to the parents and generate offspring which form the next generation.*

3.2.3. *The evolution of node transfer function*

The transfer function is often assumed to be the same for all the nodes in an ANN, at least for all the nodes in the same layer and is predefined by the human experts. But the transfer function for each node may be different and has significant impact on ANNs performance.[80–82]

Stork *et al.*[83] first applied EAs to the evolution of both topological structures and node transfer functions. The transfer function was specified in the structural genes in their genotypic representation. A simpler approach for evolving both topological structures and node transfer functions was adopted by White and Ligomenides,[72] i.e., in the initial population, 80% nodes in the ANN used the sigmoid transfer function and 20% nodes used the Gaussian transfer function. The optimal mixture between these two transfer functions evolved automatically, but parameters of the two functions did not evolve.

Liu and Yao[77] used EP to evolve ANNs with both sigmoidal and Gaussian nodes, where the growth and shrinking of the whole ANN is done by adding or deleting a node. Hwang *et al.*[79] evolved ANN topology, node transfer function, as well as connection weights for projection neural networks.

3.2.4. *Evolution of learning rules*

An ANN training algorithm/learning rules used to adjust connection weights depends on the type of architectures under investigation. Different Hebbian learning rules proposed to deal with different architectures, but designing an optimal learning rule becomes very difficult with no prior knowledge about the ANN's architecture. It is difficult to say that a rule is optimal for all ANNs. Hence an ANN should have the ability to adjust its learning rule adaptively according to its architecture and the task to be performed. Therefore the evolution of learning rules has been introduced into ANNs in order to learn their learning rules.

The relationship between evolution and learning is extremely complex. Various models have been proposed,[84-92] but most of them deal with the issue of how learning can guide evolution[84,85] and the relationship between the evolution of architectures and that of connection weights.[86-88] Algorithm 3.4 describes the evolution of learning rules. If the ANN architecture is predefined and fixed, the evolved learning rule should be optimized toward this architecture. If a near-optimal learning rule for different ANN architectures is to be evolved, the fitness evaluation should be based on the average training result from different ANN architectures in order to avoid overfitting a particular architecture.

Algorithm 3.4. *Evolution of learning rules*

(1) *Decode each individual into a learning rule.*
(2) *Construct a set of ANNs with randomly generated architecture and initial connection weights, and train them using the decoded learning rule.*
(3) *Calculate the fitness of each individual according to the average training result.*
(4) *Select parents according to their fitness.*
(5) *Apply search operators to parents to generate offspring which form the new generation.*

3.2.5. *Evolution of algorithmic parameters*

The adaptation of BP parameters such as the learning rate and momentum through evolution may be considered as the first step of the evolution of learning rules.[71,93] Harp *et al.*[71] evolved the BP's parameters along with ANN's architecture. The simultaneous evolution of both algorithmic parameters and architectures facilitate exploration of interactions between the learning algorithm and architectures such that a near-optimal combination of BP with an architecture can be found.

Other researchers[60,78,93] evolved the BP parameters while the ANN's architecture was kept fixed. The parameters evolved in this case tend to be optimized toward the architecture rather than being generally applicable to learning.

3.3. Evolving Neural Network using Swarm Intelligence

J. Kennedy and R.C. Eberhart[94] proposed a new evolutionary computation technique called the particle swarm optimization (PSO). It is inspired by insect swarms and has proven to be a competitor to genetic algorithm (GA) when it comes to optimization problems.[94,95] In comparison with GA, PSO has some attractive characteristics. It retains previous useful information; whereas GA destroys the previous knowledge of the problems once the population changes. PSO encourages constructive cooperation and information sharing between particles, which enhance the search for a global optimal solution. Successful applications of PSO to some optimization problems such as function minimization[94,95] and ANN design,[96–101] have demonstrated its potential. It is considered to be capable of reducing the ill effect of the BP algorithm of feedforward ANNs, because it does not require gradient and differentiable information. Salerno[96] used PSO to evolve parameters (i.e., weights and bias of neurons) of ANNs for solving the XOR problem and parsing natural language. Lu et al.[97] adopted PSO to train MLPs to predict pollutant levels of air and their tendency. Their results demonstrated that PSO-based ANN has a better training performance, faster convergence rate, as well as a better predicting ability than BP-based ANN. Juang[99] proposed a hybrid of GA and PSO (HGAPSO) for training recurrent networks. HGAPSO used PSO to enhance the elites generated by GA to generate higher quality individuals. The performance of HGAPSO was compared to both GA and PSO in recurrent networks design problems, demonstrating its superiority. Da and Ge[98] proposed an improved PSO-based ANN with simulated annealing (SA) technique for solving a rock-engineering problem. Their results showed that SAPSO-based ANN has a better training and generalization performance than PSO-based ANN. Comparisons between PSO and GA for evolving recurrent ANNs were done analytically by Settles et al.[100] Their comparisons indicated that the GA is more successful on larger networks and the PSO is more successful on smaller networks. However, in comparison with the wide applications of GA in evolutionary ANNs, the applications of PSO for evolving ANNs are relatively sparse.

These references indicated that PSO-based ANN algorithms were successful in evolving ANNs and achieved the generalization performance comparable to or better than those of standard BP networks (BPNs) or GA-based ANNs. However, they used PSO to evolve the parameters (i.e., weights and bias) of ANNs without considering the optimization of structure of the ANNs. Thus, the problem of designing a near optimal ANN structure by using PSO for an application remains unsolved. However, this is an important issue because the information processing capability of an ANN is determined by its structure.

Although these researches have shown that PSO performs well for global search because it is capable of quickly finding and exploring promising regions in the search space, they are relatively inefficient in fine-tuning solutions.[94,95] Moreover, a potentially dangerous property in PSO still exists: stagnation due to the lack of momentum, which makes it impossible to arrive at the global optimum.[95] To avoid these drawbacks of the basic PSO, some improvements such as the time-varying parameters and random perturbation (e.g., velocity resetting)[95] have been proposed. These improvements can enhance convergence of PSO toward the global optimum, to find the optimum solution efficiently. Yu *et al.* proposed evolutionary ANN algorithm ESPNet based on an improved PSO/DPSO with a self-adaptive ES. This integration of PSO and DPSO enables the ANN to dynamically evolve its structure and adapt its parameters simultaneously.[101]

3.3.1. *Particle swarm optimization*

The particle swarm algorithm is an optimization technique inspired by the metaphor of social interaction observed among insects or animals.[94,95] The kind of social interaction modeled within a PSO is used to guide a population of individuals (so called particles) moving towards the most promising area of the search space. In a PSO algorithm, each particle is a candidate solution equivalent to a point in a d-dimensional space, so the ith particle can be represented as $x_i = (x_{i1}, x_{i2}, \ldots, x_{id})$. Each particle "flies" through the search space, depending on two important factors, $p_i = (p_{i1}, p_{i2}, \ldots, p_{id})$, the best position the current particle has found so far; and $p_g = (p_{g1}, p_{g2}, \ldots, p_{gd})$, the global best position identified from the entire population (or within a neighbourhood).

The rate of position change of the ith particle is given by its velocity $v_i = (v_{i1}, v_{i2}, ..., v_{id})$. Equation (2) updates the velocity for each particle in the next iteration step, whereas equation (3) updates each particle's position in the search space:[98]

$$v_{id}(t) = \tau(v_{id}(t-1) + \phi_1(p_{id} - x_{id}(t-1)) + \phi_2(p_{gd} - x_{id}(t-1))) \quad (3.2)$$

$$x_{id}(t) = x_{id}(t-1) + v_{id}(t) \quad (3.3)$$

where $\tau = \frac{2}{|2-\phi-\sqrt{\phi^2-4\phi}|}$ and $\phi = \phi_1 + \phi_2, \phi > 4.0$

Two common approaches of choosing p_g are known as gbest and lbest methods. In the gbest approach, the position of each particle in the search space is influenced by the best-fit particle in the entire population; whereas the lbest approach only allows each particle to be influenced by a fitter particle chosen from its neighborhood. Kennedy and Mendes studied PSOs with various population topologies,[102] and have shown that certain population structures could give superior performance over certain optimization functions.

3.3.2. Swarm intelligence for evolution of neural network architecture

It has been seen that evolution can be introduced to ANN at different stages with possible merits and demerits. Here we will demonstrate only one example of evolving the ANN architecture and its connection weights simultaneously.[29,69,103] An approach is presented here where the number of hidden layers and number of neurons in the respective layer and set of weights are adaptively adjusted using Swarm Intelligence. In this approach, both the architecture and the set of weights are encoded in particles and evolved simultaneously i.e., each particle represents a candidate solution of the architecture and weight space. In abstract view, Algorithm 3.5 shows the simultaneous evolution of architecture and weights.

Algorithm 3.5. Evolving neural network using PSO

(1) *Evaluate each particle based on the predefined criterion.*
(2) *Find out the personal best (pbest) of each particle and global best (gbest) from the swarm.*
(3) *Update particle velocity.*
(4) *If the performance is satisfactory then stop, otherwise go to step 1.*

In this swarm approach, evolving neural network is used to evolve feed forward neural networks with a characteristic function. However, this is not an inherent constraint. In fact, we have considered here the minimal constraint on the type of artificial neural networks, which may be evolved. The feed forward ANNs do not have to be strictly layered or fully connected between adjacent layers. They may also contain hidden nodes with different transfer functions. Let us verify how this approach is representing the particles as well as evaluating the fitness of each particle.

3.3.2.1. *Particle representation*

For representing the particles we have to set the protocols such as maximum number of hidden layers denoted as Lmax, and maximum number of nodes for a particular hidden layer, denoted as Nmax apriori. Based on these values the particle can be represented as given in Fig. 3.2.

The first attribute P_{i1} of the particle represent the number of hidden layers in the architecture. The value of P_{i1} lies between 0 to Lmax. The feature from P_{i2} to $P_{(iLmax+1)}$ tells about the number of neurons in the respective hidden layer. The next features store the weights between input layer and 1st hidden layer and so on except the last feature of the particle P_{ib}. The last feature i.e., P_{ib} stores the weight values of bias unit. Figure 3.3 shows a clear mapping of architecture and weights to a particle.

3.3.2.2. *Fitness evaluation*

The fitness of each individual particle of the proposed approach is solely determined by the miss-classification rate based on the confusion matrix. The complete set of instructions for the proposed approach is as follows:

(1) Generate an initial swarm of N particles at random. The number of hidden layers and the respective number of nodes generate at random within a certain range. Uniformly distribute the set of weights inside a small range.

P_{i1}	P_{i2}	P_{i3}	P_{i4}	$\bullet \ \bullet \ \bullet$	P_{ib}

Fig. 3.2.   A typical instance of a particle.

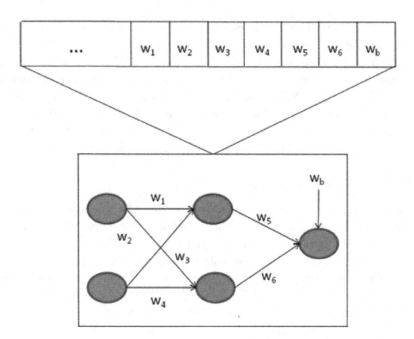

Fig. 3.3.   Mapping of architecture and weights of a particle.

(2) Evaluate the fitness of each particle by using the given training set based on miss-classification error rate obtained from confusion matrix.

(3) For each particle, if the fitness value (pbest) is better than the best fitness value in history then set current value as the new pbest.

(4) Choose the particle with the best fitness value of all the particles as the gbest.

(5) For each particle

    (a) Calculate particle velocity according to equation (3.2).

    (b) Update particle position according to equation (3.3).

(6) Continue step 2–7 until maximum iterations or minimum error criteria is not attained.

3.3.3. *Simulation and results*

The Evolution of Artificial Neural Network with PSO has been experimented with different benchmark datasets. Here we present the

Table 3.1.   Description of datasets.

Dataset	Patterns	Attributes	Classes	Patterns in class 1	Patterns in class 2	Patterns in class 3
AUSTRA	690	14	2	307	383	—
BALANCE	625	4	3	288	49	288
CREDIT(GERMAN)	1000	20	2	700	300	—
HABERMAN	306	3	2	225	81	—
HOUSE	435	16	2	267	168	—
IRIS	150	4	3	50	50	50
MONK	124	6	2	62	62	—
PIMA	768	8	2	268	500	—
WBC	699	9	2	458	241	—
WINE	178	13	3	59	71	48

results of ten different datasets collected from UCI Repository of Machine Learning database.[104] A brief description of the properties of these dataset is presented in Table 3.1.

For these simulations, we have preferred the two-fold cross validation. Each database is divided into two sets. For the division, the records are segregated depending on their class labels. Randomly we pick up the records belonging to a class and place it in one of the sets. The distribution of patterns to different sets of the databases is summarized in Table 3.2.

We have used PSO technique to evolve the architecture of the ANN for the purpose of classification of the databases presented in Table 3.2. While one set is used to evolve architecture, the other set is used for the purpose of validation. Alternately both the sets are used to evolve the architecture and for validation. The parameters of PSO used for the purpose of simulation are presented in Table 3.3.

We have used ten real life databases for the purpose of evolving ANN with PSO. The classification accuracies obtained from the training set and testing set are presented in Table 3.4. The results obtained from the training sets and test sets of a data base are averaged and the comparison of the performance is presented in Fig. 3.4. The x-axis values $1, 2, 3, \ldots, 10$ shown in Fig. 3.4 represents the databases AUSTRA, BALANCE, CREDIT, HABERMAN, HOUSE, IRIS, MONK, PIMA, WBC, WINE respectively.

Further, for the purpose of evolution of the ANN architecture, we have restricted the number of hidden layers maximum to three and the number of hidden neurons in each hidden layer to ten. The details of the architecture

Table 3.2.   Divison of dataset and its pattern distribution.

Datasets	Patterns	Patterns in class 1	Patterns in class 2	Patterns in class 3
AUSTRA				
Set1	345	153	192	—
Set2	345	154	191	—
BALANCE				
Set1	313	144	25	144
Set2	312	144	24	144
CREDIT				
Set1	500	350	150	—
Set2	500	350	150	—
HABERMAN				
Set1	153	112	41	—
Set2	153	113	40	—
HOUSE				
Set1	217	133	84	—
Set2	218	134	84	—
IRIS				
Set1	75	25	25	25
Set2	75	25	25	25
MONK				
Set1	62	31	31	—
Set2	62	31	31	—
PIMA				
Set1	384	134	250	—
Set2	384	134	250	—
WBC				
Set1	350	229	121	—
Set2	349	229	120	—
WINE				
Set1	89	29	36	24
Set2	89	30	35	24

Table 3.3.   Parameters of PSO considered for simulation.

Parameters	Values
Population Size 30 Maximum Iterations	1000
Inertia Weight	0.729844
Cognitive Parameter	1.49445
Social Parameter	1.49445
Constriction Factor	1.0

Table 3.4.   Classification accuracy obtained from ENN.

Databases	Hit Percentage in the training set	Hit percentage in the test set
AUSTRA		
Set1	94.78	87.24
Set2	93.33	86.66
Average	**94.05**	**86.95**
BALANCE		
Set1	73.07	64.21
Set2	68.05	75.32
Average	**70.56**	**69.76**
CREDIT		
Set1	82.00	75.60
Set2	83.00	73.20
Average	**82.50**	**74.40**
HABERMAN		
Set1	75.16	74.51
Set2	75.16	72.54
Average	**75.16**	**73.52**
HOUSE		
Set1	97.70	94.47
Set2	94.47	94.03
Average	**96.08**	**94.25**
IRIS		
Set1	100.00	97.33
Set2	97.33	97.33
Average	**98.66**	**97.33**
MONK		
Set1	79.03	61.29
Set2	100.00	91.93
Average	**89.51**	**76.61**
PIMA		
Set1	85.41	73.43
Set2	82.81	75.26
Average	**84.11**	**74.34**
WBC		
Set1	97.70	96.85
Set2	97.42	97.13
Average	**97.56**	**96.99**
WINE		
Set1	100.00	96.62
Set2	93.25	97.75
Average	**96.62**	**97.19**

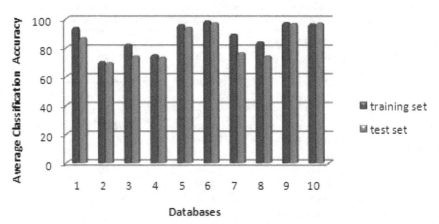

Fig. 3.4. Comparison of average classification accuracy of ENN using PSO for the training set and test set.

evolved for each set of the database are presented below in Table 3.5. From the results it can be seen that BALANCE, HABERMAN, IRIS databases perform well without using a hidden layer. A single hidden layer is found sufficient to map the non-linear relation in almost all other cases.

3.4. Evolving Polynomial Network (EPN) using Swarm Intelligence

In comparison to ANN, relatively less work has been done on polynomial neural network (PNN). It is a self-organizing architecture for neural network, introduced in,[105,106] based on the principle of Group Method of Data Handling (GMDH).[106] PNN structure exhibits distinct advantages over other methods of nonlinear modeling techniques. PNN consist of a layered structure with each layer having nodes known as partial descriptions (PD) describing partial mathematical models of the complete modeling problem. Each PD possesses high degree of flexibility and realizes a polynomial type of mapping (linear, quadratic and cubic) between input and output variables. PNN has no fixed network architecture, where model/layer development is achieved through learning. Thus, PNN is a

Table 3.5. Architectures evolved for different sets of data.

Datasets	Number of hidden layers	Number of neurons in hidden layers		
		Layer 1	Layer 2	Layer 3
AUSTRA				
Set1	1	5	—	—
Set2	1	10	—	—
BALANCE				
Set1	0	—	—	—
Set2	0	—	—	—
CREDIT				
Set1	1	3	—	—
Set2	1	1	—	—
HABERMAN				
Set1	0	—	—	—
Set2	0	—	—	—
HOUSE				
Set1	1	2	—	—
Set2	0	—	—	—
IRIS				
Set1	0	—	—	—
Set2	0	—	—	—
MONK				
Set1	0	—	—	—
Set2	1	10	—	—
PIMA				
Set1	1	10	—	—
Set2	1	10	—	—
WBC				
Set1	0	—	—	—
Set2	1	5	—	—
WINE				
Set1	3	10	10	3
Set2	0	—	—	—

self-organizing network. In each layer, a set of qualified PDs is retained based on magnitude of modeling error. The outputs of these retained PDs are manipulated in the subsequent layer PDs for further modeling error minimization. New layers are introduced till the modeling error reaches some pre set level.

3.4.1. GMDH-type polynomial neural network model

The GMDH belongs to the category of inductive self-organization data driven approaches. It requires small data samples and is able to optimize models' structure objectively. Relationship between input-output variables can be approximated by Volterra functional series, the discrete form of which is Kolmogorov–Gabor Polynomial[107]:

$$y = C_0 + \sum_{k1} C_{k1}x_{k1} + \sum_{k1k2} C_{k1k2}x_{k1}x_{k2} + \sum_{k1k2k3} C_{k1k2k3}x_{k1}x_{k2}x_{k3} \quad (3.4)$$

where C_k denotes the coefficients or weights of the Kolmorgorov-Gabor polynomial and x vector is the input variables. This polynomial can approximate any stationary random sequence of observations and it can be solved by either adaptive methods or by Gaussian Normal equations. This polynomial is not computationally suitable if the number of input variables increase and there are missing observations in input dataset. Also it takes more computation time to solve all necessary normal equations when the input variables are large.

A new algorithm called GMDH is developed by Ivakhnenko[108,109] which is a form of Kolmogorov-Gabor polynomial. He proved that a second order polynomial i.e.:

$$y = a_0 + a_1x_i + a_2x_j + a_3x_ix_j + a_4x_i^2 + a_5x_j^2 \quad (3.5)$$

which takes only two input variables at a time and can reconstruct the complete Kolmogorov-Gabor polynomial through an iterative procedure. The GMDH algorithm has the ability to trace all input-output relationship through an entire system that is too complex. The GMDH-type Polynomial Neural Networks are multilayered model consisting of the neurons/active units/Partial Descriptions (PDs) whose transfer function is a short term polynomial described in equation (3.5). At the first layer $L = 1$, an algorithm, using all possible combinations by two from m inputs variables, generates the first population of PDs. Total number of PDs in first layer is $n = m(m - 1)/2$. The output of each PD in layer $L = 1$ is computed by applying the equation (3.5). Let the outputs of first layer be denoted as $y_1^1, y_2^1, \ldots, y_n^1$. The vector of coefficients of the PDs are determined by least square estimation approach.

Depending on the growth of the PNN layers the number of PDs in each layer also grows, which requires pruning of PDs so as to avoid the computational complexity. From the experimental studies it has been observed that two best PDs does not join to produce better result, rather a PD giving better result joins with another inferior result giving PD yields the best result in the next layer. As the number of PDs grow exponentially over the layers, preserving all the PDs are not practicable. Further a substantial number of PDs need to be preserved to obtain better performance. As a result the program implementation requires large memory and computation time.

PNN layers are grown based on the error at each level. Performance of the model is evaluated at each level of the generation of the layers. At times the error level decreases gradually even up to the 10th layer. However, while evaluating the performance of the model with unknown input data results drop off beyond 3rd or 4th layer. This is due to overtraining by the chosen training data. Moreover, the growth of the layers beyond 3rd or 4th requires a lot of memory and computational time. However obtaining a suitable trade off is hard to determine, as it is not an iterative method.

3.4.2. *Evolving polynomial network (EPN) using PSO*

Evolution has been introduced to PNN at different levels by different researchers.[23-27] Some of them have tried to evolve the optimal set of inputs to each PD, some of them have evolved optimal type of the polynomial required, selection of PDs for the next layer, optimal architecture design, etc.

In most of these cases the polynomial used to develop the PDs are of Ivakhnenko's model. Generally the PDs are developed from a predefined set of standard polynomials. These standard polynomial may take two or three input and may be linear, quadratic or cubic. The combinations of these standard polynomials may not always be a good choice to generate the optimal model.

To alleviate these problems, in this section we suggest an evolving technique that will not take any standard polynomial input, the number and structure of PDs will be evolved. In addition to the number of inputs to each neuron, what are the inputs to each neuron, what are the degrees of each input in a neuron; along with the required biased weights will be evolved.[110]

In this approach we have used particle swarm optimization technique to evolve polynomials to classify the data set. The representation of a particle is shown at Fig. 3.5.

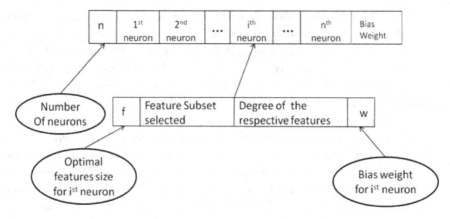

Fig. 3.5.   Representation of a particle.

First cell of the particle decides the number of neurons required for the network. Accordingly the rest of the particle space is allocated to the neurons. The space allocated for a neuron can be further divided into four parts. First cell of this space is used for deciding the optimal number of features required for this neuron and the last cell is used for the bias weight of the neuron. Rest of the cell is divided into two parts, first part of which decides the features to be selected and the second part decides the respective degrees of the features.

The architecture design of the evolving polynomial network model is given at Fig. 3.6. It can be seen that there are four distinct modules:

(1) Optimal set of neurons,
(2) optimal subset of features for each neuron,
(3) optimal degree of each feature in each neuron, and
(4) bias weight.

The first module decides the optimal size of the neurons required for the network. Accordingly the second module decides how many features and what are the features required for each neuron. The third module determines the degree of each feature in each neuron. And the fourth module works out the bias value required for each neuron and the final output unit.

Swarm Intelligence is above all to guide the different modules by obtaining the error value from the output unit. Each neuron gets the feature values and respective degrees. ℗ represents the raising of the feature

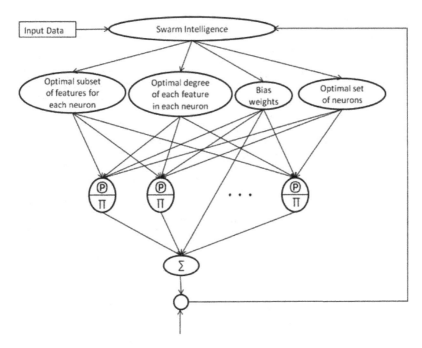

Fig. 3.6. Architecture of evolving polynomial network.

values to the power of their respective degrees. The bias value is raised to power one only. Then they are passed through a multiplier unit represented by $\prod$. Finally the output of all the neurons are summed up and passed through a linear function to the output unit. Then these estimated values are compared with the actual target output to generate the mean square error. This error signal is passed to the Swarm Intelligence module to guide different modules for appropriate training of the network.

3.4.3. *Parameters of evolving polynomial network (EPN)*

In our proposed EPN approach we evolve a set of polynomial equations to classify the data set. The polynomial equation considered in our approach can be expressed as:

$$y = C_0 + \sum_{i=1}^{n} C_i \prod_{j=1}^{p} x_r^q \qquad (3.6)$$

where n is the number of polynomial terms chosen randomly from a suitable range, p is the number of features in each term chosen randomly from the given set of features for the dataset under consideration, r is the index of feature a random integer value between 1 and number of features in the respective dataset, and q is the degree of the feature, a random integer value chosen from a suitable range.

Our proposed model is a mimic of the PNN model. We have analyzed the PNN model,[111] to obtain the suitable ranges for n, p and q.

3.4.3.1. *Highest degree of the polynomials*

While developing the models for different data sets using the Polynomial Neural Network (PNN) algorithm,[111] we have observed that many of the models are generated with satisfactory classification accuracy at the layer 3 or layer 4. Each PD in the model develops an output equation in the form

$$y = c_0 + c_1 x_i + c_2 x_j + c_3 x_i x_j + c_4 x_i^2 + c_5 x_j^2$$

where i and j take values from the range of 1 and number of features in the data set under study, where i is not equal to j, and x being the feature value or the output of the PD in the previous layer. We have observed that in many of the cases the competitive classification accuracy is obtained at 4th layer. A biquadratic polynomial equation having highest degree 2 is used for our PNN approach. Hence in each subsequent layer it gets doubled and at 4th layer the maximum degree of the polynomial is 16.

Figure 3.7 describes the possible generation of highest degree of polynomials at different layers. Considering the performance of PNN model, we have chosen the degree of polynomials in our EPN model to be in the range of 0 to 16.

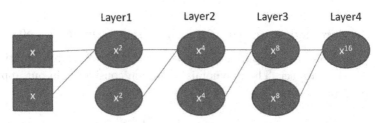

Fig. 3.7.   Highest possible degree of any feature in the PDs of different layer.

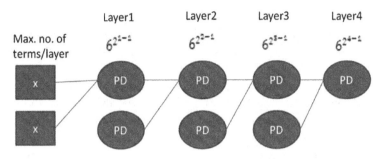

Fig. 3.8.   Highest possible number of terms in the polynomial equation.

3.4.3.2. *Number of terms in the polynomials*

For construction of PDs of first layer in the PNN model the biquadratic polynomials (5) used consists of 6 terms. The second layer takes two such inputs from the first layer, so the maximum number of terms possible in layer 2 is $6*6$ i.e. 36. In general the maximum number of terms that can be generated in any layer is , where l is the number of layer. Figure 3.8 shows the possibility of generations of maximum number of terms at different layers. However, we know that if all the features belong to unique categories, then generation of maximum terms may be possible. For example, let us consider a, b, c and d are the four unique features, then multiplication of polynomial of two terms generate four terms i.e.:

$$(a + b) * (c + d) = ac + ad + bc + bd$$

But if we consider only a and b, it will generate three terms i.e.:

$$(a + b) * (a + b) = a^2 + b^2 + 2ab$$

In our PNN models[111] each PDs from layer 2 onwards get inputs which are combinations of outputs from PDs of first layer and original inputs given to layer 1. For example in layer 2, if the output of one such PDs is produced by taking features x_1 and x_2 i.e.

$$c_0 + c_1 x_i + c_2 x_j + c_3 x_i x_j + c_4 x_i^2 + c_5 x_j^2$$

and the other input is feature, then the polynomial equation generated out of it after ignoring the coefficients is as follows:

$$1 + x_1 + PD + x_1 PD + x_1^2 + PD^2 = 1 + x_1 + (1 + x_1 + x_2 + x_1 x_2 + x_1^2 + x_2^2) + x_1(1 + x_1 + x_2 + x_1 x_2 + x_1^2 + x_2^2) + x_1^2 + (1 + x_1 + x_2 + x_1 x_2 + x_1^2 + x_2^2)^2 = 3 + 5x_1 + 4x_2 + 4x_1 x_2 + 5x_1^2 + 4x_2^2 + 5x_1^2 x_2 + 3x_1^3 + 7x_1 x_2^2 + 2x_2^3 + 3x_1^2 x_2^2 + 2x_1^3 x_2 + 2x_1 x_2^3 + x_1^4 + x_2^4$$

The maximum number of terms expected is 51 but number of terms actually generated is only 15. Further, as we always feed the different combinations of the same group of features that is available in the dataset, the number of polynomial terms is much less than the maximum which is expected. From experimentations it has been revealed that depending on the size of input features, a range of 10 to 30 numbers of polynomial terms are enough to approximate the non-linear dataset.

3.4.3.3. *Maximum unique features in each term of the polynomials*

The polynomial equation we have considered for the PNN models can have at best two unique features at layer 1. If layer 2 gets input from two PDs of layer 1, without any common features then at layer 2 any of the polynomial terms can have maximum 4 unique features. Figure 3.9 shows the possibility of unique features in each term up to layer 3. So if we consider our best result within layer 4, maximum unique features may be up to 16 in each polynomial term. From simulation of different datasets using PNN we have seen maximum of 4 to 8 unique features (subject to availability of features in the dataset) are enough to approximate the non-linearity of the data sets under investigation.

3.4.4. *Experimental studies for EPN*

The EPN technique has been experimented with databases presented at Table 3.1 and the division of the data set with distribution of records to classes has been presented at Table 3.2. The parameters of PSO considered for training of the evolving polynomial network model is given in Table 3.6.

For the construction of the EPN models, maximum limits for different modules have been fixed.

The percentage of correct classification for each data set using the EPN model is presented in the Table 3.7.

The averages of the hit percentages for the training set and test set has been compared in Fig. 3.10. The x-axis values $1, 2, 3, \ldots, 10$ shown in figures represents the databases AUSTRA, BALANCE, CREDIT, HABERMAN,

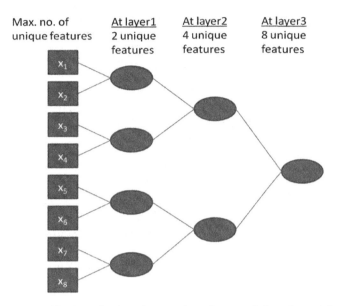

Fig. 3.9. Number of unique features in each term of the polynomial.

Table 3.6. Parameters of PSO considered for simulation.

Parameters	Values
Population Size	40
Maximum Iterations	200
Inertia Weight	0.729844
Cognitive Parameter	1.49445
Social Parameter	1.49445
Constriction Factor	1.0

HOUSE, IRIS, MONK, PIMA, WBC, WINE respectively. From the figure it can be revealed that the performance of the known database (training set) and the unknown database (test set) are comparable.

Further the results of ENN have been compared with the results of the EPN. Figure 3.11 shows the comparison of performance of the known databases with ENN against EPN. Similarly Fig. 3.12 shows the comparison for the unknown databases.

B. B. Misra, P. K. Dash and G. Panda

Table 3.7.   Classification accuracy obtained from EPN.

Databases	Hit Percentage in the training set	Hit percentage in the test set
AUSTRA		
set1	84.64	86.96
set2	87.54	84.64
Average	86.09	85.80
BALANCE		
set1	63.78	63.26
set2	63.14	59.10
Average	63.46	61.18
CREDIT		
set1	73.20	72.60
set2	71.00	71.60
Average	72.10	72.10
HABERMAN		
set1	79.09	75.16
set2	79.09	75.16
Average	79.09	75.16
HOUSE		
set1	94.93	94.95
set2	94.47	91.28
Average	94.70	93.11
IRIS		
set1	100	93.70
set2	100	96.85
Average	100	95.27
MONK		
set1	75.80	75.80
set2	74.19	75.81
Average	74.99	75.80
PIMA		
set1	75.80	75.80
set2	74.19	75.81
Average	74.99	75.80
WBC		
set1	93.98	95.71
set2	95.99	94.29
Average	94.98	95.00
WINE		
set1	85.00	81.64
set2	87.64	85.39
Average	86.32	83.51

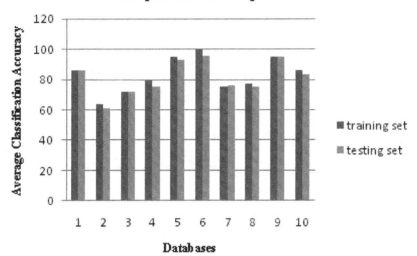

Fig. 3.10. Comparison of average classification accuracy of EPN for the training set and test.

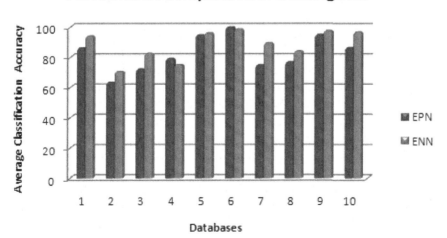

Fig. 3.11. Comparison of average classification accuracy of EPN and ENN for the training sets.

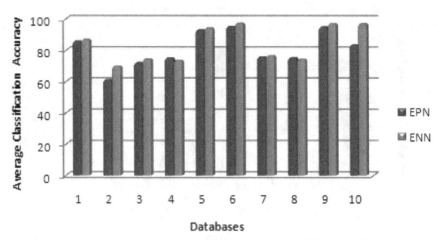

Fig. 3.12.   Comparison of average classification accuracy of EPN and ENN for the test sets.

3.5. Summary and Conclusions

The process of adaptation of evolutionary techniques for the generation of evolving neural network and polynomial network has been discussed in this chapter. The designing of ANN architecture for a specific problem encounters a number of uphill tasks. The number of hidden layers optimal for the architecture, the number of neurons optimal for each hidden layer, what should be the best node transfer function, is a single node transfer function suitable for neurons or different functions required for different nodes, what is the best learning rule for it, what should be the parameters for the algorithm and what is its optimal value, the optimal values of the connection weights between the nodes of different layers, are some of the tasks a designer of the ANN architecture needs to resolve. Further none of these tasks can be resolved in isolation, i.e., each one of it depends on others, making it a NP-Hard problem. Normally the designer adapts a trial and error method to solve it and forced to compromise with one of the possibilities he could able to experiment with the available resources. A suitable alternative is to employ the evolutionary approach to solve such complex problems. Discussion has been made on the research to solve the components of the problem in isolation as well as few of the components of the entire problem simultaneously and rest of the complexities are solved as usual i.e., by hit and trial or by depending on the domain knowledge of the designer.

A lot of research has been conducted on the use of GA to solve such problems. The application of swarm intelligence to this area is relatively new. In this chapter we have presented one of the techniques for evolving the ANN architecture and the connection weights using particle swarm optimization. The results obtained from the experimental studies are also presented for reference.

Further, we have also discussed the use of evolutionary computation to polynomial neural network (PNN). The help of evolutionary technique has been taken to solve different components of the problem by different researchers such as selection of optimal subset of inputs to a neuron/partial description (PD), selection of optimal set of PDs for the next layer, selection of appropriate polynomial function for PD, etc. We have presented a technique used for the evolutionary approach to design evolving polynomial network (EPN). We have not used any standard polynomials to develop the PDs, rather, all the components of a PD or neuron are evolved using swarm intelligence. We have used particle swarm optimization (PSO) to generate an optimal set of neurons for the network, optimal number of features and the different features needed for each neuron, the degree of each feature in the neuron, and the biased weights.

Experiments have been conducted with different bench mark datasets for the task of data classification. Few of them have been presented for reference. The results obtained from ENN and EPN are also compared to evaluate their relative performance for solving the task of data classification.

References

1. G. E. P. Box. Evolutionary operation: a method for increasing industrial productivity, *App Stat.* **6**(2), 81–101, (1957).
2. G. E. P. Box and J. S. Hunter. Condensed calculations for evolutionary operation programs, *Technometrics.* **1**, 77–95, (1959).
3. D. B. Fogel. *Evolutionary Computation: The Fossil Record.* (IEEE Press, Piscataway, NJ, 1998).
4. R. M. Friedberg. A learning machine: I, *IBM J Res Dev.* **2**, 2–13, (1958).
5. R. M. Friedberg, B. Dunham, and J. H. North. A learning machine. ii, *IBM J Res Dev.* **3**, 282–287, (1959).
6. I. Rechenberg. Cybernetic solution path of an experimental problem. In *Farborough Hants: Royal Aircraft Establishment, Library Translation 1122, August 1965. English Translation of lecture given at the Annual Conference of the WGLR at Berlin in (Sept. 1964)*, (1964).

7. I. Rechenberg. *Evolutions strategie: Optimierung technischer Systeme nach Prinzipien der biologischen Evolution.* (Stuttgart: Frommann-Holzboog, 1973).

8. H. P. Schwefel. Kybernetische evolution als strategic der experimentelen forschung in der stromungstechnik. Master's thesis, Technical University of Berlin, (1965).

9. H. P. Schwefel. *Evolutionsstrategie und numerische Optimierung.* PhD thesis, Technische Universitat Berlin (May, 1975).

10. J. H. Holland. Outline for a logical theory of adaptive systems, *J. ACM.* **9**(3), 297–314, (1962).

11. J. H. Holland. *Adpatation in Natural and Artificial Systems.* (Ann Arbor, MI: University of Michigan Press, 1975).

12. L. J. Fogel. Autonomous automata, *Ind Res.* **4**, 14–19, (1962).

13. L. J. Fogel, A. J. Owens, and M. J. Walsh. *Artificial Intelligence through Simulated Evolution.* (Wiley, New York, 1966).

14. X. Yao and Y. Liu. A new evolutionary system for evolving artificial neural networks, *IEEE Trans. Neural Networks.* **8**(3), 694–713, (1997).

15. P. A. Castillo, J. Carpio, J. J. Merelo, A. Prieto, V. Rivas, and G. Romero. G-prop: global optimization of multilayer perceptrons using gas, *Neurocomputing.* **35**, 149–163, (2000).

16. P. P. Palmes, T. C. Hayasaka, and S. Usui. Mutation-based genetic neural network, *IEEE Trans. Neural Networks.* **16**(3), 587–600, (2005).

17. N. E. Mitrakis and J. B. Theocharis. A self-organizing fuzzy polynomial neural network–multistage classifier. In *International Symposium on Evolving Fuzzy Systems*, pp. 74–79, (2006).

18. D. W. Kim and G. T. Park. Hybrid architecture of the neural networks and self-organizing approximator technique: a new approach to nonlinear system modeling systems. In *IEEE International Conference on Man and Cybernetics*, pp. 774–779, (2003).

19. D. W. Kim, J. H. Park, and G. T. Park. Combination of fuzzy rule based model and self-organizing approximator technique: a new approach to nonlinear system modeling. In *The 12th IEEE International Conference on Fuzzy Systems, 2003, FUZZ '03, Vol. 2*, pp. 1363–1367, (2003).

20. D. W. Kim and G. T. Park. A novel design of self-organizing approximator technique: an evolutionary approach. In *IEEE International Conference on Systems, Man and Cybernetics, 2003, Vol. 5*, pp. 4643–4648, (2003).

21. S. K. Oh, T. C. Ahn, and W. Pedrycz. A study on the self-organizing polynomial neural networks. In *International Conference 2001. Joint 9th IFSA World Congress and 20th NAFIPS, Vol. 3*, pp. 1690–1695, (2001).

22. S. K. Oh and W. Pedrycz. Self-organizing polynomial neural networks based on polynomial and fuzzy polynomial neurons: analysis and design, *Fuzzy Sets and Systems.* **142**, 163–198, (2004).

23. S. K. Oh, W. Pedrycz, and H. S. Park. A new approach to the development of genetically optimized multilayer fuzzy polynomial neural networks, *IEEE Transactions on Industrial Electronics.* **53**(4), 1309–1321, (2006).

24. B. J. Park, W. Pedrycz, and S. K. Oh. Fuzzy polynomial neural networks: hybrid architectures of fuzzy modeling, *IEEE Transactions on Fuzzy Systems.* **10**(5), 607–621, (2002).
25. B. Kim, D. W. Kim, and G. T. Park. Prediction of plasma etching using a polynomial neural network, *IEEE Transactions on Plasma Science.* **31**(6, Part 2), 1330–1336, (2003).
26. S. K. Oh, W. Pedrycz, and H. S. Park. Genetically optimized fuzzy polynomial neural networks, *IEEE Transactions on Fuzzy Systems.* **14**(1), 125–144, (2006).
27. S. B. Roh, W. Pedrycz, and S. K. Oh. Genetic optimization of fuzzy polynomial neural networks, *IEEE Transactions on Industrial Electronics.* **54**(4), 2219–2238, (2007).
28. X. Yao. Evolving artificial neural networks, *proceedings of the IEEE(invited paper).* **87**(9), 1423–1447, (1999).
29. X. Yao. A review of evolutionary artificial neural networks, *Int. J. Intell. Syst.* **8**(4), 539–567, (1993).
30. X. Yao. Evolutionary artificial neural networks, *Int. J. Neural Syst.* **4**(3), 203–222, (1993).
31. G. E. Hinton. Connectionist learning procedures, *Artificial Intell.* **40**(1), 185–234, (1989).
32. J. Hertz, A. Krogh, and R. G. Palmer. *Introduction to the Theory of Neural Computation.* (Addison-Wesley, 1996).
33. H.-P. Schwefel. *Numerical Optimization of Computer Models.* (Wiley, Chichester, U.K., 1981).
34. H.-P. Schwefel. *Evolution and Optimum Seeking.* (Wiley, New York, 1995).
35. D. B. Fogel. *System Identification Through Simulated Evolution: A Machine Learning Approach to Modeling.* (Needham Heights, MA: Ginn, 1991).
36. D. B. Fogel. *Evolutionary Computation: Toward a New Philosophy of Machine Intelligence.* (Wiley, 2006).
37. D. E. Goldberg. *Genetic Algorithms in Search, Optimization, and Machine Learning.* (Addison-Wesley, MA, 1989).
38. D. B. Fogel. An introduction to simulated evolutionary optimization, *IEEE Trans. Neural Networks.* **5**, 3–14, (1994).
39. T. Back, U. Hammel, and H.-P. Schwefel. Evolutionary computation: Comments on the history and current state, *IEEE Trans. Evolutionary Computation.* **1**, 3–17, (1997).
40. D. R. Hush and B. G. Horne. Progress in supervised neural networks, *IEEE Signal Processing Mag.* **10**, 8–39, (1993).
41. D. E. Rumelhart, G. E. Hinton, and R. J. Williams. *Learning internal representations by error propagation, in Parallel Distributed Processing,* In eds. D. E. Rumelhart and J. L. McClelland, *Explorations in the Microstructures of Cognition,* Vol. I, pp. 318–362. MIT Press, (1986).
42. M. F. Moller. A scaled conjugate gradient algorithm for fast supervised learning, *Neural Networks.* **6**(4), 525–533, (1993).

43. D. Whitley, T. Starkweather, and C. Bogart. Genetic algorithms and neural networks: Optimizing connections and connectivity, *Parallel Comput.* **15**(3), 347–361, (1990).
44. D. B. Fogel, L. J. Fogel, and V. W. Porto. Evolving neural networks, *Biological Cybern.* **63**(3), 487–493, (1990).
45. R. K. Belew, J. McInerney, and N. N. Schraudolph. Evolving networks: Using genetic algorithm with connectionist learning. Technical report, Comput. Sci. Eng. Dep. (C-014), Univ. of California, San Diego (Feb., 1991).
46. Y. Ichikawa and T. Sawa. Neural network application for direct feedback controllers, *IEEE Trans. Neural Networks.* **3**, 224–231, (1992).
47. L. Meeden. Incremental approach to developing intelligent neural network controllers for robots, *IEEE Trans. Syst., Man, Cybern. B.* **26**, 474–485, (1996).
48. S. Baluja. Evolution of an artificial neural network based autonomous land vehicle controller, *IEEE Trans. Syst., Man, Cybern. B.* **26**, 450–463, (1996).
49. V. W. Porto, D. B. Fogel, and L. J. Fogel. Alternative neural network training methods, *IEEE Expert.* **10**, 16–22, (1995).
50. G. W. Greenwood. Training partially recurrent neural networks using evolutionary strategies, *IEEE Trans. Speech Audio Processing.* **5**, 192–194, (1997).
51. W. Kinnebrock. Accelerating the standard backpropagation method using a genetic approach, *Neurocomput.* **6**(5–6), 583–588, (1994).
52. S. L. Hung and H. Adeli. Parallel genetic/neural network learning algorithm for mimd shared memory machines, *IEEE Trans. Neural Networks.* **5**, 900–909, (1994).
53. S. Jain, P.-Y. Peng, A. Tzes, and F. Khorrami. Neural network design with genetic learning for control of a single link flexible manipulator, *J. Intell. Robot. Syst.: Theory Applicat.* **15**(2), 135–151, (1996).
54. S.-K. Lee and D. Jang. Translation, rotation and scale invariant pattern recognition using spectral analysis and hybrid geneticneural-fuzzy networks, *Comput. Ind. Eng.* **30**, 511–522, (1996).
55. Y. M. Chen and R. M. O'Connell. Active power line conditioner with a neural network control, *IEEE Trans. Ind. Applicat.* **33**, 1131–1136, (1997).
56. R. S. Sexton, R. E. Dorsey, and J. D. Johnson. Toward global optimization of neural networks: A comparison of the genetic algorithm and backpropagation, *Decision Support Syst.* **22**(2), 171–185, (1998).
57. B. Yoon, D. J. Holmes, and G. Langholz. Efficient genetic algorithms for training layered feedforward neural networks, *Inform. Sci.* **76**(1–2), 67–85, (1994).
58. S. Park, L.-J. Park, and C. Park. A neuro-genetic controller for nonminimum phase systems, *IEEE Trans. Neural Networks.* **6**, 1297–1300, (1995).
59. I. Erkmen and A. Ozdogan. Short term load forecasting using genetically optimized neural network cascaded with a modified kohonen clustering process. In *IEEE Int. Symp .Intelligent Control*, pp. 107–112, (1997).

60. J. J. Merelo, M. Paton, A. Canas, A. Prieto, and F. Moran. Optimization of a competitive learning neural network by genetic algorithms. In *Int. Workshop Artificial Neural Networks (IWANN'93), Lecture Notes in Computer Science, Vol. 686. Berlin, Germany: Springer-Verlag*, pp. 185–192, (1993).

61. S. E. Fahlman and C. Lebiere. *The cascade-correlation learning architecture,* In ed. D. S. Touretzky, *Advances in Neural Information Processing Systems,* pp. 524–532. 2. Morgan Kaufmann, (1990).

62. M. Frean. The upstart algorithm: A method for constructing and training feedforward neural networks, *Neural Computation.* **2**(2), 198–209, (1990).

63. M. C. Mozer and P. Smolensky. Skeletonization: A technique for trimming the fat from a network via relevance assessment, *Connection Sci.* **1**(1), 3–26, (1989).

64. J. Sietsma and R. J. F. Dow. Creating artificial neural networks that generalize, *Neural Networks.* **4**(1), 67–79, (1991).

65. Y. Hirose, K. Yamashita, and S. Hijiya. Back-propagation algorithm which varies the number of hidden units, *Neural Networks.* **4**(1), 61–66, (1991).

66. Y. LeCun, J. S. Denker, and S. A. Solla. *Optimal brain damage,* In ed. D. S. Touretzky, *Advances in Neural Information Processing Systems,* pp. 598–605. 2. Morgan Kaufmann, (1990).

67. A. Roy, L. S. Kim, and S. Mukhopadhyay. A polynomial time algorithm for the construction and training of a class of multilayer perceptrons, *Neural Networks.* **6**(4), 535–545, (1993).

68. J. N. Hwang, S. S. You, S. R. Lay, and I. C. Jou. What's wrong with a cascaded correlation learning network: A projection pursuit learning perspective. Technical report, Dep. Elect. Eng., Univ. Washington, Seattle, (1993).

69. P. J. Angeline, G. M. Sauders, and J. B. Pollack. An evolutionary algorithm that constructs recurrent neural networks, *IEEE Trans. Neural Networks.* **5**, 54–65, (1994).

70. G. F. Miller, P. M. Todd, and S. U. Hegde. Designing neural networks using genetic algorithms. In *3rd Int. Conf. Genetic Algorithms and Their Applications, J. D. Schaffer, Ed. San Mateo, CA: Morgan Kaufmann,* pp. 379–384, (1989).

71. S. A. Harp, T. Samad, and A. Guha. Toward the genetic synthesis of neural networks. In *3rd Int. Conf. Genetic Algorithms and Their Applications, J. D. Schaffer, Ed. San Mateo, CA: Morgan Kaufmann,* pp. 360–369, (1989).

72. D. White and P. Ligomenides. Gannet: A genetic algorithm for optimizing topology and weights in neural network design. In *Int. Workshop Artificial Neural Networks (IWANN'93), Lecture Notes in Computer Science,* pp. 322–327, (1993).

73. L. A. Belfore, II and A.-R. A. Arkadan. Modeling faulted switched reluctance motors using evolutionary neural networks, *IEEE Trans. Ind. Electron.* **44**, 226–233, (1997).

74. J. Fang and Y. Xi. Neural network design based on evolutionary programming, *Artificial Intell. Eng.* **11**(2), 155–161, (1997).

75. V. Maniezzo. Genetic evolution of the topology and weight distribution of neural networks, *IEEE Trans. Neural Networks.* **5**, 39–53, (1994).
76. Y. Liu and X. Yao. A population-based learning algorithm which learns both architectures and weights of neural networks, *Chinese J. Advanced Software Res.* **3**(1), 54–65, (1996).
77. Y. Liu and X. Yao. Evolutionary design of artificial neural networks with different nodes. In *IEEE Int. Conf. Evolutionary Computation (ICEC'96)*, pp. 670–675, (1996).
78. D. Patel. Using genetic algorithms to construct a network for financial prediction. In *SPIE: Applications of Artificial Neural Networks in Image Processing, Bellingham, WA*, pp. 204–213, (1996).
79. M. W. Hwang, J. Y. Choi, and J. Park. Evolutionary projection neural networks. In *IEEE Int. Conf. Evolutionary Computation, ICEC'97*, pp. 667–671, (1997).
80. G. Mani. Learning by gradient descent in function space. In *IEEE Int. Conf. System, Man, and Cybernetics, Los Angeles, CA*, pp. 242–247, (1990).
81. D. R. Lovell and A. C. Tsoi. The Performance of the Neocognitron with Various S-Cell and C-Cell Transfer Functions. Technical report, Intell. Machines Lab., Dep. Elect. Eng., Univ., Queensland (Apr., 1992).
82. B. DasGupta and G. Schnitger. Efficient approximation with neural networks: A comparison of gate functions. Technical report, Dep. Comput. Sci., Pennsylvania State Univ., University Park, (1992).
83. D. G. Stork, S. Walker, M. Burns, and B. Jackson. Preadaptation in neural circuits. In *Int. Joint Conf. Neural Networks, Vol. I, Washington, DC*, pp. 202–205, (1990).
84. R. K. Belew. Evolution, learning and culture: Computational metaphors for adaptive algorithms. Technical report, Comput. Sci. Eng. Dep. (C-014), Univ. of California, San Diego (Sept., 1989).
85. S. Nolfi, J. L. Elman, and D. Parisi. Learning and evolution in neural networks. Technical report, Center Res. Language, Univ. California, San Diego (July, 1990).
86. H. Muhlenbein and J. Kindermann. *The dynamics of evolution and learning-Toward genetic neural networks*, In ed. R. Pfeifer *et al.*, *Connectionism in Perspective*, pp. 173–198. Elsevier, (1989).
87. H. Muhlenbein. *Adaptation in open systems: Learning and evolution*, In eds. J. Kindermann and C. Lischka, *Workshop Konnektionismus*, pp. 122–130. Germany: GMD, (1988).
88. J. Paredis. The evolution of behavior: Some experiments. In eds. J. Meyer and S. W. Wilson, *1st Int. Conf. Simulation of Adaptive Behavior: From Animals to Animats,* Cambridge, MA: MIT Press, (1991).
89. J. F. Fontanari and R. Meir. Evolving a learning algorithm for the binary perceptron, network, *Network.* **2**(4), 353–359, (1991).
90. D. H. Ackley and M. S. Littman. *Interactions between learning and evolution,* In eds. C. G. Langton, C. Taylor, J. D. Farmer, and S. Rasmussen, *Artificial*

Life II, SFI Studies in the Sciences of Complexity, Vol. X, pp. 487–509. Addison-Wesley, (1991).

91. J. Baxter. *The evolution of learning algorithms for artificial neural networks*, In eds. D. Green and T. Bossomaier, *Complex Systems*, pp. 313–326. Amsterdam, The Netherlands: IOS, (1992).

92. P. Turney, D. Whitley, and R. Anderson. Evolutionary computation, *Special Issue on the Baldwin Effect*. **4**(3), 312–329, (1996).

93. H. B. Kim, S. H. Jung, T. G. Kim, and K. H. Park. Fast learning method for back-propagation neural network by evolutionary adaptation of learning rates, *Neurocomput.* **11**(1), 101–106, (1996).

94. J. Kennedy and R. Eberhart. Particle swarm optimization. In *IEEE International Conference on Neural Networks,* Piscataway, NJ, pp. 1942–1948, (1995).

95. A. Ratnaweera, K. Saman, and H. Watson. Self-organizing hierarchical particle swarm optimizer with time-varying acceleration coefficients, *IEEE Trans. Evol. Comput.* **8**(3), 240–255, (2004).

96. J. Salerno. Using the particle swarm optimization technique to train a recurrent neural model. In *Ninth International Conference on Tools With Artificial Intelligence (ICTAI'97),* IEEE Press, (1997).

97. W. Lu, H. Fan, and S. Lo. Application of evolutionary neural network method in predicting pollutant levels in downtown area of hong kong, *Neurocomputing.* **51**, 387–400, (2003).

98. Y. Da and X. Ge. An improved pso-based ann with simulated annealing technique, *Neurocomput. Lett.* **63**, 527–533, (2005).

99. C. F. Juang. A hybrid genetic algorithm and particle swarm optimization for recurrent network design, *IEEE Trans. Syst. Man Cybernet.* **32**, 997–1006, (2004).

100. M. Settles, B. Rodebaugh, and T. Soule. Comparison of genetic algorithm and particle swarm optimizer when evolving a recurrent neural network. In eds. E. Cantu-Paz, *et al. Genetic and Evolutionary Computation-GECCO-2003*, Vol. 2723, pp. 148–149. Chicago, Springer, New York, (2003).

101. J. Yu, S. Wang, and L. Xi. Evolving artificial neural networks using an improved pso and dpso, *Neurocomputing Letters.* **71**, 1054–1060, (2008).

102. J. Kennedy and R. Mendes. Population structure and particle swarm performance. In *International Proceedings of the 2002 Congress on Evolutionary Computation.* pp. 1671–1675. Piscatawat, NJ: IEEE Service Center, (2002).

103. S. Dehuri, B. B. Misra, and S. B. Cho. A notable swarm approach to evolve neural network for classification in data mining. In eds. M. Koppen *et al. ICONIP 2008, Part I, LNCS 5506*, pp. 1115–1122, (2009).

104. C. L. Blake and C. Merz. Uci repository of machine learning databases, (2009). http://www.ics.uci.edu/~mlearn/MLRepository.html.

105. S. K. Oh, W. Pedrycz, and B. J. Park. Polynomial neural network architecture: Analysis and design, *Computers and Electrical Engineering.* **29**, 703–725, (2003).

106. A. G. Ivahnenko. Polynomial theory of complex systems, *IEEE Transactions on Systems, Man, and Cybernetics.* **1**, 364–378, (1971).
107. H. R. Madala and A. G. Ivakhnenko. *Inductive Learning Algorithm for complex systems Modelling.* (Bocaraton: CRC Inc, 1994).
108. J. A. Muller, F. Lemke, and A. G. Ivakhnenko. Gmdh algorithms for complex systems modeling, *Math and Computer Modeling of Dynamical Systems.* **4**, 275–315, (1998).
109. S. J. Farlow. *The GMDH algorithm,* In ed. S. Farlow, *Self-organizating methods in modelling: GMDH type algorithm,* pp. 1–24. New York: Marcel Dekker, (1984).
110. B. B. Misra, S. C. Satapathy, N. Hanoon, P. K. Dash, and G. Panda. Particle swarm optimized polynomials for data classification. In *Sixth International Conference on Intelligent Systems Design and Applications (ISDA'06),* pp. 649–654, (2006).
111. B. B. Misra, S. C. Satapathy, B. N. Biswal, P. K. Dash, and G. Panda. Pattern classification using polynomial neural network. In *IEEE International Conferences on Cybernetics & Intelligent Systems (CIS) and Robotics, Automation & Mechatronics (RAM) (CIS-RAM 2006),* (2006).

Chapter 4

DESIGN OF ALLOY STEELS USING MULTI-OBJECTIVE OPTIMIZATION

M. CHEN[*], V. KADIRKAMANATHAN[†,‡] and P. J. FLEMING[†,§]

School of Electrical Engineering,
Chongqing University,
Chongqing, 400044, China
minyouchen@cqu.edu.cn

†*Department of Automatic Control and Systems Engineering,*
University of Sheffield,
Sheffield, S1 3JD, UK
‡*visakan@shef.ac.uk*
§*p.fleming@shef.ac.uk*

In this chapter, a multi-objective optimization approach is used to address the alloy design problem, which concerns finding optimal processing parameters and the corresponding chemical compositions to achieve certain pre-defined mechanical properties of alloy steels. Neurofuzzy modeling has been used to establish the property prediction models for use in the multi-objective optimal design approach which is implemented using Particle Swarm Optimization (PSO). PSO is used as the search algorithm, because its population-based approach fits well with the needs of multi-objective optimization. An evolutionary adaptive PSO algorithm is introduced to improve the performance of the standard PSO. Based on the established tensile strength and impact toughness prediction models, the proposed optimization algorithm has been successfully applied to the optimal design of heat-treated alloy steels. Experimental results show that the algorithm can locate the constrained optimal solutions quickly and provide a useful and effective guide for alloy steels design.

4.1. Introduction

Multi-objective optimization (MOO) problems are commonly encountered in science and engineering due to the multi-criteria nature of many application problems. In many scientific and engineering fields, it is very common to face a design challenge where there are several criteria or design objectives to be met simultaneously. If these objectives conflict each other, then the problem becomes one of finding the best possible designs that satisfy the competing objectives under some trade-off scenarios. In the steel industry, optimal metal design is a challenging multi-objective problem requiring a search for optimal processing parameters and the corresponding chemical compositions to obtain the pre-defined mechanical properties of the steels.

Over the past 15 years, the use of evolutionary algorithms for multi-objective optimization has grown significantly, and a wide variety of algorithms[1,2] have been developed. One of the goals of MOO algorithm designers is to improve the efficiency of both the operation of the algorithms and the data structures used to store non-dominated vectors. This is particularly challenging in real-world problems with many conflicting objectives.[3] Similar to evolutionary computation, particle swarm optimization (PSO) is based on a biological metaphor and this heuristic global optimization technology mimics swarm intelligence; it was proposed, in 1995, by Kennedy and Eberhart et al.[4] Unlike evolutionary algorithms, which are based on the principle of survival of the fittest, PSO is motivated by the simulation of the social behavior of flocks. As Kennedy states,[3] the algorithm is based on a metaphor of social interaction, searches a space by adjusting the trajectories of individual vectors, called "particles", which are conceptualized as moving points in multi-dimensional space. At every iteration, the individual particles evaluate their positions relative to a goal. They are drawn stochastically towards the positions of their own previous best performance and the best previous performance of their companions. The PSO algorithm has been shown to be a successful optimiser for a wide range of functions.[5] Its concise conception and convenient realization was demonstrated to the evolutionary computation research community[6,7] and was subsequently effectively applied to constrained optimization, power system optimization, the Travelling Salesperson Problem, neural network training, traffic accident detection and system identification.[8-12] The integration of its self-adaptation, parameter optimization, neighbourhood topology with other intelligent optimizing algorithms led to improved exploration and experimental simulations.[13-19] PSO has proved successful in a wide variety of optimization tasks, but until recently it had not been extended to deal with multiple objectives.[20] PSO seems particularly well suited to multi-objective optimization on account of its population-based approach and the speed of convergence that the algorithm achieves for single-objective optimization.[5]

In this chapter, we combine neurofuzzy modeling and Particle Swarm Optimization to deal with the multi-objective optimal alloy design problem. An evolutionary PSO algorithm[19] is introduced to improve the performance of the standard PSO. Based on the established tensile strength and impact toughness fuzzy prediction models,[21–23] the proposed optimization algorithm has been successfully applied to the optimal design of heat-treated alloy steels. The experimental results show that the algorithm can locate the constrained optimal solutions quickly and is a useful and effective tool for alloy steels design.

4.2. The Alloy Optimal Design Problem

In the development of alloy materials, the combined design and control of chemical composition and the details of thermomechanical processing schedules to develop optimum mechanical properties invariably constitute a complex exercise. The required mechanical properties of modern alloy steels are achieved by obtaining an optimum microstructure through a careful combination of alloy compositions, rolling schedules and heat treatment. In the steel industry, heat treatments (containing hardening and tempering stages) are commonly used to develop the required mechanical properties in a range of alloy steels. The mechanical properties of the material are dependent on many factors, including the tempering temperature, the quench temperature, the types of quench medium, the content of chemical compositions of the steel and the geometry of the bar. Determining the optimal heat treatment regime and the required weight percentages for the chemical composites to obtain the pre-defined mechanical properties of steel is a challenge for the steel industry. To address this problem, a metal design paradigm which combines mechanical property prediction with an optimization mechanism has been established,[22] as shown in Fig. 4.1. It can be seen that the design optimization consists of two important components: a reliable prediction model and an efficient optimization paradigm. As the available physical knowledge of the heat treatment process is not enough to allow one to compute the mechanical properties, it is crucially important to establish reliable property prediction models. These will be obtained through elicited data-driven models, such as neural network models[24–26] and neurofuzzy models.[21–23] These models are then used to predict the mechanical properties of steel such as the Tensile Strength (TS), the Reduction of Area (ROA), Elongation and Impact Toughness.

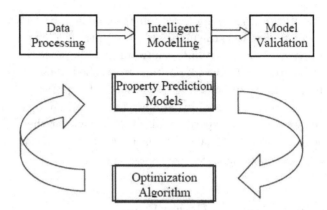

Fig. 4.1.   Metal design optimization.

The predicted properties can be used as objectives in optimal metal design. In this study, the emphasis is on impact toughness and tensile strength-based alloy design. Fuzzy models for impact toughness prediction are used to support the optimization process for multi-objective approaches. PSO is used as the optimization mechanism for alloy design. This chapter combines two challenging problems — impact toughness prediction and multi-objective optimization — into a unified framework and provides a case study example for multi-objective industrial design problems.

4.3. Neurofuzzy Modeling for Mechanical Property Prediction

Fuzzy modeling is one of the most active research fields in fuzzy logic systems. Compared with mathematical modeling and neural network modeling, fuzzy modeling possesses some distinctive advantages, such as the facility for explicit knowledge representation in the form of if-then rules (the mechanism of reasoning in human-understandable terms), the capacity for taking linguistic information from human experts and combining it with numerical data, and the ability to approximate complicated non-linear functions with simpler models. Also, the rapid development of hybrid approaches based on fuzzy logic, neural networks and genetic algorithms has enhanced fuzzy modeling technology significantly.

A variety of different fuzzy modeling approaches have been developed and applied in engineering practice.[27–31] The approaches provide powerful tools for solving complex non-linear system modeling and control problems.

However, most existing fuzzy modeling approaches place emphasis on model accuracy, paying less attention to simplicity and interpretability of the obtained models, a property which is considered to be a primary benefit of fuzzy rule-based systems. In many cases, users require the model not only to predict the system's output accurately but also to provide useful physical descriptions of the system that generated the data. Such descriptions can be elicited and possibly combined with the knowledge of domain experts, helping not only to understand the system but also to validate the model acquired from data. In material engineering, it is important to establish an appropriate composition-processing condition-property model for materials development. This study aims to develop a simple and interpretable prediction model with satisfactory accuracy, which is practical and useful in industrial applications.

4.3.1. *General scheme of neurofuzzy models*

A fuzzy model is a system description in terms of fuzzy numbers or fuzzy sets associated with linguistic labels. The general form of a fuzzy model can be represented by a set of fuzzy rules:

$$R_i: \text{If } x_1 \text{ is } A_{i1} \text{ and } x_2 \text{ is } A_{i2}, \ldots, \text{ and } x_m \text{ is } A_{im} \text{ then } y_i = z_i(x),$$

where $x = (x_1, x_2, \ldots, x_m) \in U$ and $y \in V$ are linguistic variables, A_{ij} are fuzzy sets of the universes of discourse $U_i \in R$, and $z_i(x)$ is a function of input variables.

Typically, z takes the following three forms: singleton, fuzzy set or a linear function. Fuzzy logic systems with centre of average defuzzification, product-inference-rule and singleton fuzzification have the following form:

$$y = \frac{\sum_{i=1}^{n} z_i [\prod_{j=1}^{m} \mu_{ij}(x_j)]}{\sum_{i=1}^{n} \sum_{j=1}^{m} \mu_{ij}(x_j)}, \tag{4.1}$$

where $\mu_{ij}(x)$ denotes the membership function of x_j belonging to the ith rule. Very commonly, a Gaussian function is chosen as the membership function, i.e.

$$\mu_{ij}(x_j) = \exp\left(-\frac{(x_j - c_{ij})^2}{\sigma_{ij}^2}\right) \tag{4.2}$$

Thus, Equation (2) can be rewritten as:

$$y = \frac{\sum_{i=1}^{p} z_i m_i(x)}{\sum_{i=1}^{p} m_i(x)}, \qquad (4.3)$$

where $m_i(x) = \exp(-\|x - c_i\|^2/\sigma_i^2)$ represents the matching degree of the current input x to the ith fuzzy rule. Using the Fuzzy Radial Basis Function (FRBF) definition:

$$g_i(x) = \frac{m_i(x)}{\sum_{i=1}^{p} m_i(x)} \qquad (4.4)$$

The input-output relationship (2) can be represented as:

$$y = \sum_{i=1}^{p} z_i g_i(x). \qquad (4.5)$$

Then, the fuzzy system model can be represented as a RBF network with p hidden neurons, as shown in Fig. 4.2.

Because of the functional equivalence between the fuzzy inference system shown above and a RBF network,[32] we can merge the merits of both systems together. According to the neurofuzzy modeling paradigm proposed in Chen and Linkens,[21] a fuzzy modeling problem is equivalent to solving the problem of generating an initial fuzzy rule-base from data, selecting the important input variables, determining the optimal number of fuzzy rules (i.e., the number of hidden neurons in the RBF network), optimizing the parameters both in the antecedent part and consequent part of the rules and optimizing the acquired fuzzy model by removing the redundant

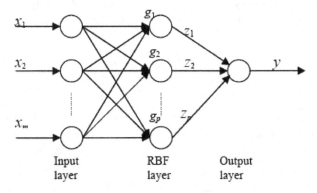

Fig. 4.2.   General architecture of a fuzzy RBF network model.

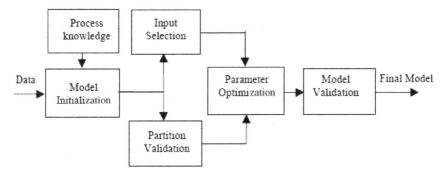

Fig. 4.3. General scheme of neurofuzzy modeling.

membership functions. Thus, a neurofuzzy model can be viewed as a neural network-based fuzzy logic system whose rules are automatically generated and optimized through network training. Compared with pure neural network models, neuralfuzzy models possess some distinctive advantages, such as the capacity for taking linguistic information from human experts and combining it with numerical data, and the ability of approximating complicated non-linear functions with simpler models. The general scheme of the neurofuzzy modeling framework is depicted in Fig. 4.3. According to the neurofuzzy modeling paradigm proposed by Chen and Linkens,[21] the modeling procedure consists of four stages. In the first stage, data pre-processing including data cleaning, data transformation and normalization, and model initialization should be undertaken. In this stage, data processing techniques and prior knowledge about the modeled process are needed for model initialization, such as determining the type of the fuzzy model, and choosing the type of membership functions. The second stage involves structure identification. There are two challenging problems in this stage:

(1) input selection, that is, to select the important inputs that affect the system output significantly among all possible input variables; and
(2) fuzzy partition validation, which is to determine the optimal number of rules for the fuzzy model.

The task of parameter optimization is carried out in stage 3. An effective learning strategy should be used to find the optimal parameters for the model. Stage 4 concerns the task of model validation. The acquired fuzzy model should be validated under certain performance indices, such as accuracy, generality, complexity, interpretability, etc. If the model performance is not good enough, further modification including structure and parameter optimization would be required. Once the model performance achieves the pre-defined criteria, the final model is produced.

4.3.2. *Incorporating knowledge into neurofuzzy models*

As previously mentioned, neurofuzzy modeling has the advantage of combinning expert knowledge with numerical data, helping not only to understand the system but also to validate the model acquired from data. This section presents a hybrid modeling method which incorporates knowledge-based components, elicited from human expertise, into underlying data-driven neurofuzzy network models.[33]

In the modeling of engineering processes, there are two kinds of information available. One is numerical information from measurements and the other is linguistic information from human experts. The aforementioned neuralfuzzy model is designed for data-driven models and cannot directly deal with fuzzy information. To enable the model to utilize expert knowledge presented by fuzzy if-then rules, an information processing mechanism must be established.

The use of linguistic qualitative terms in the rules can be regarded as a kind of information quantization. Generally, there are two different ways to incorporate knowledge into neuralfuzzy models, as shown in Fig. 4.4. The first one is to encode expert knowledge in the form of If-Then rules into input-output fuzzy data, and then to use both numerical and fuzzy data to train the neuralfuzzy model, as shown in Fig. 4.4(a). In cases where the data obtained from the system are incomplete but some expert knowledge with regard to the relationship between system input and output is available, this method can be used to incorporate linguistic knowledge into data-driven neuralfuzzy models. Fuzzy sets can be defined by a collection of α-cut sets according to the resolution identity theorem. Linguistic information can be represented by α-cut sets of fuzzy numbers. Expert knowledge represented in the form of If-Then rules can be converted to fuzzy clusters in the input and output spaces. The neuralfuzzy model can be trained using both numerical data and fuzzy data which complement each other.

On the other hand, in many cases the knowledge that links the system input and output is not available or not sufficient to generate fuzzy relations between system input and output. However, it is still possible to use expert knowledge to improve model performance if some knowledge about model

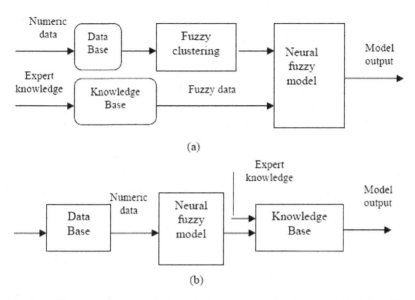

Fig. 4.4. Two approaches to the knowledge incorporation into neuralfuzzy models.

output assessment and adjustment rules is available from domain experts. In such cases, the fuzzy rule-base is generated from expert knowledge. Firstly, the neurofuzzy model is trained using numerical data, and then the obtained model output is assessed and adjusted by the established fuzzy rule-base, as shown in Fig. 4.4(b). This method is useful for knowledge-based model modification, and will be demonstrated in alloy property prediction.

4.3.3. *Property prediction of alloy steels using neurofuzzy models*

In material engineering, it is important to establish an appropriate property prediction model for materials design and development. For many years the steel research community has been developing methods for reliably predicting the mechanical properties of steels. Much of this work has concentrated on the generation of structure-property relationships based on linear regression models.[34,35] These linear models are developed for a specific class of steels and specific processing routes, and are not sophisticated enough to account for more complex interactions. Recently, some neural-network-based models have been developed to predict mechanical properties of hot rolled steels.[24-26] These models provide complex non-linear mapping and give more accurate prediction than traditional linear regression models. However, the development of these kinds of model is usually specific-problem-dependent and time-consuming. Developing a fast, efficient and systematic data-driven modeling framework for material property prediction is still needed.

The problem concerning the modeling of hot-rolled metal materials can be broadly stated as: *Given a certain material which undergoes a specified set of manufacturing processes, what are the final properties of this material?*

Typical final properties in which we are interested are the mechanical properties, such as tensile strength, yield stress, elongation, impact toughness, etc. By using the proposed neural fuzzy modeling approach, we have developed composition-microstructure-property and composition-processing-property models for a wide range of hot-rolled steels.

In the steel industry, it is important to build a reliable composition-processing-property model for alloy development. Particular emphases are placed on tensile strength and impact toughness, which are two crucially important mechanical properties in alloy steels. To build empirical models capable of predicting mechanical test results for steels, more than 3000 experimental data points from different types of alloy steels have been used to train and test the neurofuzzy model, which relates the chemical compositions and process parameters with the mechanical properties. Root-Mean-Square-Error (RMSE) was used to evaluate the performance of the fuzzy models developed. Property prediction results for different types of steels are given as follows.

4.3.3.1. Tensile strength prediction for heat-treated alloy steels

The proposed neurofuzzy modeling approach has been used to construct composition-processing-property models for Ultimate Tensile Strength (UTS) prediction of heat treated alloy steels. Using the proposed fuzzy model-based input selection mechanism[36] and the related metallurgical knowledge, 13 out of 23 possible input variables, including steel plate size (thickness and width), chemical compositions (C, Si, Mn, S, Cr, Mo, Ni, V, Ti), processing variables QT (Quenching Temperature) and TempT (Tempering Temperature), were selected as the model inputs to predict UTS. Over 400 industrial testing data points from 22 different types of

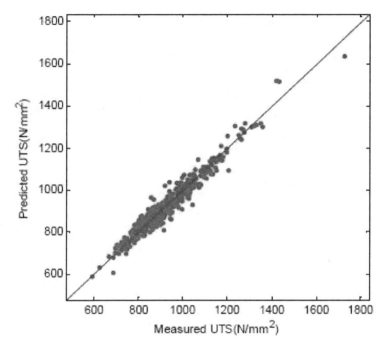

Fig. 4.5.   UTS prediction of the six-rule fuzzy model with RMSE = 33.1 (N/mm^2).

steels were used to develop the prediction models. 70% of the data were used for model training and 30% of the data for model testing.

Based on the neurofuzzy modeling approach mentioned in previous sections, a six-rule fuzzy model with confidence interval estimation was developed.[19] A comparison of the model predicted UTS with the measured UTS is shown in Fig. 4.5, (where Root Mean Square Error RMSE = 33.1 N/mm^2), while Fig. 4.6 shows the prediction results of the training and testing data respectively. 95% confidence intervals for testing data are also displayed. It is seen that the model can not only predict UTS accurately but can also provide the confidence measure for model output. The produced confidence intervals have very good coverage, i.e., almost all testing data are covered by the confidence bounds.

4.3.3.2. *Impact toughness prediction for heat-treated alloy steels*

In recent years, various models have been developed for tensile strength prediction. However, there has not been much work done on impact

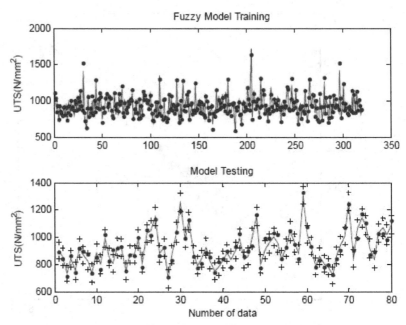

Fig. 4.6. Tensile strength prediction of the neuralfuzzy model (Dot: measured UTS; Solid line: predicted UTS; Cross: confidence bounds).

toughness prediction. The neurofuzzy modeling approach has being used to construct composition-processing-property models for both tensile strength and impact toughness prediction.

One of the most important characteristics of alloy steels, toughness, is assessed by the Charpy V-notch impact test. The absorbed impact energy and the transition temperature defined at a given Charpy energy level are regarded as the common criteria for toughness assessment. Charpy energy versus temperature curve for the test is often used to characterize the ductile-brittle transition in steels.[37] However, a value of Charpy impact energy only allows a rather qualitative description of toughness because of its complex and subtle connection with material composition and microstructure. Recent years have seen work attempting to unravel this through Charpy impact test modeling, such as instrumented Charpy test,[38] modeling of Charpy impact energy data using statistical analyses[35] and numerical modeling of the ductile-brittle transition.[37,39] However, not much work has been done to date on establishing generic composition-processing-impact toughness models. In this study, the fuzzy modeling approach has been used to establish generic toughness prediction models which link materials compositions and processing conditions with Charpy impact properties for heat-treated alloy steels.

The proposed hybrid neuralfuzzy model has been used for impact toughness prediction for low alloy steels. 408 experimental data points, including 22 types of steels, were used to develop the prediction models. The data set contains chemical compositions, processing parameters and Charpy energy $C_v(J)$ tested at different temperatures (between $-120°C$ and $60°C$). 70% of the data were used for model training and 30% of the data were used as testing data. Steel compositions C, Si, Mn, S, Ni, Nb, V, processing variables RHT (Reheating Temperature), FRT (Finish Rolling Temperature) and Charpy test temperature were selected as the model inputs.

Based on the data-driven neuralfuzzy modeling approach mentioned in previous sections, a six-rule fuzzy model was developed to predict Charpy impact energy. The predicted result at $-50°C$ with Root-Mean-Square-Error RMSE $= 22.5(J)$ is shown in Fig. 4.7. The resultant mean transition curve of Charpy impact energy versus test temperature is displayed in Fig. 4.8. This curve was generated on the basis of fixing all input variables at their mean values while the test temperature was varied from $-120°C$ to $60°C$. It can be seen that the model prediction is quite satisfactory

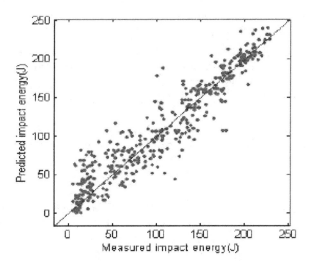

Fig. 4.7.   Impact energy prediction for TMCR steels.

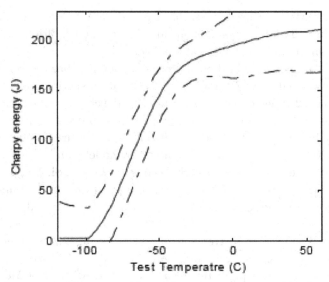

Fig. 4.8.   Impact transition curve with confidence interval generated by the neuralfuzzy model.

for intrinsically scattered Charpy test data. Since the developed neural fuzzy model can generate the full brittle to ductile transition curves for specific steels, we can apply the same model to predict Impact Transition Temperature (ITT) at a pre-defined impact energy level without model re-training. ITT_p, in Table 4.1, shows the predicted ITT of AM8 steels at 60 J energy level. It is seen that the predicted ITT values based on the Charpy energy prediction model are scattered and non-conservative (i.e., generally, ITT prediction is below the actual values). To improve the model performance, we incorporated a small knowledge-base into the obtained fuzzy model, which consists of three knowledge-based fuzzy rules:

R1: If *RHT is Low* and *FRT is Low* Then *increase ITT by about X%*

R2: If *RHT is Medium* and *FRT is Medium* Then *increase ITT by about Y%*

R3: If *RHT is High* and *FRT is High* Then *increase ITT by about Z%*

The membership functions of terms Low, Medium and High are defined by expert knowledge, with Gaussian functions used as the membership functions. The values of X, Y and Z in the consequent part of the rules were initialized by prior knowledge and then optimized via a simulated annealing algorithm. The knowledge-base was incorporated into a data-based fuzzy

Table 4.1. Charpy impact properties prediction for different steels.

Steel Type	Charpy Energy ($-50°$C)			ITT (60 J)		
	Measured	Predicted	CI	ITT	ITTK	ITTP
A8M101 (V-Ti)	204, 178	185	33	-70	-64	-75
A8M98(V)	154, 148	152	30	-65	-66	-71
A8M90 (Nb-Ni)	125, 62	84	44	-50	-55	-64
A8M94 (Nb-V-Ni)	80, 54	83	28	-45	-50	-53
A8M95 (Nb-Ni)	98, 63	81	28	-50	-48	-56
A8M96(V-Ni)	176, 152	171	27	-80	-84	-89
A8M100 (0.045%Nb-V)	97, 51	75	38	-45	-55	-60
A8M102(Nb-V)	170, 135	143	47	-55	-65	-74
A8M105(Nb-V-Ti)	192, 176	190	35	-80	-80	-89
A8M104 (0.2%Mo-Nb-V)	104, 85	84	20	-45	-50	-54
A8M92(Low C Mn-Nb-V)	185, 184	182	23	-70	-70	-82
A8M93(Low C Nb-V)	206, 197	200	21	-70	-75	-83
A8M99 (LowC 0.045%Nb-V)	199, 194	196	37	-85	-78	-89
A8M97(Nb-Ni-Ti)	186, 173	168	34	-90	-87	-101
A8M91(Cu-Nb-V)	157, 138	136	35	-75	-70	-74

model in the second mode shown in Fig. 4.4(b). After knowledge-based model modification, the RMSE of the ITT predictions was reduced from 8.5°C to 6.2°C. In Table 4.1, the ITT predictions with knowledge incorporation are represented by ITTK. The model predictions without knowledge incorporation are denoted by ITTP. It can be seen that compared with ITTP, the modified ITT predictions, ITTK, are more accurate and reasonable. Based on the developed fuzzy model, we can predict impact energy and transition temperature effectively. Table 4.1 shows the predicted impact energies of different steels at a temperature of −50°C with corresponding 95% confidence intervals, CI, and the transition temperature at 60 J energy level. It is seen that the model predicted energy values are between the two measured Charpy test energy values, and the prediction of ITT(60 J) is also quite encouraging. In the proposed modeling framework, expert knowledge in the form of If-Then rules can be incorporated into data-driven RBFN models in different way. Simulation experiments show that the developed FRBFN model has satisfactory prediction accuracy and good interpretation properties. The model performance can be improved by knowledge incorporation. The proposed modeling approach has been successfully applied to alloy toughness prediction. Experimental results show that the developed impact toughness prediction model not only predicts the impact properties of alloy steels, but also provides a useful description of the link between composition-process conditions and Charpy toughness. The developed knowledge-based neurofuzzy models are used to facilitate the multi-objective optimal design of alloy steels.

4.4. Introduction to Multi-Objective Optimization

Multi-objective optimisation recognizes that most practical problems invariably require a number of design criteria to be satisfied simultaneously, viz: $min_{x\in\Omega}F(x)$, where $x = [x_1, x_2, \ldots, x_q]$, Ω defines the set of free variables, x, subject to any constraints and $F(x) = [f_1(x), f_2(x), \ldots, f_n(x)]$ contains the design objectives to be minimized.

Clearly, for this set of functions, $f_i(x)$, it is unlikely that there is one ideal 'optimal' solution, rather a set of Pareto-optimal solutions for which an improvement in one of the design objectives will lead to a degradation in one or more of the remaining objectives. Such solutions are also known as non-inferior or non-dominated solutions to the multi-objective optimisation problem.

The concept of Pareto optimality in the two-objective case is illustrated in Fig. 4.9. Here, points A and B are two examples of non-dominated solutions on the Pareto front. Neither is preferred to the other. Point

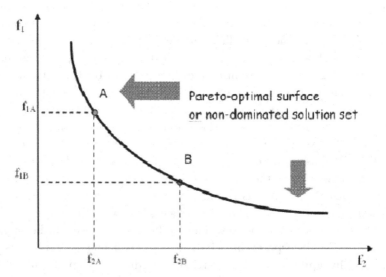

Fig. 4.9. Pareto-optimal surface or non-dominated solution set for a 2-objective problem.

A has a smaller value of f_2 than point B, but a larger value of f_1. Correspondingly, point B has a smaller value of f_1 than point A, but a larger value of f_2. Single-objective optimization has been widely used to address multi-objective optimization problems but it has a limited capability. Objectives are often non-commensurable and are frequently in conflict with one another. Within a single-objective optimization framework, multiple objectives are often tackled by the "weighted-sum" approach of aggregating objectives. This has a number of significant shortcomings, not least of which is the difficulty of assigning appropriate weights to reflect the relative importance of each objective.

Besides providing the desired family of solutions approximating to the non-dominated solution set, the multi-objective particle swarm optimizer uses dynamic weights instead of fixed weights to obtain the Pareto solutions.

4.5. Particle Swarm Algorithm for Multi-Objective Optimization

As mentioned in Section 4.3, alloy design is a challenging multi-objective optimization problem, which consists of finding the optimal chemical compositions and processing parameters for a pre-defined property requirement. Neurofuzzy modeling has been used to establish the properties prediction models which facilitate the Particle Swarm Optimization (PSO) based multi-objective optimization mechanism. An evolutionary adaptive PSO algorithm has been developed to improve the performance of the standard PSO.

Based on the established tensile strength and impact toughness fuzzy prediction models, the proposed optimization algorithm has been successfully applied to the optimal design of heat-treated alloy steels. The experimental results have shown that the algorithm can locate the constrained optimal solutions quickly and provide a useful and effective guide for alloy steels design.

4.5.1. *Particle swarm optimization algorithm*

The particle swarm algorithm works by "flying" a population of co-operating potential solutions, called particles, through a problem's solution space, accelerating particles towards better solutions. The particles in PSO consist of a d-dimensional position vector x, and a m-dimensional velocity vector v, so the ith member of a population's position is represented as $x_i = [x_{i1}, x_{i2}, \ldots, x_{im}]$, and its velocity as $v_i = [v_{i1}, v_{i2}, \ldots, v_{im}]$, $i = 1, 2, \ldots, N$, where N is the number of particles in the population. Individuals interact with one another while learning from their own experience(s), and gradually, the population members move into better regions of the problem space. The algorithm is simple — it can be described in one straightforward formula — but is able to circumvent many of the obstacles that optimization problems usually present, including those associated with Genetic Algorithms (GA). The original formula, which was developed by Kennedy and Eberhart,[4] was later improved by Shi and Eberhart by introducing an inertia weight w, in order to balance the local and global search during the optimization process.[40] During each iteration, the particle's position is modified according to the following equations:

$$v_i(t) = wv_i(t-1) + c_1 r_1(p_i - x_i(t-1)) + c_2 r_2(p_g - x_i(t-1)) \quad (4.6)$$

$$x_i(t) = v_i(t) + x_i(t-1), \quad (4.7)$$

where w is the inertia weight, c_1 and c_2 are positive constants, and r_1 and r_2 are random numbers obtained from a uniform random distribution function in the interval $[0, 1]$. The parameter p_i represents the best previous position of the ith particle and p_g denotes the best particle among all the particles in the population.

In PSO, the search toward the global optimal solution is guided by two stochastic acceleration factors (the cognitive part and the social part). It has been observed that PSO quickly finds a good local solution but sometimes remains in a local optimum solution for a considerable number of iterations without improvement. To handle this problem, many modified PSO algorithms have been proposed. Theoretical analysis of PSO has revealed the influence of the inertia weight and constants on convergence, but has not produced useful selection guidelines.[41] Most of the previous empirical developments of PSO are based on either the inertia weight or the constriction factor method.[6,15,16,40] However, for a complex multimodal function, the control of the diversity of the population with a linearly varying inertia weight may lead the particles to converge to a local optimum prematurely. On the other hand, the constriction factor method is ineffective for complex multimodal functions, despite its ability to converge to stopping criteria at a significantly faster rate for unimodal functions.

Recently, hybrid PSO algorithms have been produced by introducing evolutionary computation, such as selection and mutation. Mutation operators introduce new individuals into a population by creating a variation of a current individual, thus adding variability into the population and preventing stagnation of the search in local optima. Several modified PSO algorithms with mutation operators have been proposed[17,18,42–44] to improve the global search capability of PSO. They use a mutation operator to change a particle dimension value using a random number drawn from a probability distribution, such as Gaussian or Cauchy distribution. A particle is selected for mutation using a mutation rate that is decreased during a run, i.e., as the number of iterations increases, the effect of the mutation operator decreases.

4.5.2. *Adaptive evolutionary particle swarm optimization (AEPSO) algorithm*

To enhance the global exploratory capability of PSO while maintaining a fast rate of convergence, especially in the context of multi-objective optimization, we incorporate non-dominated sorting, adaptive inertia weight and a special mutation operator into the particle swarm optimization algorithm.[17] With this strategy, the particle's velocity in Equation (4.6) is modified as follows:

$$v_i(t+1) = wv_i(t) + [r_1(p_i - x_i(t)) + r_2(p_g - x_i(t))] + v_m(t). \qquad (4.8)$$

The second term in Equation (4.8) can be viewed as an acceleration term, which depends on the distances between the current position x_i, the personal best p_i, and the global best p_g. The acceleration factor is defined as follows:

$$\alpha = \alpha_0 + \frac{t}{N_t}, \quad t = 1, 2, \ldots, N_t, \qquad (4.9)$$

where N_t denotes the number of iterations, t represents the current generation, and the suggested range for α_0 is $[0.5, 1]$.

As can be seen from Equation (4.9), the acceleration term will increase as the number of iterations increases, which will enhance the global search ability as the search proceeds and help the algorithm to jump out of local optima, especially in the case of multimodal problems.

Furthermore, instead of using a linearly-decreasing inertia weight, we use a random number, which has been shown by Zhang *et al.*[16] to improve the performance of the PSO in some benchmark functions. Hence, in this study, we change the inertia weight at every generation via the following formula:

$$w = w_0 + r(w_1 - w_0), \qquad (4.10)$$

where $w_0 \in [0, 1]$, $w_1 > w_0$ are positive constants, and r is a random number uniformly distributed in $[0, 1]$. The suggested range for w_0 is $[0, 0.5]$, which makes the weight w randomly vary between w_0 and w_1. In this way, we can obtain a uniformly distributed random weight combination, which is generated at every iteration. The idea here is to use dynamic weights instead of fixed weights to obtain the Pareto solutions.

The third term $v_m(t)$ in Equation (4.8) is a mutation operator, which is set proportionally to the maximum allowable velocity V_{max}. If the historic optimal position, p_i, of the particle swarm is not improving with the increasing number of generations, this may indicate that the whole swarm is becoming trapped in a local optimum from which it becomes impossible to escape. Because the global best individual attracts all particles of the swarm, it is possible to lead the swarm away from a current location by mutating a single individual. To this end, a particle is selected randomly and then a random perturbation (mutation step size) is added to a randomly selected modulus of the velocity vector of that particle by a mutation probability. The mutation term is produced as follows:

$$v_m(t) = sign(2rand - 1)\beta V_{max}. \qquad (4.11)$$

where $\beta \in [0, 1]$ is a constant, $rand$ is a random number uniformly distributed in $[0, 1]$, and the sign function is defined as $sign(x) = 1$ if $x \geq 0$ and $sign(x) = -1$ if $x < 0$, which is used to decide the particle's moving direction. It is noted that the mutation rate in this algorithm is not decreased during a run. On the contrary, the mutation effect is enhanced at the late stages of search. This special mutation operator can encourage particles to move away from a local optimum and maintain the diversity of the population.

In order to evaluate the performance of individual particles, an appropriate evaluation function should be defined to select local best and global best. We simply use a weighted aggregation approach to construct the evaluation function F for multi-objective optimization:

$$F = \sum_{i=1}^{m} w_i f_i; \quad \sum_{i=1}^{m} w_i = 1, \qquad (4.12)$$

where m is the number of objectives, $i = 1, 2, \ldots, m$.

To approximate the Pareto front instead of a certain Pareto solution, the weights w_i for each objective are changed systematically and normalized as follows:

$$w_i = \frac{\lambda_i}{\sum_{i=1}^{m} \lambda_i}, \quad \lambda_i = rand, \tag{4.13}$$

where, again, *rand* is a random number uniformly distributed in $[0, 1]$. In this way, we can obtain a uniformly distributed random weight combination, which is generated at every generation. The idea is to use dynamic weights instead of fixed weights to obtain the Pareto solutions. This dynamically weighted aggregation approach was introduced for the selection of the best p_i and p_g.

Finally, in order to strengthen the convergence properties of the multi-objective optimization, the "non-dominated sorting" technique, which was proposed and improved by Deb[45,46] and then introduced into the PSO algorithm by Li,[47] has been also used in our AEPSO algorithm. In the light of the above considerations, the proposed algorithm can be summarized as follows:

(1) Initialization. Set the population size N and the maximum no. of iterations, N_t. Initialize the position x_i and velocity v_i of the particles within the pre-defined decision variable range. V_{max} is set to be the maximum allowable velocity. Set the personal best position $p_i = x_i$, and the iteration count, $t = 0$.

(2) Evaluation. Set $t = t + 1$. Evaluate each particle in the current population using a Pareto-based fitness assignment strategy. Update individual best p_i and global best p_g.

(3) New particles generation. Calculate the new velocity NV_i and new position NX_i based on the current $x_i, (i = 1, 2, \ldots, N)$, using equations (9) and (8), and the objective function values for all the new particles. Combine all x_i and NX_i (2N particles) together and store them in a temporary list *tempList*.

(4) Non-dominated Sorting. (a) Identify non-dominated solutions in *tempList* and store them in a matrix *PFront* (Pareto front). Set front number $k = 1$. (b) Remove the non-dominated particles from *tempList*. (c) Set $k = k + 1$. Identify non-dominated solutions in the remaining *tempList* and store them in a matrix *Frontk* (front k). (d) Repeat (b) and (c) until all 2 N particles are ranked into different fronts.

(5) Select particles for next iteration. If *PFront* size $> N$, then randomly select N particles from *PFront* and store them as *NextX*. Otherwise,

store *PFront* as *NextX* then randomly select particles in next front (*Frontk*) and add them to *NextX* until *NextX* size = N.

(6) Set the *NextX* as the current positions x for the next iteration.

(7) If $|x_t - x_{t-1}| < \epsilon$, execute the mutation operation as follows, otherwise go to Step 8. a) A mutation term $v_m(t)$, calculated by equation (12), is added to a randomly selected modulus of the velocity vector of that particle by a mutation probability, store in *Xtemp*. b) Evaluate the *Xtemp* and find the particles which dominate any particles in the current Pareto front. Use these dominating particles to replace the corresponding particles in the current x.

(8) If $t < N_t$, go to Step 2.

(9) Store the non-dominated solutions from the final population.

We will show that this proposed approach works very well with both multi-objective optimization test problems and our industry-related problem.

4.5.3. *Comparing AEPSO with some leading multi-objective optimization algorithms*

Multi-objective optimization is becoming more and more the focus of active research for many real-world problems, most of which are indeed "multi-objective" in nature. A good multi-objective optimization algorithm should not only converge to the global optima but also find as many well-distributed Pareto optimal solutions as possible, to provide the final user with the possibility of choosing the right solution following his/her own criteria. In order to demonstrate the effectiveness of the proposed EPSO algorithm, we used a set of commonly recognised benchmark functions (ZDT1 ZDT4 functions[45]) as test problems of multi-objective optimization. The test functions are defined as:

$$\text{Minimise } F(x) = (f_1(x), f_2(x))$$
$$\text{Subject to } f_1(x_1) = x_1,$$
$$f_2(x) = g(x_2, \ldots, x_m)h(f_1(x_1), g(x_2, \ldots, x_m))$$

where $x = (x_1, x_2, \ldots, x_m)$

ZDT1-Convex: $g(x_2, \ldots, x_m) = 1 + 9\sum_{i=2}^{m} x_i/(m-1), m = 30, x_i \in [0,1]$
$h(f_1, g) = 1 - \sqrt{f_1/g}$

ZDT2-Non-Convex: $g(x_2, \ldots, x_m) = 1 + 9 \sum_{i=2}^{m} x_i/(m-1), m = 30, x_i \in [0, 1]$

$h(f_1, g) = 1 - (f_1/g)^2$

ZDT3-Non-Continuous: $g(x_2, \ldots, x_m) = 1 + 9 \sum_{i=2}^{m} x_i/(m-1), m = 30, x_i \in [0, 1]$

$h(f_1, g) = 1 - \sqrt{f_1/g} - (f_1/g)sin(10\Pi f_1)$

ZDT4-Multimodal: $g(x_2, \ldots, x_m) = 1 + 10(m-1) + \sum_{i=2}^{m}[x_i^2 - mcos(4\Pi x_i)]$

$m = 10, x_1 \in [0, 1], x_i \in [-5, 5], i = 2, 3, \ldots, m$

$h(f_1, g) = 1 - \sqrt{(f_1/g)}$

The function ZDT1 has a convex Pareto front while ZDT2 has a concave Pareto front. Discontinuities in the Pareto front for ZDT3 cause difficulties in finding a diverse set of solutions. ZDT4 is a multimodal problem; the multiple local Pareto fronts cause difficulties for many algorithms to converge to the true Pareto-optimal front. For all test functions, we set $w_0 = 0.5, w_1 = 1, \alpha_0 = 0.5$, the population size $N = 100$ and the number of iterations $N_t = 300$. The test results are shown in Fig. 4.10. It can be seen that the proposed algorithm performed very well and converged to the Pareto-optimal with a high accuracy while maintaining a good diversity among the Pareto solutions. To compare the performance of the AEPSO to other recently developed evolutionary algorithms, such as the non-dominated sorting genetic algorithm-II (NSGA II),[45] the strength Pareto evolutionary algorithm (SPEA)[48] and NSPSO,[47] two performance metrics, namely the Generational Distance (GD) and the Spread S, which are described in,[49] were used. GD measures the distance of the obtained Pareto solution set Q from a known set of the Pareto-optimal set P^*, which is defined as follows:

$$GD = \frac{(\sum_{i=1}^{|Q|} d_i^m)^{\frac{1}{m}}}{|Q|}. \tag{4.14}$$

For a two-objective problem ($M = 2$), d_i is the Euclidean distance between the solution $i \in Q$ and the nearest member of P^*. A set of P^* (comprising 500 uniformly distributed Pareto-optimal solutions) is used to calculate the closeness metric GD.

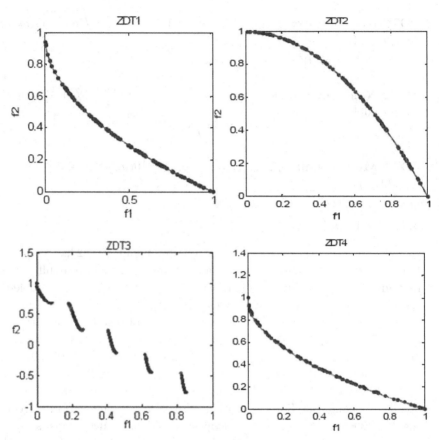

Fig. 4.10.   Pareto solutions of EPSO on ZDT1 ZDT4 solid line: Global optimal front; Dots: EPSO optimal solutions.

The Spread S measures the diversity of the solutions along the Pareto front in the final population and is defined as follows:

$$S = \frac{\sum_{m=1}^{M} d_m^e + \sum_{i=1}^{|Q|} |d_i - \bar{d}|}{\sum_{m=1}^{M} d_m^e + |Q|\bar{d}} \qquad (4.15)$$

where d_i is distance between the neighbouring solutions in the Pareto solution set Q, $\bar{d}$ is the mean value of all d_i, and d_m^e is the distance between the extreme solutions of P^* and Q along the mth objective. It is worth noting that for an ideal distribution of the solutions (uniform distribution), $S = 0$.

Table 4.2.   Mean and variance values of the convergence measure, GD.

Algorithm	ZDT1		ZDT2		ZDT3		ZDT4	
	GD	σ^2	GD	σ^2	GD	σ^2	GD	σ^2
SPEA	1.25e-3	0	3.04e-3	2.00e-5	4.42e-2	1.90e-5	9.514	11.321
NSGA II	8.94e-4	0	8.24e-4	0	4.34e-2	2.20e-5	2.92e-2	4.67e-2
NSPSO	7.53e-4	4.18e-5	8.05e-4	3.05e-5	3.40e-3	2.54e-4	7.82e-4	6.91e-5
MOPSO	1.33e-3	0	8.91e-4	0	4.18e-3	0	7.37e-1	5.48e-1
AEPSO	9.12e-5	2.61e-9	1.21e-4	1.40e-9	4.78e-4	2.85e-9	6.52e-4	4.08e-5

Table 4.3.   Mean and variance values of the diversity measure, S.

Algorithm	ZDT1		ZDT2		ZDT3		ZDT4	
	S	σ_Δ^2	S	σ_Δ^2	S	σ_Δ^2	S	σ_Δ^2
SPEA	0.730	9.07e-3	0.678	4.48e-3	0.666	6.66e-4	0.732	1.13e-2
NSGA II	0.463	4.16e-2	0.435	2.46e-2	0.576	5.08e-3	0.655	1.98e-1
NSPSO	0.767	3.00e-2	0.758	2.77e-2	0.869	5.81e-2	0.768	3.57e-2
MOPSO	0.683	1.32e-2	0.639	1.12e-3	0.832	8.92e-3	0.962	1.11e-2
AEPSO	0.759	1.70e-3	0.622	4.90e-3	0.867	1.10e-2	0.636	7.04e-3

In order to establish repeatability, the AEPSO algorithm was run ten times independently. The average performance metric values and the corresponding variance, σ^2 are summarized in Tables 4.2 and 4.3 respectively. In the Tables, the compared results for SPEA, NSGA-II and NSPSO were obtained from Deb[49] and Li[47] respectively. Results from using the multi-objective PSO algorithm, MOPSO, proposed in Coello *et al.*[20] are also shown in the Tables. It can be seen that the proposed algorithm, AEPSO, performed well as far as convergence and diversity are concerned. From Table 4.2 we can see that AEPSO has achieved a better convergence while maintaining a diverse population and achieving a well distributed trade-off front. The results indicate that the approach is highly competitive and that it can be considered a viable alternative to solve multi-objective optimization problems.

4.6. Multi-Objective Optimal Alloy Design Using AEPSO

Having established the effectiveness of the algorithm, it was applied to the optimal design for heat-treated alloy steels. In this section, details relating to the optimization of Charpy impact toughness and tensile strength using the AEPSO algorithm are presented and discussed. The decision vector consists of the weight percentages for the chemical composites, namely: Carbon (C), Manganese (Mn), Chromium (Cr), Molybdenum (Mo), Nickle (Ni) and Tempering temperature (Temp) respectively. All optimization experiments are based on the neurofuzzy property prediction models.

4.6.1. Impact toughness oriented optimal design

Companies in the steel industry value highly the achievement of the required levels of toughness properties of hot rolled steel products. The optimal alloy toughness design aims at finding the appropriate chemical compositions and tempering temperature with the criterion of a minimum Charpy impact energy of 54 J at $-20°C$, which is equivalent to the ductile-brittle transition temperature at 54 J energy level which is below $-20°C$. On the other hand, we should consider the production costs of heat-treated steels, including the costs of the addition of alloying elements, such as Cr, Mo, V, etc., and the costs of energy consumption during the heat-treatment process. In this experiment, five factors: C, Mn, Cr, Mo and Tempering Temperature, have been considered although other composites and temperatures could also be included. According to the contribution of the chemical composites and annealing to the cost of heat-treated steels, two objective functions are defined for impact toughness optimal design as below:

Minimize:

$$f_1 = \begin{cases} 100C_v & \text{if } C_v < 1.5C_{v_0} \\ 2C_{v_0}/C_v & \text{if } C_v \geq 1.5C_{v_0} \end{cases}, \quad \text{where } C_{v_0} = 54\,\text{J} \qquad (4.16)$$

$$f_2 = 18\text{Mn} + 21\text{Cr} + 52.25\text{Mo3} + 4.88\text{Temp}/600. \qquad (4.17)$$

The first objective function f_1 indicates that the ideal solutions should make the Charpy energy greater than 1.5 times of the target value, C_{v_o}, the greater the better. The second objective function represents the production cost which includes the costs of addition of alloying elements, such as Mn, Cr, Mo, etc. and the costs of energy consumption during the heat-treatment process. The optimal alloy design is to find the suitable compositions and tempering temperatures which ensure that the alloy product has a good trade-off between high impact energy and low production cost.

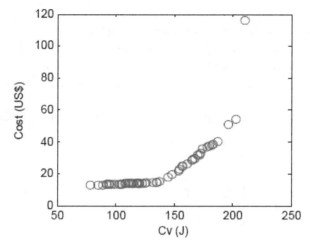

Fig. 4.11.   Obtained Pareto solutions in the objective space.

Table 4.4.   Selected Pareto solutions for two-objective optimization.

No.	C	Mn	Cr	Mo	Temp	Cv	Cost$
1	0.1203	0.3498	0.0500	0.0102	691	126	14.5
2	0.1202	1.4231	0.0501	0.0979	730	183	38.8
3	0.1200	0.3679	0.0500	0.1908	728m	157	24.6
4	0.1200	0.8445	0.0500	0.1310	730	168	30.1
5	0.1201	1.7200	0.0500	0.2303	709	197	50.8

Figure 4.11 displays the optimization result in objective space using the proposed AEPSO algorithm. It indicates that the two objectives are in conflict, as any improvement in one objective causes deterioration in the other. Table 4.4 displays different solutions selected from the Pareto solutions. It can be seen that the algorithm converged to an optimal solution front that provided optional solutions with different production costs while meeting the pre-defined toughness requirement.

4.6.2. *Optimal alloy design with both tensile strength and impact toughness*

This experiment aims at finding the optimal chemical compositions and heat-treatment process parameters to obtain the required tensile strength

(TS) and impact toughness (Cv) while pursuing the lowest possible production cost. In order to achieve the pre-defined tensile strength and toughness requirement, the model prediction error band should be taken into account in the selection of objectives. It is worth noting that the error band, which depends on model accuracy and training data density, provides an accurate guide to the model prediction error. The objective functions for alloy tensile strength and impact toughness design are defined as:

$$\text{Minimize: } F = (f_1, f_2, f_3, f_4, f_5)$$

where

$$f_1 = \begin{cases} |TS - TS_t| & \text{if } |TS - TS_t| < 0.1\,TS_t \\ 100|TS - TS_t| & \text{otherwise} \end{cases} \tag{4.18}$$

$$f_2 = EB_T \tag{4.19}$$

$$f_3 = \begin{cases} 100 C_v & \text{if } C_v < 1.5 C_{v_0} \\ 2 C_{v_o}/C_v & \text{if } C_v \geq 1.5 C_{v_0} \end{cases}, \quad \text{where } C_{v_0} = 54\,\text{J} \tag{4.20}$$

$$f_4 = EB_c \tag{4.21}$$

$$f_5 = 18\text{Mn} + 21\text{Cr} + 52.25\text{Mo3} + 4.88\text{Temp}/600. \tag{4.22}$$

In this case, the 95% confidence error band for the prediction models EBT and EBC, corresponding to TS and toughness respectively, are included in the objective functions, i.e., f_2 and f_4. The target value for TS is set to $TS_t = 800(\text{N/mm}^2)$. Among the five objectives, the first objective function f_1 indicates that the ideal solutions should be close to the target TS value, TS_t, and the acceptable variation is 10% of TS_t. A penalty is assigned to solutions that exceed the 10% variation range of the target. Objectives f_3 and f_5 are defined as in the previous subsection for f_1 and f_2.

Taking the above factors into account, the optimization experiment has been conducted based on the objective functions f_1 and f_5 defined by Equations (4.19)–(4.23) using the AEPSO algorithm. The Pareto-solutions were obtained in the objective space with the tensile strength target value $TS_t = 800\,(\text{N/mm}^2)$ and Charpy impact energy target value $C_{v_0} = 54\,\text{J}$. Again, five different solutions around the tensile strength target value are selected from the Pareto solutions and listed in Table 4.5. It can be seen that the algorithm converged to the region close to the pre-defined TS target values and also provided different solutions which meet the toughness and cost requirements of the alloy steels. It is also seen that the optimization

Table 4.5.   Selected Pareto solutions for two-objective optimization.

No.	C	Mn	Cr	Mo	Temp	TS	EBt	Cv	EBc	Cost$
1	0.341	0.800	0.806	0.225	602	819	22	92	28	66.4
2	0.347	0.887	1.350	0.144	651	809	37	97	28	85.5
3	0.344	0.841	0.558	0.308	592	803	28	90	29	59.5
4	0.375	0.839	1.119	0.011	640	794	56	289	28	67.8
5	0.298	0.985	1.202	0.252	655	817	57	117	30	86.7

method provides useful, practical composition and tempering temperature levels, with acceptable mechanical property requirement, model reliability and overall costs incurred. It indicates that the produced solutions are very consistent and always converged to a specific area that minimized the above objective functions.

4.7. Conclusions

A multi-objective alloy design approach was used to determine the optimal heat treatment regime and the required weight percentages for the chemical composites to obtain the desired mechanical properties of steel. Based on data-driven neurofuzzy models, the tensile strength and Charpy impact toughness can be predicted effectively and then used to facilitate optimal alloy design. The alloy design experimental results have shown that the optimization algorithm can locate the constrained minimum design with very good convergence, and also provide a range of optional solutions which fit the pre-defined property requirement while securing a reasonable production cost. Simulations also indicate that the algorithm produced very consistent solutions and can be effectively used in other industrial optimization problems.

An adaptive evolutionary Particle Swarm Optimization approach was described and successfully applied to this multi-objective optimal design of heat-treated alloy steels. Using a new PSO algorithm, AEPSO, we overcame problems commonly encountered in the standard PSO algorithm which related to its shortcomings for effective local search in the early stages of the run coupled with its shortcomings for effective global search during the late stages of the run. The introduction of an adaptive inertia weight and a special mutation operator improved the diversity of the Pareto solutions and the exploratory capability while keeping the algorithm simple. Compared with some recently developed algorithms, the proposed algorithm can achieve improved convergence while maintaining good diversity. (The well-known functions ZDT1 ZDT4 were used for benchmark testing).

Further work on the multi-objective optimization method, AEPSO, will seek to improve the ability of the algorithm to distribute more uniformly along the Pareto front. There is a very strong continuing interest in the literature on the use of PSO for multi-objective optimization. Important recent papers include research into distributed co-evolutionary PSO,[50] improvements using crowding, mutation and epsilon-dominance[51] and an approach which draws heavily from the experience of evolutionary multi-objective optimization research.[52] Developing new optimization algorithms with high performance on convergence, diversity and user preference[53] is our goal for future work.

Acknowledgments

The authors would like to thank the financial support from Education Ministry of China via the "111 Project".

References

1. C. Fonseca and P. Fleming. An overview of evolutionary algorithms in multi-objective optimization, *Evolutionary Computation*. **3**(1), 1–16, (1995).
2. C. A. C. Coello, D. A. V. Veldhuizen, and G. B. Lamont. *Evolutionary Algorithms for Solving Multiobjective Problems*. (Norwell, MA: Kluwer, 2002). ISBN 0-3064-6762-3.
3. R. Purshouse and P. Fleming. On the evolutionary optimization of many conflicting objectives, *IEEE Transactions on Evolutionary Computation*. **11**(6), 770–784, (2007).
4. J. Kennedy and R. C. Eberhart. Particle swarm optimization. In *Proc. of IEEE International Conference on Neural Networks*, pp. 1942–1948, (1995).
5. J. Kennedy. The particle swarm: Social adaptation of knowledge. In *Proc. of International Conference on Evolutionary Computation*, pp. 303–308, (1997).
6. Y. Shi and R. Eberhart. Empirical study of particle swarm optimization, *Evolutionary Computation*. **SE-13**, 1945–1950, (1999).
7. R. Eberhart and Y. Shi. Particle swarm optimization: developments, applications and resources. In *Proc. Congress on Evolutionary Computation, Seoul, Korea*, (2001).
8. R. Eberhart and X. Hu. Human tremor analysis using particle swarm optimization. In *Proc. Congress on Evolutionary Computation, Washington, DC*, pp. 1927–1930, (1999).
9. Y. Fukuyama and H. Yoshida. A particle swam optimization for reactive power and voltage control in electric power systems. In *Proc. Congress on Evolutionary Computation, Seoul, Korea*, (2001).

10. J. Ke and J. Qian. Nonlinear system identification using particle swarm optimization, *Journal of Circuits and System.* **8**(4), 12–15, (2003).
11. F. van den Bergh and A. P. Engelbrecht. Cooperative learning in neural networks using particle swarm optimizers, *South African Computational Journal.* **26**, 8490, (2000).
12. S. Naka, T. Grenji, T. Yura and Y. Fukuyama. Practical distribution state estimation using hybrid particle swam optimization. In *Proc. IEEE PES Winter Meeting, Columbus, Ohio, USA*, (2001).
13. Z. He, C. Wei and L.Yang. Extracting rules from fuzzy neural network by particle swam optimization. In *Proc. IEEE Int. Conf. on Evolutionary Computation, Anchorage, USA*, (1998).
14. H. Fan. A modification to particle swarm optimization algorithm, *Engineering Computations.* **19**(8), 970–989, (2002).
15. Y. Shi and R. Eberhart. Fuzzy adaptive particle swarm optimization. In *Proc. of IEEE Congress on Evolutionary Computation, Seoul, Korea*, pp. 101–106, (2001).
16. L. Zhang and S. Hu. A new approach to improve particle swarm optimization, *Lecture Notes in Computer Science.* **2723**, 134–139, (2003).
17. A. Stacey, M. Jancic, and I. Grundy. Particle swarm optimization with mutation. In *Proc. of IEEE Congress on Evolutionary Computation*, pp. 1425–1430, (2003).
18. P. S. Andrews. An investigation into mutation operators for particle swarm optimization. In *Proc. of IEEE Congress on Evolutionary Computation*, pp. 1044–1050, (2006).
19. M. Chen, C. Wu, and P. J. Fleming. An evolutionary particle swarm algorithm for multi-objective optimization. In *Proc IEEE World Cong. Intelligent Control and Automation*, pp. 3269–3274, (2008).
20. C. Coello, G. Pulido, and M. Lechuga. Handling multiple objectives with particle swarm optimization, *IEEE Transaction on Evolutionary Computation.* **8**(3), 256–279, (2004).
21. M.-Y. Chen and D. Linkens. A systematic neuro-fuzzy modeling framework with application to material property prediction, *IEEE Transactions on SMC-B.* **31**(5), 781–790, (2001).
22. D. Chen, M-Y. and Linkens and A. Bannister. Numerical analysis of factors influencing charpy impact properties of tmcr structural steels using fuzzy modelling, *Materials Science and Technology.* **20**(5), 627–633, (2004).
23. M.-Y. Chen, D. Linkens, D. A. and Howarth, and J. Beynon. Fuzzy model-based charpy impact toughness assessment for ship steels, *ISIJ International.* **44**(6), 1108–1113, (2004).
24. H. Tsuei, D. Dunne, and H. Li. *Sci. Technol. Weld. Join.* **8**(3), 205–212, (2003).
25. D. Dunne, H. Tsuei, and Z. Sterjovski. Artificial neural networks for modelling of the impact toughness of steel, *ISIJ International.* **44**(9), 1599–1607, (2004).
26. S. M. K. Hosseini, A. Z. Hanzaki, M. J. Y. Panah, and S. Yuec. Ann model for prediction of the effects of composition and process parameters on tensile

strength and percent elongation of simn trip steels, *Materials Science and Engineering A.* **374**, 122–128, (2004).

27. E. Kim, M. Park, and S. Ji. A new approach of fuzzy modelling, *IEEE Trans. Fuzzy Systems.* **5**(3), 586–590, (1997).

28. Y. Jin. Fuzzy modeling of high-dimensional systems: complexity reduction and interpretability improvement, *IEEE Trans. Fuzzy Systems.* **8**(2), 212–221, (2000).

29. E. Vandewalle. Constructing fuzzy models with linguistic integrity from numerical dataafreli algorithm, *IEEE Trans. Fuzzy Systems.* **8**(5), 591–600, (2000).

30. M. Chen and D. Linkens. Rule-base self-generation and simplification for data-driven fuzzy models, *Fuzzy Sets and Systems.* **142**(2), 243–265, (2004).

31. H.-M. Feng. Self-generating fuzzy modeling systems through hierarchical recursive-based particle swarm optimization, *Cybernetics and Systems.* **36**(6), 623–639, (2005).

32. J. Jang and C. Sun. Functional equivalence between radial basis function network and fuzzy inference systems, *IEEE Trans. Neural Networks.* **4**(1), 156–159, (1993).

33. M. Chen, W. Wang, and Y. Yang. A hybrid knowledge-based neuralfuzzy network model with application to alloy property prediction, *Lecture Notes in Computer Science.* **4491**, 532–539, (2007).

34. P. Hodgson. Microstructure modelling for property prediction and control, *Journal of Materials Processing Technology.* **60**, 27–33, (1996).

35. R. Moskovic and P. Flewitt. *Metallurgical and Materials Transactions A.* **28**, 2609, (1997).

36. D. Linkens and M. Chen. Input selection and partition validation for fuzzy modelling using neural networks, *Fuzzy Sets and Systems.* **107**, 299–308, (1999).

37. A. Needleman and V. Tvergaard. Numerical modeling of the ductile-brittle transition, *International Journal of Fracture.* **101**(1–2), 299–308, (2000).

38. M. Tahar, R. Piques, and P. Forget. In *Proc. 11th Biennial European Conference on Fracture UK*, p. 1945, (1996).

39. M. Todinov, M. Novovic, P. Bowen, and J. Knott. Numerical modeling of the ductile-brittle transition, *Materials Science and Engineering A.* **A287**, 116, (2000).

40. R. C. Eberhart and Y. Shi. Comparing inertia weights and constriction factors in particle swarm optimization. In *Proc. Congress on Evolutionary Computation, IEEE Press*, pp. 84–88, (2000).

41. S. F. Adra, I. Griffin, and P. J. Fleming. *A convergence acceleration technique for multi-objective optimization.* In eds. C. K. Goh, Y. S. Ong and K. C. Tan, *Multi-Objective Memetic Algorithms.* Geophys. Mono. Springer, (2009).

42. N. Higashi and H. Iba. Particle swarm optimization with gaussian mutation. In *Proc. IEEE Swarm Intelligence Symposium*, pp. 72–79, (2003).

43. N. Li, Y. Q. Qin, D. B. Sun, and T. Zou. Particle swarm optimization with mutation operator. In *Proc. 3rd Int. Conf. on Machine Learning and Cybernetics, Shanghai 26–29*, pp. 2251–2256, (2004).

44. L. S. Coelho and R. A. Krohling. Predictive controller tuning using modified particle swarm optimization based on cauchy and gaussian distributions. In *Proc. 8th On-Line World Conference on Soft Computing in Industrial Applications*, pp. 254–257, (2003).
45. K. Deb, Agrawal, A., A. Pratap, and T. Meyarivan. A fast elitist non-dominated sorting genetic algorithm for multi-objective optimization: Nsga-ii, *Springer*. **PPSN VI**, 849–858, (2000).
46. K. Deb and T. Goel. Controlled elitist non-dominated sorting genetic algorithms for better convergence, *Lecture Notes in Computer Science*. **1993**, 67–81, (2001).
47. X. Li. A non-dominated sorting particle swarm optimizer for multi-objective optimization, *Lecture Notes in Computer Science*. **2723**, 37–48, (2003).
48. E. Zitzler and L. Thiele. Multiobjective evolutionary algorithms: A comparative case study and the strength pareto approach, *IEEE Transactions on Evolutionary Computation*. **3**(6), 257–271, (1999).
49. K. Deb. *Multi-Objective Optimization Using Evolutionary Algorithms*. (New York; Chichester: Wiley, 2001).
50. D. Liu, K. Tan, and W. Ho. A distributed co-evolutionary particle swarm optimization algorithm. In *Proc. 2007 IEEE Congress On Evolutionary Computation, Singapore*, pp. 3831–3838, (2007).
51. M. Sierra and C. Coello. Improving pso-based multi-objective optimization using crowding, mutation and epsilon-dominance, evolutionary multi-criterion optimization. In *Third International Conference, EMO 2005, Guanajuato, Mexico, Proceedings*, (2005).
52. Y. Liu. A fast and elitist multi-objective particle swarm algorithm: Nspso. In *Proc 2008 IEEE Int Conf on Granular Computing, Hangzhou, PRC*, pp. 470–475, (2008).
53. V. Kadirkamanathan, K. Selvarajah, and P. J. Fleming. Stability analysis of the particle dynamics in particle swarm optimizer, *IEEE Transactions on Evolutionary Computation*. **10**(3), 245–255, (2006).

Chapter 5

AN EXTENDED BAYESIAN/HAPSO INTELLIGENT METHOD IN INTRUSION DETECTION SYSTEM

S. DEHURI* and S. TRIPATHY†

*Department of Information and Communication Technology,
Fakir Mohan University, Vyasa Vihar,
Balasore-756019, ORISSA, India
satchi.lapa@gmail.com

†Department of Computer Science and Engineering,
Indian Institute of Technology, Patna, India
somanath@gmail.com

This chapter presents a hybrid adaptive particle swarm optimization (HAPSO)/Bayesian classifier to construct an intelligent and more compact intrusion detection system (IDS). An IDS plays a vital role of detecting various kinds of attacks in a computer system or network. The primary goal of the proposed method is to maximize detection accuracy with a simultaneous minimization of number attributes, which inherently reduces the complexity of the system. The proposed method can exhibits an improved capability to eliminate spurious features from huge amount of data aiding researchers in identifying those features that are solely responsible for achieving high detection accuracy. Experimental results demonstrate that the hybrid intelligent method can play a major role for detection of attacks intelligently.

5.1. Introduction

An intrusion detection system (IDS) is a program to detect various kinds of misuse in computer system or network. An intrusion is defined as any non-empty set of actions that attempt to compromise the integrity, confidentiality or availability of a resource. Intrusion detection can be grouped into two classes such as misuse intrusion detection and anomaly intrusion detection.[1] Misuse intrusion detection uses well defined patterns of the attack and exploit weaknesses in system and application software to identify the intrusions. These patterns are encoded in advance and used to match against the user behavior to detect intrusions. Anomaly intrusion detection uses the normal usage behavior patterns to identify the intrusions.

The normal usage patterns are constructed from the statistical measures of the system features. The behavior of the user is observed and any deviation from the constructed normal behavior is detected as an intrusion.[2]

The main goal of the IDS is to find intrusions among normal audit data and this can be considered as a classification problem. One of the main problems with IDS is the overhead which can become positively high. As network speed becomes faster, there is an emerging need for security techniques that will be able to keep up with the increased network throughput.[3,4] Several machine learning, soft computing and computational intelligence techniques have been investigated for the design of IDS, e.g., neural networks,[5] linear genetic programming,[6] support vector machine (SVM), Bayesian networks, multivariate adaptive regression splines (MARS),[7] fuzzy inference systems (FISs),[8] hybrid intelligent systems (HISs),[9] etc. All these aforesaid efforts are primarily focussed on high detection rates, which completely ignoring the computational complexity aspect. In view of this the proposed method tried to make an intelligent IDS which is lightweight, while guaranteeing high detection rates. The present method tried to solve that by figuring out important intrusion features through hybrid adaptive particle swarm optimization (HAPSO). Feature selection is one of the important and frequently used techniques in data preprocesing for IDS.[10] It reduces the number of features, removes irrelevant, redundant or noisy features, and brings the immediate effects for IDS. In this research the hybrid method HAPSO objective is two folds: (i) learning of Bayesian coefficients and (ii) selection of optimal set of intrusion features. HAPSO is based on the idea of adaptive PSO[11] for continuous search space exploration and binary PSO[12] for discrete search space exploration.

In terms of feature selection, many researchers have proposed identifying important intrusion features through wrapper, filter and hybrid approaches. Wrapper method exploits a machine learning algorithm to evaluate the goodness of features or feature set. In the present study we use HAPSO learnable extended Bayesian classifier[13] to evaluate the optimality of features or feature set.

The rest of the chapter is organized as follows. Section 5.2 provides the related research. Preliminary materials are presented in Sec. 5.3. Section 5.4 comprises of HAPSO/Bayesian classifier for IDS. Experimental results and analysis is presented in Secs. 5.5 and 5.6 concludes the chapter with a possible feature research directions.

5.2. Related Research

With the proliferation of distributed and networked computers and then the Internet, their security has become a hot cake in research community. Anderson in 1980[14] proposed that audit trails can be used to monitor threats. The importance of such data was not comprehended at that time and all the available system security procedures were focused on denying access to sensitive data from an unauthorized source. Dorothy[2] proposed the concept of intrusion detection as a solution to the problem of providing a sense of security in computer systems. This intrusion detection model is independent of system, type of intrusion and application environment. This model served as an abstract model for further developments in the field and is known as the generic intrusion detection model. Various techniques and approaches have been used in later developments. The techniques used are statistical approaches, predictive pattern generation, expert systems, keystroke monitoring, model-based intrusion detection, state transition analysis, pattern matching, and data mining.

Statistical approaches compare the recent behavior of a user of a computer system with observed behavior and any significant deviation is considered as intrusion. This approach requires construction of a model for normal user behavior. Any user behavior that deviates significantly from this normal behavior is flagged as an intrusion. Intrusion detection expert system (IDES)[15] exploited the statistical approach for the detection of intruders. It uses the intrusion detection model proposed by Denning[2] and audit trails data as suggested in Anderson.[14] Attacks, which occur by sequential dependencies, cannot be detected, as statistical analysis is insensitive to order of events.[16] Predictive pattern generation uses a rule base of user profiles defined as statistically weighted event sequences.[17] This method of intrusion detection attempts to predict future events based on events that have already occurred.

The state transition analysis approach uses the state transitions of the system to identify intrusions. This method constructs the state transition diagram, which is the graphical representation of intrusion behavior as a series of state changes that lead from an initial secure state to a target compromised state. State transition diagrams list only the critical events that must occur for the successful completion of the intrusion. Using the audit trail as input, an analysis tool can be developed to compare the state changes produced by the user to state transition diagrams of known penetrations. State transition diagrams are written to correspond to the states of an actual computer system, and these diagrams form the basis of a rule-based expert system for detecting penetrations, called the state transition analysis tool (STAT).[18] The STAT prototype is implemented in UNIX state transition analysis tool (USTAT)[19] on UNIX-based systems.

The keystroke monitoring technique utilizes a users keystrokes to determine the intrusion attempt. The main approach is to pattern match the sequence of keystrokes to some predefined sequences to detect the intrusion. The main problems with this approach is a lack of support from the operating system to capture the keystroke sequences. Furthermore, there are also many ways of expressing the sequence of keystrokes for the same attack. Some shell programs like bash, ksh have the user definable aliases utility. These aliases make it difficult to detect the intrusion attempts using this technique unless some semantic analysis of the commands is used. Automated attacks by malicious executables cannot be detected by this technique as they only analyze keystrokes.

In an expert system, knowledge about a problem domain is represented by a set of rules. These rules consist of two parts, antecedent, which defines when the rule should be applied and consequent, which defines the action(s) that should be taken if its antecedent is satisfied. A rule is fired when pattern-matching techniques determine that observed data matches or satisfies the antecedent of a rule. The rules may recognize single auditable events that represent significant danger to the system by themselves, or they may recognize a sequence of events that represent an entire penetration scenario. There are some disadvantages with the expert system method. An intrusion scenario that does not trigger a rule will not be detected by the rule-based approach. Maintaining and updating a complex rule-based system can be difficult. Since the rules in the expert system have to be formulated by a security professional, the system performance would depend on the quality of the rules. The model-based approach attempts to model intrusions at a higher level of abstraction than audit trail records. The objective is to build scenario models that represent the characteristic behavior of intrusions. This allows administrators to generate their representation of the penetration abstractly, which shifts the burden of determining what audit records are part of a suspect sequence to the expert system. This technique differs from current rule-based expert system techniques, which simply attempt to pattern match audit records to expert rules.

The model-based approach of Garvey and Lunt[20] consists of three parts, namely, anticipator, planner and interpreter. The anticipator generates the next set of behaviors to be verified in the audit trail based on the current active models and passes these sets to the planner. The planner determines how the hypothesized behavior is reflected in the audit data and translates it into a system-dependent audit trail match. The interpreter then searches for this data in the audit trail. The system collects the information in this manner until a threshold is reached, and then it signals an intrusion attempt. Some of the drawbacks are that the intrusion patterns must always occur in the behavior it is looking for and patterns for intrusion must always be distinguishable from normal behavior and also easily recognizable.

The pattern matching[21] approach encodes known intrusion signatures as patterns that are then matched against the audit data. Intrusion signatures are classified using structural inter relationships among the elements of the signatures. These structural interrelationships are defined over high level events or activities, which are themselves, defined in terms of low-level audit trail events. This categorization of intrusion signatures is independent of any underlying computational framework of matching. Model of pattern matching is implemented using colored petrinets in IDIOT.[22]

The data mining approach to intrusion detection was first implemented in mining audit data for automated models for intrusion detection (MADAMID).[23] Since then data mining algorithms are applied by various researchers to create models to detect intrusions.[24] Data mining algorithms includes rule-based classification algorithm (RIPPER), meta-classifier, frequent episode algorithm and association rules. These algorithms are applied to audit data to compute models that accurately capture the actual behavior of intrusions as well as normal activities. The main advantage of this system is automation of data analysis through data mining, which enables it to learn rules inductively replacing manual encoding of intrusion patterns. The problem is it deals mainly with misuse detection, hence some novel attacks may not be detected. Audit data analysis and mining (ADAM)[25] also uses data mining methods. Combination of association rules and classification algorithm were used to discover attacks in audit data. Association rules are used to gather necessary knowledge about the nature of the audit data as the information about patterns within individual records can improve the classification efficiency.

Artificial neural networks (ANNs) are another data mining approaches considered as an alternative tool in intrusion detection.[26] Neural networks have been used both in anomaly intrusion detection as well as in misuse intrusion detection. In Debar *et al.*,[27] the system learns to predict the next command based on a sequence of previous commands input by a user. Neural network intrusion detector (NNID)[28] identifies intrusions based on the distribution of commands used by the user. A neural network for misuse detection is implemented in two ways.[29] The first approach incorporates the neural network component into the existing or modified expert system. This method uses the neural network to filter the incoming data for suspicious events and forwards them to the expert system. This improves the effectiveness of the detection system. The second approach uses the neural network as a stand alone misuse detection system. In this method, the neural network receive data from the network stream and analyzes it for misuse intrusion.

SVM are learning machines that plot the training vectors in high-dimensional feature space, labeling each vector by its class. SVMs classify data by determining a set of support vectors, which are members of the set of training inputs that outline a hyper plane in the feature space. SVM have proven to be a good candidate for intrusion detection because of their speed. SVM are scalable as they are relatively insensitive to the number of data points. Therefore the classification complexity does not depend on the dimensionality of the feature space; hence, they can potentially learn a larger set of patterns and scale better than neural networks.[5] Peddabachigari *et al.*,[9] have presented two hybrid approaches for modeling IDS like DT-SVM (i.e., a combination of decision tree and support vector machine) and an ensemble approach combining the base classifiers. As a result of hybridization and an ensemble their proposed IDS provide high detection accuracy.

Neurofuzzy (NF) computing combines fuzzy inference with neural networks.[30] Knowledge expressed in the form of linguistic rules can be used to build a fuzzy inference system (FIS). With data, ANNs can be built. For building an FIS, the user has to specify the fuzzy sets, fuzzy operators and the knowledge base. Similarly for constructing an ANN for an application the user needs to specify the architecture and learning algorithm. An analysis reveals that the drawbacks pertaining to these approaches are complementary and therefore it is natural to consider building an integrated system combining these two concepts. While the learning capability is an advantage from the viewpoint of FIS, the formation of linguistic rule base is an advantage from the viewpoint of ANN. An adaptive neurofuzzy IDS is proposed in Shah *et al.*,[8] Abraham *et al.*,[31] has proposed a three fuzzy rule based classifier to detect intrusion in a network. Further a distributed soft computing based IDS has modeled by Abraham *et al.*,[31] as a combination of different classifiers to model lightweight and more accurate (heavy weight) IDS.

MARS is an innovative approach that automates the building of accurate predictive models for continuous and binary-dependent variables. It excels at finding optimal variable transformations and interactions, and the complex data structure that often hide in high-dimensional data. An IDS based on MARS technology is proposed in Mukkamala *et al.*,[7] LGP is a variant of the conventional genetic programming (GP) technique that acts on linear genomes. An LGP-based IDS is presented in Mukkamala *et al.*[6]

Intrusion detection systems based on the human immunological system have been proposed in Esponda *et al.*,[32] and Hofmeyr and Forrest.[33] Hofmeyr and Forrest proposed a formal framework for anomaly detection in computer systems, inspired by the characteristics of the natural immune system. Hofmeyr and Forrest[33] applied the concepts derived from natural immune system to design and test an artificial immune system to detect network intrusion.

5.3. Preliminaries

5.3.1. *Naive Bayesian classifier*

Classification is considered as the task of assigning a sample to one of the k classes, $\{C_1, C_2, C_3, \ldots, C_k\}$, based on the n-dimensional observed feature vector $\overrightarrow{x}$. Let $p(\overrightarrow{x}|C_i)$ be the probability density function for the feature vector, $\overrightarrow{x}$, when the true class of the sample is C_i. Also, let $P(C_i)$ be the relative frequency of occurrence class C_i in the samples. If no feature information is available, the probability that a new sample will be of class C_i is $P(C_i)$ this probability is referred to as the a priori or prior probability. Once the feature values are obtained, we can combine the prior probability with the class-conditional probability for the feature vector, $p(\overrightarrow{x}|C_i)$, to obtain the posteriori probability that a pattern belongs to a particular class. This combination is done using Bayes theory:

$$P(C_i|\overrightarrow{x}) = \frac{p(\overrightarrow{x}|C_i)P(C_i)}{\sum_{j=1}^{k} p(\overrightarrow{x}|C_j)P(C_j)}. \tag{5.1}$$

Once the posterior probability is obtained for each class, classification is a simple matter of assigning the pattern to the class with the highest posterior probability. The resulting decision rule is Bayes decision rule:

$$\text{given } \vec{x}, \text{ decide } C_i \quad \text{if } P(C_i|\vec{x}) > P(C_j|\vec{x}) \, \forall j$$

When the class-conditional probability density for the feature vector and the prior probabilities for each class are known, the Bayes classifier can be shown to be optimal in the sense that no other decision rule will yield a lower error rate. Of course, these probability distributions (both a priori and a posteriori) are rarely known during classifier design, and must instead be estimated from training data. Class-conditional probabilities for the feature values can be estimated from the training data using either a parametric or a non-parametric approach. A parametric method assumes that the feature values follow a particular probability distribution for each class and estimate the parameters for the distribution from the training data. For example, a common parametric method first assumes a Gaussian distribution of the feature values, and then estimates the parameters μ_i and σ_i for each class, C_i, from the training data. A non-parametric approach usually involves construction of a histogram from the training data to approximate the class-conditional distribution of the feature values.

Once the distribution of the feature values has been approximated for each class, the question remains how to combine the individual class-conditional probability density functions for each feature, $p(x_1|C_i)$, $p(x_2|C_i), \ldots, p(x_d|C_i)$ to determine the probability density function for the entire feature vector: $p(\vec{x}|C_i)$. A common method is to assume that the feature values are statistically independent:

$$p(\vec{x}|C_i) = p(x_1|C_i) \times p(x_2|C_i) \times \cdots \times p(x_n|C_i) \quad (5.2)$$

The resulting classifier, often called the naive Bayes classifier, has been shown to perform well on a variety of data sets, even when the independence assumption is not strictly satisfied.[34] The selection of the prior probabilities for the various categories has been the subject of a substantial body of literature.[35] One of the most common methods is to simply estimate the relative frequency for each class from the training data and use these values for the prior probabilities. An alternate method is to simply assume equal prior probabilities for all categories by setting $P(C_i) = \frac{1}{k}$, $i = 1, 2, \ldots, k$.

The naive Bayesian classifier is summarized using the following computational procedure:

- Classifier Construction
  (1) Determine the probabilities, $P(C_j)$ using the training data.
  (2) Use training data to determine the category means and variances for continuous variables and category conditional probabilities for discrete variable.

- Classification of Unknown Sample, $\vec{x}$
  (1) Calculate $p(x|C_i)P(C_i)$ for each C_i.
  (2) Assign $\vec{x}$ to the category attaining the largest score.

5.3.2. *Intrusion detection system*

With the proliferation of inter connections among computers and the internet, their security has become a crucial issue. Protection against unauthorized disclosure of information, modification of data and denial of services (DOS) attacks through providing the security services confidentiality, integrity and availability is mandatory. In general, preventive methods are being used for designing a secure system. However, attackers can know the prevention techniques a prior, and exploit the design clue and/flaw to compromise the security of the system by developing sophisticated attacks and malwares. Intrusion Detection System (IDS) the last line of defense, therefore, has become an important component in the security infrastructure toolbox.

IDS is not an emerging research filed, but a specialized commercial area as well. Recall that the concept of developing an IDS was evolved in 1980 by Anderson[14] followed by a model designed by Denning in 1986.[2] Denning's model is a generic intrusion detection model regards as a rule-based pattern matching system. The IDS model has an event generator and the events may include audit records, network packets or other activities. Activity profile contains description of a subjects normal behavior with respect to a set of intrusion detection measures. Profiles are updated periodically allowing the system to learn new behavior. The audit record is matched against profiles. Then type information in the matching profiles determines what rules apply to update the profile and check for abnormal behavior; reports if anomalous detected. In 1988, some prototypes[36] are proposed with the idea that intrusion behavior involves abnormal usage of the system. Thereafter, both the researchers and commercial persons were motivated to develop IDS using various techniques include statistical approaches, predictive pattern generation, expert systems, keystroke monitoring, state transition analysis, pattern matching, and data mining techniques.

The goal of an IDS is to monitor, detect and respond the unauthorized activities referred as intrusion arises due to the inside or outside attackers. Anderson[14] identified three broad categories of intruders based on their behaviors: Masquerader: Unauthorized individuals penetrates the system's access control to exploit a legitimate users account. Misfeasor: A legitimate user misuses his/her priviliges. Clandestine user: An individual who seizes supervisory control of the system and uses this control of the system and uses this control to avoid auditing and access control.

The existing IDS schemes can be divided into two broad categories depending on the detection mechanism: Misuse detection and anomaly detection. Misuse detection detects the intrusion (user behavior that deviates from the normal behavior) without using the behavior profile. Here the decision is made on the basis of the definition of misuse of computer resources called signature. So known intrusions can be detected efficiently but, these techniques fail easily while faces unknown intrusions. Regularly updating the knowledge base using supervised learning algorithm could be an alternative solution. Unfortunately, data set for this purpose are expensive.

The alternate detection mechanism anomaly detection recognizes a particular (suspicious) incident by scanning the behavior of active user and issue an appropriate alert. Apparently, it would be possible if an intrusion exhibits the characteristics distinct from typical legitimate/normal activities. A normal activity is characterized by user behavior profiles which need to be updated continually. Therefore, this type of detection has the capacity of recognizing new types of attacks and requires only the normal data while building the profiles. The major difficulties of such a system is for demarkation of normal and abnormal behaviors boundaries.

5.3.2.1. *Architecture of IDS*

An intrusion detection system can be considered as an automated auditing mechanism comprises of the following four phases of tasks.

Data Collection: The first phase of an IDS is to collect or gather data from various sources which is to be used for analysis. NIDSs collect data from network traffic using sniffers as tcp-dump and HIDSs glean data observing process activities, memory usage, system call using ps, netstat commands in unix based systems.

Feature Selection: The collected data is usually large and it slows down the training and testing process if whole data is passed to analysis phase. Therefore, a subset of the creating feature vectors that represent most of the collected data is to be selected.

Analysis: The selected data is analyzed to determine if attack occurs by observing the attack signature (in misuse detection) or comparing with the normal behavior and finding the anomaly (in anomalous detection).

Action: The IDS alerts the system administrator for a possible attack. Sometimes IDS participate actively to stop or control the intrusion by closing network ports or killing process.

5.3.2.2. *Efficiency of IDS*

An IDS that is functionally correct but, much slower in operation to detect, may be of little or no use. Therefore, the efficiency of an IDS is evaluated by its effectiveness and performance.

5.3.2.3. *Effectiveness*

The effectiveness of an IDS is its capability to mark an event correctly as normal or intrusion. But, there are four possible predictions of an IDS at any instant: true positive (TP), true negative (TN), false positive (FP) and false negative (FN). True positive and true negative correspond to a correct operation of the IDS i.e., events are correctly identified as intrusion or normal respectively. False positive refers to normal events marked as intrusion while false negative refers to intrusions marked as normal events. To evaluate the effectiveness, the following parameters need to be determined by observing the outcomes of IDS for some time.

- True Negative Rate (TNR): $\frac{TN}{TN+FP}$
- True Positive Rate (TPR): $\frac{TP}{TP+FN}$
- False Negative Rate (FNR): $\frac{FN}{FN+TP}$
- False Positive Rate (FPR): $\frac{FP}{FP+TN}$
- Accuracy: $\frac{TN+TP}{TN+TP+FN+FP}$

The TPR are called detection rate (DR) and FPR are called as false alarm rate (FAR) are two most popular performance metrics for evaluating an IDS. An optimal IDS should have high DR and low FAR as possible.

5.3.2.4. *Performance of IDS*

The performance of an intrusion-detection system is the rate at which audit events are processed. The IDS performance requirements include the following:

- The IDS should be fast enough that it can detect the presence of intrusion in real-time and report it immediately to avoid the damage of resources and loss of privacy.
- The IDS should be scalable enough to handle the additional computational and communication loads.

5.3.3. *Feature selection*

In general an IDS deals with huge data, some times include irrelevant and redundant data which can introduce noise data lead to drop the detection accuracy and slow down training and testing process. Removing these irrelevant features usually increases performance of classifiers. At the same time, care must be taken such that the prediction accuracy of the classifier is maintained while finding the subset of features.

Feature selection method involves four necessary steps. The process begins with subset generation to generate a suitable feature subset. It is essentially a heuristic search either (forward selection) initialize by an empty set and a feature is added on at each iteration or (backward selection) starts with full subset shrinking at each iteration. Besides this, search may include both forward and backward selection. Each newly generated subset in the subset generation stage is evaluated by an evaluation criteria. The process stops once the terminating criteria is reached. Finally the result is validated with some prior knowledge of data. Thus any feature selection method must consider the following four basic issues:[10] (i) a starting point in the search space; (ii) organization of the search; (iii) evaluation strategy of the generated subset; (iv) terminating criterion for search.

Evaluation criteria is the most important issue in feature selection process. The selected subset is evaluated considering the target concept and the learning algorithm. Depending on the evaluation criteria three different approaches for the feature selection methods were reported in Ref. 37:

- wrapper approach
- filter approach
- embedded approach.

Wrapper Approach: In this approach, the selection algorithm searches for a good subset of features using some induction algorithm. Once the induction algorithm is fixed, train with these feature subset by the search algorithm and estimate the error rate. The error rate can be assigned as the value of the evaluation function of the feature subset. Thus in this approach the selection of feature is based on the accuracy of the classifier.

Kohavi and John[38] introduced wrappers for feature selection and the approach is tailored to a particular learning algorithm and a particular training set. The selection algorithm in a wrapper approach depends on both the number of features and number of instances.

The major drawback of the wrapper approach would be feeding with an arbitrary feature into the classifier may lead to biased results and therefore the accuracy can not be guaranteed. Another drawback is that for a large set of features trying all possible combinations to feed the classifier may not be feasible. Therefore, some researchers are motivated to alleviate the excessive loading of the training phase avoiding the evaluation of many subsets exploiting intrinsic properties of the learning algorithms.[39]

Filter Approach: This approach evaluates the goodness of the feature set in regards only to the intrinsic properties of the data, ignoring the induction algorithm. Since filter is applied to the algorithm to select relevant features considering the data and the target concept to be learned, the approach is referred as filter approach. Obviously, filter method would be faster than the wrapper approach. Filter method feature selections are appropriate for the huge database while wrapper methods are infeasible[40]

Embedded Approach: This approach has been identified in.[10] In this case the feature selection process is done inside the induction algorithm itself.

5.3.4. *Particle swarm optimization*

Particle swarm optimization technique is considered as one of the modern heuristic algorithm for optimization introduced by James Kennedy and Eberhart in 1995.[41] A swarm consists of a set of particles moving around the search space, each representing a potential solution (fitness). Each particle has a position vector $(x_i(t))$, a velocity vector $(v_i(t))$, the position at which the best fitness $(pbest_i)$ encountered by the particle, and the index of the best particle $(gbest)$ in the swarm. Moreover, each particle knows the best value so far in the group (gbest) among pbests. Each particle tries to modify its position using the following information along with their previous velocity:

(1) The distance between the current position and pbest,
(2) The distance between the current position and gbest.

In each generation, the velocity of each particle is updated to their best encountered position and the best position encountered by any particle using Equation (5.3):

$$v_i(t) = v_i(t-1) + c_1 * r_1(t) * (pbest_i - x_i(t)) + c_2 * r_2(t) * (gbest - x_i(t)) \quad (5.3)$$

The parameters c_1 and c_2 are called acceleration coefficients, namely cognitive and social parameter, respectively. $r_1(t)$ and $r_2(t)$ are random values, uniformly distributed between zero and one and the value of $r_1(t)$ and $r_2(t)$ is not same for every iteration. The position of each particle is updated every generation. This is done by adding the velocity vector to the position vector, as given in Equation (5.4):

$$x_i(t) = x_i(t - 1) + v_i(t) \quad (5.4)$$

However, in the first version of PSO, there was no actual control over the previous velocity of the particles. In the later versions of PSO, this shortcoming was addressed by incorporating two new parameters, called inertia weight introduced by Shi and Ebherhart[42] and constriction factor (χ) introduced by Clerc and Kennedy[43] addressed in Equations (5.5) and (5.6) respectively:

$$v_i(t) = w * v_i(t-1) + c_1 * r_1(t) * (pbest_i - x_i(t)) + c_2 * r_2(t) * (gbest - x_i(t)), \quad (5.5)$$

where w is called the inertia weight.

$$v_i(t) = \chi\{v_i(t - 1) + c_1 * r_1(t) * (pbest_i - x_i(t)) + c_2 * r_2(t) * (gbest - x_i(t))\} \quad (5.6)$$

$$\chi = \frac{2}{|2 - c - \sqrt{c^2 - 4c}|}, \quad (5.7)$$

where $c = c_1 + c_2, c > 4$.

Shi and Eberhart[42] have found a significant improvement in the performance of PSO with the linearly decreasing inertia weight over the generations, time-varying inertia weight (TVIW) which is given in Equation (5.8):

$$w = w_2 + \left(\frac{maxiter - iter}{maxiter} \right) * (w_1 - w_2), \qquad (5.8)$$

where w_1 and w_2 are the higher and lower inertia weight values and the values of w will decrease from w_1 to w_2. *iter* is the current iteration (or generation) and *maxiter* is the maximum number of iteration (or total number of generation).

Then, Ratnaweera and Halgamuge[44] introduced a time varying acceleration co-efficient (TVAC), which reduces the cognitive component, c_1 and increases the social component, c_2 of acceleration co-efficient with time. With a large value of c_1 and a small value of c_2 at the beginning, particles are allowed to move around the search space, instead of moving toward pbest. A small value of c_1 and a large value of c_2 allow the particles converge to the global optima in the latter part of the optimization. The TVAC is given in Equations (5.9) and (5.10):

$$c_1 = (c_{1i} - c_{1f}) * \left(\frac{maxiter - iter}{maxiter} \right) + c_{1f} \qquad (5.9)$$

$$c_2 = (c_{2i} - c_{2f}) * \left(\frac{maxiter - iter}{maxiter} \right) + c_{2f} \qquad (5.10)$$

where c_{1i} and c_{2i} are the initial values of the acceleration coefficient c_1 and c_2 and c_{1f} and c_{2f} are the final values of the acceleration co-efficient c_1 and c_2, respectively.

Thus far we have discussed PSO for continuous space, however, many optimization problems including the problem to be solved in this chapter are set in a space featuring discrete, qualitative distinctions between variables and between levels of variables.

5.4. HAPSO for Learnable Bayesian Classifier in IDS

5.4.1. *Adaptive PSO*

In the standard PSO method, the inertia weight is made constant for all the particles in a single simulation, but the most important parameter that

moves the current position towards the optimum position is the inertia
weight (w). In order to increase the search ability, the algorithm should be
redefined in a manner that the movement of the swarm should be controlled
by the objective function. In adaptive PSO,[11] the particle position is
adjusted such that the highly fitted particle (best particle) moves slowly
when compared to the less fitted particle. This can be achieved by selecting
different w values for each particle according to their rank, between w_{min}
and w_{max} as in the following form:

$$w_i = w_{min} + \frac{w_{max} - w_{min}}{Tpop} \times rank_i. \qquad (5.11)$$

where $Tpop$ is denoted as size of the swarm. From Equation (5.11), it can
be seen that the best particle assigned with first takes the inertia weight of
minimum value while that for the lowest fitted particle takes the maximum
inertia weight, which makes that particle move with a high velocity.

The velocity of each particle is updated using Equation (5.3), and
if any updated velocity goes beyond V_{max}, it is limited to V_{max} using
Equation (5.12):

$$v_{ij}(t) = sign(v_{ij}(t-1)) * min(|v_{ij}(t-1)|, V_{jmax}). \qquad (5.12)$$

The new particle position is obtained by using Equation (5.8), and if
any particle position goes beyond the range specified, it is adjusted to its
boundary using Equations (5.13) and (5.14):

$$x_{ij}(t) = min(x_{ij}(t), range_{jmax}), \qquad (5.13)$$

$$x_{ij}(t) = max(x_{ij}(t), range_{jmin}), \qquad (5.14)$$

Furthermore the concept of re-initialization in APSO algorithm is
introduced to escape the algorithm from premature convergence to a local
optimum and further improvement is not noticeable.

5.4.2. *Hybrid APSO*

Most of the applications have been concentrated on solving continuous
optimization problems. However, in this research the problem space is
defined as the combination of continuous and discrete optimization. In
addition to invention of PSO for continuous search space, Kennedy and
Eberhart[12] also developed a binary version of PSO for discrete optimization

problems. The discrete PSO essentially differs from the original (or continuous) PSO in two characteristics. First the particle is composed of the binary variable. Second the velocity represents the probability of bit x_{ij} taking the value 1. In otherwords if $v_{ij} = 0.3$, then there is a 30% chance that x_{ij} will be a 1, and a seventy percent chance it will be zero. Since the velocity vector contains all the probabilistic values, therefore it must be constrained to the interval $[0.0, 1.0]$.

In this research, we combined the best effort of adaptive PSO (APSO) and binary PSO (BPSO) to explore the continuous and discrete search space simultaneously. Like PSO, APSO is initialized with a group of random particles (solutions) from continuous and discrete domain and then searches for optima by updating each iteration. In every iteration, each particle is updated by following two best values. The first one is the local best solution a particle has obtained so far. This value is called personal best solutions. Another, best value is that the whole swarm has obtained so far. This value is called global best solution.

The representation of the Bayesian coefficients (discussed in Sec. 5.3) on the particle is fairly direct– a real value from $[0, 1]$. In order to infer the minimal set of features required for accurate classification, it is desirable to promote parsimony in the discriminant function, that is, as many coefficients should be reduced to zero (specifically nth and $(n-1)$th coefficients) as possible without sacrificing classification accuracy. While the cost function encourages parsimony by penalizing a coefficient vector for each non-zero value, a simple real valued representation for the coefficients themselves does not provide an easy means for the APSO to reduce coefficients to zero. Several method were tested to aid the search for a minimal feature set, including reducing weight vales below a predefined threshold value to zero, and including a penalty term in the cost function for higher weight values. the method that proved most effective, however, was a hybrid representation that incorporates both the ideas like PSO for continuous domain (APSO) and PSO for discrete domain i.e., called binary PSO. In this representation, a mask field is associated with each coefficients. The contents of the mask field determine whether the coefficient is included in the classifier or not. A single bit mask is assigned to each coefficients. The particle representation is given below.

Coefficients(Real Values)	w_1	w_2	w_3	w_4
Mask (0/1)	m_1	m_2	m_3	m_4

If the value of m_i, $i = 1(1)5$ is 1, then the coefficient is weighted and included in the classifier. If on the other hand, the mask bit for a coefficient was set to 0, then the weight was treated effectively as zero, eliminating the coefficient from consideration by the classifier.

In a nutshell, the particle swarm formula:

$$\vec{v}_i(t) = \vec{v}_i(t-1) + c_1 \otimes r_1 \otimes (\overrightarrow{pbest_i} - \vec{x}_i(t))$$
$$+ c_2 \otimes r_2 \otimes (\overrightarrow{gbest} - \vec{x}_i(t)), \tag{5.15}$$

remains unchanged. The position of each particle is changed by the following rule:

The coefficient vector is changed like standard PSO, where as the mask vector is changed like BPSO. However, the velocity of each particle contains the probability, must be constrained to the interval $[0,1]$. A logistic transformation $S(v_{ij})$ can be used to change the mask vector of each particle.

if $(\text{rand}() < s(v_{ij}))$
$x_{ij} = 1;$
else
$x_{ij} = 0;$

where the function $s(.)$ is a sigmoidal limiting transformation and $rand()$ is a quasirandom number selected from a uniform distribution in $[0,1]$.

5.4.3. *Learnable Bayesian classifier in IDS*

The more general family of naive Bayesian classifier can be constructed using the following formulation:

$$P(\vec{x}|C_i) = \sum_{j=1}^{n} w_j \left(\prod_{k=1}^{j} P(x_k|C_i) \right), \tag{5.16}$$

where $P(x_k|C_i)$ is the kth largest of the $P(x_j|C_i)$ and $w_j \in [0,1]$, $\sum_{j=1}^{n} w_j = 1$.

Let us look at this formulation for some special cases of the weights. In the case where $w_n = 1$ and $w_j = 0$ for $j \neq n$ we get the original naive Bayesian classifier. At the other extreme is the case when $w_1 = 1$ and $w_j = 0$ for $j \neq 1$. In this case, the a priori probability $P(\vec{x}|c_i)$ is using the one feature value of the object $\vec{x}$ that most strongly supports as being a member of the class C_i. Another special case is when $w_j = 1/n$. In this case $P(\overrightarrow{x}|C_i) = \frac{1}{n}(\sum_{j=1}^{n}(\prod_{k=1}^{j} P(x_k|C_i)))$.

The introduction of this more general classifier formulation provides us with additional degrees of freedom in the form of the associated weights. While the inclusion of the additional terms provides for a more general model it brings with the problem of determining the values of these weights. The hybrid APSO can be used as a suitable tool to obtain these weights by using the training set. In the pure naive Bayesian classifier, no attempt is made to assure that the training set itself will be correctly classified, the training set is just used to determine the probabilities.

During the execution of HAPSO, each particle is passed to the classifier for evaluation, and a cost score is computed, based primarily on the accuracy obtained by the parameterized generalized Bayesian formulation in classifying a set of samples of known class. Since the HAPSO seeks to maximize the cost score, the formulation of the cost function is a key element in determining the quality of the resulting classifier. Coefficients are associated with each term in the APSO cost function that allow control of each run. The following cost function is computed during the evaluation of particle fitness:

$$f(\overrightarrow{x}) = A_c \times CL_{acc} + \frac{A_f}{S_{fr}}, \tag{5.17}$$

where $S_{fr} = m_i * \sum_{i=1}^{n} * rank(w_i)$, A_c is the weight factor associated with CL_{acc} (Classification Accuracy) and A_f is the weight factor associated with selected number of weights. Additionally, we assign a rank to each weight factor– particularly highest rank to the weight factor associated with the first largest of the $P(x_j|C_i)$ and so on.

The coefficients determine the relative contribution of each part of the fitness function in guiding the search. The values for the cost function coefficients are determined empirically in a set of initial experiments for each data set. Typical values for these coefficients are $A_c = 20.0$ and $A_f = 10.0$.

5.5. Experiments

5.5.1. Description of intrusion data

In the 1998 DARPA intrusion detection evaluation program, an environment was set up to acquire raw TCP/IP dump data for a network by simulating a typical US Air Force LAN. The LAN was operated like a real environment, but being blasted with multiple attacks. For each

TCP/IP connection, 41 various quantitative and qualitative features were extracted.[45] Of this database a subset of 494021 data were used, of which 20% represent normal patterns. The four different categories of attack patterns are as follows.

5.5.1.1. *Probing*

Probing is a class of attacks where an attacker scans a network to gather information or find known vulnerabilities. An attacker with a map of machines and services that are available on a network can use the information to look for exploits. There are different types of probes: some of them abuse the computers legitimate features; some of them use social engineering techniques. This class of attacks is the most commonly heard and requires very little technical expertise. Different types of probe attacks with same mechanism known as *abuse of feature* are shown in Table 5.1.

5.5.1.2. *Denial of service attacks*

DoS is a class of attacks where an attacker makes some computing or memory resource too busy or too full to handle legitimate requests, thus denying legitimate users access to a machine. There are different ways to launch DoS attacks: by abusing the computers legitimate features; by targeting the implementations bugs; or by exploiting the systems misconfigurations. DoS attacks are classified based on the services that an attacker renders unavailable to legitimate users. Some of the popular attack types are shown in Table 5.2.

5.5.1.3. *User to root attacks*

User to root (U2R) exploits are a class of attacks where an attacker starts out with access to a normal user account on the system and is able to exploit vulnerability to gain root access to the system. Most common exploits in

Table 5.1.   Probe attacks.

Type of Attack	Service	Effect of the Attack
Ipsweep	Icmp	Identifies Active Machines
Mscan	Many	Looks for Known Vulnerabilities
Nmap	Many	Identifies Active Ports on a Machine
Saint	Many	Looks for Known Vulnerabilities
Satan	Many	Looks for Known Vulnerabilities

Table 5.2. Denial of service attacks.

Attack Type	Service	Mechanism	Effect of the Attack
Apache2	http	Abuse	Crashes httpd
Back	http	Abuse/Bug	Slows down server response
Land	http	Bug	Freezes the machine
Mail bomb	N/A	Abuse	Annoyance
SYN flood	TCP	Abuse	Denies service on one or more ports
Ping of death	Icmp	Bug	None
Process table	TCP	Abuse	Denies new processes
Smurf	Icmp	Abuse	Slows down the network
Syslogd	Syslog	Bug	Kills the Syslogd
Teardrop	N/A	Bug	Reboots the machine
Udpstrom	Echo/Chargen	Abuse	Slows down the network

this class of attacks are regular buffer overflows, which are caused by regular programming mistakes and environment assumptions. Table 5.3 presents some of the attack types in this category whose service and effect of the attack type is *user session* and *Gains root shell* respectively for all type of attacks.

5.5.1.4. *Remote to user attacks*

A remote to user (R2U) attack is a class of attacks where an attacker sends packets to a machine over a network, then exploits machines vulnerability to illegally gain local access as a user. There are different types of R2U attacks: the most common attack in this class is done using social engineering. Some of the R2U attacks are presented in Table 5.4.

5.5.2. *System parameters*

Complex relationships exist between features, which are difficult for humans to discover. The IDS must therefore reduce the amount of data to be

Table 5.3. User to root attacks.

Type of Attacks	Mechanism
Eject	Buffer overflow
Ffbconfig	Buffer overflow
Fdformat	Buffer overflow
Loadmodule	Poor environment sanitation
Perl	Poor environment sanitation
Ps	Poor temp file management
Xterm	Buffer overflow

Table 5.4.   Remote to user attacks.

Attack Type	Service	Mechanism	Effect of the Attack
Dictionary	Telnet, rlogin, pop, ftp, imap	Abuse feature	Gains user access
Ftp-write	Ftp	Misconfig.	Gains user access
Guest	Telnet, rlogin	Misconfig.	Gains user access
Imap	Imap	Bug	Gains root access
Named	Dns	Bug	Gains root access
Phf	Http	Bug	Executes commands as http user
Sendmail	Smtp	Bug	Executes commands as root
Xlock	Smtp	Misconfig.	Spoof user to obtain password
Xnsoop	Smtp	Misconfig.	Monitor key stokes remotely

processed. This is very important if real-time detection is desired. The easiest way to do this is by doing an intelligent input feature selection. Certain features may contain false correlations,which hinder the process of detecting intrusions. Further, some features may be redundant since the information they add is contained in other features. Extra features can increase computation time, and can impact the accuracy of IDS. Feature selection improves classification by searching for the subset of features, which best classifies the training data. Feature selection is done based on the contribution the input variables made to the construction of the HAPSO learnable Bayesian classifier.

The data set has 41 attributes for each connection record plus one class label. R2U and U2R attacks don't have any sequential patterns like DOS and Probe because the former attacks have the attacks embedded in the data packets whereas the later attacks have many connections in a short amount of time. Therefore, some features that look for suspicious behavior in the data packets like number of failed logins are constructed and these are called content features. Our experiments have two phases, namely, a training (or model building) and a testing phase. In the training phase the system constructs a model using the training data to give maximum generalization accuracy (accuracy on unseen data) with a compact set of features. The test data is passed through the constructed model to detect the intrusion in the testing phase. Besides the four different types of attacks mentioned above we also have to detect the normal class. The data set for our experiments contained a subset of 11982 records (KDD cup 99 Intrusion detection data set), which were randomly generated from the MIT data set. Random generation of data include the number of data from each class proportional to its size, except that the smallest class is completely included. This data set is again divided into training data with 5092 records and testing data with 6890 records. All the intrusion detection models are trained and tested with the same set of data. As the data set has five different classes we perform a five-class classification. The normal data belongs to class one, probe belongs to class two, denial of service (DoS) belongs to class three, user to root (U2R) belongs to class four and remote to local (R2U) belongs to class five.

HAPSO parameters have been choosen without performing a preliminary tuning phase, rather they have been set on the basis of the experience gained of multivariate optimization problem. Namely their values are the following:

Swarm size, N	50
c_1	2.0
c_2	1.8
Inertia weight, w_{min}	0.4
Inertia weight, w_{max}	0.9

5.5.3. *Results*

The accuracy of the classifier is measured through the confusion matrix. As it is a stochastic algorithm we reported the average training set results obtained on ten simulations in Table 5.4. The top-left entry of the following matrix shows that 1394 of the actual normal test set were detected to be normal; the last column indicates that 99.57% of the actual normal data points were detected correctly. In the same way, for Probe 658 of the actual attack test set were correctly detected; the last column indicates that 94.00% of the actual Probe data points were detected correctly. Similarly for Dos 98.22% of the actual DoS test data points were detected correctly. 64.00% of the U2Su test data points are correctly classified. In the case of R2U class 95.71% of the test data points are correctly classified. The bottom row shows that 96.87% of the test set said to be normal indeed were normal and 89.52% of the test set classified, as probe indeed belongs to probe. The overall accuracy of the classification is 97.69%.

The most evident aspect of the results on this dataset is the feature selection capability demonstrated by the HAPSO/Bayesian classifier. The

Table 5.5. Classification accuracy on training set with
a selected set of features.

Attack Type	Accuracy	Optimal Set of Features
Normal	99.97	12
Probe	99.63	9.42
DoS	99.96	10.03
U2Su	99.64	8.15
R2L	99.98	11.75

CF	Normal	Probe	DoS	U2Su	R2L	Class Acc.
Normal	1394	5	1	0	0	99.57%
Probe	40	658	2	0	0	94.00%
DoS	4	70	4127	1	0	98.22%
U2Su	0	1	6	16	2	64.00%
R2L	1	1	4	18	536	95.71%
%	96.87%	89.52%	99.69%	45.71%	99.63%	

number of features selected for each class of the dataset ranges from seven
to twelve with a average training accuracy of 99.83%.

5.6. Conclusions and Future Research Directions

Effective intrusion detection and management systems are critical
components of cyber infrastructure as they are in the forefront of the
battle against cyber-terrorism. In this chapter we presented a HAPSO
learnable Bayesian classifier for simultaneous intrusion features selection
and detection.

The experimental results demonstrated that on an average 99.83% of
detection accuracy is obtained during training of the system. Additionally,
the features selected against each class ranges from seven to twelve. With
the increasing incidents of cyber attacks, building an effective and intelligent
intrusion detection models with good accuracy and real-time performance
are essential. This field is developing continuously. More swarm intelligence
techniques with possible hybridization should be investigated and their
efficiency should be evaluated as intrusion detection models.

Our future research will be directed towards developing more accurate
base classifiers particularly for the detection of U2R type of attacks.

References

1. S. Mukkamala, A. Sung, and A. Abraham. Intrusion detection using ensemble of soft computing and hard computing paradigms, *Journal of Network and Computer Applications.* **28**(2), 167–182, (2005).
2. D. Denning. An intrusion detection model, *IEEE Transactions on Software Engineering.* **SE-13**(2), 222–232, (1987).
3. R. C. Summers. *Secure Computing: threats and safeguards.* (McGraw Hill, New York, 1997).
4. C. Kruegel and F. Valeur. Stateful intrusion detection for high-speed networks. In *Proc. IEEE Symposium on Research on Security and Privacy*, pp. 285–293, (2002).
5. S. Mukkamala, A. H. Sung, and A. Abraham. Intrusion detection using ensemble of soft computing paradigms. In *Proc. 3rd International Conference on Intelligent Systems Design and Applications, Advances in Soft Computing*, pp. 239–248, Germany, (2003).
6. S. Mukkamala, A. H. Sung, and A. Abraham. Modeling intrusion detection systems using linear genetic programming approach. In *Proc. 17th International Conference on Industrial and Engineering Applications of Artificial Intelligence and Expert Systems, Innovations in Applied Artificial Intelligence*, pp. 633–642, Germany, (2004).
7. S. Mukkamala, A. H. Sung, A. Abraham, and V. Ramos. Intrusion detection systems using adaptive regression splines. In *Proc. 6th International Conference on Enterprise Information Systems (ICEIS'04)*, pp. 26–33, Portugal, (2004).
8. K. Shah, N. Dave, S. Chavan, S. Mukharajee, A. Abraham, and S. Sanyal. Adaptive neurofuzzy intrusion detection system. In *Proc. IEEE International Conference on Information Technology:Coding and Computing(ITCC'04)*, pp. 70–74, USA, (2004).
9. S. Peddabachigari, A. Abraham, C. Grosan, and J. Thomas. Modeling intrusion detection system using hybrid intelligent system, *Journal of Network and Computer Applications.* **30**, 114–132, (2007).
10. A. L. Blum and P. Langley. Selection of relevant features and examples in machine learning, *Artificial Intelligence.* **97**, 245–271, (1997).
11. B. K. Panigrahi, V. R. Pandi, and S. Das. Adaptive particle swarm optimization approach for static and dynamic economic load dispatch, *Energy Conversion and Management.* **49**, 1407–1415, (2008).
12. J. Kennedy and R. C. Eberhart. A discrete binay version of the particle swarm algorithm. In *Proc. of the World Multiconference on Systemics, Cybernetics and Informatics*, pp. 4104–4109, NJ: Pisacataway, (1997).
13. R. R. Yagar. An extension of the naive bayesian classifier, *Information Sciences.* **176**, 577–588, (2006).
14. J. P. Anderson. Computer Security Threat Monitoring and Surveillance. Technical report, James P. Anderson Co., Fort Washington, Pennsylvania (April, 1980).

15. T. Lunt. Detecting intruders in computer systems. In *Proc. of the Conference on Auditing and Computer Technology*, (1993).

16. T. Lunt, A. Tamaru, F. Gilham, R. Jagannathan, P. Neumann, and H. Javitz. A real time intrusion detection expert system (IDES). Technical report, Computer Science Laboratory, SRI International, Menlo Park, California (February, 1992).

17. H. S. Teng, K. Chen, and S. C. Lu. Security audit trail analysis using inductively generated predictive rules. In *Proc. IEEE of the 11th National Conference on Artificial Intelligence Applications*, pp. 24–29, NJ: Pisacataway, (1990).

18. P. A. Porras. STAT: a state transition analysis tool for intrusion detection. Master's thesis, Computer Science Department, University of California, Santa, Barbara, (1992).

19. K. Ilgun. USTAT: a real-time intrusion detection system for unix. Master's thesis, Computer Science Department, University of California, Santa, Barbara, (1992).

20. T. D. Garvey and T. F. Lunt. Model based intrusion detection. In *Proc. of the 14th National Conference on Computer Security*, pp. 372–385, (1991).

21. S. Kumar. *Classification and Detection of Computer Intrusions*. PhD thesis, Department of Computer Science, Purdue University (Aug., 1995).

22. S. Kumar and E. H. Spafford. An application of pattern matching in intrusion detection. Technical report, Purudue University, (1994).

23. W. Lee. *A data mining framework for constructing features and models for intrusion detection systems*. PhD thesis, Department of Computer Science, Columbia University (June, 1999).

24. R. Grossman, S. Kasif, R. Moore, D. Rocke, and J. Ullman. Data mining research: Opportunities and challenges. In *Proc. of three NSF Workshops on Mining Large, Massive, and Distributed Data* (Jan, 1998).

25. W. Lee, S. Stolfo, and K. Mok. A data mining framework for building intrusion detection models. In *Proc. of the IEEE Symposium on Security and Privacy*, (1999).

26. K. L. Fox, R. R. Henning, J. H. Reed, and R. Simonian. A neural network approach towards intrusions detection. In *Proc. of the 13th National Computer Security Conference*, pp. 125–134, Washington, DC (Oct., 1990).

27. H. Debar, M. Becke, and D. Siboni. A neural network component for an intrusion detection system. In *Proc. IEEE Computer Society Symposium on Research in Security and Privacy*, (1992).

28. R. J., L. M. J., and M. R. Intrusion detection with neural networks, *Advances in Neural Information Processing Systems*. **10**, (1998).

29. J. Cannady. Artificial neural networks for misuse detection. In *Proc. National Information Systems Security Conference*, (1998).

30. S. X. Wu and W. Bonzhaf. The Use of Computational Intelligence in Intrusion Detection Systems: A review. Technical Report 2008-05, Department of Computer Science, Memorial University of Newfoundland, St. John's, NL, Canada A1B3X5 (November, 2008).

31. A. Abraham, R. Jain, J. Thomas, and S. Y. Han. D-SCIDS: Distributed soft computing intrusion detection system, *Journal of Network and Computer Applications.* **30**, 81–98, (2007).
32. F. Esponda, S. Forrest, and P. Helman. A formal framework of positive and negative detection, *IEEE Transactions on Systems, Man, and Cybernetics-Part B.* **34**(1), 357–373, (2004).
33. S. A. Hofmeyr and S. Forrest. Immunity by design: an artificial immune system. In *Proc. GECCO Conference*, (1999).
34. R. O. Duda, P. E. Hart, and D. G. Stork. *Pattern classification.* (Wiley, New York, 2001).
35. J. Han and M. Kamber. *Data mining: Concepts and techniques.* (Morgan Kaufmann, UK, 2001).
36. D. S. Bauer and M. E. Michael. NIDX: an expert system for real time network intrusion detection. In *Proc. of the Computer Networking Symposium*, pp. 90–106, (1988).
37. S. Das. Filters, wrappers and a boosting-based hybrid for feature selection. In *Proc. 18th Intl. Conf. on Machine Learning*, (2001).
38. R. Kohavi and G. John. Wrapers for feature subset selection, *Artificial Intelligence.* **97**(1–2), 273–324, (1997).
39. R. Caruana and D. Freitag. Greedy attribute selection. In *Proc. of the 11th Intl. Conf. on Machine Learning*, p. 2532, (1994).
40. H. Liu and H. Motoda. *Feature Selection for Knowledge Discovery and data Mining.* (Kluwer Academic Press, 1998).
41. J. Kennedy and R. C. Eberhart. Particle swarm optimization. In *Proc. of IEEE International Conference on Neural Networks*, pp. 1942–1948, (1995).
42. Y. Shi and R. Eberhart. Empirical study of particle swarm optimization. In *Proc. of IEEE World Conference on Evolutionary Computation*, pp. 6–9, (1999).
43. M. Clerc and J. Kennedy. The particle swarm explosion, stability and convergence in a multidimensional complex space, *Transactions on Evolutioanry computation.* **6**(1), 58–73, (2002).
44. A. Ratnaweera, S. K. Halgamuge, and H. C. Watson. Self-organizing hirarchical particle swarm optimizer with time varying acceleration coefficients, *IEEE Transactions on Evolutionary Computation.* **8**(3), 240–255, (2004).
45. K. cup 99. Intrusion detection dataset, (1999). /http://kdd.ics.uci.edu/databases/kddcup99/kddcup.data_10_percent.gz.

Chapter 6

MINING KNOWLEDGE FROM NETWORK INTRUSION DATA USING DATA MINING TECHNIQUES

M. PANDA* and M. R. PATRA[†]

*Department of ECE,
Gandhi Institute of Engineering and Technology,
Gunupur, Orissa, India
mrutyunjaya.2007@rediffmail.com

[†]Department of Computer Science,
Berhampur University, Berhampur, Orissa, India
mrpatra12@gmail.com

Today networking of computing infrastructures across geographical boundaries has made it possible to perform various operations effectively irrespective of application domains. But, at the same time the growing misuse of this connectively in the form of network intrusions has jeopardized the security aspect of both the data that are transacted over the network and maintained in data stores. Research is in progress to detect such security threats and protect the data from misuse. A huge volume of data on intrusion is available which can be analyzed to understand different attack scenarios and devise appropriate counter-measures. The DARPA KDDcup'99 intrusion data set is a widely used data source which depicts many intrusion scenarios for analysis. This data set can be mined to acquire adequate knowledge about the nature of intrusions thereby one can develop strategies to deal with them. In this work we discuss on the use of different data mining techniques to elicit sufficient information that can be effectively used to build intrusion detection systems.

6.1. Introduction

Network intrusion refers to any activity that tries to compromise the security of information stored in computers connected to a network. A wide range of activities falls under this definition, including attempts to de-stabilize the network, gain un-authorized access to files or privileges or simply misuse of network resources. Intrusion Detection Systems (IDS) are being developed to deal with such attacks and facilitate appropriate actions in order to safeguard against possible damage to vital information resources. One of the major challenges in building IDS is its ability to report suspicious and malicious network activities in real-time.

In a much cited survey on IDS, Axelsson[1] depicts a generalized model of a typical intrusion detection system as shown in Fig. 6.1, where the solid arrows indicate data/control flow and the dotted arrows indicate a response to intrusive activity. According to Axelsson, the generic architectural model of an intrusion detection system contains the following modules:

Audit data collection: This module is used during the data collection phase. The data collected in this phase is analyzed by the intrusion detection algorithm to find traces of suspicious activity. The source of the data can be host/network activity logs, command based logs, application based logs, etc.

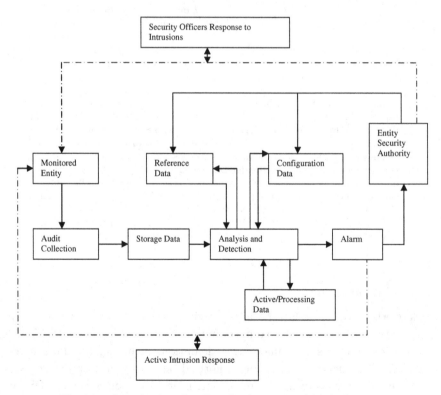

Fig. 6.1. Organization of a generalized intrusion detection system.

Audit data storage: Typical intrusion detection systems store the audit data either indefinitely or for a sufficiently long time for later reference. The volume of data is often exceedingly large. Hence, the problem of audit data reduction is a major research issue in the design of intrusion detection systems.

Analysis and detection: The processing block is the heart of an intrusion detection system where the algorithms to detect suspicious activities are implemented. Algorithms for the analysis and detection of intrusions have been traditionally classified into three broad categories: signature (or misuse) detection, anomaly detection and hybrid detection.

Configuration data: The configuration data is the most sensitive part of an intrusion detection system. It contains information that pertains to the operation of the intrusion detection system, namely; information on how and when to collect audit data, how to respond to intrusions, etc.

Reference data: The reference data storage module stores information about known intrusion signatures (in case of signature detection) or profiles of normal behavior (in case of anomaly detection). In the latter case, the profiles are updated whenever new knowledge about the system behavior is available.

Active/processing data: The processing element must frequently store intermediate results such as information about partially fulfilled intrusion signatures.

Alarm: This part of the system deals with all output produced from the intrusion detection system. The output may be either an automated response to an intrusion or a suspicious activity that is informed to a system security officer.

6.2. Mining Knowledge Using Data Mining Techniques

Huge amount of data is generated through the day-to-day functioning of organizations. Many times vital information is hidden in such large volumes of data which can influence the decision-making process of any organization. Exploring knowledge from the available data sources in order to guide our actions, be it in business, science or engineering, is an interesting domain of research. Data mining is a technique which tries to automatically extract the predictive information from data sources that is not apparently visible. The data mining process drills through huge volume of data, to discover the hidden key facts in order to assist in the decision making process.[2] In other words, data mining discovers patterns of data that can generate new knowledge for organizational use. This of course entails huge computations, and therefore, the process must be automated. For ensuring meaningful results, the foremost requirement is that the data must have been expressed in a well-understandable format. The first step in data mining is to describe the data by summarizing its statistical attributes. The data description alone does not provide any action plan. A predictive model must be built based on the patterns determined from known results. Then the model is tested on results outside the original sample of data.

A complete data mining process is depicted in Fig. 6.2 wherein historical data is used for training the data mining algorithms which is later evaluated on a subset of the same data set. Later, this learned model is used for the purpose of prediction in case of any new data. The learning process is broadly classified as: (i) supervised, and (ii) unsupervised. In supervised learning, a tutor must help the system in the construction of the model, by defining classes and providing positive and negative examples of objects

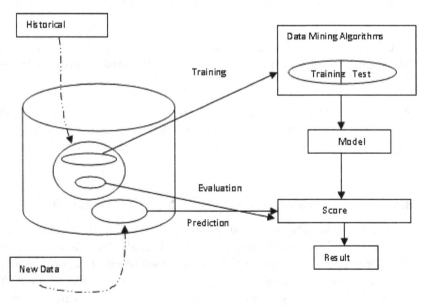

Fig. 6.2.   Data mining process.

belonging to these classes. Thus, supervised learning is a function fitting algorithm.

In unsupervised learning, there is no tutor which defines the classes a priori. The system must itself find some way of clustering the objects into classes, and find appropriate descriptions for these classes. Thus, unsupervised learning is a cluster finding algorithm.

Some of the most frequently used data mining techniques are as follows:

- Association Rule Mining.
- Classification.
- Clustering.

6.3. Association Rule Mining

Association rules[3,4] are one of many data mining techniques that describe events that tend to occur together. The concept of association rules can be understood as follows:

Association rule mining: Association rule mining finds interesting association or correlation relationships among a large set of data items.[4] The association rules are considered interesting if they satisfy both a minimum support threshold and a minimum confidence threshold.[5] A more formal definition is the following.[6] Let $I = \{I_1, I_2, I_3, \ldots, I_m\}$ be a set of items. Let D, the task relevant data, be a set of database transactions where each transaction T is a set of items such that $T \subseteq I$. An association rule is an implication in the form of $X \rightarrow Y$, where $X, Y \subset I$ are sets of items called item sets, and $X \cap Y = \phi$. X is called antecedent while Y is called consequent; the rule means X implies Y. There are two important basic measures for association rules, support(s) and confidence(c). Since the database is large and users concern about only those frequently occurred items, usually thresholds of support and confidence are pre-defined by users to drop those rules that are not so interesting or useful. The two thresholds are called minimal support and minimal confidence respectively, additional constraints of interesting rules also can be specified by the users. The two important measures for Association Rule Mining (ARM), support and confidence, can be defined as follows.

The support(s) of an association rule is the ratio (in percent) of the records that contain X Y to the total number of records in the database. Support is the statistical significance of an association rule.

The confidence(c) can be defined as the ratio (in percent) of the number of records that contain X Y to the number of records that contain X. Confidence is a measure of a rule's strength. Often a large confidence is required for association rules.

The problem of mining association rules can be decomposed into two sub problems[7] as stated in Algorithm 6.1, shown in Fig. 6.3. The first step in Algorithm 6.1 finds large or frequent item sets. Item sets other than those are referred as small item sets. Here an item set is a subset of the total set of items of interest from the database. An interesting (and useful) observation about the large item sets is that: if an item set X is small, any superset of X is also small. Of course the contra positive of this statement (if X is a large item set than so is any subset of X) is also important to remember. The second step in Algorithm 6.1 finds association rules using large item sets in the first step. In this, it is desired to generate strong association rules from the frequent item sets. By definition these rules must satisfy both minimum support and minimum confidence. Association rule mining is to find out association rules that satisfy the pre-defined minimum support and confidence from a given database.[7] The problem is usually decomposed into two sub problems. One is to find those item sets whose occurrences exceed a pre-defined threshold in the database, those item sets are called frequent or large item sets. The second problem is to generate association rules from those large item sets with

---

Input:

    I, D, s, c

Output:

    Association rules satisfying s and c

Algorithm

1. *Find all sets of items which occur with a frequency that is greater than or equal to the user specified threshold support s.*

2. *Generate the desired rules using the large item sets, which have user specified threshold confidence, c.*

Fig. 6.3.   Basic association rule mining algorithms.

the constraints of minimal confidence. Suppose one of the large item sets is L_k, $L_k = \{I_1, I_2, \ldots, I_{k-1}, I_k\}$, association rules with this item sets are generated in the following way: the first rule is $\{I_1, I_2, \ldots, I_{k-1}\} \rightarrow \{I_k\}$, by checking the confidence this rule can be determined as interesting or not. Then other rules are generated by deleting the last items in the antecedent and inserting it to the consequent, further the confidences of the new rules are checked to determine their interestingness. Those processes iterated until the antecedent becomes empty. Since the second sub problem is quite straight forward, most of the researches focus on the first sub problem.

Apriori algorithm: Apriori is a great improvement in the history of association rule mining, Apriori algorithm was first proposed in Agrawal and Srikant.[7] Apriori is efficient during the candidate generation process for two reasons: it employs a different candidate generation method and a new pruning technique. Figure 6.4 gives an overview of the Apriori algorithm for finding all frequent item sets from the database.[8] The Apriori generates the candidate item sets by joining the large item sets of the previous pass and deleting those subsets which are small in the previous pass without considering the transactions in the database. By only considering large item sets of the previous pass, the number of candidate large item sets is significantly reduced. The first pass of the algorithm simply counts item occurrences to determine the large 1-itemsets. A subsequent pass, say pass k, consists of two phases. First, the large item sets L_{k-1} found in the $(k-1)$th pass are used to generate the candidate item sets C_k, using the Apriori candidate generation function as described above. Next, the database is scanned and the support of candidates in C_k is counted. A hash-tree data structure[7] is used for this purpose. The Apriori-gen function takes as argument L_{k-1}, the set of all large $(k-1)$-item sets. It returns a superset of the set of all large k-item sets, as described in Agrawal and Srikant.[7]

Extended association rule: Previous work as described earlier has focused on mining association rules in large databases with single support. Since a single threshold support is used for the whole database, it assumes that all items in the data are of the same nature and/or have similar frequencies. In reality, some items may be very frequent while others may appear rarely in a data set. However, the latter may be more informative and more interesting than the other. For example, it could be some items in a super market which are sold less frequently but more profitable, for example food processor and cooking pan.[9] Therefore, it might be very

```
Input: database D
              Minimum Support s
              Minimum Confidence c
Output:
              R_t All association rules
Algorithm:
              L_1 = {large 1-itemsets};
              for (k=2, L_{k-1}≠ø; k++) do begin
              C_k=apriori-gen (L_{k-1});  //New Candidates
              for all transactions t D do begin
                    C_t=subset (C_k, t);
                    //Candidates contained in t
                    For all candidates c C_t do
                              c.count++;
                    end
              L_k = {cC_k|c.count≥minsupport}
              end
              L_f=_k L_k;
        R_t = Generate Rules (L_f, c)
```

Fig. 6.4. Apriori algorithm.

interesting to discover a useful rule food Processor → Cooking Pan with a support of 2%. If the threshold support is set too high, rules involving rare items will not be found. To obtain the rules involving both frequent and rare items, the threshold support has to be set very low. Unfortunately, this may cause combinatorial explosion, producing too many rules, because those frequent items will be associated with other items in all possible ways and many of them may be meaningless. This dilemma is known as "rare item problem".[9] Therefore single threshold support for the entire database is inadequate to discover important association rules because it cannot capture the inherent natures and/or frequency differences in the database. In Liu and Ma,[9] the existing association rule model is extended to allow the user to specify multiple threshold supports. The extended new algorithm is named as MSApriori, as shown in Fig. 6.5. In this method, the threshold support is expressed in terms of minimum item support (MIS) of the items that appear in the rule. The main feature of this technique is that the user can specify a different threshold item support for each item. Therefore, this technique can discover rare item rules without causing frequent items to generate too many unnecessary rules.

M=sort (I, MS); /* according to MIS (i)'s stored in MS*/

F=Init-pass (M, T); /*make the first pass over T*/

L_1= {<f>|fF, f.count ≥MIS (f)};

For (k=2; L_{k-1}≠ø; k++) do

        If k=2 then C_2=level2-candidate-gen (F)

        else C_k=candidate-gen (L_{k-1})

        end

        for each transaction t € T do

        C_t=subset (C_k, t);

        For each candidate c € C_t do

        c.count++;

end

L_k={cC_k|c.count≥MIS(c [1])}

end

L_f=$_k$$L_k$;

R_t=Generate Rules (L_f c)

Fig. 6.5.   MS Apriori algorithm.

MS Apriori algorithm: Let L_k denotes the set of large k-item sets. Each item set c, is of the following form $\langle c[1], c[2], \ldots, c[k] \rangle$ which consists of items $c[1], c[2], \ldots, c[k]$, where $MIS(c[1]) \leq MIS(c[2]) \leq, \ldots, \leq MIS(c[k])$. The algorithm is illustrated as follows:

Similar to conventional algorithms, the MS Apriori generates all large item sets by making multiple passes on the data. In the first pass, it counts the supports of individual items and determines whether they are large. In each subsequent pass, it uses large item sets of the previous pass to generate candidate item sets. Computing the actual supports of these candidate sets, the MS Apriori determines which of the candidate sets are actually large at the end of the pass. However, the generation of large item sets in the second pass differs from other algorithms. A key operation in the MS Apriori is the sorting of the items I in ascending order of their MIS values. This ordering is used in the subsequent operation of the algorithm.

A comparison between Apriori and MS Apriori algorithm with respect to execution time is shown in Fig. 6.6. From this, it is evident that the MS Apriori algorithm with multiple support threshold values is faster than the conventional Apriori algorithm with a single minimum threshold, while building a network intrusion detection model.

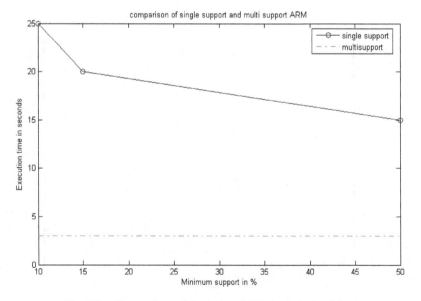

Fig. 6.6. Comparison of Apriori and MS Apriori algorithm.

6.4. Measuring Interestingness

The number of discovered association rules using Apriori is very large and many of the discovered rules do not have much meaning. Therefore, it is important to implement pruning and interestingness measures so as to obtain the most interesting generalized profile association rules. Here we discuss about the implementation of a template based pruning technique and interestingness measure to select the most interesting profile rules among a set of generalized rules. More details can be found in Panda and Patra.[10]

Template based pruning: One way of selecting association rules that are of interest is to specify template information in which we can explicitly specify what is interesting and what is not. An implementation of the template based pruning to extract relevant set of association rules can be found in Giha *et al.*[11] This technique is useful because not all rules that passed the min.support and min.confidence values are interesting. This technique filters the discovered association rules and selects the ones that match some specified template criteria, while rejecting others. It is a fact that strong association rules are not necessarily interesting.[12] Several measures, besides confidence, have been proposed to better measure the correlation between X and Y. Some of them are as follows: Chi-Square testing, lift, correlation, conviction and cosine.

Chi-Square testing: To perform the Chi-Square test, a table of expected frequencies is first calculated using $P(X)$ and $P(Y)$ from the contingency table. The expected frequency for $(X$ and $Y)$ is given by the product of $P(X)P(Y)$. Performing a grand total over observed frequencies versus expected frequencies gives a number which we denote by Chi. we use chi-square (χ^2) test to measure the degree of independence between two different attributes by comparing their observed patterns of occurrence (actual support) with the expected pattern of occurrence (expected support). (χ^2) value is calculated as follows:

$$\chi^2 = \Sigma(f_o - f_e)^2 / f_e, \tag{6.1}$$

where f_o represents an observed frequency (actual support) and f_e is an expected frequency (expected support). The contingency table is a frequency table in which a sample from the population is classified according to two or more attributes. The expected support is that all expected frequencies of the presence or absence of an item will be equal in a category or not. The expected support/confidence is calculated as a product of corresponding row and column totals divided by the total number of elements in the lower right cell of the observed support/confidence table. The calculated value of χ^2 is compared with the table value of χ^2 for given degrees of freedom at a specified level of significance. If at the stated level (generally 5% level is selected), the calculated value of χ^2 is more than the table value of χ^2, the difference between theory and observed is considered significant, i.e., it could not have arisen due to fluctuations of simple sampling. If on the other hand, the calculated value of χ^2 is less than the table value, the difference between theory and observed is not considered as significant, i.e., it is regarded as due to fluctuations of simple sampling and hence ignored. The observed value of χ^2 is compared with a cut-off value read from a Chi-Square table/Surf stat Chi-Square calculator. The degree of freedom in this case is calculated as $(r-1)(c-1)$, where, r and c represents the total number of rows and columns are present in the contingency table under consideration. For the probability value of 0.05 with one degree of freedom, the cut-off value is measured. If χ value is greater than this, X and Y are regarded as correlated with a 95% confidence level. Otherwise, they are regarded as non-correlated also with a 95% confidence level.

R-interesting measures: this technique uses the information provided in taxonomies to find the interesting rules among its ancestors, based on the assumption of statistical independence and strength of the latter rule. R is a threshold value specified by the user. A rule $X \to Y$ is interesting if it passed the R-specified threshold with respect to its ancestors. This technique is based on the idea implemented in Srikant and Agrawal[13] and states that: A rule $(X \to Y)$ is considered to be interesting in a given set of rules, if it has no ancestors or it is R-interesting with respect to its ancestor $X \to \widetilde{Y}$. We call a rule $X \to Y$ R-interesting with respect to ancestor $X \to \widetilde{Y}$, if the support of the rule $X \to Y$ is R-times the expected support based on $X \to \widetilde{Y}$, or the confidence is R-times the expected confidence based on $X \to \widetilde{Y}$.

Lift $(X \to Y)$ $= conf(X \to Y)/P(Y)$, an equivalent definition is: $P(X, Y)/P(X)P(Y)$. Lift is a symmetric measure. A lift well above one indicates a strong correlation between X and Y. A lift around one says that $P(X, Y) = P(X)P(Y)$. In terms of probability, this means that the occurrences of X and the occurrence of Y in the same transaction are independent events; hence X and Y are not correlated. Another definition can be found in Webb.[14]

Correlation $(X \rightarrow Y)$ $= \frac{[P(X,Y)-P(X)P(Y)]}{\sqrt{[P(X)P(Y)(1-P(X))(1-P(Y))]}}$. Correlation is a symmetric measure. A correlation around 0 indicates that X and Y are not correlated, a negative figure indicates that X and Y are negatively correlated and a positive figure that they are positively correlated. Note that the denominator of the division is positive and smaller than 1. Thus the absolute value $|cor(X \rightarrow Y)|$ is greater than $|P(X,Y) - P(X)P(Y)|$. In other words, if the lift is around 1, correlation can still be significantly different from 0.

Conviction $(X \rightarrow Y)$ $= [1 - P(Y)]/[1 - conf(X \rightarrow Y)]$. Conviction is not a symmetric measure. A conviction around 1 says that X and Y are independent, while conviction is infinite as $conf(X \rightarrow Y)$ is tending to 1. It is to be noted that if p(Y) is high, 1-P(Y) is small. In that case, even if $conf(X \rightarrow Y)$ is strong, conviction $(X \rightarrow Y)$ may be small.

Cosine$(X \rightarrow Y)$ $= \frac{P(X,Y)}{\sqrt{[P(X)P(Y)]}}$, where $\sqrt{[P(X)P(Y)]}$ means the square root of the product $P(X)P(Y)$. An equivalent definition is:

$$Cosine(X \rightarrow Y) = \sqrt{\frac{|t_i|t_i \ contains \ both \ X \ and \ Y|}{[|t_i \ containing \ X||t_i \ containing \ Y|]}}. \qquad (6.2)$$

Cosine is a number between 0 and 1. This is due to the fact that both $P(X,Y) \leq P(X)$ and $P(X,Y) \leq P(Y)$. A value close to 1 indicates a good correlation between X and Y. Contrasting with the previous measures, the total number of transactions n is not taken into account by the cosine measure. Only the numbers of transactions containing both X and Y, the number of transactions containing X and the number of transactions containing Y are used to calculate the cosine measure. The results after considering some of the above discussed interesting measures in network intrusion detection data is provided in Table 6.1.

6.5. Classification

An intrusion detection system that classifies audit data as normal or anomalous based on a set of rules, patterns or other affiliated techniques

Table 6.1. Measuring interestingness {Con:Confidence, Exp. Con:Expected Confidence}.

Rule	Support	Expected Support	Con.	Exp. Con	Chi-square	R ≥ 1.1
Service=Ntp_u → class=normal	151	113	1	0.72	50.778	—
Flag=SH → class=nmap	103	0.226	1	0.71	46839.447	0.9115
Service=auth → class=normal	84	63	1	0.71	28	371.681
Service=other → class=normal	15	11	1	0.71	5.454	0.238
Flag=RSTOS0 → class=port sweep	10	0.002	1	0.07	49990	0.909
Service=smtp → class=normal	3083	2306	0.99	0.71	1038.8	1541500
Service=domain_u → class=normal	1236	925	0.99	0.71	415.56	0.5359
Service=ftp_data → class=normal	1079	807	0.99	0.71	363.677	1.1664
Service=ecr_i → class=smurf	11258	2708	0.98	0.071	35545	13.9504
Service=finger → class=normal	156	117	0.98	0.70	52	0.0576
Service=ftp → class=normal	146	110	0.96	0.69	47.78	1.2478
Service=pop_3 → class=normal	29	22	0.96	0.68	9.596	0.2636
Flag=S0 → class=neptune	416	3.702	0.96	0.06	46330.62	18.909
Service=http → class=normal	29036	21724	0.94	0.66	9774.79	7843.3279

can be broadly defined as a classification based intrusion detection system. The classification process typically involves the following steps:

(1) Identify class attributes and classes from training data;
(2) Identify attributes for classification;
(3) Learn a model using the training data; and
(4) Use the learned model to classify the unknown data samples.

A variety of classification techniques have been proposed. Those include inductive rule generation techniques, fuzzy logic, genetic algorithms, neural networks, ensemble classifier, and hybrid algorithms.

Inductive rule generation algorithms: It typically involves the application of a set of association of rules and frequent episode patterns to classify the audit data. In this context, if a rule states that "if event X occurs, then event Y is likely to occur", then events X and Y can be described as set of (variable, value)-pairs where the aim is to find the sets X and Y such that X implies Y. In the domain of classification, we fix Y and attempt to find sets of X which are good predictors for the right classification. While supervised classification typically only derives rules relating to a single attribute, general rule induction techniques, which are typically unsupervised in nature, derive rules relating to any or all the attributes. The advantage of using rules is that they tend to be simple and intuitive, unstructured and less rigid. As the drawbacks they are difficult to maintain, and in some cases, are inadequate to represent many types of information. A number of inductive rule generation algorithms have been proposed by many researchers. Some of them first construct a decision tree and then extract a set of classification rules from the decision tree. Other algorithms like RIPPER,[15] C4.5[16] directly induce rules from the data by employing a divide-and-conquer approach. A post learning stage involving either discarding (as in C4.5) or pruning (RIPPER) some of the learnt rules is carried to increase the classifier accuracy. RIPPER has been successfully used in a number of data mining based anomaly detection algorithms to classify incoming audit data and detect intrusions. One of the primary advantages of using RIPPER is that the generated rules are easy to use and verify. Lee *et al.*,[17-19] used RIPPER to characterize sequences occurring in normal data by a smaller set of rules that capture the common elements in those sequences. During monitoring, sequence violating these rules is treated as anomalies.

Decision tree: These are powerful and popular tools for classification and prediction. The attractiveness of tree-based methods is largely due to the fact that, in contrast to neural networks, decision trees represent rules. A decision tree is a tree that has three main components: nodes, arcs, and leaves. Each node is labeled with a feature attribute which is most informative among the attributes not yet considered in the path from the root, each arc out of a node is labeled with a feature value for the node's feature and each leaf is labeled with a category or class. A decision tree can then be used to classify a data point by starting at the root of the tree and moving through it until a leaf node is reached. The leaf node would then provide the classification of the data point.

Fuzzy logic: These techniques have been in use in the area of computer and network security since the late 1990s.[20] Fuzzy logic has been used for intrusion detection for two primary reasons.[21] Firstly, several quantitative parameters that are used in the context of intrusion detection e.g., CPU usage time, connection interval, etc., can potentially be viewed as fuzzy variables. Secondly, as stated by Bridges *et al.*,[21] the concept of security is fuzzy in itself. In other words, the concept of fuzziness helps to smooth out the abrupt separation of normal behaviour from abnormal behavior. That is, a given data point falling outside/inside a defined "normal interval", will be considered anomalous/normal to the same degree regardless of its distance from/within the interval.

Genetic algorithms: It is a search technique used to find approximate solutions to optimization and search problems. This has also been extensively employed in the domain of intrusion detection to differentiate normal network traffic from anomalous connections. The major advantage of genetic algorithms is their flexibility and robustness as a global search method. In addition, a genetic algorithm search converges to a solution from multiple directions and is based on probabilistic rules instead of deterministic ones. In the domain of network intrusion detection, genetic algorithms have been used in a number of ways. Some approaches have used genetic algorithms directly to derive classification rules, while others use genetic algorithms to select appropriate features or determine optimal parameters of related functions, while different data mining techniques are then used to acquire the rules. While the advantage of the genetic approach was that it used numerous agents to monitor a variety of network based parameters, lack of intra-agent communication and a lengthy training process were some issues that were not addressed.

Neural network: Neural network based intrusion detection systems have traditionally been host based systems that focus on detecting deviations in program behaviour as a sign of an anomaly. In the neural network approach to intrusion detection, the neural network learns to predict the behaviour of the various users and daemons in the system. The main advantage of neural networks is their tolerance to imprecise data and uncertain information and their ability to infer solutions from data without having prior knowledge of the regularities in the data. This in combination with their ability to generalize from learned data has made them an appropriate approach to intrusion detection. However, the neural network based solutions have several drawbacks. First, they may fail to find a satisfactory solution either because of lack of sufficient data or because there is no learnable function. Secondly, neural networks can be slow and expensive to train. The lack of speed is partly because of the need to collect and analyze training data and partly because the neural network has to manipulate the weights of the individual neurons to arrive at the correct solution. Anomaly detection schemes also involve other data mining techniques such as support vector machines (SVM) and other types of neural network models. Because data mining techniques are data driven and do not depend on previously observed patterns of network/system activity, some of these techniques have been very successful at detecting new kinds of attacks. However, these techniques often have a very high false positive rate.

Bayesian network: A Bayesian network is a graphical model that encodes probabilistic relationships among variables of interest. When used in conjunction with statistical techniques, Bayesian networks have several advantages for data analysis.[22] Firstly, because Bayesian networks encode the interdependencies between variables, they can handle situations where data is missing. Secondly, Bayesian networks have the ability to represent causal relationships. Therefore, they can be used to predict the consequences of an action. Lastly, because Bayesian networks have both causal and probabilistic relationships, they can be used to model problems where there is a need to combine prior knowledge with data. Several researchers have adapted ideas from Bayesian statistics to create models for anomaly detection.[23–25] The Bayesian network is a restricted network that has only two layers and assumes complete independence between the information nodes (i.e., the random variables that can be observed and measured). These limitations result in a tree shaped network with a single hypothesis node (root node) that has arrows pointing to a number of information nodes (child node). All child nodes have exactly one parent node, that is, the root node, and no other causal relationship between nodes are permitted. The naive Bayesian networks have some disadvantages. First, as pointed out in,[23] the classification capability of naive Bayesian networks is identical to a threshold based system that computes the sum of the outputs obtained from the child nodes. Secondly, because the child nodes do not interact between themselves and their output only influences the probability of the root node, incorporating additional information becomes difficult as the variables that contain the information cannot directly interact with the child nodes. Another area, within the domain of anomaly detection, where Bayesian networks have been frequently used is the classification and suppression of false alarms. Although using the Bayesian for the intrusion detection or intruder behavior prediction can be very appealing, there are some issues that one should be concerned about them. Since the accuracy of this method is dependant on certain assumptions that are typically based on the behavioral model of the target system, deviating from those assumptions will decrease its accuracy. Selecting an accurate model will lead to an inaccurate detection system. Therefore, selecting an accurate behavioral model is not an easy task as typical systems and/or networks are complex.

Principal component analysis: Typical data sets for intrusion detection are typically very large and multidimensional. With the growth of high speed networks and distributed network based data intensive applications storing, processing, transmitting, visualizing and understanding the data is becoming more complex and expensive. To tackle the problem of high dimensional datasets, researchers have developed a dimensionality reduction technique known as Principal component analysis (PCA).[26–28] In mathematical terms, PCA is a technique where n correlated random variables are transformed into $d < n$ uncorrelated variables. The uncorrelated variables are linear combinations of the original variables and can be used to express that data in a reduced form. Typically, the first principal component of the transformation is the linear combination of the original variables with the largest variance. In other words, the first principal component is the projection on the direction in which the variance of the projection is maximized. The second principal component is the linear combination of the original variables with the second largest variance and orthogonal to the first principal component, and so on. In many data sets, the first several principal components contribute most of the variance in the original data set, so that the rest can be disregarded with minimal loss of the variance for dimensional reduction of the dataset. PCA has been widely used in the domain of image compression, pattern recognition and intrusion detection. In case of an anomaly detection scheme, PCA was used as an outlier detection scheme and was applied to reduce the dimensionality of the audit data and arrive at a classifier that is a function of the principal components. They measured the mahalanobis distance of each observation from the centre of the data for anomaly detection. The mahalanobis distance is computed based on the sum of squares of the standardized principal component scores. In Shyu *et al.*,[29] the authors have evaluated these methods over KDDcup1999 data and have demonstrated that it exhibits better detection rate than other well known outlier based anomaly detection algorithms such as the local outlier factor "LOF" approach, the Nearest Neighbour approach and the kth Nearest Neighbour approach.

Markov models: A hidden markov model is a statistical model, where the system being modeled is assumed to be a Markov process with unknown parameters. The challenge is to determine the hidden parameters from the observable parameters. Unlike a regular Markov model, where the state transition probabilities are the only parameters and the state of the system is directly observable, in a hidden Markov model, the only visible elements are the variables of the system that are influenced by the state of the system, and the state of the system itself is hidden. A hidden Markov model's state represents some unobservable condition of the system being modeled. In each state, there is a certain probability of producing any of the observable system outputs and a separate probability indicating the likely next states. By having different output probability distributions in each of the state, and allowing the system to change states over time, the model is capable of representing non-stationary sequences. To estimate the parameters of a hidden Markov model for modeling normal system behaviour, sequences of normal events collected from normal system operation are used as training data. An expectation-maximization (EM) algorithm is used to estimate the parameters. Once a hidden Markov model has been trained, when confronted with test data, probability measures can be used as thresholds for anomaly detection. In order to use hidden Markov models for anomaly detection, three key problems need to be addressed. The first problem, also known as the evaluation problem, is to determine given a sequence of observations, what is the probability that the observed sequence was generated by the model. The second is the learning problem which involves building from the audit data, a model or set of models, that correctly describes the observed behavior. Given a hidden Markov model and the associated observations, the third problem, also known as the decoding problem, involves determining the most likely set of hidden states that have led to those observations. The major drawback of using hidden Markov models in anomaly detection technique is that it is computationally expensive, because it uses parametric estimation techniques based on the Bayes algorithm for learning the normal profile of the host/network under consideration.

6.6. Ensemble of Classifier

Ensembles of classifiers are often better than any individual classifier. This can be attributed to three key factors.[30]

Statistical: Machine learning algorithms attempt to construct a hypothesis that best approximates the unknown function that describes the data, based on the training examples provided. Insufficient training data can lead an algorithm to generate several hypotheses of equal performance. By taking all of the candidate hypotheses and combining them to form an ensemble, their votes are averaged and the risk of selecting incorrect hypotheses is reduced.

Computational: Many machine learning approaches are not guaranteed to find the optimal hypotheses; rather, they perform some kind of local search which may find local minima (rather than the global minimum, or the optimal hypothesis). For example, decision trees and ANNs can often produce sub-optimal solutions. By starting the local search in different locations, an ensemble can be formed by combining the resulting hypotheses; therefore, the resulting ensemble can provide a better approximation of the true underlying function.

Representational: The statistical and computational factors allow ensembles to locate better approximations of the true hypothesis that describes the data; however, this factor allows ensembles to expand the space of representable functions beyond that achievable by any individual classifier. It is possible that the true function may not be able to be represented by an individual machine learning algorithm, but a weighted sum of the hypotheses within the ensemble may extend the space of representable hypotheses to allow a more accurate representation.

These factors represent three key advantages that machine learning ensembles hold; they also represent three of the major limitations often recognized in specific machine algorithms. It is for this reason that ensembles have the potential to deliver better performance in terms of detection accuracy than many individual machine learning algorithms.

Ensemble of Classifiers which comes under Decision committee learning has demonstrated spectacular success in reducing classification error from learned classifiers. These techniques develop a classifier in the form of a committee of subsidiary classifiers. The committee members are applied to a classification task and their individual outputs combined to create a single classification from the committee as a whole. This combination of outputs is often performed by majority vote. Three decision committee learning approaches, AdaBoost, Multi Boosting and Bagging have received extensive attention. They are recent methods for improving the predictive power of classifier learning systems. Some classification methods are unstable in the sense that small perturbations in their training sets may result in large changes in the changes in the constructed classifier. Breiman[31] proved that decision tress with neural networks are unstable during classification. Unstable classifications can have their accuracy improved by perturbing and combining, i.e., generating a series of classifiers by perturbing the training set, and then combining these classifiers to predict together. Boosting is one of the efficient perturbing and combining methods. Though a number of variants of boosting are available, we use the most popular form of boosting, known as AdaBoost (Adaptive Boosting) for our experimentation. Multi-Boosting is an extension to the highly successful AdaBoost technique for forming decision committees. MultiBoosting can be viewed as combining AdaBoost with Wagging. It is able to harness both AdaBoost's high bias and variance reduction with Wagging's superior variance reduction. Bagging (Bootstrapped Aggregating) on the other hand, this combined voting with a method for generating the classifiers that provide the votes. The simple idea was based on allowing each base classifier to be trained with a different random subset of the patterns with the goal of bringing about diversity in the base classifiers. Databases can have nominal, numeric or mixed attributes and classes. Not all classification algorithms perform well for different types of attributes, classes and for databases of different sizes. In order to design a generic classification tool, one should consider the behaviour of various existing classification algorithms on different datasets.

AdaBoost boosting is a general method for improving the accuracy of any given learning algorithm. Boosting refers to a general and provably effective method of producing a very accurate prediction rule by combining rough and moderately inaccurate rules of thumb. Boosting has its roots in a theoretical framework for studying machine learning called the "PAC" learning model, due to Valiant[32] and Kearns and Vazirani,[33] for a good introduction to this model. They were the first to pose the question of whether a "weak" learning algorithm which performs just slightly better than guessing in the PAC model can be "boosted" into an arbitrary accurate "strong" learning algorithm. Finally, the AdaBoost algorithm, introduced by Freund and Schapiro,[34] solved many of the practical difficulties of the earlier boosting algorithms, and is the focus of this chapter. The algorithm takes as input a training set $\{(x_1, y_1), \ldots, (x_m, y_m)\}$, where each belongs to some domain or instance space X, and each label is in some label set Y. Foremost of this chapter, it is assumed $Y = \{-1, +1\}$; later, we discuss extensions to the multiclass case. AdaBoost calls a given weak or base learning algorithm repeatedly in a series of rounds $t = 1, \ldots, T$. One of the main ideas of the algorithm is to maintain a distribution or set of weights over the training set. The weight of this distribution on training example i on round t is denoted $D_t(i)$. Initially, all weights are set equally, but on each round, the weights of incorrectly classified examples are increased so that the weak learner is forced to focus on the hard examples in the training set. The weak learner's job is to find a weak hypothesis $h_t \colon X \to -1, +1$ appropriate for the distribution D_t. The goodness of a weak hypothesis is measured by its error:

$$E(t) = P_{r_i \subset D_t}[h_t(x_i) \neq y_i] = \Sigma_{i:h_{(t)}(x_i) \neq y_i} D_t(i) \qquad (6.3)$$

Notice that the error is measured with respect to the distribution D_t on which the weak learner was trained. In practice, the weak learner may be an algorithm that can use the weights D_t on the training examples. Alternatively, when this is not possible, a subset of the training examples can be used to train the weak learner. Once the weak hypothesis h_t has been received, AdaBoost chooses a parameter α_t. Intuitively, α_t measures the importance that is assigned to h_t. Note that $\alpha_t \geq 0$ if $\varepsilon_t \leq 1/2$ (which can be used without loss of generality), and that α_t gets larger as ε_t gets smaller. The distribution D_t is next updated using the rule specified. The effect of this rule is to increase the weight of examples misclassified by h_t, and to decrease the weight of correctly classified examples. Thus, the weight tends to concentrate on "hard" examples. The final hypothesis H is a weighted majority vote of the T weak hypotheses where α_t is the weight assigned to h_t.

MultiBoosting: MultiBoosting is an extension to the highly successful AdaBoost technique for forming decision committees. MultiBoosting can be viewed as combining AdaBoost with Wagging.[35] MultiBoosting can be considered as wagging committees formed by AdaBoost. A decision has to be made as to how many sub-committees should be formed for a single run, and the size of those sub-committees. In the absence of an a-priori reason for selecting any specific values for these factors, the current implementation of MultiBoosting, takes as an argument a single committee size T, from which it by default sets the number of sub-committees and the size of those sub-committees to $\sqrt{(T)}$. As both these values must be whole numbers, it is necessary to round off the result. For ease of implementation, this is achieved by setting a target final sub-committee member index, where each member of the final committee is given an index, starting from one. This allows the premature termination of boosting one sub-committee, due to too great or too low error, to lead to an increase in the size of the next sub-committee. If the last sub-committee is prematurely terminated, an additional sub-committee is added with a target of completing the full complement of committee members. If this sub-committee also fails to reach the target, this process is repeated; adding further sub-committees until the target total committee size is achieved. In addition to the bias and variance reduction properties that this algorithm may inherit from each of its constituent committee learning algorithms, MultiBoost has the potential computational advantage over AdaBoost that the sub-committees may be learned in parallel, although this would require a change to the handling of early termination of learning a sub-committee. The AdaBoost process is inherently sequential, minimizing the potential for parallel computation. However, each classifier learned with wagging is independent of the rest, allowing parallel computation, a property that MultiBoost inherits at the sub-committee level.

Bagging: Bootstrapped Aggregating (Bagging) combines voting with a method for generating the classifiers that provide the votes. The simple idea was based on allowing each base classifier to be trained with a different random subset of the patterns with the goal of bringing about diversity in the base classifiers. Devising different ways of generating base classifiers that perform well but are diverse (i.e., make different errors) has historically been one of the most active subtopics within ensemble methods which comes under Meta classifier research. Bagging is a simple example of one such method of generating diverse base classifiers; therefore, we discuss it in more details here. Bagging generates multiple bootstrap training sets from the original training set and uses each of them to generate a classifier for inclusion in the ensemble. The algorithms for bagging and doing the bootstrap sampling (sampling with replacement) are shown in Fig. 6.7. In Fig. 6.7, T is the original training set of N examples, M is the number of base models to be learned, L_b is the base model learning algorithm, the hi's are the classification functions that take a new example as input and return the predicted class from the set of possible classes Y, random integer (a, b) is a function that returns each of the integers from a to b with equal probability, and $I(A)$ is the indicator function that returns 1 if event A is true and 0 otherwise. To create a bootstrap training set from a training set of size N, we perform N multinomial trials, where in each trial; we draw one of the N examples. Each example has probability $\frac{1}{N}$

Input: n data objects, number of clusters

Output: membership value of each object in each cluster

Algorithm:

1. Select the initial location for the cluster centers

2. Generate a new partition of the data by assigning each data point to its closest centre.

3. Calculate the membership value of each object in each cluster.

4. Calculate new cluster centers as the centroids of the clusters.

5. If the cluster partition is stable then stop, otherwise go to step2 above.

Fig. 6.7. Bagging algorithm.

of being drawn in each trial. The Bagging algorithm shown in Fig. 6.7 does exactly this-N times; the algorithm chooses a number r at random from 1 to N and adds the rth training example to the bootstrap training set S. Clearly, some of the original training examples will not be selected for inclusion in the bootstrapped training set and others will be chosen one time or more. On average, each generated bootstrapped training set will contain $0.63\,N$ unique training examples even though it will contain N actual training examples. In bagging, we create M such bootstrap training sets and then generate classifiers using each of them. Bagging returns a function $h(x)$ that classifies new examples by returning the class y that gets the maximum number of votes from the base models $\{h_1, h_2, \ldots, h_M\}$. In bagging, the M bootstrap training sets that are created are likely to have some differences. If these differences are enough to induce noticeable differences among the M base models while leaving their performances reasonably good, then the ensemble will probably perform better than the base models individually.

Random Forest: Random forest is an ensemble of unpruned classification or regression trees, induced from bootstrap samples of the training data, using random feature selection in the tree induction process. Prediction is made by aggregating (majority vote for classification or averaging for regression) the predictions of the ensemble. Random forest generally exhibits a substantial performance improvement over the single tree classifier such as CART and C4.5. It yields generalization error rate that compares favorably to AdaBoost, yet is more robust to noise. However, similar to most classifiers, random forest can also suffer from the curse of learning from extremely imbalanced training data set. As it is constructed to minimize the overall error rate, it will tend to focus more on the prediction accuracy of the majority class, which often results in poor accuracy, for the minority class.

In random forests, there is no need for cross validation or a test set to get an unbiased estimate of the test error. Since each tree is constructed using the bootstrap sample, approximately $\frac{1}{3}$rd of the cases are left out of the bootstrap samples and not used in training. These cases are called out of bag (oob) cases. These oob cases are used to get a run-time unbiased estimate of the classification error as trees are added to the forest.

The error rate of a forest depends on the correlation between any two trees and the strength of each tree in the forest. Increasing the correlation increases the error rate of the forest. The strength of the tree relies on the error rate of the tree. Increasing the strength decreases the error rate of the forest. When the forest is growing, random features are selected at random out of the all features in the training data. The more discussion about this along with the comparison of the results can be obtained from Panda and Patra.[36]

Support Vector Machines (SVM): SVMs are becoming increasingly popular in the machine learning and computer vision communities. Training a Support Vector Machine (SVM) requires the solution of a very large quadratic programming (QP) optimization problem. In this chapter, we use a variant of SVM for fast training using sequential minimal optimization (SMO).[37] SMO breaks this large QP problem into a series of smallest possible QP problems avoiding large matrix computation. The amount of memory required for SMO is linear in the training set size, which allows SMO to handle very large training sets. SMO's computation time is dominated by SVM evaluation; hence SMO is fastest for linear SVMs and sparse data sets. SVM ensembles can improve the limited classification performance of the SVM. In boosting, each individual SVM is trained using training samples chosen according to the sample's probability distribution, which is updated in proportion to the degree of error of the sample.

Boost-SMO: We apply boosting to SMO algorithm which is the most efficient state-of-the art technique for training SVMs. Shortly, SMO decomposes the quadratic programming (QP) problem arising in SVM training into a sequence of minimal QP problems involving only two variables, and each of these problems is solved analytically. SMO heuristically selects a pair of variables for each problem and optimizes them. This procedures repeats until all the patterns satisfy the optimality conditions. A direct way to use the probability distribution over examples in training SVMs is to create sub samples of data or the so-called boosting sets. The boosting set that will be used for training the classifier on the th iteration can be created by sampling examples from the original data set according to probability distribution. Each individual SVM is trained using regular SMO; hence it achieves maximum margin separability on the corresponding boosting set. But because of the limited amount of data used to train individual SVMs, their decision boundaries may be far from the global optimal solution. However, the ensemble effect of a sequence of SVMs (normally an order of 10–15) allows for a boosted classifier to have a high

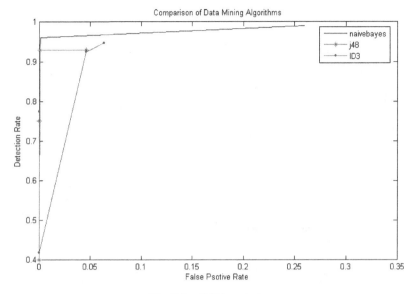

Fig. 6.8.   ROC analysis.

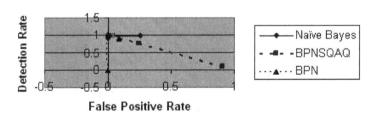

Fig. 6.9.   Comparison of data mining techniques.

generalization performance. Since, the boosting algorithm also has the effect
of improving the margin, Boost-SMO is capable to find a global solution
which is comparable in terms of accuracy to that obtained by the standard
SVM training algorithms. More details about this can be obtained from
Williums *et al.*[37] and Panda and Patra.[38] Some of the results based on
decision trees (ID3 and J48), naive bayes and neural network are shown in
Figs. 6.8 and 6.9. In Tables 6.2 and 6.3, the comparison of the ensemble
classifiers with different datasets and hybrid approach is done in order to
obtain high accuracy respectively.

Table 6.2.   Comparison of ensemble of classifiers over different data sets.

Ensemble of Classifiers	Iris Dataset	Waveform Dataset	Students Dataset	KDDCup'99 IDS Dataset
Bagging + C4.5	94.8	94.47	94.47	Not provided
AdaBoost + C4.5	82.81	83.32	83.73	
MultiBoosting + C4.5	86.49	81.44	81.68	
Bagging + Decision Stump	70.33	57.41	87.22	67.94
AdaBoost + Decision Stump	95.07	67.68	87.16	77.68
MultiBoosting + Decision Stump	94.73	66.44	86.95	77.67
Bagging + REP tree	Not provided	Not provided	Not provided	99.37
AdaBoost + REP tree				99.26
MultiBoosting + REP tree				99.257

Table 6.3.   Performance comparison of classifiers {Acc: Accuracy}.

Attack Type	Hybrid DT + SVM Acc (%)	SMO Acc (%)	AdaBoost + SMO Acc (%)	MultiBoost + SMO Acc (%)
Normal	99.7	97.47	98.8	97.88
Probe	98.57	66.20	71.0	71.00
DoS	99.92	100.00	99.41	99.00
U2R	48.00	54.3	45.00	67.00
R2L	37.80	38.1	29.42	30.00

6.7. Clustering

Clustering can be considered the most important unsupervised learning problem; so, as every other problem of this kind, it deals with finding a structure in a collection of unlabeled data. A loose definition of clustering could be "the process of organizing objects into groups whose members are similar in some way". The basic clustering process is shown in Fig. 6.10.

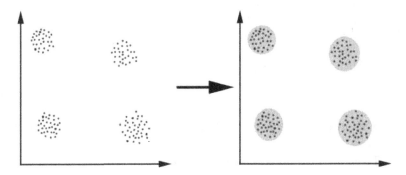

Fig. 6.10.   Basic clustering process.

A cluster is therefore a collection of objects which are "similar" between them and are "dissimilar" to the objects belonging to other clusters. We can show this with a simple graphical example: In this case we easily identify the four clusters into which the data can be divided; the similarity criterion is distance: two or more objects belong to the same cluster if they are "close" according to a given distance (in this case geometrical distance). This is called distance-based clustering. Another kind of clustering is conceptual clustering: two or more objects belong to the same cluster if this one defines a concept common to all objects. In other words, objects are grouped according to their fit to descriptive concepts, not according to simple similarity measures. So, the goal of clustering is to determine the intrinsic grouping in a set of unlabeled data. But how to decide what constitutes a good clustering? It can be shown that there is no absolute "best" criterion which would be independent of the final aim of the clustering. Consequently, it is the user which must supply this criterion, in such a way that the result of the clustering will suit their needs. For instance, we could be interested in finding representatives for homogeneous groups (data reduction), in finding "natural clusters" and describe their unknown properties ("natural" data types), in finding useful and suitable groupings ("useful" data classes) or in finding unusual data objects (outlier detection).

Types of Clustering Algorithms:

The *k*-means algorithm: So, with intrusion detection we want to define two clusters, and classify each observation (object) according to the closest cluster (class). Initially, we don't know what the clusters looks like. Therefore we choose the *k*-means algorithm to find these clusters, and to assign one cluster to each observation. The k-means algorithm is a simple and good candidate.

Algorithm description:

(1) First we select two observations randomly. These will act as an initial mean vector, or centroids, for each cluster. They are simply two different plots in Euclidian space (R^n) where n is number of features (metrics) used.

(2) Then, for each observation, we calculate the distance to each centroid. The smallest distance from an observation to each of the clusters decides which cluster the observation belongs to. Like in the example above, where three individuals aged 10, 60, and 70 should be classified as "Old" and "Young". If vector (read: individual, object or observation) 10 was selected as centroid for cluster one, and vector 60 for cluster two, the vector 70 would be closer to cluster two and should belong to this cluster. Vector 10 and 60 will of course be located in the same clusters where they are selected as centroids (null-distance).

(3) When all observations have been grouped together in their nearest cluster, a new centroid is calculated for each cluster as the average value of the vectors they contain. This will change the centre location (centroid) of both clusters. In our age-example, cluster one 10 will include only one observation and still have the centroid 10. For cluster two, the new centroid will be $(60 + 70)/2 = 65$. Calculating new centroids based on vector averages; If a cluster contains two vectors (x_1, x_2, x_3) and (y_1, y_2, y_3) then the new centroid will be (z_1, z_2, z_3) where $z_1 = (x_1 + y_1)/2$, $z_2 = (x_2 + y_2)/2$ and $z_3 = (x_3 + y_3)/2$.

(4) Now we should try a new iteration with the new centroids (jump to two). If all observations remain in their already assigned clusters after the next iteration, the algorithm ends.

We now have two clusters with defined centers (centroids), and a number of observations (vectors) in each cluster. It can be proved that the k-means algorithm always terminates, but it does not necessarily find the best solution. The selection of initial centroids might result in more or less optimal results.

Example: For our three individuals aged 10, 60, and 70 we want to find two clusters where we want to group "Old" and "Young". If 10 and 60 are selected as initial centroids, we end up with two clusters with centroids 10 and 65. Ok, these might be candidates for "Old" and "Young". But, if 60 and 70 are selected as initial cluster centroids, vector 10 will be grouped together with 60 and we end up with two clusters with centroids 35 and 70 which might be a less optimal definition. The main advantage of the k-means algorithm is its simplicity and speed, a good feature if and IDS want to use clustering techniques in real-time. Also, its complexity increases in a linear matter with an increase in the number of features used. Other algorithm exists and these too could be candidates for automatic clustering, like; (i) The Fuzzy C-means algorithm, (ii) Hierarchical clustering, (iii) Mixture of Gaussians.

Fuzzy c-Means (FCM) Clustering: Fuzzy c-Means (FCM) algorithm, also known as fuzzy ISODATA, was introduced by Bezdek[39] as extension to Dunn's algorithm to generate fuzzy sets for every observed feature. The fuzzy c-means clustering algorithm is based on the minimization of an objective function called c-means functional. Fuzzy c-means algorithm is one of the well known relational clustering algorithms. It partitions the sample data for each explanatory (input) variable into a number of clusters. These clusters have "fuzzy" boundaries, in the sense that each data value belongs to each cluster to some degree or other. Membership is not certain, or "crisp". Having decided upon the number of such clusters to be used, some procedure is then needed to location their centers (or more generally, mid-points) and to determine the associated membership functions and the degree of membership for the data points. Fuzzy clustering methods allow for uncertainty in the cluster assignments. FCM is an iterative algorithm to find cluster centers (centroids) that minimize a dissimilarity function. Rather that partitioning the data into a collection of distinct sets by fuzzy partitioning, the membership matrix (U) is randomly initialized according to Equation (6.2).

$$\sum_{i=1}^{c} u_{ij} = 1, \quad \forall j = 1, 2, 3, \dots, n. \tag{6.4}$$

The dis-similarity function (or more generally the objective function), which is used in FCM in given Equation (6.3).

$$J(U, c_1, c_2, \dots, c_c) = \sum_{i=1}^{c} J_i = \sum_{i=1}^{c} \sum_{j=1}^{n} u_{ij}^m d_{ij}^2, \tag{6.5}$$

where, U_{ij} is between 0 and 1; c_i is the centroids of cluster i; d_{ij} is the Euclidean distance between ith centroids c_i and jth data point. $m \in [1, \infty]$ is a weighting exponent. There is no prescribed manner for choosing the exponent parameter, m. In practice, $m = 2$ is common choice, which is equivalent to normalizing the coefficients linearly to make their sum equal to 1. When m is close to 1, then the cluster centre closest to the point is given much larger weight than the others and the algorithm is similar to k-means. To reach a minimum of dissimilarity function there are two conditions. These are given in (6.4) and (6.5).

$$c_i = \frac{\sum_{j=1}^{n} u_{ij}^m x_j}{\sum_{j=1}^{n} u_{ij}^m}, \tag{6.6}$$

$$u_{ij} = \frac{1}{\sum_{k=1}^{c} \left(\frac{d_{ij}}{d_{kj}}\right)^{\frac{2}{m-1}}}. \tag{6.7}$$

This algorithm determines the following steps in Fig. 6.11. By iteratively updating the cluster centers and the membership grades for each

Input: *n data objects, number of clusters*

Output: *membership value of each object in each cluster*

Algorithm:

1. Select the initial location for the cluster centers

2. Generate a new partition of the data by assigning each data point to its closest centre.

3. Calculate the membership value of each object in each cluster.

4. Calculate new cluster centers as the centroids of the clusters.

5. If the cluster partition is stable then stop, otherwise go to step2 above.

Fig. 6.11.   Fuzzy c-Means Clustering Algorithm.

data point, FCM iteratively moves the cluster centers to the "right" location within a dataset. FCM does not ensure that it converges to an optimal solution, because the cluster centers are randomly initialized. Though, the performance depends on initial centroids, there are two ways as described below for a robust approach in this regard.

(1) Using an algorithm to determine all of the centroids.
(2) Run FCM several times each starting with different initial centroids.

EM (Expectation Maximization) Clustering

Extensions and generalizations: The EM (expectation maximization) algorithm extends the k-means approach to clustering in two important ways:

(1) Instead of assigning cases or observations to clusters to maximize the differences in means for continuous variables, the EM clustering algorithm computes probabilities of cluster memberships based on one or more probability distributions. The goal of the clustering algorithm then is to maximize the overall probability or likelihood of the data, given the (final) clusters.
(2) Unlike the classic implementation of k-means clustering, the general EM algorithm can be applied to both continuous and categorical variables (note that the classic k-means algorithm can also be modified to accommodate categorical variables).

The EM Algorithm: The EM algorithm for clustering is described in detail in Fig. 6.12. The basic approach and logic of this clustering method is as follows. Suppose you measure a single continuous variable in a large sample of observations. Further, suppose that the sample consists of two clusters of observations with different means (and perhaps different standard deviations); within each sample, the distribution of values for the continuous variable follows the normal distribution. The resulting distribution of values (in the population) may look like this:

Details about the clustering algorithms can be found in Panda and Patra.[40]

Self-organizing Maps: Self-organizing map (SOM) is a data visualization technique invented by Professor Teuvo Kohenen,[41] which reduces the dimensions of data through the use of self-organizing neural

1. Initialization: $\mu_A^0, \sigma_{A,}^0, P_A^{0}, \mu_B^0, \sigma_B^0$, and P_B^{0}, ϵ;

2. At iteration j: compute the probabilities

$$Pr[A|x] = \frac{Pr^j[x|A]P_A^j}{Pr^j[x]}, Pr^j[B|x] = \frac{Pr^j[x|B]P_B^j}{Pr^j[x]}$$

3. Update the new mixture parameters:

$$P_A^{j+1} = \frac{1}{n}\sum_x Pr[A|x], \qquad P_B^{j+1} = \frac{1}{n}\sum_x Pr[B|x];$$

$$\mu_A^{j+1} = \frac{\sum_x xPr[A|x]}{\sum_x Pr[A|x]}, \qquad \mu_B^{j+1} = \frac{\sum_x xPr[B|x]}{\sum_x Pr[B|x]};$$

$$\sigma_A^{j+1} = \frac{\sum_x P[A|x](x-\mu_A^{j+1})^2}{\sum_x P[A|x]}, \qquad \sigma_B^{j+1} = \frac{\sum_x P[B|x](x-\mu_B^{j+1})^2}{\sum_x P[B|x]};$$

4. Compute the log estimate $E_j = \sum_x \log(Pr^j(x))$. Stop if $|E_j - E_{j+1}| \le \epsilon$; Otherwise set $j = j+1$ and go to Step 2.

Fig. 6.12. EM algorithm.

networks. The problem that data visualization attempts to solve is that humans simply cannot visualize high dimensional data as is, so techniques are created to help us understand this high dimensional data. The SOMs can reduce dimensions by producing a map of usually one or two dimensions which plot the similarities of the data by grouping similar data items together. So, SOMs accomplish two things, they reduce dimensions and display similarities. A winning neuron is one of neurons such that very similar or close to the neighborhood data in which later on can be classified as or belong to clusters. In this way, the SOM can provide specialized platform for data representation of the input space.

A SOM consists of a grid shaped set of nodes. Each node j contains a prototype vector $m_j \in R^n$, where n is also the dimension of the input data. SOM is trained iteratively. For each sample x_i of the training data, the best matching unit (BMU) in the SOM is located:

$$c = \arg\min_j\{\|x_i - v_j\|\}. \tag{6.8}$$

Index c indicates the corresponding prototype (BMU) vector m_c. The Euclidean norm is usually chosen for the distance measure. The BMU m_c and its neighboring prototype vectors in this SOM grid are then updated towards the sample vector in the input space.

$$m_j(t+1) = m_j(t) + h_{cj}(t)[x_i - m_j(t)]. \tag{6.9}$$

Equation (6.8) states that each prototype is turned towards the sample vector x_i according to the neighborhood function $h_{cj}(t)$. Most commonly used neighborhood function is the Gaussian neighborhood.

$$h_{cj}(t) = \alpha(t) \cdot \exp\left(\frac{\|n_c - n_j\|^2}{2\sigma^2(t)}\right) \qquad (6.10)$$

The neighborhood is centered on the BMU. Norm $\|n_c - n_j\|$ is the topological distance between prototypes c and j in the SOM grid. The factors $\alpha(t)$ and $\sigma(t)$ are the learning rate factor and the neighborhood width factor, respectively. Both of these factors decrease monotonically as training proceeds.

COBWEB Algorithm for Incremental Clustering: Whereas iterative distance-based clustering, such as K-Means, iterate over the whole dataset until convergence in the clusters is reached, COBWEB works incrementally, updating the clustering instance by instance. The clustering COBWEB creates is expressed in the form of a tree, with leaves representing each instance in the tree, the root node representing the entire dataset, and branches representing all the clusters and sub clusters within the tree. In fact, that there is no limit to the total number of sub clusters except the limit imposed by the size of the dataset. COBWEB starts with a tree consisting of just the root node. From there, instances are added one by one, with the tree updated appropriately at each stage. When an instance is added, one of the four possible actions is taken: The option with the greatest category utility is chosen. Category utility is defined by the function:

$$CU(C_1, C_2, \ldots, C_k) = \frac{\sum_l Pr[C_l] \sum_i \sum_j (Pr[a_i = v_{ij}|C_l]^2 - Pr[a_i = v_{ij}]^2)}{k}$$

$$(6.11)$$

where $C_1, C_2, \ldots, C_k$ are the k clusters; the outer summation is over each of the clusters, which is later divided by k to provide a "per cluster" figure; the next inner summation sums over the attributes, and the inner-most summations sums over the possible values; a_i is the ith attribute, and it takes on values which are dealt with by the sum over j. $Pr[A]$ refers to the probability of event A occurring and $Pr[A|B]$ refers to the probability of event A occurring conditional on event B. Thus the difference ($Pr[a_i = v_{ij}|C_l]^2 - Pr[a_i = v_{ij}]^2$) refers to the difference between the probability that a_i has value v_{ij} for an instance in cluster C_l and the probability that

a_i has value v_{ij}. The larger this value, the more good the clustering does in terms of classification.

This category utility formula only applies to categorical attributes (if it didn't, the set $v_{i1}, v_{i2}, \ldots$ would be infinite, and the summation could not be evaluated by conventional evaluation of a summation). However, it is easily extended to numeric attributes by assuming their distribution is normal, with an observed mean μ and standard deviation σ. Using the probability density function yields the logical equivalency.

$$\sum_i \sum_j (Pr[a_i = v_{ij}|C_l]^2 - Pr[a_i = v_{ij}]^2)$$

$$\Leftrightarrow \sum_i \left(\int f(a_i|C_l)^2 \, da_i - \int f(a_i)^2 \, da_i \right) \tag{6.12}$$

where,

$$\sum_i \left(\int f(a_i|C_l)^2 \, da_i - \int f(a_i)^2 \, da_i \right) = \frac{1}{2\sqrt{\pi}.\sigma_i} \sum_i \left(\frac{1}{\sigma_{il}} - \frac{1}{\sigma_i} \right) \tag{6.13}$$

note that, if the standard deviation estimate is ever 0, an infinite value is produced for the real-valued category utility function. To overcome this potential problem, COBWEB allows one to set the acuity to a value which is the minimum of the standard deviations. Table 6.4 shown a comparison of clustering algorithms for intrusion detection.[42]

Table 6.4.   Comparison of clustering algorithms for intrusion detection {NC: Nearest Cluster, FFT10: FFT for 10 clusters, FFT50: FFT with 50 clusters, SVM100: SVM using K-means with 100 clusters}.

Attack/Method	Probe		DoS		U2R		R2L	
	DR	FPR	DR	FPR	DR	FPR	DR	FPR
KDD Cup Winner	0.833	0.006	0.971	0.003	0.123	3E-5	0.084	5E-5
SOM Map	0.643	***	0.951	***	0.229	***	0.113	***
Linear GP	0.857	***	0.967	***	0.013	***	0.093	***
K-Means	0.876	0.026	0.973	0.004	0.298	0.004	0.064	0.001
NC	0.888	0.005	0.971	0.003	0.022	6E-6	0.034	1E-4
COBWEB	0.364	0.059	0.812	0.248	0.0	0.026	0.611	0.03
FFT10	0.28	0.066	1.0	0.0	0.17	0.021	0.611	0.034
FFT50	0.37	0.06	0.812	0.25	0.34	0.017	0.56	0.036
SVM100	0.67	0.05	0.99	0.05	0.0	0.05	0.29	0.05

6.8. Conclusion

Building intrusion detection systems has been a real challenge as new types of attacks are encountered every day. No single technique can effectively deal with the growing intrusion scenarios. In this work we have applied different data mining techniques to analyze available intrusion data sets to extract knowledge about the nature of intrusions so that suitable counter-measures can be developed to deal with them. We have discussed the association rule mining with various interestingness measures in order to obtain the best rules for the detection of intrusions. Results show that the use of multiple minimum supports can enhance the performance compared to the single minimum support threshold. It is observed that unsupervised clustering algorithms like COBWEB and FFT provide promising results in detecting network intrusions. Further, the ensemble classifiers can still improve the accuracy of intrusion detection in many cases.

References

1. S. Axelsson. Research in intrusion detection system: A survey. Computing Science Technical Report 98-17, http://citeseer.ist.psu.edu/axellson98 research.html, (1998).
2. S. Christennsen, D. Zerkle, and K. Hermiz. A data mining analysis of rtid alarms, *Computer networks.* **34**, 571–577, (2000).
3. R. Agarwal, T. Imielinski, and A. Swami. Mining association rules between sets of items in large databases. In *Proc. of the ACM SIGMOD conf. on management of data*, pp. 207–216, (1993).
4. J. Hipp, U. Gntzer, and G. Nakhaeizadeh. Algorithms for association rule mining–a general survey and comparison. In *Proc. of the ACM SIGKDD Intl. conf. on KDDM*, Vol. 2, pp. 58–64, (2000).
5. C. Gyorod and R. Gyorodi. Mining association rules using large databases. In *Proceedings of Oradea EMES'02*, pp. 45–50, Oradea, Romania, (2002).
6. R. Gyorodi and C. Gyorodi. Architecture of data mining system. In *Proceedings of Oradea ENES'02*, pp. 141–146, Oradea, Romania, (2002).
7. R. Agrawal and R. Srikant. Fast algorithms for mining association rules in large databases. In *Proceedings of the 20th International Conference on VLDB*, pp. 487–499, Santiago, Chile, (1994).
8. Q. Zhao and S. S. Bhowmik. Association rule mining: A survey. CAIS 2003116, Nayang Technological University, Singapore, (2003).
9. W. H. B. Liu and Y. Ma. Mining association rules with multiple supports. In *Proceedings of the ACM SIGKDD International Conference on Knowledge Discovery and Data Mining (KDD-99)*, pp. 337–341, San Diego, CA, USA, (August, 1999).

10. M. Panda and M. Patra. Discovering significant rules for building a network intrusion detection model, *IJAER*, **4**(3), 381–398, (2009). Research India Publication, India.
11. F. E. Giha, Y. P. Singh, and H. T. Ewe. Mining generalized customer profiles. In *Proc. of the AIML'06 International conference*, pp. 141–147, (June, 2006).
12. P. N. Tan, V. Kumar, and J. Srivastava. selecting the right interestingness measure for association patterns. In *Proc. of the 8th ACM SIGKDD International conference on knowledge discovery and data mining*, pp. 67–76, San Fransisco, USA, (2001).
13. R. Srikant and R. Agrawal. Mining generalized association rules. In *Proceeding of the 21st International conference on VLDB*, Vol. 13, pp. 161–180, Switzerland (September, 1995).
14. G. I. Webb. Discovering significant rules. In *Proceedings of the 12th ACMSIGKDD International Conference on Knowledge Discovery and Data Mining, Aug. 20–23*, pp. 434–443, Philadelphia, USA, (2006).
15. W. W. Cohen. Fast effective rule induction. In eds. A. Prieditid and S. Russel, *Proc. of the 12th Intl. Conf. on Machine Learning*, pp. 115–123. Morgan Kauffmann, (1995).
16. J. R. Quinlan. *C4.5: Programs for machine learning*. (Morgan Kaufman Series in Machine Learning, 1993).
17. W. Lee, R. Nimbalkar, K. K. Yee, S. B. Patil, P. H. Desai, T. T. Tran, and S. J. Stolfo. A data mining and cidf based approach for detecting novel and distributed intrusions. In eds. L. H. Debar and S. F. Wu. *Proc. of the 3rd. Intl. Workshop on Recent Advances in Intrusion Detection*, Vol. 1907, pp. 49–65. LNCS, Springer-Verlag, (2007).
18. W. Lee and S. J. Stolfo. Data mining approaches for intrusion detection. In *Proc. of 7th USENIX Association*, (1996).
19. W. Lee, S. J. Stolfo, and K. W. Mok. A data mining framework for building intrusion detection models. In *Proc. of IEEE Symposium on Security and Privacy*, pp. 120–132. IEEE Press, (1999).
20. H. H. Hosmer. Security is funny! Applying the fuzzy logic paradigm to the multi policy paradigm. In *Proc. of Workshop on New Security Paradigms*. ACM Press, (1993).
21. S. M. Brodges. Fuzzy data mining and genetic algorithms applied to intrusion detection. In *Proc. of National Information Security Conference* (2000, 1993).
22. D. Hackermann. A tutorial on learning with bayesian networks. Microsoft research MSR-TR-95-06, (1995).
23. C. Kragel, T. Toth, and E. Kirda. Service specific anomaly detection for network intrusion detection. In *Proc. of ACM Symposium on Applied Computing*, pp. 201–208, Madrid, Spain, (2002). ACM Press.
24. A. Valdes and K. Skinner. Adaptive model based monitoring for cyber attack detection. In *Recent Advances in Intrusion Detection*, pp. 80–92. LNCS 1907, Springer Verlag, (2000).
25. N. Ye, M. Xu, and S. M. Emran. Probabilistic networks with undirected links for anomaly detection. In *Proc. of IEEE Systems, Man and Cybernetics Information Assurance and Security Workshop*, West Point, NY, (2000).

26. R. A. Calvo, M. Partridge, and M. A. Jabri. A comparative study of pca techniques. In *Proc. of 19th Australian Conference on Neural Networks*, (1998).

27. H. Hotelling. Analysis of a complex statistical variables into principal components, *Journal of educational psychology*. **24**, 417–441, 498–520, (1933).

28. W. Wang and R. Battiti. Identifying intrusions in computer networks with principal component analysis. In *Proc. of 1st Intl Conf. on Availability, Reliability and Security*, pp. 270–279, (2006).

29. M. L. Shyu, S. C. Chen, K. Sarinnapakorn, and L. Chang. A novel anomaly detection scheme based on principal component classifier. In *Proc. of IEEE Foundations and New Directions of Data Mining Workshop*, pp. 172–179, (2003).

30. T. Dietterich, Ensemble methods in machine learning, *Lecture Notes in Computer Science (LNCS)*. **1857**, 1–15, (2000).

31. L. Breimn. A theory of the learnable, *Machine Learning*. **24**(3), 123–140, (1996).

32. L. Valient. Bagging predictors, *Comm. ACM*. **27**(11), 1134–1142, (1984).

33. K. M. J. and U. Vazirani. *An Introduction to Computational Learning Theory*. (MIT Press, 1994).

34. Y. Freund and R. Schapire. A decision- theoretic generalization of on-line learning and an application to boosting, *J. Compu. Syst. Sci, Academic Press Inc.* **55**(1), 119– 139, (1997).

35. G. Webb. Multiboosting: A technique for combining boosting and wagging. **40**, (2000).

36. M. Panda and M. Patra. Evaluating machine learning algorithms for detecting network intrusions, *IJRTE*, **1**(1), 472–477, (2009), Academy Publisher, Finland.

37. N. Williums, S. Zonder, and G. Armitage. Evaluating machine learning algorithms for automated network applications. CAIA 060410B, (2006).

38. M. Panda and M. R. Patra. Anomaly based intrusion detection using boosting support vector classifiers. In *Proc. of IEEE Advance Computing Conference (IACC-09)*, Patiala, India, (2009). IEEE Press, USA.

39. J. Bezdek. *Pattern Recognition with Fuzzy Objective Function Algorithm*. (Plennum Press, 1981).

40. M. Panda and M. R. Patra. A comparative study of clustering algorithms for building a network intrusion detection model, *Karpagam J. Computer Sci.*, **9**(5), (2009). India (In press).

41. T. Kohenen, *Self-Organizing Maps*. (3rd edition, Springer Berlin, 2000).

42. M. Panda and M. R. Patra. Unsupervised anomaly based network intrusion detection using farthest first and hierarchical conceptual clustering. In *Proc. of 4th Indian International Conference on Artificial Intelligence (IICAI-09)*, Bangalore, India, pp. 1646–1658, (2009). DBLP.

Chapter 7

PARTICLE SWARM OPTIMIZATION FOR MULTI-OBJECTIVE OPTIMAL OPERATIONAL PLANNING OF ENERGY PLANTS

Y. FUKUYAMA*, H. NISHIDA and Y. TODAKA

Fuji Electric Systems Co. Ltd.,
No.1, Fuji-machi, Hino, Tokyo 191-8502, Japan
*fukuyama-yoshikazu@fujielectric.co.jp

This chapter presents a particle swarm optimization for multi-objective optimal operational planning of energy plants. The optimal operational planning problem can be formulated as a mix-integer nonlinear optimization problem. An energy management system called FeTOP, which utilizes the presented method, is also introduced. FeTOP has been actually introduced and operated at three factories of one of the automobile companies in Japan and realized 10% energy reduction.

7.1. Introduction

Recently, cogeneration systems (CGS) have been installed in energy plants of various factories and buildings. CGS is usually connected to various facilities such as refrigerators, reservoirs, and cooling towers. It produces various energies including electric loads, air-conditioning loads, steam loads. Since daily load patterns of the loads are different, daily optimal operational planning for an energy plant is a very important task for saving operational costs and reducing environmental loads.

In order to generate optimal operational planning for an energy plant, various loads should be forecasted, and startup and shutdown status and input values for the facilities at each control interval should be determined using facility models. Therefore, the optimal operational planning problem can be formulated as a mixed-integer linear problem (MILP) and mathematical programming techniques such as branch and bound, decomposition method, and dynamic programming have been applied conventionally.[1-3] However, the facilities may have nonlinear input-output characteristics practically, and operational rules, which cannot be expressed as mathematical forms, should be considered in actual operation. For example, steam turbines usually have plural boilers and the characteristics of the turbines cannot be expressed with only one equation and the characteristics should be expressed with combination of equations with various conditions. Therefore, when the models are constructed, we should use concept of data mining. In addition, in the problem, various objectives should be considered such as reduction of operational costs and environmental loads. Consequently, the problem cannot be solved by the conventional methods and the method for solving the multi-objective MINLP problem with complex models has been eagerly awaited.

Particle Swarm Optimization (PSO) is one of the evolutionary computation techniques.[4] PSO is suitable for the optimal operational planning for energy plants because it can handle multi-objectives, such as operation rules, constraints, and independent complex facility models easily. The Original PSO was developed by Eberhart and Kennedy.[5] Recently, various modified methods have been developed and applied to various problems.[4-14] We have been developing an optimal operational planning and control system of energy plants using PSO (called FeTOP).[15,16] FeTOP has been actually introduced and operated at three factories of one of the automobile company in Japan and realized 10% energy reduction.[17] Forecasting various loads is out of scope in this paper. However, we have already developed the analyzable structured neural network (ASNN) and other forecasting methods. The accurate load forecasting can be realized for various loads.[18] When we construct forecasting models, data mining methods should be used so that the difference of models such as weekdays and weekends can be treated. In this chapter, three PSO, based methods: Original PSO, Evolutionary PSO, and Adaptive PSO are compared for optimal operational planning problems of energy plants, which are formulated as MINLPs. The three methods are compared using typical energy plant operational planning problems.

7.2. Problem Formulation

7.2.1. *State variables*

State variables are electrical power output values of generator, heat energy output values of genelink and heat exchanger, and heat energy input values of genelink per hour (24 points a day). The detailed variables and related boundary constraints can be listed as follows:

Generator   The state variables of generators are as follows:

- P_{gni}: Electrical power output (24 points a day)
- $\delta_{gi} \in \{0, 1\}$: Startup/shutdown status, where, $P_{gnmin} \leq F_{gni} \leq F_{gnmax}$ $(i = 0, \ldots, 23, n = 1, \ldots, N_g)$,
- N_g: Number of generator,
- P_{gnmax}: Maximum output,
- P_{gnmin}: Minimum output.

Genelink   Genelink is a kind of absorption refrigerators, which can decrease adding fuels by inputting wasted heat energy of generator. The state variables of genelink are as follows:

- Q_{ggLni}: Heat input values (24 points a day)
- Q_{cgLni}: Output heat values (24 points a day)
- $\delta_{gli} \in \{0, 1\}$: Startup/shutdown status, where, $(i = 0, \ldots, 23, n = 1, \ldots, N_{gl},), (i = 0, \ldots, 23, n = 1, \ldots, N_{gl},)$,
- N_{gl}: Number of genelink,
- $Q_{ggLnimax}$: Maximum heat input values determined by output heat values,
- Q_{cdi}: Air-conditioning load,
- Q_{rcgLn}: Rated air-conditioning output.

Heat Exchanger   The state variables of heat exchanger for heating/hot water supply are as follows:

- Heat Exchanger for Heating Q_{ghni}: Heat energy input values (24 points a day) $\delta_{hexhi} \in \{0, 1\}$: Startup/shutdown status, where $0 \leq A_{hexhn}Q_{ghni} \leq Q_{hdi}, (i = 0, \ldots, 23, n = 1, \ldots, N_{hexh})$, N_{hexh}: Number of heat exchanger for heating, Q_{hdi}: Heat load, A_{hexhn}: Coefficients of facility characteristics.
- Heat Exchanger for Hot Water Supply Q_{gwi}: Heat energy input values (24 points a day) $\delta_{hexwi} \in \{0, 1\}$: Startup/shutdown status, where, $0 \leq A_{hexwn}Q_{gwni} \leq Q_{wdi}, (i = 0, \ldots, 23, n = 1, \ldots, N_{hexw})$, N_{hexw}: Number of heat exchanger for hot water supply, Q_{wdi}: Hot water supply load, A_{hexwn}: Coefficients of facility characteristics.

Outputs of each facility for 24 points of the day should be determined. Moreover, two or three variables are required for one facility (startup and shutdown status (binary or discrete variables), and output or output/input values (continuous variables)). Therefore, one state variable for one facility is composed of vectors with 48 (24 points × 2 variables) or 72 (24 points × 3 variables) elements. Therefore, for example, handling two generators, two genelinks, and two heat exchangers require 336 variables.

7.2.2. Objective function

The objective function is to minimize the operational costs and environmental loads of the day.

$$Min \; w_1 \cdot (CE + Cg + Cw) + w_2 \cdot EL \qquad (7.1)$$

where, CE: Total electricity charges of a day, Cg: Total fuel charges of a day, Cw: Total water charges of a day, EL: Environmental loads of a day, wi: weighting factors.

7.2.3. Constraints

In this chapter, the following constraints are considered. Demand and supply balance: Summation of energies supplied by facilities such as electrical power, air-conditioning energy, and heat energy should be equal to each corresponding load.

(1) **Electric Energy Balance:** Summation of purchase or sale electric energies and electric power generation values by CGS should be equal to electric loads:

$$E_{ri} + \sum_{n}^{N_g} E_{gni} = E_{di}, \quad (i = 0, \ldots, 23) \qquad (7.2)$$

where, E_{ri}: Purchase or sale electric energies, E_{gni}: Electric power generation values, E_{di}: Electric loads.

(2) **Air-conditioning Energy:** Balance Summation of air-conditioning energies should be equal to air-conditioning loads.

$$\sum_{n=1}^{N_{gl}} Q_{cgLni} = Q_{cdi}, \quad (i = 0, 1, \ldots, 23) \qquad (7.3)$$

(3) **Heat Energy Balance:** Summation of heat energy inputs and heat energies produced by boilers should be equal to heat loads.

$$Q_{hi} + \sum_{n=1}^{N_{bh}} Q_{bhni} = Q_{hdi}, \quad (i = 0, 1, \ldots, 23) \tag{7.4}$$

$$Q_{hi} = \sum_{n=1}^{N_{hexh}} A_{hexhn} Q_{ghni}, \quad (i = 0, 1, \ldots, 23), \tag{7.5}$$

where, N_{bh}: Number of boiler for heating, Q_{bhni}: Output of boiler for heating.

(4) **Hot Water Supply Balance:** Summation of hot water inputs and hot waters produced by boilers should be equal to hot water loads.

$$Q_{wi} + \sum_{n=1}^{N_{bw}} Q_{bwni} = Q_{wdi}, \quad (i = 0, 1, \ldots, 23) \tag{7.6}$$

$$Q_{wi} = \sum_{n=1}^{N_{hexw}} A_{hexw} Q_{gwni}, \quad (i = 0, 1, \ldots, 23), \tag{7.7}$$

where, N_{bw}: Number of boiler for hot water supply.

(5) **Heat Balance:** Summation of the heat energy consumptions at genelinks, for heat and hot water loads, and radiation values at cooling towers should be equal to the (wasted) heat energy produced by CGSs.

$$\sum_{n=1}^{N_g} Q_{gni} = \sum_{n=1}^{N_{gl}} Q_{ggLni} + \sum_{n=1}^{N_{hexh}} Q_{ghni} + \sum_{n=1}^{N_{hexw}} Q_{gwni} + \sum_{n=1}^{N_g} Q_{ctni}, \tag{7.8}$$

$$Q_{gni}^k = f(F_{gni}), \tag{7.9}$$

where, Q_{ctni}: Radiation value at cooling tower, Q_{gni}: Heat output of generator.

(6) **Facility constraints:** Various facility constraints including the boundary constraints with state variables should be considered. Input-output characteristics of facilities should be also considered as facility constraints. For example, the characteristic of genelink is nonlinear practically and the nonlinear characteristic should be considered in the problem.

(7) **Operational rules:** If the facility is startup, then the facility should not be shutdowned for a certain period. (Minimum up time). If the

facility is shutdowned, then the facility should not be startup for a certain period. (Minimum down time).

Facility models are constructed using the facility constraints and the operational rules. The models are independent and all states of the energy plant are calculated when all of the facility states are input from PSO. Then, the operational costs and the environmental loads for the days can be calculated. When we construct facility models using actual operation data, we have to construct plural models even for one facility using data mining concepts because we have to use various operating points for facilities so that supply and demand balance of various energies should be maintained. Namely, actual operation data can be divided into several groups and facility models are constructed for each group using data mining concepts.

7.3. Particle Swarm Optimization

PSO has been developed through simulation of simplified social models. The features of the method are as follows: (a) The method is based on research about swarms such as fish schooling and a flock of birds. (b) It is based on a simple concept. Therefore, the computation time is short and it requires few memories. (c) It was originally developed for nonlinear optimization problems with continuous variables. However, it is easily expanded to treat problems with discrete variables. Therefore, it is applicable to a MINLP with both continuous and discrete variables such as the optimal operational planning of energy plants. The above feature (c) is suitable for the target problem because practically efficient methods have not been developed for the planning problem with both continuous and discrete variables.

According to the research results for a flock of birds, birds find food by flocking (not by each individual). The observation leads the assumption that every information is shared inside flocking. Moreover, according to observation of behavior of human groups, behavior of each individual (agent) is also based on behavior patterns authorized by the groups such as customs and other behavior patterns according to the experiences by each individual. The assumption is a basic concept of PSO. PSO is basically developed through simulation of a flock of birds in two-dimension space. The position of each agent is represented by XY-axis position and the velocity (displacement vector) is expressed by vx (the velocity of X-axis) and vy (the velocity of Y-axis). Modification of the agent position is realized by using the position and the velocity information.

7.3.1. *Original PSO*

The original PSO is a population based stochastic optimization technique developed by Kennedy and Eberhart.[5,19] The current searching points are modified using the following state equations:

$$v_i^{k+1} = wv_i^k + c_1 r_1 (pbest_i - s_i^k) + c_2 r_2 (gbest - s_i^k) \qquad (7.10)$$

$$s_i^{k+1} = s_i^k + v_i^{k+1} \qquad (7.11)$$

where, v_i^k: Velocity of particle i at iteration k, w: Weighting function, c_i: Weighting coefficients, r_i: Random number between 0 and 1, s_i^k: Current position of particle i at iteration k, $pbest_i$: pbest of particle i, $gbest$: gbest of the group.

The original PSO algorithm can be expressed as follows:

(1) State variables (searching point): State variables (states and their velocities) can be expressed as vectors of continuous numbers. PSO utilizes multiple searching points as agents for search procedures.
(2) Generation of initial searching points: Initial conditions of searching points in the solution space are usually generated randomly within their allowable ranges.
(3) Evaluation of searching points: The current searching points are evaluated by the objective function of the target problem. Pbests (the best evaluated value so far of each agent) and gbest (the best of pbest) can be modified by comparing the evaluation values of the current searching points, and current pbests and gbest.
(4) Modification of searching points: The current searching points are modified using the state equations of PSO.
(5) Stop criterion: The search procedure can be stopped when the current iteration number reaches the predetermined maximum iteration number. For example, the last gbest can be output as a solution.

7.3.2. *Evolutionary PSO EPSO*

The idea behind EPSO[11,12] is to grant a PSO scheme with an explicit selection procedure and with self-adapting properties for its parameters. At a given iteration, consider a set of solutions or alternatives that we will keep calling particles. The general scheme of EPSO is the following:

(1) REPLICATION — each particle is replicated R times.
(2) MUTATION — each particle has its weights mutated.

(3) REPRODUCTION — each mutated particle generates an offspring according to the particle movement rule.
(4) EVALUATION — each offspring has its fitness evaluated.
(5) SELECTION — by stochastic tournament the best particles survive to form a new generation.

The velocity of the state equations for EPSO is the following:

$$v_i^{k+1} = w_{i0}^* + w_{i1}^*(pbest_i - s_i^k) + w_{i2}^*(gbest^* - s_i^k) \qquad (7.12)$$

So far, this seems like PSO; the movement rule keeps its terms of inertia, memory and cooperation. However, the weights undergo mutation.

$$w_{ik}^* = w_{ik} + \tau \cdot N(0,1) \qquad (7.13)$$

where, $N(0,1)$ is a random variable with Gaussian distribution, 0 mean, variance 1, and τ is the learning parameters.

7.3.3. *Adaptive PSO(APSO)*

The adaptive PSO is based on the results of the analysis and the simulations on the basis of the stability analysis in discrete dynamical systems. The new parameters (p) are set to each particle. The weighting coefficients are calculated as follows. If the particle becomes pbest:

$$c_2 = \frac{2}{p}, \quad c_1 = any. \qquad (7.14)$$

If the particle is not pbest:

$$c_2 = \frac{1}{p}, \quad c_1 = c_2 \cdot \frac{|gbest - s|}{|pbest - s|} \qquad (7.15)$$

The search trajectory of PSO can be controlled by the parameter (p). Concretely, when the value is enlarged more than 0.5, the particle may move close to the position of gbest. The adaptive procedure can be expressed as follows:

(1) If the particle becomes gbest, the weighting coefficient (w) is set to 1. Besides, w is set to 0.
(2) When the particle goes out the feasible region, the parameter (p) is set to 0.5 or more so that the particle may convergence.

(3) When the objective function value of pbest of the particle is improved for a certain period, the parameter (p) is reduced more than 0.5 so that the particle may divergence.

7.3.4. *Simple expansion of PSO for optimal operational planning*

In order to reduce the number of state variables, the following simple expansion of PSO is utilized. Namely, all of the state variables can be expressed as continuous variables. If the input value for a facility is under the minimum input value, then the facility is recognized as shutdown. Otherwise, the facility is recognized as startup and the value is recognized as the input of the facility. The reduction method can reduce the number of state variables to half, and drastic improvement of PSO search procedures can be expected.

7.4. Optimal Operational Planning for Energy Plants Using PSO

All of state variables have 24 elements and one state in the solution space can be expressed as an array with number of all facilities multiplied by 24 elements. A flow chart is shown in Fig. 7.1.

The whole algorithm can be expressed as follows:

(1) Step 1: Generation of initial searching points (states): States and velocities of all facilities are randomly generated. The upper and lower bounds of facilities are considered.
(2) Step 2: Evaluation of searching points: The current states are input to facility models and the total operational costs are calculated as the objective function value. The pbests and gbest are updated based on the value.
(3) Step 3: Modification of searching points: The current searching points (facility states) are modified using the state equations. The upper and lower bounds of facilities are considered when the current states are modified.
(4) Step 4: Stop criterion: The search procedure can be stopped when the current iteration number reaches the predetermined maximum iteration number. Otherwise, go to Step 2. The last gbest is output as a solution.

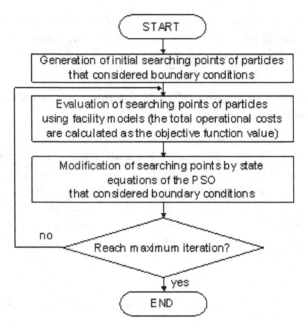

Fig. 7.1.   A flow chart of optimal operational planning for energy plants using PSO.

7.5. Numerical Examples

The proposed method is applied to the typical CGS system.

7.5.1. *Simulation conditions*

An office load model with 100,000 [m²] total floor spaces is utilized in the simulation. Two CGS generators (750 [kW]/unit) and two genelinks (4700 [kW]/unit) are assumed to be installed. At most, two genelinks can be startup in summer season, one genelink in winter season, and one genelink in intermediate season. The efficient rate of the heat exchanger is 0.975 and the rate of the boiler is 0.825. The rated capacity of the cooling tower is 1050 [kW]/unit. The cooling tower is installed for each CGS generator. The forecasted loads for three represented days are shown in Figs. 7.2–7.4. Only daily costs are considered in the simulation for the sake of simplicity. Number of particles is set to 200. The iteration number is set to 100. Twenty trials are compared. The numbers may be able to be optimized and the further investigation should be performed.

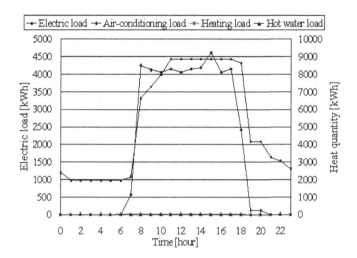

Fig. 7.2.   Energy loads in summer season (August).

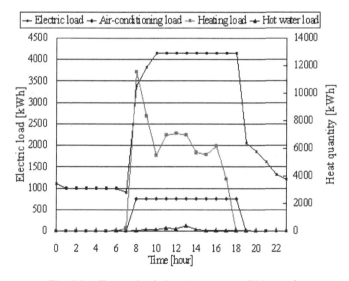

Fig. 7.3.   Energy loads in winter season (February).

7.5.2. *Simulation results*

Table 7.1 shows comparison of costs by three PSO based method and the conventional rule based planning method. According to the results, the total operational cost is reduced compared with the conventional method. EPSO and APSO can generate better average results than original PSO.

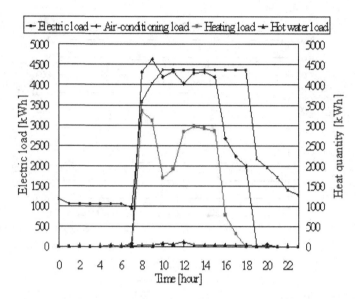

Fig. 7.4.   Energy loads in intermediate season (November).

Table 7.1.   Comparison of costs by the original PSO, EPSO, and APSO methods.

Method	Minimum	Average	Maximum
Conventional	100.0	—	—
Original PSO	98.68	98.80	98.86
Evolutionary PSO	97.96	97.97	98.00
Adaptive PSO	98.12	98.14	98.18

Many heat energies are input to genelink, and heating and hot water loads are supplied by boilers using the original PSO method. On the contrary, many heat energies are input to heat exchangers for heating load and air-conditioning loads are supplied by fuel input in genelink by the evolutionary PSO methods.

7.6. FeTOP — Energy Management System

An energy management system, called FeTOP, has been developed. It provides an optimal operational planning and control scheme of energy plants. It consists of three functions: an energy forecasting function, an optimal operational planning function of the facilities such as a cogeneration system, and a simulation function of the energy plant. Figure 7.5 shows

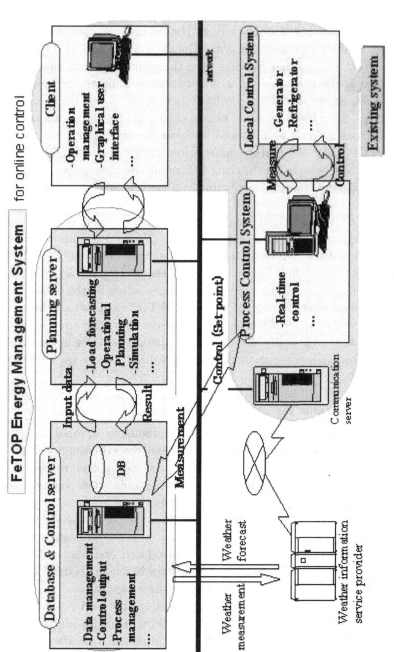

Fig. 7.5. An example of practical system structure using FeTOP.

an example of practical system structure using FeTOP. The functions of FeTOP are installed in the PC servers. Data management and control signal output functions are installed in the Database & Control server. The load forecasting, the optimal planning, and the plant simulation functions are installed in the Planning server. The two servers and the process control system communicate through the local area network inside the factories and buildings. Since the forecasting results of weather conditions are necessary for the load forecasting functions, the weather forecast results are input to FeTOP from the weather information service provider. The planning results can be observed in the client PC installed in the energy management office by the operators. The operators can modify the next control signal if necessary.

FeTOP inputs measurement values of various sensors and consistency of the sensor information is important for realizing real optimal planning. The authors have developed the sensor diagnosis functions for FeTOP.[20] The functions can find the sensors which should be fixed and modify the sensors' measurement values to the consistent values by the other sensors' measurement values. Using the functions, FeTOP can continue the optimal control even if some of the sensor measurement values are inconsistent. FeTOP has been actually introduced and operated at three factories of one of the automobile company in Japan and realized 10% energy reduction.[17]

7.7. Conclusions

This paper compares three PSO based methods for optimal operational planning of energy plants: the original PSO, the evolutionary PSO, and the adaptive PSO. The proposed methods are applied to operational planning of a typical energy plant and the simulation results indicate practical applicability of advanced particle swarm optimizations for the target problems. Following the comparison, an energy management system, called FeTOP, using the advanced particle swarm optimization has been developed. FeTOP has been actually introduced and operated at three factories of one of the automobile companies in Japan. Manual operation by expertised operators has been done in three factories and realized 10% energy reduction by introduction of an automatic and optimal control system, FeTOP. As a future work, the target planning problem will be formulated as a multi-objective function problem with Pareto optimal solutions.

References

1. H. Ravn. Optimal scheduling of co-production with a storage, *Journal of engineering.* **22**, 267–281, (1994).
2. K. Ito and R. Yokoyamaet. Optimal operation of a co-generation plant in combination with electric heat pumps, *Transaction of the ASME.* **116**, 56–64, (1994).
3. R. Yokoyama and K. Ito. A revised decomposition method for milp problems and its application to operational planning of thermal storage systems, *Journal of Energy Resources Technology.* **118**, 277–284, (1996).
4. D. Manolas, C. Frangopoulos, T. Gialamas and D. Tsahalis. Operation optimization of an industrial cogeneration system by a genetic algorithm, *Energy Conversion and Management.* **38**(15–17), 1625–1636, (1997).
5. J. Kennedy and R. Eberhart. Particle swarm optimization. In *Proceedings of IEEE International Conference on Neural Networks*, Vol. IV, pp. 1942–1948, Perth, Australia, (1995).
6. A. Córdobaa and L. González-Monroya. Genetic algorithms to optimize energy supply systems, *Computer Physics Communications.* **121–122**, 43–45, (1999).
7. K. P. Wong and C. Algie. Evolutionary programming approach for combined heat and power dispatch, *Electric Power Systems Research.* **61**(3), 227–232 (April, 2002).
8. Y. Fukuyama. Foundation of particle swarm optimization. In *Tutorial text on Modern Heuristic Optimization Techniques with Application to Power Systems*, IEEE Power Engineering Society Winter Power Meeting (January, 2002).
9. Y. Fukuyama, *et al.* A particle swarm optimization for reactive power and voltage control considering voltage security assessment, *IEEE Trans. on Power.* **15**(4), 1232–1239 (November, 2000).
10. X. Hu, R. Eberhart, and Y. Shi. Recent advances in particle swarm. In *Proc. of IEEE CEC2004*, Portland, Oregon, USA, (2004).
11. V. Miranda and N. Fonseca. New evolutionary particle swarm algorithm (epso) applied to voltage/var control. In *Proceedings of PSCC'02*, Sevilla, Spain (June, 2002).
12. V. Miranda and N. Fonseca. Epso—best of two world of meat-heuristic applied to power system problems. In *Proceedings of the 2002 Congress of Evolutionary Computation*, (2002).
13. K. Yasuda, *et al.* Adaptive particle swarm optimization. In *Proc. of IEEE International Conference on Systems, Man, and Cybernetics*, (2003).
14. A. Ide and K. Yasuda. A basic study of the adaptive particle swarm optimization, *IEEJ (Institute of Electrical Engineers of Japan) Transactions on Electronics, Information and Systems.* **124**(2), 550–557, (2004).
15. T. Tsukada, T. Tamura, S. Kitagawa and Y. Fukuyama. Optimal operational planning for cogeneration system using particle swarm optimization. In *Proc. of the IEEE Swarm Intelligence Symposium 2003*, Indianapolis, Indiana, USA, (2003).

16. S. Kitagawa, Y. Fukuyama, *et al.* Fetop-energy management system: Optimal operational planning and control of energy plants. In *Proc. of the IPEC-Niigata 2005*, Niigata, Japan, (2005).
17. Y. Fukuyama, *et al.* Optimal operation of energy utility equipment and its application to a practical system, *Fuji Electric Journal.* **77**(2), (2004).
18. Y. Fukuyama, *et al.* Intelligent technology application to optimal operation for plant utility equipment, *Journal of the Society of Plant Engineers Japan.* **14**(3), (2002).
19. J. Kennedy and R. Eberhart. *Swarm Intelligence.* (Morgan Kaufmann Publishers, 2001).
20. S. Kitagawa, Y. Fukuyama, *et al.* Sensor diagnostic system for plant utility equipment. In *Proc. of Annual Conference of IEE of Japan*, 4–180, (2004).

Chapter 8

SOFT COMPUTING FOR FEATURE SELECTION

A. K. JAGADEV[*,†], S. DEVI[*] and R. MALL[‡,§]

*Department of Computer Science and Engineering,
ITER, SOA University, Bhubaneswar, India
†a_jagadev@yahoo.co.in

‡Department of Computer Science and Engineering,
Indian Institute of Technology, Kharagpur-721302, India
§rajib@cse.iitkgp.ernet.in

Feature selection has been the focus of interest for quite some time and much work has been done. It is in demand in areas of application for high dimensional datasets with tens or hundreds of thousands of variables available. This survey is a comprehensive overview of many existing methods from the 1970s to the present; considering both soft and non-soft computing paradigm. The strengths and weaknesses of different methods are explained and methods are categorized according to generation procedures and evaluation functions. The objective of feature selection is three fold: improving the prediction performance of the predictors, providing faster and more cost-effective prediction and providing a better understanding of the underlying process that generated the data. This survey identifies future research areas in feature subset selection and introduces newcomers to this field.

8.1. Introduction

A universal problem that all intelligent agents must face is where to focus their attention, e.g., a problem-solving agent must decide which aspects of a problem are relevant and so forth. The majority of real-world classification problems require supervised learning where the underlying class probabilities and class-conditional probabilities are unknown and each instance is associated with a class label, i.e., relevant features are often unknown a priori. In many applications, the size of a dataset is so large that learning might not work as well before removing these unwanted features. Theoretically, having more features implies more discriminative power in classification. Many reduction algorithms have been developed during past years. Generally, they can be divided into two broad

categories:[1] feature transform (or feature extraction) and feature selection
(or variable selection). Feature transform constructs new features by
projecting the original feature space to a lower dimensional one. Principal
component analysis and independent component analysis are two widely
used feature transform methods.[2] Although feature transform can obtain
the least dimension, its major drawbacks lie in that its computational
overhead is high and the output is hard to be interpreted for users. Feature
selection is the process of choosing a subset of the original feature spaces
according to discrimination capability to improve the quality of data.
Unlike feature transform, the fewer dimensions obtained by feature selection
facilitate exploratory of results in data analysis. Due to this predominance,
feature selection has now been widely applied in many domains, reducing
the number of irrelevant redundant features which drastically reduces the
running time of a learning algorithm and yields a more general concept.
In our opinion, there are typically four basic steps in a feature selection
method shown in Fig. 8.1:

(1) A generation procedure to generate the next candidate subset.
(2) An evaluation function to evaluate the subset under examination.
(3) A stopping criterion to decide when to stop, and
(4) A validation procedure to check whether the subset is valid.

The issue of feature selection comes to the spotlight because of the vast
amounts of data and increasing needs of preparing data for data mining

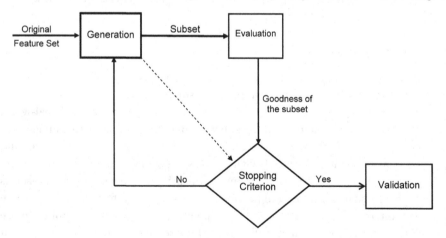

Fig. 8.1.   Feature selection process with validation.

applications. More often than not, we have to perform feature selection in order to obtain meaningful results.[3] Feature selection has the following prominent functions:

Enabling: Feature selection renders the impossible possible. As we know, every data mining algorithm is somehow limited by its capability in handling data in terms of sizes, types, formats. When a data set is too huge, it may not be possible to run a data mining algorithm or the data mining task cannot be effectively carried out without data reduction.[4] Feature selection reduces data and enables a data mining algorithm to function and work effectively with huge data.

Focusing: The data includes almost everything in a domain (recall that data is not solely collected for data mining), but one application is normally only about one aspect of the domain. It is natural and sensible to focus on the relevant part of the data for the application so that the search is more focused and the mining is more efficient.

Cleaning: The GIGO (garbage-in-garbage-out) principle[5] applies to almost all, if not all, data mining algorithms. It is therefore paramount to clean data, if possible, before mining. By selecting relevant instances; we can usually remove irrelevant ones as well as noise and/or redundant data. The high quality data will lead to high quality results and reduced costs for data mining.

This procedure generates a subset of features that are relevant to the target concept.[6] There are basically three kinds of generation procedure which are listed below.

If the original feature set contains N number of features, then the total number of competing candidate subsets to be generated are 2^N. This is a huge number even for medium-sized N. There are different approaches for solving this problem, namely: complete, heuristic, and random.

Complete: This generation procedure does a complete search for the optimal subset according to the evaluation function used. An exhaustive search is complete. However, Schimmer argues[7] that "just because the search must be complete do not mean that it must be exhaustive." Different heuristic functions are used to reduce the search without jeopardizing the chances of finding the optimal subset.[8] Hence, although the order of the search space is $O(2^N)$, a fewer subsets are evaluated. The optimality of the feature subset, according to the evaluation function, is guaranteed because the procedure can backtrack. Backtracking[9] can be done using various techniques, such as branch and bound, best first search, and beam search.

Heuristic: In each iteration of this generation procedure, all remaining features yet to be selected (rejected) are considered for selection (rejection). There are many variations to this simple process, but generation of subsets is basically incremental[10] (either increasing or decreasing). The order of the search space is $O(N^2)$ or less; some exceptions are Relief, DTM[11] that are discussed in detail in the next section. These procedures are very simple to implement and very fast in producing results, because the search space is only quadratic in terms of the number of features.

Random: This generation procedure is rather new in its use in feature selection methods compared to the other two categories. Although the search space is $O(2^N)$, these methods typically search a fewer number of subsets than 2^N by setting a maximum number of iterations possible.[12,13] Optimality[14] of the selected subset depends on the resources available. Each random generation procedure would require values of some parameters. Assignment of suitable values to these parameters are an important task for achieving good results.

8.1.1. *Definition*

In this chapter, different existing FS methods are generalized and compared. The following lists those that are conceptually different and cover a range of definitions.

(1) Idealized: Find the minimally sized feature subset that is necessary and sufficient to the target concept.[15]
(2) Classical: Select a subset of M features from a set of N features, $M < N$, such that the value of a criterion function is optimized over all subsets of size M.[16]
(3) Improving Prediction accuracy: The aim of feature selection is to choose a subset of features for improving prediction accuracy or decreasing the size of the structure without significantly decreasing prediction accuracy of the classifier built using only the selected features.[17]
(4) Approximating original class distribution: The goal of feature selection is to select a small subset such that the resulting class distribution,

given only the values for the selected features, is as close as possible to the original class distribution given all feature values.[18]

Definition 1: Feature selection in supervised learning: feature selection in supervised learning is the process of choosing a subset of the original features that optimizes the predictive performance of a considered model by eliminating the redundant features and those with little or no predictive information.

Definition 2: Feature selection in unsupervised learning: feature selection in unsupervised learning is the process of choosing a subset of the original variables that forms a high quality clustering for the given number of clusters.

Consulting the above matter of fact, the approaches for selection of relevant features are categorized below.

(1) Embedded Approach: It embeds the selection within the basic induction algorithm usually weighting schemes is considered.[19,20]
(2) Filter Approach: This method filters out irrelevant attributes before induction occurs. FOCUS and RELIEF follow feature selection with decision tree construction. In RELIEF, features are given weights but as the redundant features have same weight so the method may select a duplicate feature which increases complexity,[21] where as FOCUS implements exhaustive search. PCA (Principal Component Analysis)[22] can reduce dimensionality. The approach is well described in Fig. 8.2.

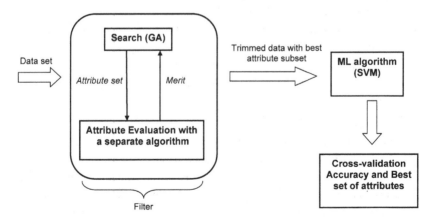

Fig. 8.2.   Filter approach in attribute selection.

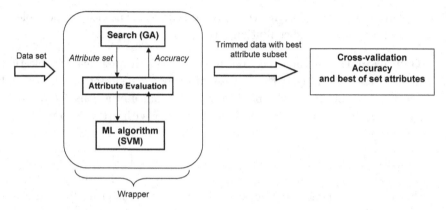

Fig. 8.3.   Wrapper approach in attribute selection.

Wrapper Approach: Here Feature selection occurs outside the induction method but it uses that method as a subroutine rather than as a post processor.[23] It induces high computational cost as induction algorithm is called for each subset of feature. There are two wrapper (classifier-specific) methods: sequential forward selection (SFS) and sequential forward feature selection (SFFS).[24] Both SFS and SFFS take an iterative approach, and the computation cost quickly becomes prohibitive for large-scale problems like expression-based classification.[25] Fig. 8.3 describes the approach.

Procedure:

(1) Input all features of the domain as the input.
(2) Generate a candidate feature subset.
(3) Run a classification algorithm with the feature subset generated in Step 2.
(4) Measure performance of the algorithm.
(5) If performance satisfactory then stop and go to Step 6 otherwise go to Step 2.
(6) Output a feature subset.

OBLIVION[26] is a type of wrapper approach which uses backward elimination and leave-one-out cross validation to estimate the accuracy of subsets. In this approach induction algorithm is considered as a black box i.e., no knowledge of algorithm is needed; only the interface has value. The induction algorithm runs on a selected optimal subset of features that generate a classifier such that accuracy of classifier[27] is maximal, but the optimal feature subset may not be unique. This approach conducts a search in the space of possible parameters. A search requires a state space,[28] an initial state, a termination condition and a search engine (either hill climbing or best first search). For n features size of search space is $O(2^n)$. The drawbacks of wrapper methods are significant as well.

(1) In the mining contest, the number of features with which we have to deal is quite large when the FS process is carried out as a preprocessing stage in these mining tasks. The complexity and the execution time make the task unfeasible.
(2) As the feature selection depends on the classification algorithm, we lose generality because of the behavior of the classification algorithm[29] in terms of accuracy and efficiency as the good performance of the system depends directly on the goodness of the classification algorithm chosen. Furthermore the selection of a classification method slightly suitable for a certain problem may give rise to choose or eliminate features wrongly.
(3) The combination of the wrapper methods with Soft Computing[30] techniques such as GAS and Neural Networks to carry out the FS process make it turns into a tough problem especially when the sets of examples (and/or) features are large.

8.2. Non-Soft Computing Techniques for Feature Selection

In this Section we will discuss few of the classical non-evolutionary[31] feature selection methods.

8.2.1. *Enumerative algorithms*

- **Exhaustive Search**. All the possible $^D C_d$ subsets are evaluated and the best one among them is chosen. This guarantees the optimal solution, but the computational time is intractable when the problem size is not small.
- **Branch and Bound**.[32] This algorithm generates a search tree that identifies the features being removed from the original set. It achieves a substantial reduction in the number of subset evaluations by pruning[21] those sub trees that will never be superior to the current best solution. However, the main problem with this algorithm is its exponential time complexity. Additionally, this algorithm requires the strict assumption of monotonicity,[33] i.e., adding new features never degrades the performance.

8.2.2. *Sequential search algorithms*

- **Sequential forward search:** This search starts with a candidate feature subset that is the empty set. Then it iteratively adds one feature at a time to the candidate feature subset, as long as some measure of performance-say predictive accuracy[34] is improved. At each iteration the feature added to the current feature subset is the feature whose inclusion maximizes the measure of performance.

- **Sequential backward search:** It is just opposite strategy of sequential forward search. It starts with a candidate feature subset that is the entire set of available features. Then it iteratively removes one feature at a time from the candidate attribute subset, as long as some measure of performance is improved. At each iteration the feature removed from the current feature subset is the feature whose removal maximizes the measure of performance.

Note that both forward selection and backward selection are greedy strategies,[35] which can be trapped in local maxima in the search space. To reduce this possibility one can use more robust search strategies. The next section discusses how evolutionary based feature selection can work in view of robustness.

8.2.3. *Sampling*

A spontaneous response to the challenge of feature selection is, without fail, some form of sampling. Although it is an important part of feature selection, there are other approaches that do not rely on sampling, but resort to search or take advantage of data mining algorithms.[36]

Sampling is a procedure that draws a sample S_i by a random process in which each S_i receives its appropriate probability p_i[37] of being selected. In practice, we seldom draw a probability sample by writing down the S_i and p_i because it is intolerably laborious with a large dataset, where sampling may produce billions of possible samples. The draw is most commonly made by specifying probabilities of inclusion for the individual instances and drawing instances, one by one or in groups until the sample of desired size is constructed.[38] It is not without a reason that people tend to first think of sampling as a tool for instance selection. Sampling methods are useful tools,[39] have existed for quite many years and are available in many system packages.

Sampling does not consciously search for relevant instances. One can't help asking "how are the three functions (enabling, focusing, and cleaning)[40] of feature selection accomplished in sampling?" What does the wonder is the random mechanism underlying every sampling method. Enabling[41] and cleaning are possible as the sample is usually smaller than the original data and noise and irrelevant instances in the sample will become accordingly less if sampling is performed appropriately. Although it does not take into account the task at hand, some forms of sampling can, to a limited extent, help focusing. We present some commonly used sampling methods below.

Purposive Sampling: It is a method in which the sample instances are selected with definite purpose in view. For example, if we want to give the picture that the knowledge of students in the P.G. Department of Information and Communication Technology has increased, then we may take individuals in the sample from students who are securing the marks >60% and ignoring the rest. Hence this purposive sampling is a type of favoritism sampling. This sampling suffers from the drawback of favoritism and nepotism and does not give a representative sample of the population.

Random Sampling: In this case the sample instances are selected at random[42] and the drawback of purposive sampling is completely overcome. A random sample is one in which each unit of population has an equal chance of being included in it. Suppose we want to select n instances out of the N such that every one of the $^N C_n$ distinct samples has an equal chance of being drawn. In practice, a random sample is drawn instance by instance. Since an instance that has been drawn is removed from the data set for all subsequent draws, this method is also called random sampling without replacement. Random sampling with replacement is feasible: at any draw, all N instances of the dataset are given an equal chance of being drawn, no matter how often they have already been drawn.

Stratified Sampling: In this sampling the heterogeneous data set of N instances is first divided into $n_1, n_2, \ldots, n_k$ homogenous subsets. The subsets are called strata. These subsets are non-overlapping, and together they comprise the whole of the dataset (i.e., $\sum_{i=1}^{k} n_i = N$).[17] The instances are sampled at random from each of these stratums; the sample size in each stratum varies according to the relative importance of the stratum in the population. The sample, which is the aggregate of the sampled instances of each of the stratum, is termed as a stratified sample and the technique of drawing this sample is known as stratified sampling.[43] If a sample is taken randomly in each stratum, the whole procedure is described as stratified random sampling.

Adaptive sampling: In many sampling applications, one may feel inclined to make decision on further sampling based on what has been observed so far. Adaptive sampling refers to a sampling procedure for selecting instances to be included in the sample that depends on results obtained from the sample. The primary purpose of adaptive sampling[44] is to take advantage of data characteristics in order to obtain more precise estimates. It can be considered as sampling and mining are performed side by side to take advantage of the result of preliminary mining for more effective sampling[45] and vice versa. Its variant can be found in sequential sampling and progressive sampling.

The simplest way of applying sampling is to go through the data once and obtain a sample, then work on the sample only. However, better results can often be achieved following the common pattern below:

- Obtain some approximate mining result with a sufficiently large samples.
- Refine the result with the whole data N.

The above pattern is an ideal case, as we need to scan the whole data set twice. However, in some cases, a few samples may be needed in the first step so that sampling is conducted a few times. In some cases, the above pattern (both steps) may be repeated a few times. If a mining algorithm is data hungry and memory intensive,[46] it is obvious that one should maximize the use of the data obtained in Step 1 and minimize the use of the whole data; the ideal case would be going through Step 2 only once.

Determining a sample size: There are sampling theories and learning theories that tell us how large the sample should be for what kind of results we expect. In general, the more precise the result we want, the larger the sample size. Examples can be found in[117] which PAC learning theory,[47] the VC dimension,[48] and Chernoff Bounds are mentioned for determining sample sizes. Some more examples can be found in Refs. 49 and 50.

Moreover, in data mining applications, we are often constrained by the computers memory capacity in processing data with a limited size. Besides the efficiency issue of the mining algorithm, we often end up using as much data as the computer can take. In other words, theoretical bounds help little in this situation. With increased memory capacity, we will be better and better guided by theoretical bounds in determine sample size.

Sample size[51] is also related to mining quality. However, samples of the same size could vary in terms of their qualities. In particular, some samples are more representative or resemble the original data more than others. Hence, there is a need for measuring sample quality; we then wish to establish the positive correlation between sample quality and mining quality.

8.2.4. *Feature selection based on information theory*

This method is a practical and efficient method which eliminates a feature that gives little information. The proposed method addresses both theoretical and empirical aspects of feature selection i.e., a filter approach[55] which can serve more features. It is a type of probabilistic approach i.e., for each instance:

$$Pr(C/F = f), \tag{8.1}$$

where C is the class, F denotes the features, f is a tuple.

This method uses cross-entropy (KL-dist) to select G such that $Pr(C/G = f_G)$ is close as previous.

Now:

$$\Delta_G = \sum Pr(f)\partial_G(F) \tag{8.2}$$

and:

$$\partial_G(F) = D(Pr(C/f), Pr(C/f_G)) \tag{8.3}$$

i.e., it employs backward elimination (eliminate F_i which would cause smallest increase in triangle).

Working principle:

- If $Pr(A = a|X = x, B = b) = Pr(A = a|X = x)$, then B gives us no information.
- M is markov blanket for a feature F if M does contain F.

With these two measures, two new feature selection algorithms, called the quadratic MI-based feature selection (QMIFS) approach and the MI-based constructive criterion (MICC) approach. In classificatory analysis, such a criterion tries to measure the ability of a feature or a feature subset to discriminate the different classes. Up to now, various criteria like distance, dependence, and consistency measures have been used for feature selection.[56–59] But these measures may be very sensitive to the concrete values of the training data; hence they are easily affected by the noise or outlier data. Whereas the information measures, such as the entropy or mutual information, investigate the amount of information or the uncertainty of a feature for classification. It depends only on the probability distribution of a random variable rather than on its concrete values. Fano[60] has revealed that maximizing the mutual information between the feature data and the desired target can achieve a lower bound to the probability of error. Inspired by this idea, Battiti developed his greedy feature selection method, MIFS.[61] This method evaluates mutual information between individual feature and class labels, and selects those features that have maximum mutual information with class labels but less redundant among the selected features. However, because of large errors in estimating the mutual information, the performance of MIFS is degraded. Kwak and Choi[62] enhanced the MIFS method under the assumption of uniform distributions of information of input features, and presented an algorithm called MIFS-U. MIFS-U[55] makes a better estimation of the mutual information criterion than MIFS, but it still fails to give the accurate estimation formula without the parameter β to be preset by users, which is related to the redundancy of selected features. So the problem of selecting input features can be solved by computing the mutual information between input features and output classes. This was formulated by Battiti as a "feature reduction" problem as [FRn-k].[63]

Assume S is the subset of already-selected features, that F is the subset of unselected features, $S \cap F = \Phi$, and that C is the output classes. For a feature $f_i \in F$ to be selected, the mutual information $I(C; S, f_i)$ should be the largest one among those $I(C; S, f_i)s, f_i \in F$.

Notice that the mutual information $I(C; S, f_i)$ can be represented as:

$$I(C; S, f_i) = I(C; S) + I(C; f_i|S) \qquad (8.4)$$

For a given feature subset S, since $I(C; S)$ is a constant, to maximize $I(C; S, f_i)$, the conditional mutual information $I(C; f_i|S)$ should be maximized. Furthermore, the conditional mutual information $I(C; f_i|S)$ can be represented as:

$$I(C; fi|S) = I(C; f_i) - I(C; f_i; S) \qquad (8.5)$$

To decrease the influence of parameter β on Battitis MIFS,[55] we consider a more accurate estimation of the redundant information Ir.

Proposition 1: For any $f_s \in S$, $f_i \in F$, suppose that the information is distributed uniformly throughout the regions of $H(f_s)$, $H(f_i)$, and $H(C)$,[44] and that the classes C do not change the ratio of entropy of f_s to the mutual information between f_s and f_i; if all the selected features in S are completely independent to each other, the total redundant information of the candidate feature f_i to all the selected features in subset S with respect to output classes C, denoted by I_r, can be calculated by the simple summation.

QMIFS

(1) Initialization: Set $F \leftarrow$ initial set of n features, $S \leftarrow$ empty set.
(2) Computation of the MI with the output class: $\forall f_i \in F$, compute $I(C; f_i)$.
(3) Selection the first feature: Find the feature that maximizes $I(C; f_i)$, set $F \leftarrow F \; f_i, S \leftarrow f_i$
(4) Greedy selection: Repeat until desired numbers of features are selected.

- Computation of entropy: $\forall f_s \in S$, compute $H(fs)$ if it is not yet available.
- Computation of the MI between variables: For all couples of features (f_i, f_s) with $f_i \in F$, $f_s \in S$, compute $I(f_i, f_s)$ and $\phi_{ik} = I(f_i; f_k)/H(f_k)$, if it is not yet available.
- Selection of the next feature: Choose the feature $f_i \in F$ that maximizes $I(C; f_i) - \beta \sum_{f_i I(f_i, f_s)}$, set $F \leftarrow F \; f_i, S \leftarrow f_i$.

(5) Output the set S containing the selected features.

8.2.5. *Floating search for feature selection*

Exhaustive search is computationally prohibitive. Heuristic search employs monotonic features i.e., adding a feature to the current set, does not decrease value of criterion function. But breakdown to sequential search is structural errors which can cause non-monotonicity.[64,65] So here sequential search is combined with backtracking to improve accuracy. Here number of forward and backtracking steps is dynamically controlled. The resulting feature set are not nested as in (1, r) algorithm, so there is sufficient chance to correct the decision in later steps. In general (1, r) there is no way of predicting the best values of 'l' and 'r'. In floating (l, r), there is no backward steps at all if the performance can not be improved. Thus parameter setting is not needed at all. Still there is no theoretical bound on the computational cost of the algorithm.

8.2.6. *Feature selection for SVM*

Support vector machine can be utilized as a induction algorithm for selecting features. Generally gradient descent technology can be used. Here SVM[36] takes advantage of performance increase of wrapper methods.

Working Principle:

(1) An optimal hyper plane is selected.
(2) Maximal marginal hyper plane is chosen. The decision function is $f(x) = w.\phi(x) + b$.
(3) Here performance depends upon large margin M and E (R^2/M^2) where all training tuples are within a sphere of radius R.
(4) But SVM[66] can suffer in high dimensional spaces where many features are irrelevant.

8.2.7. *Feature weighting method*

It is easier to implement in on-line incremental settings, e.g., WINNOW an algorithm that updates weights in a multiplicative manner, rather than additively as in perception rule.[67] So its behavior degrades logarithmically with the number of irrelevant features.

(1) Initialize weights $w_i, i = 1(1)n$ of the features to 1.
(2) For $(x_1, \ldots, x_n)$ output '1' if $w_1 x_1 + \cdots + w_n x_n >= n$ else '0'.
(3) If the algorithm predicts '−ve' on a '+ve' example, then for each $x_i = 1$, double the value of w_i else make $w_i/2$.
(4) Goto Step 2.

8.2.8. *Feature selection with dynamic mutual information*

DMIFS: Feature selection using dynamic mutual information.
    Input: A training dataset $T = D(F, C)$.
    Output: Selected features S.

(1) Initialize relative parameters: $F = F; S = \phi; D_u = D; D_l = \phi$.
(2) Repeat.
(3) For each feature $f \in F$ do.
(4) Calculate its mutual information $I(C; f)$ on D_u;
(5) If $I(C; f) = 0$ then $F = F - f$;
(6) Choose the feature f with the highest $I(C; f)$;
(7) $S = SUf; F = F - f$;
(8) Obtain new labeled instances D_l from D_u induced by f;
(9) Remove them from D_u, i.e., $D_u = D_u - D_l$;
(10) Until $F = \phi$ or $|D_u| = I_T$.

This algorithm works in a straightforward way. It estimates mutual information for each candidate feature in F with the label C. During calculating step, feature will be immediately discarded from F if its mutual information is zero. In this situation, the probability distribution of the feature is fully random and it will not contribute to predict the unlabeled instances Du.[70,71] After that, the feature with the highest mutual information will be chosen. It is noticed that the search strategy in DMIFS is sequential forward search. This means that the selected subset obtained by DMIFS is an approximate one.

8.2.9. *Learning to classify by ongoing feature selection*

Existing classification algorithms use a set of training examples to select classification features, which are then used for all future applications of the classifier. A major problem with this approach is the selection of a training set: a small set will result in reduced performance, and a large set will require extensive training. In addition, class appearance may change over time requiring an adaptive classification system. In this paper, we propose a solution to these basic problems by developing an on-line feature selection method, which continuously modifies and improves the features used for classification based on the examples provided so far.

Online feature selection $(n; k; e)$: Given a time point in the online learning process following the presentation of e examples and n features, find the subset with $k < n$ features that is maximally informative about the class, estimated on the e examples. For computational efficiency, an on-line selection[23,72] method will also be of use when the set of features to consider is large, even in a non-online scheme. It then becomes possible to consider initially a limited set of candidate features, and consider new ones incrementally until an optimal subset is selected. The proposed algorithm proceeds in an iterative manner: it receives at each time step either a new example or a new feature or both, and adjusts the current set of selected features. When a new feature is provided, the algorithm makes a decision regarding whether to substitute an existing feature with the new one, or maintain the current set of features, according to a value computed for each feature relative to the current feature set. The value of each feature is evaluated[73] by the amount of class information it contributes to the features in the selected set. The algorithm also keeps a fixed-size set of the most recent examples, used to evaluate newly provided features. In this way, the evaluation time of the features value, which depends only on the number of examples and the number of features in the selected set, is constant throughout the learning. Given a feature f and a set of selected features S, the desired merit value $MV(f; S)$[74] should express the additional class information gained by adding f to S. This can be measured using mutual information by:

$$MV(f; S) = I(f; S; C) - I(S; C), \qquad (8.6)$$

where I stands for mutual information.

8.2.10. *Multiclass MTS for simultaneous feature selection and classification*

Here the important features are identified using the orthogonal arrays and the signal-to-noise ratio, and are then used to construct a reduced model measurement scale. Mahalanobis distance and Taguchi's robust engineering.[75] Mahalanobis distance is used to construct a multidimensional measurement scale and define a reference point of the scale with a set of observations from a reference group. Taguchi's robust engineering is applied to determine the important features and then optimize the system. The goal of multiclass classification problems[76,77] is to find a mapping or function,$C_i = f(X)$, that can predict the associated class label $C - (i)$ of a given example vector X. Thus, it is expected that the mapping or function can accurately separate the data classes. MTS is different from classical multivariate methods in the following ways.[78,79] First, the methods used in MTS are data analytic instead of probability-based inference. This means that MTS does not require any assumptions on the distribution of input variables. Second, the Mahalanobis distance in MTS is suitably scaled and used as a measure of severity of various conditions. MTS can be used not only to classify observations into two different groups (i.e., normal and abnormal) but also to measure the degree of abnormality of an observation. Third, every example outside the normal space (i.e., abnormal example) is regarded as unique and does not constitute a separate population.

To implement MMTS, there are four main stages:

(1) Construction of a full model measurement scale with Mahalanobis[96] space of each class as the reference.
(2) Validation of the full model measurement scale.
(3) Feature selection, and
(4) Future prediction with important features.

Thus, not only the class prediction ability but also the feature selection efficiency (FSE) should be simultaneously considered when algorithms are evaluated. For this reason, a measurement of FSE[60,80] was proposed and used in this study in addition to employing balanced classification accuracy (BCA)[62,81] as the classification accuracy index. FSE is defined as the geometric mean of the feature stability and the percentage of removed features, and a higher value is preferred in the feature selection.

8.3. Soft computing for feature selection

8.3.1. *Genetic algorithm for feature selection*

Among the different categories of feature selection algorithms, the evolutionary algorithms (mainly genetic algorithm (GA)) is a rather recent development. The GA is biologically inspired and has many mechanisms mimicking natural evolution. It has a great deal of potential in scientific and engineering optimization or search problems. Furthermore, GA is naturally applicable to feature selection since the problem has an exponential search space. The individual encoding and fitness function are two important steps to be determined before proceeds into the details of genetic algorithm for feature selection. The other genetic operators are the same with the standard genetic algorithm but some authors are modified to some extent for better effectiveness of their algorithms.

The following steps are relevant for GA based feature selection.

- 1st step is to isolate most relevant associations of features.
- 2nd step is to class individuals.

• Then the crossover and mutation operations are performed to get the next candidate subset.

Generally, genetic algorithm exhibits tournament selection as the prime operation.[52] Finally a fitness function evaluates the subset. Every chromosome in the population represents an example of the set, where each gene is a feature. There is not a unique representation of the features in the chromosomes. In the case of a transactional database in database mining and the vector space model in text mining. A gene has a value $\{0, 1\}$, meaning absence/presence of that feature in the example, respectively. The weighting approach[53] is also generalized. Especially in text mining, where the features are represented by their frequency in the document or another value based on it. Nevertheless, there are not too many approaches dealing with other types of data, where the uncertainty is considered. The rest of the genetic parameters are not generally fixed. The size of the population does not seem to have a relation with the number of features, and the crossover and mutation rate utilized are the standard (0.6 and 0.001, respectively). Most of the approaches consider Wrapper methods, although the filter ones seem to be the most adequate in problems with a large number of features, especially when they are combined with GAS.[54]

8.3.2. *ELSA*

ELSA springs forms algorithms originally motivated by artificial life models of adaptive agents in ecological environments.[84] Modeling reproduction in evolving populations of realistic organisms requires that selection, like any other agent process, be locally mediated by the environments in which the agents are situated. In a standard evolutionary algorithm, an agent is selected for reproduction. Based on how its fitness compares to that of other agents. In ELSA, an agent (candidate solution) may die, reproduce, or neither based on an endogenous energy level that fluctuates via interactions with the environment. The energy level is compared against a constant selection threshold for reproduction. By relying on such local selection, ELSA reduces the communication among agents to a minimum. The competition and consequent selective pressure is driven by the environment.[85] There are no direct comparison with other agents. Further the local selection naturally enforces the diversity of the population by evaluating genetic individuals based on both quality measurements and on the number of similar individuals in the neighborhood in objective

```
Initialize population of agents, each with energy θ/2
While there are alive agents and for T iterations
    for each energy source c
        for each v(0 ..  1)
            E_envt^c (v)←2vE^c_tot
        endfor
    endfor
    for each agent a
        a'←mutate(crossover(a,randommate))
        for each energy source c
            v←Fitness(a',c)
            ΔE←min(v, E_envt^c (v))
            E_envt^c (v)← E_envt^c (v)- ΔE
            E_a←E_a+ΔE
        endfor
        E_a← E_a-E_cost
            if (E_a> θ)
                insert a' into population
                E_a'← E_a/2
                E_a← E_a- E_a'
            else if (E_a < 0 )
                    remove a from population
            endif
    endfor
endwhile
```

Fig. 8.4.   Pseudo code of ELSA.

space. The bias of ELSA toward diversity makes it ideal for multi-objective optimization, giving the decision maker a clear picture of pareto-optimal solutions from which to choose. Previous research has demonstrated the effectiveness of ELSA for feature selection in both supervised[86,87] and unsupervised[88] learning. The pseudo code for ELSA is given in Fig. 8.4.

8.3.3. *Neural network for feature selection*

The development of the artificial neural networks (ANNs) has been inspired in part by the fact that the most advanced learning system, human brains consists of millions of interconnected neurons. Contrasted with decision tree algorithms, ANNs can approximate well both real-valued and discrete-valued target functions. In particular, ANNs have proven successful in many practical problems. For example, ANNs[82] have been applied in management sciences, finance and marketing for stock market prediction, bankruptcy prediction, customer clustering and market segmentation with

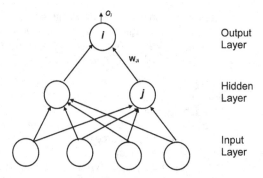

Fig. 8.5. A typical neural network model.

some success. It was proved in that any function can be approximated to arbitrary accuracy by a network with three layers of units when the output layer uses linear units and the hidden layer uses sigmoid units. The back propagation algorithm is the most common network learning algorithm. Typically the neural network model consists of a number of neurons which are connected by weighted links. We show a representative model with three layers, an input layer, a hidden layer and an output layer in Fig. 8.5 below. Neural networks with back propagation learning have great representational power can be very effective for both discrete valued and real valued data that are often noisy. However, it is more difficult for humans to understand the resulting models from neural networks than learned rules from decision tree algorithms. Further, the performance of ANNs also depend on many parameters such as number of training approaches, the activation functions at the hidden and output layers, learning rate and number of hidden nodes. Longer training times than decision tree algorithm is another factors that hinders the usage of ANNs for high dimensional data sets. For recurrent networks that were proposed for the analysis of time series data and[83] for optimal brain damage approach that dynamically alters network structure.

8.4. Hybrid Algorithm for Feature Selection

Genetic algorithms (GAs) and support vector machines (SVMs)[31] are integrated effectively based on a wrapper approach. Specifically, the GA component searches for the best attribute set by applying the principles of an evolutionary process. The SVM then classifies the patterns in the reduced datasets, corresponding to the attribute subsets represented by the

Fig. 8.6.   Structure of a chromosome (bit set).

GA chromosomes. SVMs use kernel[68] functions to transform input features from lower to higher dimensions. Implementation of GAs is achieved by translating the parameters into a coded string of binary digits, as is done in this proposed hybrid. These strings denote the attributes present in the data sets, with the length of the string being equal to the $N + 1$, where N is the number of attributes excluding the class attribute. A typical structure (a chromosome) is illustrated in following Fig. 8.6. After each generation, the algorithm would then check two termination criteria. Firstly, if convergence is achieved — the case when all chromosomes in the population possess the same fitness levels — the evolution process can then be halted. The maximum number of generations that the user permits the algorithm to run before stopping the process is set prior to commencement. The second criterion is based on this parameter that is decided by the user. If convergence is not reached before the maximum number of generations,[66,69] the algorithm will cease.

Comparison with pure SVM: The GA-SVM hybrid was tested with pure SVM to investigate the performance of the additional attribute selection component. Pure SVM in this case means that no attribute selection was done on the data sets. The GA-SVM hybrid incorporates the stochastic nature of genetic algorithms together with the vast capability of support vector machines in the search for an optimal set of attributes. The eradication of the redundant attributes using the GA-SVM hybrid improves the quality of the data sets and enables better classification of future unseen data.

8.4.1. Neuro-Fuzzy feature selection

This feature selection approach is shown to yield a diverse population of alternative feature subsets with various accuracy/complexity trade-off. The algorithm is applied to select features for performing classification with fuzzy model. Fuzzy[89] models involving only a few inputs can be more compact and transparent, thus offering improved interpretability of the fuzzy rule base. Such subtleties are often overlooked when feature selection is based on simple correlation tests, or on information measures such as mutual information, between the potential predictors and the output variable. VEGA (Vector Evaluated Genetic Algorithm),[90] which develops different subpopulations, optimizing each objective separately and the overall population at each generation, is formed by merging and shuffling the sub-populations.

(1) Individuals are randomly selected from the population to form a dominance tournament group.

(2) A dominance tournament sampling set is formed by randomly selecting individuals from the population.

(3) Each individual in the tournament group is checked for domination by the dominance sampling group (i.e., if dominated by at least one individual).

(4) If all but one of the individuals in the tournament group is dominated by the dominance tournament sampling group, the non dominated one is copied and included in the mating pool.

(5) If all individuals in the tournament group are dominated, or if at least two of them are nondominated, the winner which best seems to maintain diversity[91] is chosen by selecting the individual with the smallest niche count. The niche count for each individual is calculated by the following formula:

$$m(i) = \sum_{j=1}^{N} s(d_{ij}) \tag{8.7}$$

where m_i is the niche count of the ith individual in the tournament group. s is calculated by the formula:

$$s(d_{ij}) = \begin{cases} 1 - \left(\dfrac{d_{ij}}{\sigma_s}\right)^\alpha & \text{if } d_{ij} < \sigma_s \\ 0 & \text{otherwise} \end{cases} \tag{8.8}$$

where d_{ij} is the Hamming distance of the above individual with each of the N individuals already present in the mating pool and σ_s is the Hamming distance threshold, below which two individuals are considered similar enough to affect the niche count.

(6) If the mating pool is full end tournament selection; otherwise go back to Step 1.

Here we follow a fuzzy classifier design method based on cluster estimation.[92] The main characteristics of this approach are:

(1) An initial fuzzy classification model is derived by cluster estimation.
(2) The fuzzy rule base contains a separate set of fuzzy rules for each class.
(3) Double-sided Gaussian membership[89] functions are employed for the premise parts of the fuzzy rules. These are more flexible than the typical Gaussian kernel.
(4) The classification outcome is determined by the rule with the highest activation.
(5) Training is performed by a hybrid learning algorithm, which combines gradient-based and heuristic adaptation of the membership functions parameters. Only the rules with the maximum activation per class are updated for each pattern. The cost function to be minimized is a measure of the degree to which the rules for each class are activated when a pattern that belongs to that particular class is inserted. Specifically, for each pattern, the cost is defined as:

$$E = \frac{1}{2}(1 - \mu_{c,max} + \mu_{\neg c,max})^2 \qquad (8.9)$$

where $\mu_{c,max}$ is the firing strength of the rule among the set of rules belonging to the correct class, which achieves the maximum activation among the correct class rules, while[93] is the firing strength of the fuzzy rule, which belongs to the wrong class and achieves the maximum activation amongst the rules of its class. In such fuzzy models, it is straightforward to study the effect of removing an input, by simply removing all the antecedent clauses which are associated with the deleted input.

8.5. Multi-Objective Genetic Algorithm for Feature Selection

Feature selection can naturally be posed as a multi-objective search problem, since in the simplest case it involves minimization of both the subset cardinality and modeling error. Therefore, multi-objective evolutionary algorithms (MOEA) are well suited for feature selection. Evolutionary Multi-Objective Feature Selection (EMOFS)[94] is employed to handle such objectives, namely the specificity and sensitivity of classifiers (shown in Fig. 8.8). The obvious choice for assessing a classifier's performance is to estimate its misclassification rate. Yet, in many problem domains, such as in engineering or medical diagnosis, it makes more sense to optimize alternative objectives. A typical approach is to analyze the diagnostic performance by means of a confusion matrix. Instead of minimizing the misclassification rate, it is preferable to maximize the specificity and sensitivity of a diagnostic model. If a fixed hypothesis space and induction algorithm is assumed, then the feature selection problem is to select a subset S^j so that:

$$S^j(H(x)) = \arg \min_{S^j \in S}\{(J(x))\}$$

$$= \arg \min_{S^j \in S}\{[|S^j|, \text{ sensitivity, specificity}]\} \quad (8.10)$$

where the objective function $J(x)$ is a vector consisting of three terms, the subset cardinality, S^j, and the classifier's specificity and sensitivity. Typically in multi-objective optimization problems, there is no single optimal solution, but a range of Pareto optimal solutions. The key concept here is dominance: a solution J1 is said to dominate a solution J2 if and only if J1 is no worse than J2 in any of the objectives, while it is strictly better than J2 in at least one objective. Accordingly, the aim of multi-objective feature selection is to identify a set of non-dominated feature subsets, rather than a single optimal subset. Elitist Niched Pareto Genetic Algorithm (ENPGA)[95] employs a simple and computationally appealing way to obtain a reduced-size elite set. Individuals from the Archive Set are selected for inclusion in the Elite Set by tournament selection, where the winner is determined by fitness sharing. Here, binary tournaments are employed, while sharing is performed in the Hamming and subset cardinality spaces, in a way similar to that for selection for reproduction. The niche count is calculated from the distances of the competing individuals to those belonging to the partially filled Elite Set, thus encouraging diversity in both the Hamming distance as well as the subset cardinality space. The population management policy employed in ENPGA involves:

P_p, P_o: parent and offspring population respectively

P_e, P_a: elite and archive set respectively

N_p, N_{pmin}: Parent population size, and minimum allowable population size respectively.

N_o: Offspring population size is twice the parent population size

N_e, N_a: Elite and Archive set size respectively; N_{emax} is the maximum allowable elite set size. P_e is selected from P_a by tournament selection, while P_p includes P_e, with the rest of P_p's individuals selected from P_o with Pareto domination tournament selection.

A specialized crossover operator, the Subset Size-Oriented Common Features crossover (SSOCF)[96] is employed to facilitate the exploration around a wide area at the vicinity of the Pareto front, while avoiding the "averaging" effect. Figure 8.7 describes averaging effect of crossover operation.

Similarly the idea behind NSGA is that a ranking selection method is used to emphasize good points and a niche method is used to maintain stable subpopulations of good points. It varies from simple genetic algorithm only in the way the selection operator works. The crossover and mutation remain as usual. Before the selection is performed, the population is ranked on the basis of an individual's nondomination. The nondominated individuals present in the population are first identified from the current population. Then, all these individuals are assumed to constitute the first nondominated front in the population and assigned a large dummy fitness value. The same fitness value is assigned to give an equal reproductive potential to all these nondominated individuals. In order to maintain the diversity in the population, these classified individuals are then shared with their dummy fitness values.[97] Sharing is achieved by performing selection operation using degraded fitness values obtained by dividing the original fitness value of an individual by a quantity proportional to the number of individuals around it.

8.6. Parallel Genetic Algorithm for Feature Selection

Parallelization of self-adaptive genetic algorithms (GAs) has received considerable attention in recent years due to its significant speedup. GAs resembles iterative methods but they aim to search the solution space more broadly. The idea of GAs is to maintain a population of individuals, each giving a solution to the problem in hand. The quality of an individual is determined by calculating the value of a suitable fitness function. A new generation of individuals is created by applying crossover and mutation operations to the individuals. A self-adaptive genetic algorithm for clustering (SAGA)[98] is described. In this algorithm, each individual contains several parameter values in addition to the actual solution. The algorithm still has a few parameters, but their values are not critical to the result. SAGA was demonstrated to be very robust and to achieve excellent results. The main drawback of the method is the long running time. The performance of a sequential GA can often be somewhat improved

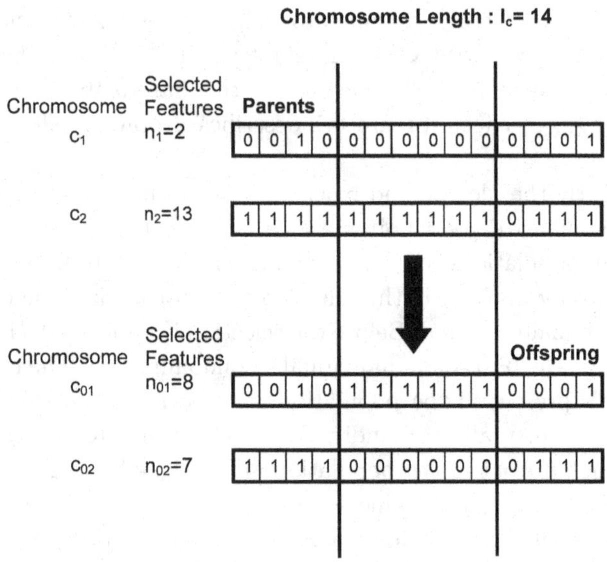

Chromosome Length : l_c= 14

Fig. 8.7.   Averaging effect of n-point cross over.

begin

    generation t=0;

    Initialisation; $P_p(t)$; has approximately uniform distribution across all features and subset sizes

    model construction/evaluation for all subsets in $P_p(t)$; fitness assignment

    extract initial non dominated front; Form $P_a(0)$.

    while termination criterion is not satisfied **do**

        t=t+1

        apply SSOCF to Produce Offspring $P'_o(t)$ from $P_p(t)$; Include $P_e(t)$.

        mutate $P'_o(t)$ to produce $P_o(t)$

        model construction/evaluation for all subsets in $P_o(t)$; fitness assignment

        extract non dominated front; Update $P_a(t)$

        if $|P_a(t)| > N_{emax}$ **then**

            select $P_e(t)$ from $P_a(t)$ by tournament selection with fitness sharing

        else $P_e(t) \leftarrow P_a(t)$

        $N_e = \min\{N_{emax}, N_a\}$

        $N_p = \min\{N_{pmin}, 10 \cdot N_e\}$

        select $P_p(t+1)$ from $P_o(t)$ with Pareto domination tournaments

        update mutation rate

    end

end

Fig. 8.8.   Pseudo code of EMOFS.

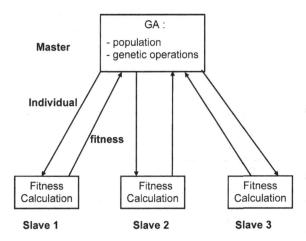

Fig. 8.9.   Master-slave model of parallelization.

by re-considering the representation of the individuals, redesigning the reproduction operators, balancing between the population size and the number of generations, introducing suitable local search operators, etc. Parallel GAs are typically classified into three classes according to their approach on parallelization: fitness level, population level and individual level parallelization. Hierarchical or hybrid parallelization models are often considered as the fourth class.

Fitness level: In the fitness level parallelization a master process distributes the evaluation of the individuals to slave processes. The master process performs all the other tasks of the GA shown in Fig. 8.9. This kind of parallelization is useful when the fitness value calculation is time-consuming so that the data transfer between the master and the slaves will not become a bottleneck of the system.

Population level: In the population level parallelization a complete GA including an entire population is placed at each process and an interconnection network between the processes is constructed, which is well described in Fig. 8.10.

Individual level: Parallelization can also be realized at individual level. Commonly, the individuals are placed in a grid. Each grid node contains a single individual.

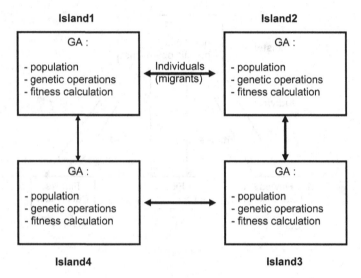

Fig. 8.10.   Island model, bidirectional ring topology.

Crossover is performed on neighboring individuals and the neighbor for crossover is selected by a suitable rule, such as tournament selection. This kind of parallel algorithms are often called cellular parallel GAs due to their resemblance of cellular automata[99] (see Fig. 8.11). The model is also called fine-grained due to the distribution of memory and genetic information among processors.

Hierarchical models: There is a rapidly growing set of parallel GA models which contain features from more than one of the above types. These are often called hierarchical or hybrid models. A hybrid model consisting of coarse grained GAs connected in a fine-grained GA style topology performed better than a plain coarse-grained or fine-grained GA. On the other hand, a coarse-grained[100] GA with a fine-grained GA on each island performed rather badly.

Parallel self-adaptive GA: Our parallel GA (ParSAGA) uses the island parallelization model, where QGAs[101] run independently and communicate with each other, see Sec. 2.2. The processes are seen as islands which occasionally send individuals ("emigrants") to other islands. We have implemented island parallelization using a gene bank model. In the gene

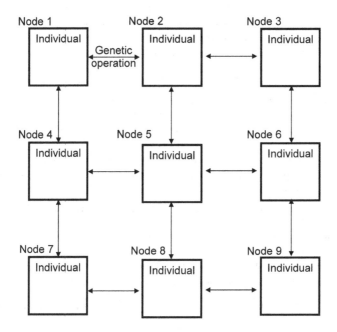

Fig. 8.11. Cellular model.

bank model, instead of sending emigrants directly to other islands, islands communicate only with the gene bank process.

Self-adaptive genetic algorithm for clustering (SAGA).

(1) Generate S random individuals to form the initial generation.
(2) Iterate the following T times.

- Select S_B surviving individuals for the new generation.
- Select $S - S_B$ pairs of individuals as the set of parents.
- For each pair of parents (L_A, L_B) do the following:
  - Determine the strategy parameter values $(\gamma_{L_n}, \psi_{L_n}, V_{L_n})$ for the offspring by crossing the strategy parameters $(\gamma_{L_a}, \psi_{L_a}, V_{L_a})$ and $(\gamma_{L_b}, \psi_{L_b}, V_{L_b})$ of the two parents.
  - Mutate the strategy parameter values of L_n with the probability (a predefined constant).
  - Create the solution ω_{L_n} by crossing the solutions of the parents. The crossing method is determined by γ_{L_n}.
  - Mutate the solution of the offspring with the probability ψ_{L_n}.

— Add noise to ω_{L_n}. The maximal noise is V_{L_n}.
— Apply k-means iterations to ω_{L_n}.
— Add L_n to the new generation.

- Replace the current generation by the new generation.

(3) Output the best solution of the final generation.

Steps added to SAGA for island processes in Step 2 above are:

- Send an individual to the gene bank.
- Receive an individual from the gene bank and add it to the current population.
- Remove an individual from the current population.

Gene bank process

(1) Select coordinates K_q for each island q.
(2) Repeat the following steps until a stopping condition is fulfilled.

- Sleep until an island process r makes a communication request.
- Receive an individual L_r from r.
- Select an individual L_s from the gene bank.
- Send L_s to island r.
- Add L_r to the gene bank.
- If the gene bank contains $B + 1$ individuals, remove the worst individual from the gene bank.

(3) Return the solution of the best individual in the gene bank.

8.7. Unsupervised Techniques for Feature Selection

Feature selection in unsupervised learning can be considered as a sub-problem of unsupervised model selection. The problem of determining an appropriate model in unsupervised learning has gained popularity in the machine learning, pattern recognition and data mining communities. Unsupervised model selection addresses either how to identify the optimal number of clusters K or how to select feature subsets while determining the correct numbers of clusters. The latter problem is more difficult because of the inter dependency between the number of clusters and the feature subsets used to form clusters. To this point, most research on unsupervised model selection has considered the problem of identifying the right number of clusters using all available features.[102,103]

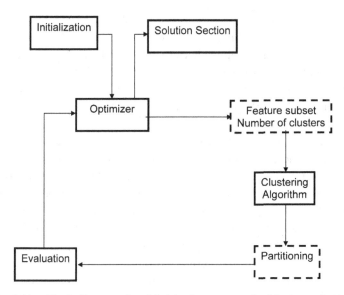

Fig. 8.12.   Block diagram of multi-objective unsupervised feature selection.

We have described a multi-objective evolutionary approach to semi-supervised clustering. In this algorithm, the concept of semi-supervision is implemented by optimizing separate objectives related to the performance with respect to internal and external information. Specifically, the algorithm works through the optimization of an internal cluster validation technique, the Silhouette Width, combined with the optimization of an external validation technique, the Adjusted Rand Index.[104] The Silhouette Width is computed across both labeled and unlabelled data, whereas the Adjusted Rand Index can be computed for the labeled data only. The optimization algorithm used is an existing multi-objective evolutionary algorithm (MOEA) from the literature, PESA-II[105] which is shown in Fig. 8.12. In order to obtain good scalability to large data sets, a specialized encoding and specialized operators are used. In particular, both the encoding and the mutation operator make use of nearest neighbor lists to restrict the size of the search space.

(1) PESA-II: The optimizer used is the elitist MOEA, PESA-II, described in detail. PESA-II updates, at each generation, a current set of non-dominated solutions stored in an externale to undergo reproduction and variation. PESA-II uses a selection policy designed to give

equal reproduction opportunities to all regions of the current non-dominated front; thus in our application, it should provide a diverse set of solutions trading off the three different objectives. No critical parameters are associated with this "niched"[106] selection policy, as it uses an adaptiv population (but limited size), and uses this to build an internal population size range equalization and normalization of the objectives.

(2) Encoding and variation operators: The application of PESA-II to feature selection requires the choice of an appropriate encoding and operators. Due to the use of k-means, there are two components of a solution that need to be coded for: the actual feature subset, and the number of clusters. A simple binary encoding is used to select/deselect[107] features: the genome comprises one bit for every feature, with a value of 1 indicating the activation of a feature and a value of 0 indicating its deactivation.

(3) Clustering algorithm: The k-means algorithm starts from a random partitioning of the data into k clusters (where k is an input parameter). It repeatedly:

- computes the current cluster centers (that is, the average vector of each cluster in data space) and
- reassigns each data item to the cluster whose centre is closest to it. It terminates when no more reassignments take place. By this means, the intra-cluster variance, that is, the sum of squares of the differences between data items and their associated cluster centers is locally minimized.

(4) Objective functions: The Silhouette value[118] for an individual data item, which reflects the confidence in this particular cluster assignment, is:

$$S(i) = \frac{b_i - a_i}{max(a_i, b_i)} \qquad (8.11)$$

8.8. Evaluation functions

An optimal subset is always relative to a certain evaluation function (i.e., an optimal subset chosen using one evaluation function may not be the same as that which uses another evaluation function). Typically, an evaluation function tries to measure the discriminating ability of a feature or a subset to distinguish the different class labels. Considering these divisions and the latest developments, we divide the evaluation functions into five categories: distance, information (or uncertainty), dependence, consistency, and classifier error rate. In the following subsections we briefly discuss each of these types of evaluation functions.

Distance measures: It is also known as separability, divergence, or discrimination measure. For a two-class problem, a feature X is preferred to another feature Y if X induces a greater difference between the two-class conditional probabilities than Y; if the difference is zero, then X and Y are indistinguishable. An example is the Euclidean distance measure.

Information measures: These measures typically determine the information gain from a feature. The information gain from a feature X is defined as the difference between the prior uncertainty[40] and expected posterior uncertainty using X. Feature X is preferred to feature Y if the information gain from feature X is greater than that from feature Y (e.g., entropy measure).[108]

Dependence measures: Dependence measures or correlation measures qualify the ability to predict the value of one variable from the value of another. The coefficient is a classical dependence measure and can be used to find the correlation between a feature and a class. If the correlation of feature X with class C is higher than the correlation[109] of feature Y with C, then feature X is preferred to Y. A slight variation of this is to determine the dependence of a feature on other features; this value indicates the degree of redundancy of the feature. All evaluation functions based on dependence measures can be divided between distance and information measures.[110,111] But, these are still kept as a separate category, because conceptually, they represent a different viewpoint.[112] More about the above three measures can be found in Ben-Basset's survey.[113]

Consistency measures: These measures are rather new and have been in much focus recently. These are characteristically different from other measures, because of their heavy reliance on the training dataset and the use of the Min-Features bias in selecting a subset of features.[114] Min-Features[115] bias prefers consistent hypotheses definable over as few features as possible. These measures find out the minimally sized subset that satisfies the acceptable inconsistency rate that is usually set by the user.

Classifier error rate measures: The methods using this type of evaluation function are called "wrapper methods", (i.e., the classifier is the evaluation function).[116] As the features are selected using the classifier that later on uses these selected features in predicting the class labels of unseen instances, the accuracy level is very high.

8.9. Summary and Conclusions

Feature-selection method can significantly reduce the computational cost and possibly find an even better feature subset than directly applying a classifier-specific feature-selection algorithm to the full feature set. In the first stage of a two-stage design,[70] a classifier-independent feature-selection algorithm is used to remove most of the non informative features. In the second stage, a classifier-specific feature-selection algorithm is applied to further refine the feature set from the first stage.

This paper illustrates the pros and cons of various methods of feature selection which are listed below.

Accuracy: The features used to describe the patterns implicitly define a pattern language. If the language is not expressive enough, it fails to capture the information necessary for classification. Hence, regardless of the learning algorithm,[31] the amount of information given by the features limits the accuracy of the classification function learned.

Required learning time: The features describing the patterns implicitly determine the search space that the learning algorithm must explore. An abundance of irrelevant features can unnecessarily increase the size of the search space and hence the time needed for learning a sufficiently accurate classification function.

Necessary number of examples: All other things being equal, the larger the number of features describing the patterns, the larger the number of examples needed to train a classification function to the desired accuracy.

Cost: In medical diagnosis, for example patterns consist of observable symptoms along with the results of diagnostic tests. These tests have various associated costs and risks; for instance, an invasive exploratory surgery can be much more expensive and risky than, say, a blood test. Those comparisons can enable new comers for more efficient work on these topics.

Finally, we outline few research directions in the area of feature selection.

(1) Define standardized evaluation criteria[113] to enable systematic comparison of existing and novel approaches.
(2) Scale up intelligent focusing approaches by combining technologies from machine learning research and the database community.
(3) Develop more intelligent focusing solutions that provide data reduction techniques beyond pure statistical sampling[46] and make use of the specific characteristics of concrete contexts in data mining.
(4) A more rigorous investigation is required to formulate and implement unsupervised feature selection as a multi-objective problem.

Much work still remains to be done. Instance and feature selection corresponds to scaling down data and reduce the feature space. When we understand better instance and feature selection, it is natural to investigate if this work can be combined with other lines of research in overcoming the problem of huge amounts of data.

References

1. J. Kittler. Feature set search algorithms, *Pattern Recognition and Signal Processing*. 835–855, (1978).
2. A. Jain and B. Chandrasekaran. Dimensionality and sample size considerations, *Pattern Recognition in Practice*. **2**, 835–855, (1982).
3. R. Setiono and H. Liu. Neurolinear: From neural networks to oblique decision rules, *Neurocomputing*. **17**, 1–24, (1997).
4. K. C. Tan, Q. Yu, and T. H. Lee. A distributed co-evolutionary classifier for knowledge discovery in data mining, *IEEE Transactions on Systems, Man and Cybernetics: Part C*. **35**(2), 131–142, (2005).
5. D. Huang and T. Chow. Effective feature selection scheme using mutual information, *Neurocomputing*. **63**, 325–343, (2005).
6. I. Guyon and A. Elisseeff. An introduction to variable and feature selection, *Journal of Machine Learning Research*. **3**, 1157–1182, (2003).
7. O. Carlborg and C. Haley. Epistasis: too often neglected in complexity studies?, *Nat. Rev. Genet.* **5**(8), 618–625, (2004).
8. H. Vafaie and K. Jong. Genetic algorithms as a tool for feature selection in machine learning. In *Proc. of the 4th International Conference on Tools with Artificial Intelligence*, (1992).
9. C. Su and Y. Hsiao. An evaluation of the robustness of mts for imbalanced data, *IEEE Trans. Knowledge and Data Engineering*. **19**(10), 1321–1332 (October, 2007).

10. S. Salcedo-Sanz, G. Camps-Valls, F. Perez-Cruz, J. Sepulveda-Sanchis, and C. Bousono-Calzon. Enhancing genetic feature selection through restricted search and walsh analysis, *IEEE Transactions on Systems, Man, and Cybernetics-Part C: Applications and Reviews.* **34**(4), 398–406, (2004).

11. P. Narendra and K. Fukunaga. A branch and bound algorithm for feature subset selection, *IEEE Trans. Computers.* **26**(9), 917–922, (1977).

12. A. Jain and A. Vailaya. Image retrieval using color and shape, *Pattern Recognition.* **29**(8), 1,233–1,244, (1996).

13. J. Mao, K. Mohiuddin, and A. Jain. Parsimonious network design and feature selection through node pruning. In *Proc. of 12th ICPR*, pp. 622–624, Jerusalem, (1994).

14. G. Wang, F. Lochovsky, and Q. Yang. Feature selection with conditional mutual information maximin in text categorization. In *Proc. of the 13th ACM International Conference on Information and Knowledge Management*, pp. 342–349, ACM, Washington, DC, USA (November, 2004).

15. Y. Hamamoto, S. Uchimura, Y. Matsunra, T. Kanaoka, and S. Tomita. Evaluation of the branch and bound algorithm for feature selection, *Pattern Recognition Letters.* **11**, 453–456 (July, 1990).

16. F. Ferri, P. Pudil, M. Hatef, and J. Kittler. Comparative study of techniques for large scale feature selection, *Pattern Recognition in Practice IV.* pp. 403–413, (1994).

17. A. Blum and P. Langley. Selection of relevant features and examples in machine learning, *Artificial Intelligence.* **97**(1–2), 245–271, (1997).

18. S. Perkins and J. Theiler. Online feature selection grafting. In *Proc. of the 20th Int. Conf. on Machine Learning*, pp. 21–24, (2003).

19. U. Alon, N. Barkai, D. Notterman, Y. S. Gish, D. Mack, and A. Levine. Broad patterns of gene expression revealed by clustering analysis of tumor and normal colon cancer tissues probed by oligonucleotide arrays, *Cell Biology.* **96**, (1999).

20. J. Pudil, P. Novovicova and J. Kittler. Floating search methods in feature selection, *Pattern Recognition Letters.* **15**, 1,119–1,125, (1994).

21. C. C. Chang and C. J. Lin. Libsvm:a library for support vector machines, (2001).

22. T. Riho, A. Suzuki, J. Oro, K. Ohmi, and H. Tanaka. The yield enhancement methodology for invisible defects using the mts+ method, *IEEE Trans. Semiconductor Manufacturing.* **18**(4), 561–568, (2005).

23. G. H.John, R. Kohavi, and K. Pfleger. Irrelevant features and the subset selection problem. In *Proc. of the Eleventh International Machine Learning Conference*, pp. 121–129, New Brunswick, NJ, (1994). Morgan Kaufman.

24. J. M. nad J. L Castro, C. J. Mantas, and F. Rojas. A neuro-fuzzy approach for feature selection. In *Proc. of Joint 9th IFSA World Congress and 20th NAFIPS International Conference*, Vol. 2, pp. 1003–8, (2001).

25. T. Joachims. Transductive inference for text classification using support vector machines. In *Proc. of the 16th International Conference on Machine*

Learning(ICML-99), pp. 200–209. Morgan Kaufmann Publishers, San Francisco, CA, (1999).

26. C. Sima and E. Dougherty. What should be expected from feature selection in small-sample settings, *Bioinformatics*. **22**(19), 2430–2436, (2006).

27. H. L. Ye and H. C. Liu. A som-based method for feature selection. In *Proc. of the 9th IEEE International Conference on Neural Information Processing*, pp. 1295–1299, Singapore, (2002).

28. M. A. Hearst, B. Schölkopf, S. Dumais, E. Osuna, and J. Platt. Trends and controversies – support vector machines, *IEEE Intelligent Systems*. **13**, 18–28, (1998).

29. J. Pearl. *Probabilistic Reasoning in Intelligent Systems: Networks of Plausible Inference*. (Morgan Kaufmann, Los Altos, CA, 1988).

30. K. J. Cherkauer and J. W. Shavlik. Growing simpler decision trees to facilitate knowledge discovery. In *Proc. of the 2nd International Conference on Knowledge Discovery and Data Mining (KDD-96)*, pp. 315–318, (1996).

31. A. Rakotomamonjy. Variable selection using svm-based criteria, *Journal of Machine Learning Research*. **3**, 1357–1370, (2003).

32. K. C. Tan, T. A. Tay, and C. M. Heng. Mining multiple comprehensible classification rules using genetic programming. In *Proc. of the IEEE Congress on Evolutionary Computation*, pp. 1302–1307, Honolulu, Hawaii, (2002).

33. S. J. Russell and P. Norvig. *Artificial Intelligence: A Modern Approach*. (Prentice Hall, New Jersey, 1995).

34. N. Kwak and C. H. Choi. Input feature selection by mutual information based on parzen window, *IEEE Transactions on Pattern Analysis and Machine Intelligence*. **24**(12), 1667–1671, (2002).

35. J. R. Quinlan. *C4.5: Programs for Machine Learning*. (CA: Morgan Kaufmann, Berlin: Springer, 1992).

36. F. Fleuret. Fast binary feature selection with conditional mutual information, *Journal of Machine Learning Research*. **5**, 1531–1555, (2004).

37. W. D. Shi and H. Liu. Feature selection for handwritten chinese character recognition based on genetic algorithms. In *Proc. of the IEEE International Conference on Systems, Man, and Cybernetics*, Vol. 5, pp. 4201–4206, (1998).

38. E. Dougherty and M. Brun. On the number of close-to-optimal feature sets, *Cancer Inf.* **2**, 189–196, (2006).

39. U. Fayyad. Data mining and knowledge discovery in databases: Implications for scientific databases. In *Proc. of the Fifteenth International Conference Machine Learning (ICML'98)*, pp. 144–151, (1998).

40. U. Sima, S. Attoor, U. Braga-Neto, J. Lowey, E. Suh, and E. Dougherty. Impact of error estimation on feature-selection algorithms, *Pattern Recognition*. **38**(12), 2472–2482, (2005).

41. P. Das and S. Datta. Exploring the effects of chemical composition in hot rolled steel product using mahalanobis distance scale under mahalanobis-taguchi system, *Computational Materials Science*. **38**(4), 671–677, (2007).

42. U. Braga-Neto and E. Dougherty. Bolstered error estimation, *Pattern Recognition.* **37**, 1267–1281, (2004).
43. K. Fukunaga and P. Narendra. A branch and bound algorithm for computing k-nearest neighbors, *IEEE Trans. Comput.* **C-24**, 750–753, (1976).
44. U. M. Fayyad and K. B. Irani. Multi-interval discretization of continuous valued attributes for classification learning. In *Proc. of the 13th International Joint Conference on Artificial Intelligence*, pp. 1022–1027, (1993).
45. N. Kwak and C. Choi. Improved mutual information feature selector for neural networks in supervised learning. In *Proc. of the 1999 Int. Joint Conf. on Neural Networks*, (1999).
46. L. Shih, J. Rennie, Y. Chang, and D. Karger. Text bundling: Statistics-based data reduction. In *Proc. of the 20th Int'l Conf. Machine Learning (ICML)*, (2003).
47. M. L. Ginsberg. *Essentials of Artificial Intelligence.* (Morgan Kaufmann, 1993).
48. D. Aha and D. Kibler. Effective feature selection scheme using mutual information, *Machine Learning.* **6**, 37–66, (1991).
49. E. R. Hruschka and N. F. F. Ebecken. A feature selection bayesian approach for extracting classification rules with a clustering genetic algorithm, *Applied Artificial Intelligence.* **17**, 489–506, (2003).
50. H. Ishibuchi, T. Nakashima, and T. Murata. Three-objective genetic-based machine learning for linguistic rule extraction, *Information Sciences.* **136**, 109–133, (2001).
51. M. Dash and H. Liu. Feature selection for classification, *In Intelligent Data Analysis.* **I**(3), 1 01, (1997).
52. D. Lowe. Distinctive image features from scale-invariant key points, *Int. J. Comput. Vision.* **60**(2), 91–110, (2004).
53. A. Gordon. A survey of constrained classification, *Computational Statistics & Data Analysis.* **21**, 17–29, (1996).
54. D. X. J. Principe and J. Fisher. *Information Theoretic Learning.* (Wiley, New York, NY, 1999).
55. R. Battiti. Using mutual information for selecting features in supervised neural net learning, *IEEE Transactions on Neural Networks.* **5**(4), 537–550, (1994).
56. R. R. F. Mendes, F. B. Voznika, A. A. Freitas, and J. C. Nievola. Discovering fuzzy classification rules with genetic programming and co-evolution. In *Proc. of the Fifth European Conference, PKDD 2001, Lecture Notes in Artificial Intelligence*, Vol. 168, pp. 314–325, (2001).
57. B. Walczk and D. Massart. Rough sets theory, *Chemometrics and Intelligent Laboratory Systems.* **47**, 1–16, (1999).
58. R. Johnson and D. Wichern. *Applied Multivariate Statistical Analysis.* (Prentice-Hall, 1998).
59. H. Kim and G. Koehler. Theory and practice of decision tree induction, *Omega.* **23**(6), 637–652, (1995).

60. R. Fano. *Transmission of Information: A Statistical Theory of Communications.* (Wiley, New York, NY, 1961).

61. J. K. Kishore, L. M. Patnaik, V. Mani, and V. K. Agrawal. Application of genetic programming for multi category pattern classification, *IEEE Transactions on Evolutionary Computation.* **4**(3), 242–258, (2001).

62. R. Kohavi and G. John. Wrappers for feature subset selection, *Artificial Intelligence.* **97**(1–2), 273–324, (1997).

63. B. Hanczar, J. Hua, and E. R. Dougherty. Decorrelation of the true and estimated classifier errors in high-dimensional settings. In *Proc. of the EURASIPJ, Bioinformatics System Biol.,* (2007).

64. J. M. Chambers, W. S. Cleveland, B. Kleiner, and P. A. Turkey. Graphical methods for data analysis, *Pacific, CA: Wadsworth and Brooks/Cole.* (1983).

65. M. Martin-Bautista and M. A. Vila. A survey of genetic feature selection in mining issues. In *Proc. of the 1999 Congress on Evolutionary Computation,* Vol. 2, pp. 13–21, (1999).

66. I. Guyon, J. Weston, S. Barnhill, and V. Vapnik. Gene selection for cancer classification using support vector machines, *Machine Learning.* **46**, 389–422, (2002).

67. B. Chakraborty. Genetic algorithm with fuzzy fitness function for feature selection. In *Proc. of the IEEE International Symposium on Industrial Electronics,* pp. 315–319, (2002).

68. S. Mukkamala, G. Janoski, and A. Sung. Intrusion detection using neural networks and support vector machines. In *Proc. of the 2002 International Joint Conference on Neural Networks,* Vol. 2, pp. 1702–1707, (2002).

69. V. Vapnik. The nature of statistical learning theory, *Springer-Verlag, New York.* **31**, 405–428, (2001).

70. W. W. Cohen. Fast effective rule induction. In *Proc. of the 12th International Conference on Machine Learning,* pp. 115–123, (1995).

71. Y. Cun, B. Boser, J. Denker, D. Hendersen, R. Howard, W. Hubbard, and L. Jackel. Back propagation applied to handwritten zip code recognition, *Neural Computation.* **1**, 541–551, (1989).

72. N. Cho, H. Jang, H. Park, and Y. Cho. Waist circumference is the key risk factor for diabetes in korean women with history of gestational diabetes, *Diabetes Research and Clinical Practice.* **71**(2), 177–183, (2006).

73. M. L. Wong, W. Lam, P. S. Leung, K. S. Ngan, and J. C. Y. Cheng. Discovering knowledge from medical databases using evolutionary algorithms, *IEEE Engineering in Medicine and Biology Magazine.* **19**(4), 45–55, (2000).

74. T. Ho and M. Basu. Complexity measures of supervised classification problems, *IEEE Trans. Pattern Analysis and Machine Intelligence.* **24**(3), 289–300 (March, 2002).

75. G. Taguchi and R. Jugulum. *The Mahalanobis-Taguchi Strategy.* (John Wiley & Sons, 2002).

76. A. Al-Ani, M. Deriche, and J. Chebil. A new mutual information based measure for feature selection, *Intelligent Data Analysis.* **7**(1), 43–57, (2003).

77. I. Kononenko. Estimating attributes: analysis and extensions of relief, *Machine Learning: ECML-94, Lecture Notes in Computer Science.* **784**, 171–182, (1994).

78. H. Liu and H. Mtotda. *Instance Selection and Construction for Data Mining.* (Kluwer Academic Publishers, 2001).

79. M. Barger and M. Bidgood-Wilson. Caring for a woman at high risk for type 2 diabetes, *J. Midwifery and Women's Health.* **51**(3), 222–226, (2006).

80. G. Taguchi, S. Chowdhury, and Y. Wu. *Taguchi's Quality Engineering Handbook.* (Wiley, 2005).

81. S. Kjos, R. Peters, A. Xiang, O. Henry, M. Montoro, and T. Buchanan. Predicting future diabetes in latino women with gestational diabetes, *Diabetes.* **44**, 586–591, (1995).

82. A. Hubert. Comparing partitions, *Journal of Classification.* **2**, 193–198, (1985).

83. P. Rousseeuw. Silhouettes: a graphical aid to the interpretation and validation of cluster analysis, *Journal of Computational and Applied Mathematics.* **20**, 53–65, (1987).

84. D. Levine. *A Parallel Genetic Algorithm for the Set Partitioning Problem.* PhD thesis, Illinois Institute of Technology, Mathematics and Computer Science Division, Argonne National Laboratory, Argonne, Illinois, USA (May, 1994).

85. A. Malhi and R. X. Gao. Pca-based feature selection scheme for machine defect classification, *IEEE Transactions on Instrumentation and Measurement.* **53**(6), 1517–1525, (2004).

86. H. Liu and H. Motoda. *Feature Selection for Knowledge Discovery and Data Mining.* (Kluwer Academic Publishers, Boston, USA, 1998).

87. B. Efron, T. Hastie, I. Johnstone, and R. Tibshirani. Least angle regression, *The Annals of Statistics.* **32**, 407–451, (2004).

88. R. Tibshirani. Regression shrinkage and selection via the lasso, *J. Royal Statistical Soc.* **58**(1), 267–288, (1996).

89. V. Vapnik. *Statistical Learning Theory.* (John Wiley and Sons, New York, NY, 1998).

90. L. Breiman, J. H. Friedman, R. A. Olshen, and C. J. Stone. Classification and regression trees, *Wadsworth International Group.* (1984).

91. E. Jantunen and K. Vähä-Pietilä. Simulation of faults in rotating machines. In *Proc. of the COMADEM 97*, Vol. 1, pp. 283–292, Helsinki, Finland, (1997).

92. K. Louisville, Q. Wu, P. Suetens, and O. A. Integration of heuristic and bayesian approaches in a pattern- classification system, *Knowledge Discovery in Databases.* pp. 249–260, (1991).

93. X. Li. Data reduction via adaptive sampling, *Comm. Information and Systems.* **2**(1), 53–68, (2002).

94. B. Metzger, N. Cho, S. Rston, and R. Radvany. Pregnancy weight and antepartum insulin secretion predict glucose tolerance five years after gestational diabetes mellitus, *Diabetes Care.* **16**, 1598–1605, (1993).

95. J. Handl and J. Knowles. Improvements to the scalability of multi-objective clustering. In *Proc. of the 2005 IEEE Congress on Evolutionary Computation*, pp. 2372–2379. IEEE Press, Anaheim, CA, (2005).

96. D. Hanisch, A. Zien, R. Zimmer, and T. Lengauer. Co-clustering of biological networks and gene expression data, *Bioinformatics.* **18**(90001), 145–154, (2002).

97. J. Handl and J. Knowles. Feature subset selection in unsupervised learning via multi-objective optimization, *International Journal on Computational Intelligence Research (to appear)*. (2006).

98. J. Pena, J. Lozana, and P. Larranaga. An empirical comparison of four initialization methods for the K-means algorithm, *Pattern Recognition Letters.* **20**(10), 1027–1040, (1999).

99. J. Horn. *The Nature of Niching: Genetic Algorithms and the Evolution of Optimal, Cooperative Populations*. PhD thesis, University of Illinois at Urbana Champaign, Urbana, Illinois, (1997).

100. C. Blake, E. Keogh, and C. J. Merz. Uci repository of machine learning databases, (1998).

101. M. Kirley and D. G. Green. An empirical investigation of optimization in dynamic environments using the cellular genetic algorithm. In eds. D. Whitley, D. Goldberg, E. Cant-Paz, L. Spector, I. Parmee, and H.-G. Beyer, *Proc. of the 2000 Genetic and Evolutionary Computation Conference (GECCO-2000)*, pp. 11–18, Las Vegas, Nevada, USA (July, 2000). Morgan Kaufmann Publishers, San Francisco, California, USA.

102. M. Vidal-Naquet and S. Ullman. Object recognition with informative features and linear classification, *ICCV,*. pp. 281–288, (2003).

103. C. Justin and R. Victor. Feature subset selection with a simulated annealing data mining algorithm, *J. Intelligent Information Systems.* **9**, 57–81, (1997).

104. R. Caruana and D. Freitag. Greedy attribute selection. In *Proc. of the Eleventh International Conference on Machine Learning*, pp. 28–36, (1994).

105. H. Vafaie and K. Jong. Genetic algorithms as a tool for restructuring feature space representations. In *Proc. of the Seventh International Conference on Tools with Artificial Intelligence*, Arlington, VA (November, 1995).

106. D. Goldberg. *Genetic Algorithms in Search Optimization and Machine Learning*. (Addison-Wesley, 1989).

107. L. Prechelt. Proben1 — a set of neural network benchmark problems and bench marking rules. Technical report 21/94, ftp://ftp.ira.uka.de/pub/neuron/proben1.tar.gz, (1994).

108. Y. H. Chang, B. Zheng, X. H. Wang, and W. F. Good. Computer-aided diagnosis of breast cancer using artificial neural networks: Comparison of back propagation and genetic algorithms. In *Proc. of International Joint Conference on Neural Networks*, Vol. 5, pp. 3674–3679, Washington, DC, USA, (1999).

109. K. J. Cios, W. Pedrycz, and R. Swiniarski. *I h f a Mining: Methods for Knowledge Discovery*. (AAA1 Press, Portland, OR, 1998).
110. I. H. Witten and E. Frank. *Data Mining-Practical Machine Learning Tools and Techniques with JAVA Implementations*. (Morgan Kaufmann, Los Altos, CA, 2005).
111. N. Vasconcelos and M. Vasconcelos. Scalable discriminant feature selection for image retrieval and recognition, *CVPR*. **2**, 770–775, (2004).
112. D. Michie, D. J. Spiegelhalter, and C. C. Taylor. *Machine Learning, Neural and Statistical Classification*. (Springer-Verlag, London: Ellis Horwood, 1994).
113. G. L. Pappa, A. A. Freitas, and C. A. A. Kaestner. A multi-objective genetic algorithm for attribute selection. In *Proc. of the Fourth International Conference on Recent Advances in Soft Computing (RASC-2002)*, pp. 116–121, (2002).
114. F. Peng, H. Long and C. Ding. Feature selection based on mutual information: criteria of max-dependency, max-relevance and min-redundancy, *IEEE Transactions on Pattern Analysis and Machine Intelligence*. **27**(8), 1226–1238, (2005).
115. K. Kira and L. Rendel. The feature selection problem: traditional methods and a new algorithm. In *Proc. of Tenth National Conference on Artificial Intelligence*, pp. 129–134, (1992).
116. Y. Su, V. Murali T. M. Pavlovic, M. Schaffer, and S. Kasif. Rank gene: identification of diagnostic genes based on expression data, *Bioinformatics*. **19**(12), 1578–1579, (2003).
117. E. Frank and I. H. Witten (1998). Generating accurate rule sets without global optimization. In *Proc. of Fifteenth International Conference Machine Learning (ICML'98)*, 144–151.
118. K. Shima, M. Todoriki, and A. Suzuki. SVM-based feature selection of latent semantic features. *Pattern Recognition Letters*. 2004, **25**(9): 1051–1057.

Chapter 9

OPTIMIZED POLYNOMIAL FUZZY SWARM NET FOR CLASSIFICATION

B. B. MISRA*, P. K. DASH[†] and G. PANDA[‡]

*Department of Information Technology,
Silicon Institute of Technology,
Bhubaneswar-751024, Orissa, India
bijanmisra@ieee.org

[†]Multidisciplinary Research Cell,
SOA University,
Bhubaneswar-751030, Orissa, India
pkdash_india@yahoo.com

[‡]School of Electrical Sciences,
Indian Institute of Technology,
Bhubaneswar, Orissa, India
ganapati.panda@gmail.com

This chapter presents a hybrid approach for solving classification problems. We have used three important neuro and evolutionary computing techniques such as Polynomial Neural Network, Fuzzy system, and Particle Swarm Optimization to design a classifier. The objective of designing such a classifier model is to overcome some of the drawbacks in the existing systems and to obtain a model that consumes less time in developing the classifier model, to give better classification accuracy, to select the optimal set of features required for designing the classifier and to discard less important and redundant features from consideration. Over and above the model remains comprehensive and easy to understand by the users.

9.1. Introduction

The classification task of data mining and knowledge discovery has received much attention in recent years and is growing very fast. In addition to classification task of data mining, there exist some more tasks like association rule mining, clustering, dependency modeling, etc., in data mining area. However, classification is a fundamental activity of data mining. Given predetermined disjoint target classes $C_1, C_2, \ldots, Cn$, a set of input features $F_1, F_2, .., F_m$ and a set of training data T with each instance taking the form $\langle a_1, a_2, \ldots, a_m \rangle$, where a_i $\langle i = 1, 2, \ldots, m \rangle$ is in the domain of attribute $A_i, i = 1, 2, \ldots, m$ and associated with a unique target class label the task is to build a model that can be used to predict the target category for new unseen data given its input attributes values.

There are many classifiers like statistical, linear discriminant, k-nearest neighbour, kernel, neural network, decision tree, and many more exist in the literature. But linear classifiers are of special interest, due to their simplicity and easy expansibility to non-linear classifiers. One of the most powerful classical methods of linear classifiers is the least mean squared error procedure with the Ho and Kashyap modification.[1] Two main disadvantages of this approach are:

(1) The use of the quadratic loss function, which leads to a non- robust method.
(2) The impossibility of minimizing the Vapnik-Chervonenkis (VC) dimension of the designed classifier.

The most important feature of the classifier is its generalization ability, which refers to producing a reasonable decision for data previously unseen during the process of classifier design (training). The easiest way to measure the generalization ability is to use a test set that contains data that do not belong to the training set. From statistical learning theory, we know that in order to achieve good generalization capability, we should select a classifier with the smallest VC dimension (complexity) and the smallest misclassification error on the training set. This principle is called the principle of Structural Risk Minimization (SRM).

In real life, noise and outliers may corrupt samples nominated for the training set. Hence the design of the classifier methods needs to be robust. According to Huber,[2] a robust method should have the following properties:

(1) Reasonably good accuracy at the assumed model.
(2) Small deviations from the model assumptions should impair the performance only by a small amount.
(3) Larger deviations from the model assumptions should not cause a catastrophe.

Many robust loss functions are discussed in Ref. 2. In this work the absolute error loss function is taken due to its simplicity.

The paper by Bellman *et al.*[3] was the starting point in the application of fuzzy set theory to pattern classification. Since then, researchers have found several ways to apply this theory to generalize the existing pattern classification methods, as well as to develop new algorithms. There are two main categories of fuzzy classifiers: fuzzy if-then rule-based and non if-then rule fuzzy classifiers. The second group may be divided into fuzzy k-nearest neighbors and generalized nearest prototype classifiers (GNPC). Several approaches have been proposed for automatically generating fuzzy if-then rules and tuning parameters of membership functions for numerical data. These methods fall into three categories: neural-network-based methods with high learning abilities, genetic (evolution)-based methods with the Michigan and Pittsburg approaches, and clustering-based methods. There are several methods that combine the above enumerated categories that have proved effective in improving classification performance.[4] Recently, a new direction in the fuzzy classifier design field has emerged: a combination of multiple classifiers using fuzzy sets,[5] which may be included into the non if-then fuzzy classifier category. In general, there are two types of the combination: classifier selection and classifier fusion. In the first approach each classifier is an expert in some local area of the feature space. In the second approach all classifiers are trained over the whole feature space. Thus, in this case, we have competition, rather than complementing, among the fuzzy classifiers. Various methods have been proposed for fuzzy classifier design; however, in contrast to statistical and neural pattern classifiers, both theoretical and experimental studies concerning fuzzy classifiers do not deal with the analysis of the influence of the classifier complexity on the generalization error.

Feature selection happens to be an intrinsic part of most of the classification methods. The task of feature selection is handled normally in two different ways. The features are selected prior to use of the classification technique or the feature selection is a part of the classification method. In this chapter we will discuss a technique called Polynomial Neural Network (PNN)[6] which requires no separate attention for features selection, rather it selects the optimal set of features required for the model on the fly.

In this Chapter we have discussed the fuzzy swarm net,[7] which is trained by the particle swarm optimization (PSO) technique. The fuzzy swarm net contains a single layer perceptron. The input data is converted to the fuzzy membership functions. These membership functions are multiplied with the weights and fed to the perceptron. A set of such nets is considered as a swarm and the mean square error (MSE) of each net is considered for training the nets using PSO.

Further this discussion has been extended by incorporating Polynomial Neural Network (PNN) to the fuzzy swarm net architecture to design the architectures for Optimal Polynomial Fuzzy Swarm Net (OPFSN).[8] To design this model at the first step different combinations of the set of input features are taken to generate linear/quadratic/cubic polynomials called Partial Descriptions (PDs). Least Square Estimation (LSE) technique is used to determine the coefficients of these PDs. The outputs of these PDs are considered as the input to the fuzzy swarm net model to design the classifier.

This chapter is organized as follows. In Sec. 9.2 the fuzzy net architecture is briefly discussed. Section 9.3 discusses the basics of particle swarm optimization. Section 9.4 describes the fuzzy swarm net (FSN) classifier design. The basic concept of PNN has been discussed in Sec. 9.5. Design of classifier with Optimized Polynomial Fuzzy Swarm Net (OPFSN) has been covered in Secs. 9.6. and 9.7 illustrates the experimental studies with fuzzy swarm net and OPFSN models. We have concluded this chapter with Sec. 9.8.

9.2. Fuzzy Net Architecture

The Multilayer Perceptron (MLP) architecture is used widely for many practical applications, but it possesses certain drawbacks. A uniform or standard model does not exist which will suit any type of application. For each application a different model needs to be designed i.e., the user should understand the complexity of the problem thoroughly and should decide the number of hidden layers and the number of hidden nodes in each layer to be taken. Understanding the complexity of a problem is not an easy job for a new user, even an experienced user may face difficulties in making correct decision about the architecture design. Therefore very often the user opts for a trial and error method to decide the MLP architecture. But it is also not viable to explore all possible designs from the vast search space to find the best one. As a result instead of searching for the best one we compromise with an architecture that is acceptable.

The user very often remains in search of a net that is free from such complexities and time consuming efforts. As an alternative approach certain flat nets are suggested such as Functional Link Artificial Neural Network

(FLANN), Fuzzy Net, etc. Such network does not possess any hidden layer and thereby completely overcomes the difficulties of deciding the number of hidden layers and the number of hidden nodes in case of MLP architecture. These flat nets normally use a single perceptron as its output layer which makes the training process very simple and less cumbersome.

Functional link Artificial neural network (FLANN) originally proposed by Pao[9] is a novel single-layer neural network capable of forming arbitrarily complex decision regions. FLANN was developed as an alternative architecture to the well-known multilayer perceptron network with application to function approximation, pattern recognition and nonlinear channel equalization.[9-24] As a computationally efficient single-layer neural network, the FLANN's nonlinearity is introduced by the functional expansion of the input pattern by linear, polynomial, trigonometric, hyperbolic, Chebyshev orthogonal polynomial, Legendre, power series and others. The main advantage of the FLANN is a reduced computational burden by increasing the dimensionality of the input signal space with a set of linearly independent nonlinear functions. These FLANN-based nonlinear networks offer better performance in terms of the MSE level, convergence rate and computational complexity over many networks such as the MLP network, the RBF network and the polynomial perceptron network (PPN).

The objective of using Fuzzy net is not only to overcome the hazards in MLP but much more. Using fuzzy set theory it is easy to model the 'fuzzy' boundaries of linguistic terms by introducing gradual memberships. In contrast to classical set theory, in which an object or a case either is a member of a given set or not, fuzzy set theory makes it possible that an object or a case belongs to a set only to a certain degree.[25] Interpretations of membership degrees include similarity, preference, and uncertainty.[26] They can state how similar an object or case is to a prototypical one, they can indicate preferences between sub optimal solutions to a problem, or they can model uncertainty about the true situation, if this situation is described in imprecise terms. In general, due to their closeness to human reasoning, solutions obtained using fuzzy approaches are easy to understand and to apply. Due to these strengths, fuzzy systems are the method of choice, if linguistic, vague, or imprecise information has to be modeled.[27]

Neural networks and fuzzy systems have established their reputation as alternative approaches to information processing. Both have certain advantages over classical methods, especially when vague data or prior knowledge is involved. However, their applicability suffered from several weaknesses of the individual models. Therefore, combinations of neural networks with fuzzy systems have been proposed, where both models complement each other. These so-called fuzzy net systems allow overcoming some of the individual weaknesses and offering some appealing features.

The basic idea of combining fuzzy systems and neural networks is to design an architecture that uses a fuzzy system to represent knowledge in an interpretable manner and the learning ability of a neural network to optimize its parameters. The drawbacks of both of the individual approaches — the black box behavior of neural networks, and the problems of finding suitable membership values for fuzzy systems — could thus be avoided. A combination can constitute an interpretable model that is capable of learning and can use problem-specific prior knowledge.[28-30]

A neuro fuzzy system[31-37] is based on a fuzzy system which is trained by a learning algorithm derived from neural network theory. The (heuristical) learning procedure operates on local information, and causes only local modifications in the underlying fuzzy system.

A fuzzy net system can be viewed as a 3-layer feedforward neural network. The first layer represents input variables, the middle (hidden) layer represents fuzzy rules and the third layer represents output variables. Fuzzy sets are encoded as (fuzzy) connection weights. It is not necessary to represent a fuzzy system like this to apply a learning algorithm to it. However, it can be convenient, because it represents the data flow of input processing and learning within the model.

A fuzzy net can be interpreted as a system of fuzzy rules. It is also possible to create the system out of training data from scratch, as it is possible to initialize it by prior knowledge in form of fuzzy rules.

A fuzzy net system approximates an n-dimensional (unknown) function that is partially defined by the training data. The fuzzy rules encoded within the system represent vague samples, and can be viewed as prototypes of the training data. A fuzzy net should not be seen as a kind of (fuzzy) expert system, and it has nothing to do with fuzzy logic in the narrow sense.

The architecture of fuzzy net model uses a single perceptron.[38] The input vector is expanded into different membership functions. The expansion input vectors effectively increases the dimensionality of the input vector and hence the hyper planes generated by the fuzzy net[39-41] provides greater discrimination capability in the input pattern space.

Let us discuss an example of designing a fuzzy net architecture. Figure 1 shows the architecture of this example of the fuzzy net. Each unit in the

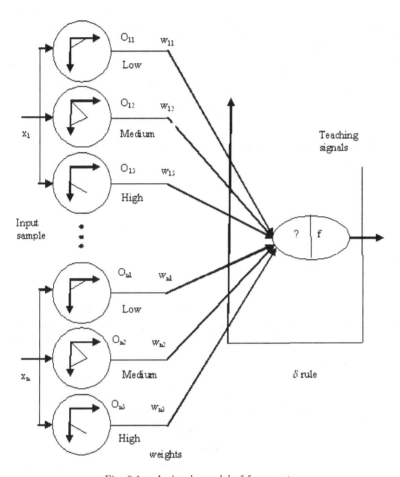

Fig. 9.1. A simple model of fuzzy net.

input layer has a triangular Gaussian membership function as its inner function, given by:

$$O_{i,1}(x_i, sm_i, th_i) = e^{-\frac{1}{2}\left(\frac{x_i - sm_i}{th_i}^2\right)} \tag{9.1}$$

$$O_{i,2}(x_i, me_i, th_i) = e^{-\frac{1}{2}\left(\frac{x_i - me_i}{th_i}^2\right)} \tag{9.2}$$

$$O_{i,3}(x_i, bg_i, th_i) = e^{-\frac{1}{2}\left(\frac{x_i - bg_i}{th_i}^2\right)} \tag{9.3}$$

where x_i is the ith input feature, sm_i is the low value of the ith input feature, bg_i is the high value of the ith input feature, me_i is the medium value of the ith input feature and th_i is taken as $(bg_i - sm_i)/3$. Each input data is the input of these membership functions (low, medium, high) and the outputs of the units $O_{i,j}$ ($i = 1 - n, j = 1, 2, 3$) are the grades of the membership functions. The inputs of the unit in the output layer are $w_{i,j}O_{i,j}$. The output unit has a sigmoid function f given by:

$$o = F(s) = \frac{1}{1 + e^{-s}} \tag{9.4}$$

where s is the sum of the inputs of the output unit i.e.:

$$s = \sum_{i=1}^{N} \sum_{j=1}^{3} O_{i,j} W_{i,j} \tag{9.5}$$

o is the output of this network. The connection weights $w_{i,j}$ are modified by the δ rule.

9.3. Particle Swarm Optimization

The particle swarm algorithm is an optimization technique inspired by the metaphor of social interaction observed among insects or animals. The kind of social interaction modeled within a PSO is used to guide a population of individuals (called particles) moving towards the most promising area of the search space.[42-47] PSO was developed and first introduced as a stochastic optimization algorithm by Eberhart and Kennedy.[48] During this period, PSO gained increasing popularity due to its effectiveness in performing difficult optimization tasks. Among other applications, it has been applied to tackle multi-objective problems,[49] minimax problems,[50,51] integer programming problems,[52] noisy and continuously changing environments,[53-55] errors-in-variables problems,[56] existence of function zeros,[57] power systems[58-64] parameter learning of neural networks (NNs),[65,66] control,[67-70] prediction,[71-73] modeling[74-76] and numerous engineering applications.[77-88]

    In a PSO algorithm, each particle is a candidate solution equivalent to a point in a d-dimensional space, so the ith particle can be represented as $x_i = (x_{i,1}, x_{i,2}, \ldots, x_{i,d})$. Each particle "flies" through the search space, depending on two important factors, $p_i = (p_{i,1}, p_{i,2}, \ldots, p_{i,d})$, the best position found so far by the current particle and $p_g = (p_{g1}, p_{g2}, \ldots, p_{gd})$, the global best position identified from the entire population (or within a neighborhood).[44]

The rate of position change of the ith particle is given by its velocity $v_i = (v_{i,1}, v_{i,2}, \ldots, v_{i,d})$. Equation (9.6) updates the velocity for each particle in the next iteration step, whereas Equation (9.7) updates each particle's position in the search space:[89]

$$v_{i,d}(t) = \tau(v_{i,d}(t-1) + \phi_1(p_{i,d} - x_{i,d}(t-1)) + \phi_2(p_{gd} - x_{i,d}(t-1))) \qquad (9.6)$$

$$x_{i,d}(t) = x_{i,d}(t-1) + v_{i,d}(t) \qquad (9.7)$$

where:

$$\tau = \frac{2}{(|2 - \phi - \sqrt{\phi^2 - 4\phi}|)}, \quad \phi = \phi_1 + \phi_2, \quad \phi > 4.0 \qquad (9.8)$$

τ is referred to as the constriction coefficient.

Two common approaches of choosing p_g are known as gbest and lbest methods. In the gbest approach, the position of each particle in the search space is influenced by the best-fit particle in the entire population; whereas the lbest approach only allows each particle to be influenced by a fitter particle chosen from its neighborhood. Kennedy and Mendes studied PSOs with various population topologies,[90] and have shown that certain population structures could give superior performance over certain optimization functions.

Further, the role of the inertia weight ϕ, in Equation (9.8), is considered critical for the PSO's convergence behaviour. Improved performance can be achieved through the application of an inertia weight applied to the previous velocity:

$$v_{i,d}(t) = \phi v_{i,d}(t-1) + \phi_1(p_{i,d} - x_{i,d}(t-1)) + \phi_2(p_{gd} - x_{i,d}(t-1)) \qquad (9.9)$$

The inertia weight is employed to control the impact of the previous history of velocities on the current one. Accordingly, the parameter ϕ regulates the trade-off between the global (wide-ranging) and local (nearby) exploration abilities of the swarm. A large inertia weight facilitates global exploration (searching new areas), while a small one tends to facilitate local exploration, i.e., fine-tuning the current search area. A suitable value for the inertia weight ϕ usually provides balance between global and local exploration abilities and consequently results in a reduction of the number of iterations required to locate the optimum solution. Initially, the inertia weight was constant. However, experimental results indicated that it is better to initially set the inertia to a large value, in order to promote global exploration of the search space, and gradually decrease it to get more refined solutions. Thus, an initial value around 1.2 and a gradual decline towards 0 can be considered as a good choice for ϕ.

During the last decade the basic PSO algorithm has been modified and new concepts have been introduced to it. Few of them improvise the general performance, and the rest improved performance of particular kinds of problems.

9.3.1. Fully informed particle swarm (FIPS)

In the basic PSO algorithm information pertaining to personal best and neighborhood best are the two main sources which influence the performance of the algorithm, whereas we ignore the information available with the remaining neighbors. How the particles should interact with its neighbors has been suggested by Mendes.[90-92] In FIPS, the particle is affected by all its neighbors and at times the personal best value does not influence the velocity for the next iteration. FIPS can be depicted as follows:

$$v_i = \chi \left(v_i + \frac{1}{K_i} \sum_{n=1}^{K_i} U(0, \phi) * (P_{nbr_n} - x_i) \right), \qquad (9.10)$$

$$x_i = x_i + v_i \qquad (9.11)$$

where K_i is the number of neighbors in the ith particle, and nbr_n is the nth neighbor of ith particle. FIPS may find better solutions in less iteration with appropriate parameter setting, but it is dependent on the population topology.

9.3.2. Binary particle swarms

Kennedy and Eberhart[93] presented a method that operates on bit-strings rather than real numbers. In this method the velocity is used as a probability threshold which determines whether x_{id} should be evaluated as a zero or a one. A logistic function is operated on x_{id} to obtain the value:

$$s(x_{i,d}) = \frac{1}{1 + e^{-x_{i,d}}} \qquad (9.12)$$

A random number r is generated for each bit and compared it to $s(x_{i,d})$. If r was less that the threshold, then $x_{i,d}$ was interpreted as 1, otherwise as 0.

Agrafiotis and Cedeno[78] performed feature selection in pattern matching task by using the particle locations as probabilities to select features. Basing on the location value of the particle each feature was assigned a slice of a roulette wheel. Depending on the selection of feature, the values are discretized to 0, 1.

Mohan and Al-Kazemi[94] suggested different methods for implementing particle swarm on binary space. They have suggested a method called "regulated discrete particle swarm," which performs well on a test problem.

In Pampara *et al.*[95] encoded each particle with small number of coefficients of a trigonometric model (angle modulation) which was then run to generate bit strings.

Clerc[96,97]: Moraglio *et al.*[98] have extending PSO to more complex combinatorial search spaces and observed some progress. However it is difficult to predict if PSO will be a better choice for such combinatorial search spaces.

9.3.3. *Hybrids and adaptive particle swarms*

Different researchers have tried to utilize the information from the environment for fine tuning the PSO parameters. Evolutionary computation and other techniques have been followed for the purpose.

Angeline[42] hybridized particle swarms in his model. He applied selection to the particles, then the "good" particles were reproduced and mutated, but the "bad" particles were eliminated. He obtained improved results with this modification.

Evolutionary strategies concept was used by Miranda and Fonseca[92] to improve the performance of PSO. They modified the particle values by adding random values distributed around a mean of zero; the variance of the distribution is evolved along with function parameters. They used Gaussian random values to perturb χ, ϕ_1, and ϕ_2, as well as the position of the neighborhood best, but not the individual best by using selection to adapt the variance. The evolutionary self-adapting particle swarm optimization method has shown excellent performance in comparison to some standard particle swarm methods. They have used it for the manufacture of optical filters and for optimization of power systems.

Breeding technique from genetic algorithm was used by Loovbjerg et al.[99] Few particles were selected and they were paired randomly. Weighted arithmetic average was used to calculate both positions and velocities from the parameters of the selected particles. To increase the diversity they divided the particle swarm into subpopulations.

Wei et al.,[100] embedded velocity information in an evolutionary algorithm. They replaced mutation with PSO velocity update technique in a fast evolutionary programming (FEP) algorithm. Their obtained results indicate that the approach is successful on a range of functions.

Krink and Loovbjerg[101] proposed a self-adaptive method where they gave option to an individual to choose one among genetic algorithm, particle swarm, or hill-climbing. An individual is allowed for this change, if it does not improve after 50 iterations.

Poli and Stephens[102] hybridized PSO with hill-climbing technique, where they have considered the particles to be sliding on a fitness landscape. They have avoided the use of particle memory and thereby overcoming the book-keeping task required for preserving the personal best values. However they have used the mass and force to guide the exploration in the fitness landscape.

Clerc[97] used adaptation of the constriction factor, population size, and number of neighbors. He obtained best performance when all three of these factors were adapted. Clerc worked with three rules:

(1) *Suicide and generation*: a particle kills itself when it is the worst and produces a clone when it is the best;
(2) *Modifying the coefficient*: increase the constriction coefficient with good local improvement otherwise decrease;
(3) *Change in neighborhood*: reduce the number of neighbors for the locally best particle and increase for poorly performing particles.

However Clerc did not performed the adaptive changes during the entire period of simulation rather allowed the adaption occasionally.

Vesterstroom et al.[103] used the idea of division of labor from insect swarm algorithms. When no improvement is noticed on the performance of a particle it was allowed for local search at the global best position of the population. However this particle was provided with a new random velocity vector. The division of labor modification performed well on unimodal problems but not on multimodal functions no significant improvement observed.

Holden and Freitas[104] proposed hybridization of PSO and ACO algorithms for hierarchical classification. They applied it to the functional classification of enzymes and obtained very promising results.

PSO was combined with differential evolution (DE) by Hendtlass.[105] He obtained mixed results for this hybridization. On one multimodal problem the hybridized algorithm performed better than PSO or DE. But PSO was found to be faster and robust than DE and hybrid models. Subsequently Zhang and Xie[106] used hybridization of PSO and DE and reported to obtain better results.

Poli *et al.*[107,108] proposed hybridization of PSO with genetic programming (GP). For the control of the particle movement GP was used to evolve new laws. This method provided better result than standard PSO methods.

9.3.4. *PSOs with diversity control*

It has been reported by different researchers that the swarm has a tendency of converging prematurely to local optima. Different approaches have been suggested to overcome the premature convergence as the swarm concentrates on a single optimum.

To help the PSO to attain more diversity and became less vulnerable to local minima, Loovbjerg[109] proposed critically self organized PSO. In his method if two particles became close to one another, a variable called the "critical value" is incremented. When the variable reaches the criticality threshold, one of the particles is allowed to relocate itself.

Some researchers have tried to diversify the particles' clustering too closely in one region of the search space. Blackwell and Bentley[110] suggested a method called the collision-avoiding swarms which achieves diversity by reducing the attraction of the swarm center.

The "spatially extended" particles were proposed by Krink *et al.*,[111] where each particle was considered to be surrounded by a sphere of some radius and if such a particle collides with another particle, it bounces off.

A negative entropy value is added to the particle swarm by Xie *et al.*[112] to discourage excessively rapid convergence towards a poor quality local optimum. Considering different conditions they have weighed the velocity, location of a particle with some random value to obtain dissipative particle swarm.

9.3.5. *Bare-bones PSO*

Kennedy[113] has proposed bare-bones PSO with an objective to move the particles according to its probability distribution rather than by addition of velocity. In other words bare-bones PSO can be termed as velocity-free PSO. Bare-bones PSO throw light on the relative importance of particle motion and the neighborhood topology. The particle update rule was replaced with a Gaussian distribution of mean $(p_i + p_g)/2$ and standard deviation $|p_i - p_g|$. This empirical distribution resembled a bell curve centred at $(p_i + p_g)/2$. This method works as well as the PSO on some problems, but less effective on other problems (Richer and Blackwell).[114]

Richer and Blackwell[114] have replaced the Gaussian distribution on bare-bones with a Levy distribution. The Levy distribution is bell-shaped like the Gaussian but with fatter tails. The Levy has a tunable parameter, α, which interpolates between the Cauchy distribution ($\alpha = 1$) and Gaussian ($\alpha = 2$). This parameter can be used to control the fatness of the tails. In a series of trials, Richer and Blackwell found that Levy bare-bones at $\alpha = 1.4$ reproduces canonical PSO behavior, a result which supports the above conjecture. Levy spring constants PSO produced excellent results (Richer and Blackwell[114]). The explanation might lie at the tails again, where large spring constants induce big accelerations and move particles away from local optima.

9.4. Fuzzy Swarm Net Classifier

To implement the fuzzy net with swarm intelligence, initially we take a set of fuzzy nets. Each net is treated as a particle and the set of fuzzy nets are treated as swarm. Each net shares the same memory in a distributed environment.[7]

At any instance of time all the nets are supplied with one input record and the respective target. All the nets in the distributed environment are initialized to random weights w_{ij} in the range [0, 1].

Let us consider that the input-output data are given by:

$$(X_i, y_i) = (x_{1,i}, x_{2,i}, \ldots, x_{n,i}, y_i),$$

where $i = 1, 2, \ldots, N$. The input-output relationship of the above data can be described in the following manner:

$$y = f(x_1, x_2, \ldots, x_N)$$

The estimated output O produced by the nets in the distributed environment can be represented as:

$$O = f(x_1, x_2, \ldots, x_N) = \frac{1}{1 + e(-s)}$$

where $s = \sum_{i=1}^{N} \sum_{j=1}^{3} O_{i,j} W_{i,j}$

Fuzzy Swarm Net architecture has been illustrated with the help of Figs. 9.2 and 9.3. Figure 9.2 represents the block diagram of the net, where $x_1, \ldots, x_n$ are the input features to the net and the fuzzy membership values of the ith input feature L_i: Low, M_i: Medium, H_i: High, are generated by the net in the 2nd layer of the FSN model. This block diagram has been considered as a component in Fig. 9.3 for presenting the FSN model.

Figure 9.3 illustrates the architecture of the FSN model. FSN trains the model taking two inputs i.e. $\overline{X}$: input vector, and $\overline{T}$: target vector. At the beginning the values $\overline{w}$: position of vector and $\overline{v}$: velocity vector are randomly initialized from the domain $[0, 1]$. After each iteration the values $\overline{w}, \overline{v}, \overline{p}$ (personal best), $\overline{p}_g$ (global best) are updated basing on e the error term associated with each particle.

We calculate the error for all the nets in the distributed environment after each iteration. The net giving minimum error is treated as the leader or gbest among all the nets. The nets also preserve the best value achieved by the respective nets during all the iterations in their local memory, which

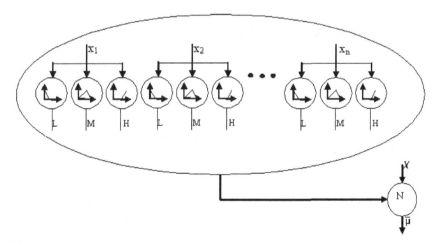

Fig. 9.2. Block diagram of the net.

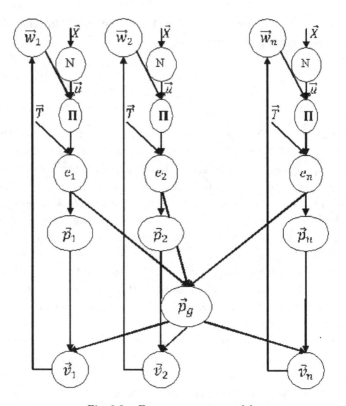

Fig. 9.3.   Fuzzy swarm net model.

is treated as the personal best or pbest of it. Each net uses both gbest and pbest values to update its weights for the next iteration as follows:

$$v_{k,d}(t) = \tau(v_{k,d}(t-1) + \phi_1(p_{k,d} - x_{k,d}(t-1)) + \phi_2(p_{gd} - x_{k,d}(t-1)))$$
$$x_{k,d}(t) = x_{k,d}(t-1) + v_{k,d}(t)$$

where k is the swarm size, $d = i * j$, $w_{i,j}$ obtains its value from $x_{k,d}$.

The stopping criterion may be allowing the nets to iterate till they converge to a single decision. However in this process, the nets get over trained leading to poor performance of the classifier. From different simulations of a dataset, a suitable range of iteration can be fixed for it. Different dataset require different range of iterations, one range may not be suitable for all the datasets. The following high-level pseudocode gives more insight view of the proposed model.

Pseudocode

(1) *Determine system's input variables.*
(2) *Form training and testing data.*
(3) *Initialize the weights to the nets in the swarm.*
(4) *Calculate the output of the nets and determine their error.*
(5) *Update gbest and pbest if required.*
(6) *If stopping criterion not met go to Step 4.*

9.5. Polynomial Neural Network

Group Methods of Data Handling (GMDH) is the realization of inductive approach for mathematical modeling of complex systems.[115,116] It belongs to the category of self-organization data driven approaches. With small data samples, GMDH is capable of optimizing structures of models objectively.[117]

The relationship between input-output variables can be approximated by Volterra functional series, the discrete form of which is Kolmogorov-Gabor Polynomial:[118]

$$y = c_0 + \sum_{k_1} c_{k_1} x_{k_1} + \sum_{k_1 k_2} c_{k_1 k_2} x_{k_1} x_{k_2} + \sum_{k_1 k_2 k_3} c_{k_1 k_2 k_3} x_{k_1} x_{k_2} x_{k_3} + \cdots \tag{9.13}$$

where c_k denotes the coefficients or weights of the Kolmogorov-Gabor polynomial and x vector is the input vector. This polynomial can approximate any stationary random sequence of observations and it can be solved by either adaptive methods or by Gaussian equations.[119] This polynomial is not computationally suitable if the number of input variables increase and there are missing observations in input dataset. Also it takes more computation time to solve all necessary normal equations when the input variables are large.

A new algorithm called GMDH is developed by Ivakhnenko[118,120,121] which is a form of Kolmogorov-Gabor polynomial. He proved that a second order polynomial i.e.:

$$y = a_0 + a_1 x_i + a_2 x_j + a_3 x_i x_j + a_4 x_i^2 + a_5 x_j^2 \tag{9.14}$$

which takes only two input variables at a time and can reconstruct the complete Kolmogorov-Gabor polynomial through an iterative procedure. The GMDH method belongs to the category of heuristic self-organization methods, where the approaches like black-box concepts, connectionism and induction concepts can be applied.[120] The black-box method is a principal approach to analyze systems on the basis of input-output samples. And the method of connection and induction can be thought of as representation of complex functions through network of elementary functions. Thus the GMDH algorithm has the ability to trace all input-output relationship through an entire system that is too complex. The GMDH-type Polynomial Neural Networks are multilayered model consisting of the neurons/active units/Partial Descriptions (PDs) whose transfer function is a short-term polynomial described in equation (9.11). At the first layer $L = 1$, an algorithm, using all possible combinations by two from m inputs variables, generates the first population of PDs. Total number of PDs in first layer is $n = m(m - 1)/2$.

The outputs of each PDs in layer $L = 1$ is computed by applying the Equation (9.11). Let the outputs of first layer be denoted as $y_1^1, y_2^1, \ldots, y_n^1$. The vector of coefficients of the PDs are determined by least square estimation approach.

The architecture of a PNN[122,123] with four input features is shown in Fig. 9.4. The input and output relationship of the above data by PNN algorithm can be described in the following manner:

$$y = f(x_1, x_2, \ldots, x_m),$$

where m is the number of features in the dataset.

This process is repeated till error decreases. Overall framework of the design procedure[6,115,124–128] of the GMDH-type PNN comes as a sequence of the following steps:

(1) *Determine system's input variables.*
(2) *Form training and testing data.*

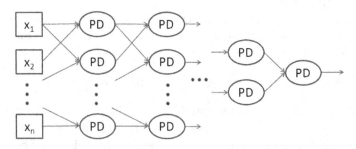

Fig. 9.4.   Basic PNN model

(3) *Choose a structure of the PNN.*
(4) *Determine the number of input variables and the order of the polynomial forming a partial description (PD) of data.*
(5) *Estimate the coefficients of the PD.*
(6) *Select PDs with the best classification accuracy.*
(7) *Check the stopping criterion.*
(8) *Determine new input variables for the next layer.*

The layers of PNN model grows as per the algorithm described above. The residual error between the estimated output and the actual output is calculated at each layer. If the error level is within the tolerable limit then the growth of the model is stopped and the final model is derived taking into account only those PDs that contribute to obtain the best result. Otherwise the next layer is grown. It is observed that the error level decreases rapidly at the first layers of PNN network and relatively slower near to optimal number of layers, and further increasing the number of layers causes increasing the value of error level because of over-fitting.[129–131] Thus during simulation the number of layers in the model increases one-by-one until the stopping rule, i.e., the tolerable error level is met at the layer r. Subsequently we take a desired PNN model of nearly optimal complexity from rth layer. Hence we preserve only those PDs that contribute to the better result. From the simulation it is seen that the output of best two PDs of previous layer not necessarily yields the best result in the next layer. Hence, a substantial number of PDs that give above average result in a layer are preserved for building the next layer. In turn, complexity of the system grows in terms of time for building a model and the computer memory required to preserve the system status at each layer of the network. A number of different techniques have been suggested[132–134] to handle such a situation without compromising the efficiency of the system.

9.6. Classification with Optimized Polynomial Neural Fuzzy Swarm Net

The Optimized Polynomial Fuzzy Swarm Net (OPFSN) model[8] is built in different steps. In the first step we use the PNN algorithm to construct the PDs for the first layer. If the number of features in the dataset is not too large, we consider all the PDs for the subsequent steps, otherwise we select a subset of PDs using one of the different pruning techniques.

At the second step of execution we obtain the fuzzy membership values for input feature. In general the output of the PDs in the first step becomes the input to the second step. But for a better generalization we can use the input features of the dataset along with the output of the PDs as the input to the second step.

The membership values, along with the PDs and the original input features of the dataset are jointly considered as input to the net consisting of a single unit of perceptron. At this stage we use the concept of swarm intelligence for two different purposes. Each particle of the swarm is treated as a net and the input to each particle is different. The particles compete among themselves to find the optimal subset of input to the third step. Along with determining the optimal subset of input the particles also optimize the weights associated with the net and for the bias. The OPFSN architecture is shown in Fig. 9.5. The error associated with each particle i.e., the error by selecting a subset of inputs and choosing a set of weight for the net in the distributed environment is calculated for each iteration. The net giving minimum error is treated as the leader or gbest among all the nets. The nets also preserve their respective best value achieved till the current iteration in their local memory, which is treated as the personal best or pbest of it. Each net uses both gbest and pbest values to update its weights for the next iteration as follows:

$$v_{k,d}(t) = \tau(v_{k,d}(t-1) + \phi_1(p_{k,d} - x_{k,d}(t-1)) + \phi_2(p_{g,d} - x_{k,d}(t-1)))$$
$$x_{k,d}(t) = x_{k,d}(t-1) + v_{k,d}(t)$$

where k is the swarm size, $d = i*j$, $w_{i,j}$ obtains its value from $x_{k,d}$. In general the stopping criterion is to allow the nets to iterate till they converge to a single decision. But for this net such a stopping criterion should not be used. For example let us consider there are m number of features in the dataset and let $k = m(m-1)/2$ be the number of PDs generated by the PNN algorithm for its first layer. Then the number of input to the fuzzy triangular membership system is $(m+k)$ and the number of fuzzy membership values generated are $3(m+k)$. We consider m features, k PDs and $3(m+k)$ membership values as the input to the net i.e., the total number of inputs to the net is say $z = 4(m+k)$. The representation of a particle for the swarm intelligence used in OPFSN model is shown at Fig. 9.6.

Basing on the selection of the binary bits, the weights are considered for evaluation of the respective nets. A large number of real valued weights

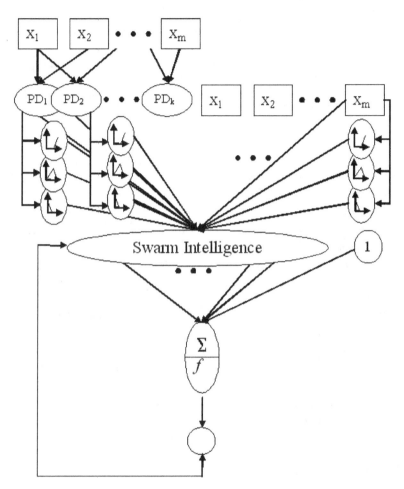

Fig. 9.5. Optimized polynomial fuzzy swarm net architecture.

remains part of the particle representation which does not takes part in the competition. Such weights will never converge to the same value or even nearby values as they are not part of the competition.

It is difficult to form a single rule which will hold good for different types of dataset. From different simulations of a dataset, a suitable range of iteration can be fixed for it. Different datasets require different range of iterations, one range may not be suitable for all the datasets. The following high-level pseudocode gives more insight to the OPFSN model.

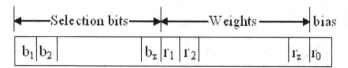

Fig. 9.6. Representation of a particle of the OPFSN model, b_i represents the binary selection bits and r_i represents the real values of the weights on the links and r_0 for the bias value.

Pseudocode

(1) *Determine system's input variables.*
(2) *Form training and testing data.*
(3) *Choose a structure of the PNN.*
(4) *Determine the number of input variables and the order of the polynomial forming the PDs.*
(5) *Estimate the coefficients of the PD taking 2/3rd of training set.*
(6) *Select PDs with the best classification accuracy using rest 1/3rd of training set.*
(7) *Generate fuzzy membership values taking output of PDs and features of training set.*
(8) *Initialize the weights to the nets in the swarm.*
(9) *Calculate the output of the nets and determine their error.*
(10) *Update gbest and pbest if required.*
(11) *If stopping criterion not met, estimate the new particle position and go to step 9.*

9.7. Experimental Studies

In this Section the performance of the FSN model is evaluated using the real world benchmark classification databases. The most frequently used in the area of neural networks and of neuro fuzzy systems are IRIS, WINE, PIMA, and BUPA Liver Disorders. All these databases are taken from the UCI machine repository.[135]

9.7.1. Description of the datasets

Let us briefly discuss the datasets, which we have taken for our experimental setup.

IRIS Plants Database: This dataset consists of $d = 4$ numerical attributes describing the length and width of sepal and petal of iris plant and $c = 3$ classes. There are $n = 150$ instances. These data relates to the classification of iris plants.

WINE recognition data: The dataset consists of $d = 13$ numerical attributes and $c = 3$ classes. There are $n = 178$ instances. These data are the results of a chemical analysis of wines grown in the same region in Italy but derived from three different cultivars.

PIMA Indians Diabetes Database: This dataset consists of $d = 8$ numerical medical attributes and $c = 2$ classes (tested positive or negative for diabetes). There are $n = 768$ instances. Further, data set related to the diagnosis of diabetes in an Indian population that lives near the city of Phoenix, Arizona.

BUPA Liver Disorders: data set related to the diagnosis of liver disorders and created by BUPA Medical Research, Ltd. The dataset consists of $d = 5$ attributes and $c = 2$ number of classes. There are $n = 345$ number of instances.

Table 9.1 presents a summary of the main features of each database that has been used in this study.

The dataset is divided into two parts. For the division of datasets, initially samples are segregated to respective classes. Randomly two samples are picked up from a class and added one to each sets. In the case of an odd number of samples, the last sample is added randomly to one of the sets or the set containing less number of samples. After distribution of all the samples between two sets, the position of samples in the dataset is shuffled. The division of datasets and its class distribution is shown in Table 9.2.

One set is used for building the model and the other part is used for testing the model. The protocol of parameters used for our simulation studies is given in Table 9.3.

The average correct classification level obtained by the OPFSN is presented in Table 9.4 for the training and testing phases. Average values of

Table 9.1. Description of datasets used.

Dataset	Patterns	Attributes	Classes	Patterns in Class 1	Patterns in Class 2	Patterns in Class 3
IRIS	150	4	3	50	50	50
WINE	178	13	3	59	71	48
PIMA	768	8	2	268	500	—
BUPA	345	6	2	145	200	—

Table 9.2.   Division of dataset and its pattern distribution.

Dataset	Patterns	Patterns in Class 1	Patterns in Class 2	Patterns in Class 3
IRIS				
Set1	75	25	25	25
Set2	75	25	25	25
WINE				
Set1	89	29	36	24
Set2	89	30	35	24
PIMA				
Set1	384	134	250	—
Set2	384	134	250	—
BUPA				
Set1	172	72	100	—
Set2	173	73	100	—

Table 9.3.   Parameters considered for simulation of OPFSN model.

Parameters	Values
Population Size	20
Maximum Iterations	500
Inertia Weight	0.729844
Cognitive Parameter	1.49445
Social Parameter	1.49445
Constriction Factor	1.0

the results have been made bold and considered for comparison with other models.

Further the same databases are presented to the MLP[136] and FSN;[7] the results obtained are presented in Table 9.5. The average result of set1 and set2 for training and testing have been made bold and used for further comparison with the OPFSN model.

The average results of MLP, FSN and OPFSN have been presented at Table 9.6 for the purpose of comparison. From the table it can be seen that OPFSN is giving better result in case of IRIS database.

The average performance of OPFSN is better in comparison to other models for WINE and PIMA databases during the training phase only. BUPA database is giving much better performance than FSN in the training

Table 9.4. Classification accuracy of datasets simulated in OPFSN model.

Data set used for testing	Hit Percentage in the training set	Hit Percentage in the test set
IRIS		
Set1	99.93	99.53
Set2	100.00	99.40
Average	99.96	99.46
WINE		
Set1	98.14	97.07
Set2	98.76	96.12
Average	98.45	96.60
PIMA		
Set1	80.24	77.33
Set2	78.88	76.05
Average	79.56	76.69
BUPA		
Set1	75.86	69.21
Set2	77.25	70.52
Average	76.56	69.86

Table 9.5. Classification accuracy obtained from MLP AND FSN.

Databases	MLP Hit Percentage in the		FSN Hit Percentage in the	
	training set	test set	training set	test set
IRIS				
Set1	97.33	100.00	94.53	100.00
Set2	97.33	97.33	95.47	97.73
Average	97.33	98.66	95.00	98.86
WINE				
Set1	96.63	100	85.39	98.09
Set2	97.75	93.26	91.24	98.31
Average	97.19	96.63	88.315	98.20
PIMA				
Set1	73.44	85.42	73.83	79.53
Set2	75.26	82.81	74.89	81.09
Average	74.35	84.11	74.36	80.31
BUPA				
Set1	77.91	78.61	70.41	77.05
Set2	76.30	79.07	68.03	75.98
Average	77.10	78.84	69.22	76.51

Table 9.6.   Comparison Performance among MLP, FSN and OPFSN.

Databases	Hit Percentage in the training set			Hit Percentage in the test set		
	MLP	FSN	OPFSN	MLP	FSN	OPFSN
IRIS	97.33	95.00	99.96	98.66	98.86	99.46
WINE	97.19	88.31	98.45	96.63	98.20	96.60
PIMA	74.35	74.36	79.56	84.11	80.31	76.69
BUPA	77.10	69.22	76.56	78.84	76.51	69.86

phase and a competitive performance with MLP. In case of test phase WINE database is giving a competitive performance, but performance of BUPA and PIMA databases is less than the performance of MLP. The best average results in Table 9.6 are made bold to distinguish it from other results.

The training phase and test phase results are also presented separately in Table. 9.6 and Fig. 9.7 for different models and for different databases.

Again the same datasets are simulated with OPFSN Model in a wrapper approach. We allow the PSO to select different sets of features starting from set cardinality one to ten. We perform 20 simulations for selection of each set of features and the average classification accuracy is considered for comparison. Figure 9.8 shows the mean value of average results obtained from exposing train and test set to the model while different sets are taken for training.

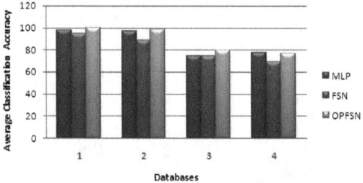

Fig. 9.7.   Comparison of average classification accuracy of MLP, FSN and OPFSN for the training sets, X-axis values represent 1: IRIS, 2: WINE, 3: PIMA, and 4: BUPA databases.

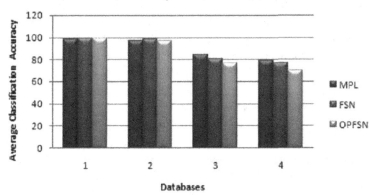

Fig. 9.8.   Comparison of average classification accuracy of MLP, FSN and OPFSN for the test sets, X-axis values represent 1: IRIS, 2: WINE, 3: PIMA, and 4: BUPA databases.

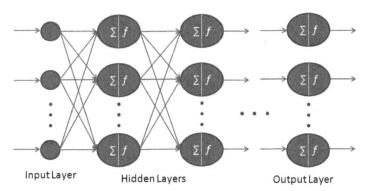

Fig. 9.9.   Comparison of performance of different datasets for selecting different size of features.

9.8. Conclusion

In this chapter, we have discussed the fuzzy swarm net (FSN) model for the task of classification in data mining. The FSN model expands the given set of inputs into three categories: low, medium and high. These inputs are fed to the single layer feed forward artificial neural network. A set of such nets is being taken to spread in a distributed environment. Swarm intelligence technique is used to train these nets.

Further we have briefed the concept of Polynomial Neural Network (PNN) algorithm and its use for handling the classification problems. The PNN model takes a subset of the features to produce a polynomial called the

Partial Description (PD), the coefficients of which are estimated using Least Square Estimation (LSE) technique. The different combinations of subset of features generate a set of PDs of the first layer of the PNN algorithm. At this stage we use certain pruning techniques to preserve a set of PDs that is most promising for generating PDs for the next layer.

In the next section, Optimized Polynomial Neural Fuzzy Swarm Net (OPFSN) model is discussed. This model at the first step generates the PDs for the first layer of the PNN and the output of these PDs along with the input features are feed to a fuzzy system in the next step. The output of the fuzzy system along with the output of the PDs and the input features are passed on to a single unit of perceptron through swarm intelligence. The particles of the Swarm compete among themselves in a distributed environment to choose the optimal set of input sets required for the net as well as to determine the weight associated with the links of this optimal network.

The experimental studies demonstrate the performance of the OPFSN model in comparison to other models for the task of classification. The efficiency of the models gets established with the fact that a very small subset of input can also perform equally well.

References

1. Y. C. Ho and R. L. Kashyap. A class of iterative procedures for linear inequalities, *J. SIAM Contr.* **4**(2), 112–115, (1966).
2. P. J. Huber. *Robust Statistics.* (Wiley, New York, 1981).
3. R. Bellman, K. Kalaba, and L. A. Zadeh. Abstraction and pattern classification, *J. Math. Anal. Appl.* **13**(1), 1–7, (1966).
4. E. Czogala and J. M. Leoski. *Fuzzy and Neuro Fuzzy Intelligent Systems.* (Springer, 2000).
5. L. I. Kuncheva. Switching between selection and fusion in combining classifiers: An experiment, *IEEE Trans. Syst. Man Cybern., Part B.* **32**(2), 146–156, (2002).
6. S. K. Oh and W. Pedrycz. The design of self-organizing polynomial neural networks, *Inf Sci.* (2002).
7. B. B. Misra, S. Dehuri, G. Panda, and P. K. Dash. Fuzzy Swarm Net for Classification in Data Mining, *CSI Journal of Computer Science and Engineering.*
8. B. B. Misra, P. K. Dash, and G. Panda. Optimal polynomial fuzzy swarm net for handling data classification problems. In *IEEE International Advance Computing Conference (IACC'09)*, pp. 1235–1240, (2009).
9. Y. Pao. *Adaptive Pattern Recognition and Neural Networks.* (Addision-Wesley, MA, 1989).

10. J. Patra and R. Pal. A functional link artificial neural network for adaptive channel equalization, *Signal Processing.* **43**(2), 181–195, (1995).

11. J. Patra, R. Pal, R. Baliarsingh, and G. Panda. Nonlinear channel equalization for qam signal constellation using artificial neural networks, *IEEE Trans. Syst. Man Cybern.-B.* **29**(2), 262–271, (1999).

12. B. B. Misra and S. Dehuri. Functional link artificial neural network for classification task in data mining, *Journal of Computer Science.* **3**(12), 948–955, (2007).

13. J. Patra, R. Pal, B. Chatterji, and G. Panda. Identification of nonlinear dynamic systems using functional link artificial neural network, *IEEE Trans. Syst. Man Cybern.-B.* **29**(2), 254–262, (1999).

14. T. T. Lee and J. T. Jeng. The chebyshev-polynomialsbased unified model neural networks for function approximation, *IEEE Trans. Syst. Man Cybern.-B.* **28**(6), 925–935, (1998).

15. J. Patra and A. Kot. Nonlinear dynamic system identification using chebyshev functional link artificial neural networks, *IEEE Trans. Syst. Man Cybern.-B.* **32**(4), 505–511, (2002).

16. A. Hussain, J. J. Soraghan, and T. S. Durrani. A new adaptive functional-link neural-network-based dfe for overcoming co-channel interference, *IEEE Trans. Commun.* **45**(11), 1358–1362, (1997).

17. W. D. Weng, C. S. Yang, and R. C. Lin. A channel equalizer using reduced decision feedback chebyshev functional link artificial neural networks, *Inf. Sci.* **177**(13), 2642–2654, (2007).

18. D. Krishnaiah, D. Reddy Prasad, A. Bono, P. Pandiyan, and R. Sarbatly. Application of ultrasonic waves coupled with functional link neural network for estimation of carrageenan concentration, *International Journal of Physical Sciences.* **3**(4), 090–096, (2008).

19. H. Zhao and J. Zhang. Functional link neural network cascaded with chebyshev orthogonal polynomial for nonlinear channel equalization, *Signal Processing.* **88**, 1946–1957, (2008).

20. J. C. Patra, G. Chakraborty, and S. Mukhopadhyay. Functional link neural network-based intelligent sensors for harsh environments, *Sensors and Transducers Journal.* **90, Special Issue**, 209–220, (2008).

21. S. Dehuri, B. B. Misra, and S. B. Cho. Genetic feature selection for optimal functional link artificial neural network in classification. In *IDEAL 2008, LNCS 5326*, pp. 156–163, (2008).

22. S. N. Singh and K. N. Srivastava. Degree of insecurity estimation in a power system using functional link neural network, *European Transactions on Electrical Power.* **12**(5), 353–359, (2007).

23. B. S. Lin, B. S. Lin, J. C. Chien, and F. C. Chon. Functional link network with genetic algorithm for evoked potentials, *Basis and Communications.* **17**, 193–200, (2005).

24. T. Marcu and B. K. Seliger. Dynamic functional — link neural networks genetically evolved applied to system identification. In *European Symposium on Artificial Neural Networks, (ESANN'2004)*, pp. 115–120, (2004).

25. L. A. Zadeh. Fuzzy sets, *Information and Control*. **8**, 338–353, (1965).
26. D. Dubois, H. Prade, and R. R. Yager. Information engineering and fuzzy logic. In *5th IEEE International Conference on Fuzzy Systems (FUZZ-IEEE'96)*, pp. 1525–1531, (1996).
27. R. Kruse, C. Borgelt, and D. Nauck. Fuzzy data analysis: Challenges and perspectives. In *IEEE Int. Conf. on Fuzzy Systems*, pp. 1211–1216, (1999).
28. C. Lin and C. Lee. *Neural Fuzzy Systems. A Neuro Fuzzy Synergism to Intelligent Systems*. (Prentice Hall, New York, 1996).
29. D. Nauck, F. Klawonn, and R. Kruse. *Foundations of Neuro Fuzzy Systems*. (Wiley, Chichester, 1997).
30. A. Klose, D. Nurnberger, A. Nauck, and R. Kruse. *Data Mining with Neuro Fuzzy Models*, In eds. A. Kandel, H. Bunke, and M. Last, *Data Mining and Computational Intelligence*, pp. 1–36. Physica-Verlag, (2001).
31. L. Arafeh, H. Singh, and S. K. Putatunda. A neuro fuzzy logic approach to material processing, *IEEE Transactions on Systems, Man, and Cybernetics, Part C: Applications and Reviews*. **29**(3), 362–370, (1999).
32. A. H. Al-Badi, S. M. Ghania, and E. F. EL-Saadany. Prediction of metallic conductor voltage owing to electromagnetic coupling using neuro fuzzy modeling, *IEEE Transactions on Power Delivery*. **24**(1), 319–327, (2009).
33. J. E. Heiss, C. M. Held, P. A. Estevez, C. A. Perez, C. A. Holzmann, and J. P. Perez. Classification of sleep stages in infants: a neuro fuzzy approach, *IEEE Engineering in Medicine and Biology Magazine*. **21**(5), 147–151, (2002).
34. S. P. Torres, W. H. Peralta, and C. A. Castro. Power system loading margin estimation using a neuro fuzzy approach, *IEEE Transactions on Power Systems*. **22**(4), 1955–1964, (2007).
35. L. Rutkowski and K. Cpalka. Designing and learning of adjustable quasi-triangular norms with applications to neuro fuzzy systems, *IEEE Transactions on Fuzzy Systems*. **13**(1), 140–151, (2005).
36. M. Panella and A. S. Gallo. An input-output clustering approach to the synthesis of anfis networks, *IEEE Transactions on Fuzzy Systems*. **13**(1), 69–81, (2005).
37. C. J. Lin, C. H. Chen, and C. T. Lin. A hybrid of cooperative particle swarm optimization and cultural algorithm for neural fuzzy networks and its prediction applications, *IEEE Transactions on Systems, Man, and Cybernetics-part C: Applications and Reviews*. **39**(1), 55–68, (2009).
38. S. Watanabe, T. Furuhashi, K. Obata, and Y. Uchikawa. A study on feature extraction using a fuzzy net for off-line signature recognition. In *Int. Joint Conf. on Neural Networks*, (1993).
39. J. Kim, Y. Moon, and B. P. Zeigler. Designing fuzzy net controllers using genetic algorithms, *IEEE Control Systems Magazine*. **15**(3), 66–72, (1995).
40. T. Kuremoto, M. Obayashi, K. Kobayashi, H. Adachi, and K. Yoneda. A reinforcement learning system for swarm behaviors. In *IEEE International Joint Conference on Neural Networks, 2008. IJCNN 2008. (IEEE World Congress on Computational Intelligence*, pp. 3711–3716, (2008).

41. E. D. Kirby, J. C. Chen, and J. Z. Zhang. Development of a fuzzy-nets-based in-process surface roughness adaptive control system in turning operations, *Expert Systems with Applications*. **30**, 592–604, (2006).

42. P. J. Angeline. *Evolutionary optimization versus particle swarm optimization: philosophy and performance differences*, In eds. V. W. Porto, N. Saravanan, D. Waagen, and A. E. Eiben, *Evolutionary Programming VII*, Vol. 1447, *Lecture Notes in Computer Science*, pp. 601–610. Springer, (1998).

43. R. C. Eberhart and Y. Shi. *Comparison between genetic algorithms and particle swarm optimization*, In eds. V. W. Porto, N. Saravanan, D. Waagen, and A. E. Eiben, *Evolutionary Programming VII*, Vol. 1447, *Lecture Notes in Computer Science*, pp. 591–600. Springer, (1998).

44. Y. Shi and R. C. Eberhart, *Parameter selection in particle swarm optimization*, In eds. V. W. Porto, N. Saravanan, D. Waagen, and A. E. Eiben, *Evolutionary Programming VII*, Vol. 1447, *Lecture Notes in Computer Science*, pp. 611–616. Springer, (1998).

45. Y. Shi and R. Eberhart. A modified particle swarm optimizer. In *IEEE Conference on Evolutionary Computation*, (1998).

46. J. Kennedy. *The behavior of particles*, In eds. V. W. Porto, N. Saravanan, D. Waagen, and A. E. Eiben, *Evolutionary Programming VII*, Vol. 1447, *Lecture Notes in Computer Science*, pp. 581–590. Springer, (1998).

47. A. Carlisle and G. Dozier. An off-the-shelf pso. In *Particle Swarm Optimization Workshop*, pp. 1–6, (2001).

48. R. C. Eberhart and J. Kennedy. A new optimizer using particle swarm theory. In *6th Symp. MicroMachine and Human Science, Nagoya, Japan*, pp. 39–43, (1995).

49. C. A. Coello Coello and M. S. Lechuga. Mopso: A proposal for multiple objective particle swarm optimization. In *IEEE Congr. Evolutionary Computation*, pp. 1051–1056, (2002).

50. E. C. Laskari and K. E. Parsopoulos. Article swarm optimization for minimax problems. In *Article Swarm Optimization for Minimax Problems*, pp. 1582–1587, (2002).

51. S. Y. and R. A. Krohling. Co-evolutionary particle swarm optimization to solve min-max problems. In *IEEE Conf. Evolutionary Computation*, pp. 1682–1687, (2002).

52. E. C. Laskari, K. E. Parsopoulos, and M. N. Vrahatis. Particle swarm optimization for integer programming. In *IEEE 2002 Congr. Evolutionary Computation*, pp. 1576–1581, (2002).

53. A. Carlisle. *Applying the particle swarm optimizer to non-stationary environments*. PhD thesis, Auburn Univ., Auburn, AL, (2002).

54. R. C. Eberhart and Y. Shi. Tracking and optimizing dynamic systems with particle swarms. In *IEEE Congr. Evolutionary Computation Seoul, South Korea*, pp. 94–100, (2001).

55. K. E. Parsopoulos and M. N. Vrahatis. *Particle swarm optimizer in noisy and continuously changing environments*, In ed. M. Hamza,

Artificial Intelligence and Soft Computing, pp. 289–294. Cancun, Mexico: IASTED/ACTA Press, (2001).

56. K. E. Parsopoulos, E. C. Laskari, and M. N. Vrahatis. *Solving norm errors-in-variables problems using particle swarm optimizer*, In ed. M. Hamza, *Artificial Intelligence and Applications*, pp. 185–190. Marbella, Spain: IASTED/ACTA Press, (2001).

57. K. E. Parsopoulos and M. N. Vrahatis. Investigating the existence of function roots using particle swarm optimization. In *IEEE 2003Congr. Evolutionary Computation*, pp. 1448–1455, (2003).

58. A. A. E. Ahmed, L. T. Germano, and Z. C. Antonio. A hybrid particle swarm optimization applied to loss power minimization, *IEEE Trans. Power Syst.* **20**(2), 859–866, (2005).

59. T. O. Ting, M. V. C. Rao, and C. K. Loo. A novel approach for unit commitment problem via an effective hybrid particle swarm optimization, *IEEE Trans. Power Syst.* **21**(1), 411–418, (2006).

60. B. Zhao, C. X. Guo, and Y. J. Cao. A multiagent-based particle swarm optimization approach for optimal reactive power dispatch, *IEEE Trans. Power Syst.* **20**(2), 1070–1078, (2005).

61. J. G. Vlachogiannis and K. Y. Lee. A comparative study on particle swarm optimization for optimal steady-state performance of power systems, *IEEE Trans. Power Syst.* **21**(4), 1718–1728, (2006).

62. C. M. Huang, C. J. Huang, and M. L. Wang. A particle swarm optimization to identifying the armax model for short-term load forecasting, *IEEE Trans. Power Syst.* **20**(2), 1126–1133, (2005).

63. Y. Liu and X. Gu. Skeleton-network reconfiguration based on topological characteristics of scale-free networks and discrete particle swarm optimization, *IEEE Transactions on Power Systems.* **22**(3), 1267–1274, (2007).

64. Y. d. Valle, G. K. Venayagamoorthy, S. Mohagheghi, J. C. Hernandez, and R. G. Harley. Particle swarm optimization: Basic concepts, variants and applications in power systems, *IEEE Transactions on Evolutionary Computation.* **12**(2), 171–195, (2008).

65. M. M. Jannett and T. C. Jannett. Simulation of a new hybrid particle swarm optimization algorithm. In *36th Southeastern Symp. Syst. Theory*, pp. 150–153, (2004).

66. C. Zhang, H. Shao, and Y. Li. Particle swarm optimization for evolving artificial neural network. In *IEEE Int. Conf. Syst., Man, Cybern.*, Vol. 4, pp. 2487–2490, (2000).

67. Y. Song, Z. Chen, and Z. Yuan. New chaotic pso-based neural network predictive control for nonlinear process, *IEEE Trans. Neural Netw.* **18**(2), 595–601, (2007).

68. Y. S. Wang, K. J. Wang, J. S. Qu, and Y. R. Yang. Adaptive inverse control based on particle swarm optimization algorithm. In *IEEE Int. Conf. Mechatronics, Autom.*, pp. 2169–2172, (2005).

69. L. dos Santos Coelho and B. M. Herrera. Fuzzy identification based on a chaotic particle swarm optimization approach applied to a nonlinear yo-yo motion system, *IEEE Transactions on Industrial Electronics.* **54**(6), 3234–3245, (2007).

70. V. Kadirkamanathan, K. Selvarajah, and P. J. Fleming. Stability analysis of the particle dynamics in particle swarm optimizer, *IEEE Transactions on Evolutionary Computation.* **10**(3), 245–255, (2006).

71. W. Liu, K. Wang, B. Sun, and K. Shao. A hybrid particle swarm optimization algorithm for predicting the chaotic time series mechatronics and automation. In *IEEE Int. Conf. Mechatronics*, pp. 2454–2458, (2006).

72. C. J. Lin, C. H. Chen, and C. T. Lin. A hybrid of cooperative particle swarm optimization and cultural algorithm for neural fuzzy networks and its prediction applications, *IEEE Transactions on Systems, Man, and Cybernetics, Part C: Applications and Reviews.* **39**(1), 55–68, (2009).

73. W. C. Liu. Design of a multiband cpw-fed monopole antenna using a particle swarm optimization approach, *IEEE Transactions on Antennas and Propagation.* **53**(10), 3273–3279, (2005).

74. R. Marinke, E. Araujo, L. S. Coelho, and I. Matiko. Particle swarm optimization (pso) applied to fuzzy modeling in a thermal-vacuum system. In *5th Int. Conf. Hybrid Intell. Syst.*, pp. 67–72, (2005).

75. Y. Liu and X. He. Modeling identification of power plant thermal process based on PSO algorithm. In *Amer. Control Conf.*, Vol. 7, pp. 4484–4489, (2005).

76. R. Saeidi, H. R. S. Mohammadi, T. Ganchev, and R. D. Rodman. Particle swarm optimization for sorted adapted gaussian mixture models, *IEEE Transactions on Audio, Speech, and Language Processing.* **17**(2), 344–353, (2009).

77. M. A. Abido. Optimal design of power system stabilizers using particle swarm optimization, *IEEE Trans. Energy Conversion.* **17**, 406–413, (2002).

78. D. K. Agrafiotis and W. Cedeno. Feature selection for structure-activity correlation using binary particle swarms, *J. Medicinal Chem.* **45**(5), 1098–1107, (2002).

79. A. R. Cockshott and B. E. Hartman. Improving the fermentation medium for echinocandin b production Part II: Particle swarm optimization, *Process Biochem.* **36**, 661–669, (2001).

80. P. C. Fourie and A. A. Groenwold. The particle swarm optimization algorithm in size and shape optimization, *Struct. Multidisc. Optim.* **23**, 259–267, (2002).

81. W. Z. Lu, H. Y. Fan, A. Y. T. Leung, and J. C. K. Wong. Analysis of pollutant levels in central hong kong applying neural network method with particle swarm optimization, *Environ. Monitoring Assessment.* **79**, 217–230, (2002).

82. C. O. Ourique, E. C. Biscaia, and J. C. Pinto. The use of particle swarm optimization for dynamical analysis in chemical processes, *Comput. Chem. Eng.* **26**, 1783–1793, (2002).

83. K. E. Parsopoulos, E. I. Papageorgiou, P. P. Groumpos, and M. N. Vrahatis. A first study of fuzzy cognitive maps learning using particle swarm optimization. In *IEEE 2003 Congr. Evolutionary Computation*, pp. 1440–1447, (2003).
84. T. Ray and K. M. Liew. A swarm metaphor for multi-objective design optimization, *Eng. Opt.* **34**(2), 141–153, (2002).
85. A. Saldam, I. Ahmad, and S. Al-Madani. Particle swarm optimization for task assignment problem, *Microprocess. Microsyst.* **26**, 363–371, (2002).
86. V. Tandon, H. El-Mounayri, and H. Kishawy. Nc end milling optimization using evolutionary computation, *Int. J. Mach. Tools Manuf.* **42**, 595–605, (2002).
87. J. C. Tillett, R. M. Rao, F. Sahin, and T. M. Rao. Particle swarm optimization for the clustering of wireless sensors. In *SPIE*, Vol. 5100, *Orlando, FL*, (2003).
88. S. E. Easter Selvan, S. Subramanian, and S. T. S. Theban Solomon. Novel technique for pid tuning by particle swarm optimization. In *7th Annu. Swarm Users/Researchers Conf. (SwarmFest 2003), Notre Dame, IN*, (2003).
89. J. Kennedy and R. Eberhart. *Swarm Intelligence*. (Morgan Kaufmann Academic Press, 2001).
90. J. Kennedy and R. Mendes. Population structure and particle swarm performance. In *The Congress on Evolutionary Computation, Piscatawat, Honolulu, HI. Piscataway: IEEE.*, pp. 1671–1676, (2002).
91. R. Mendes, P. Cortes, M. Rocha, and J. Neves. Particle swarms for feedforward neural net training. In *The International Joint Conference on Neural Networks, Honolulu, HI. Piscataway: IEEE*, pp. 1895–1899, (2002).
92. V. Miranda and N. Fonseca. New evolutionary particle swarm algorithm (epso) applied to voltage/var control. In *The 14th Power Systems Computation Conference (PSCC), Seville, Spain*, pp. 1–6, (2002).
93. J. Kennedy and R. C. Eberhart. A discrete binary version of the particle swarm algorithm. In *The Conference on Systems, Man, and Cybernetics, Piscataway: IEEE.*, pp. 4104–4109, (1997).
94. C. K. Mohan and B. Al-Kazemi. Discrete particle swarm optimization. In *The Workshop on Particle Swarm Optimization, Indianapolis, IN, Purdue School of Engineering and Technology, IUPUI*, (2001).
95. G. Pampara, N. Franken, and A. P. Engelbrecht. Combining particle swarm optimization with angle modulation to solve binary problems. In *The IEEE Congress on Evolutionary Computation (CEC), Piscataway: IEEE*, pp. 225–239, (2005).
96. M. Clerc. *Discrete particle swarm optimization, illustrated by the traveling salesman problem*, In eds. B. V. Babu and G. C. Onwubolu, *New optimization techniques in engineering*, pp. 219–239. Berlin: Springer, (2004).
97. M. Clerc. *Particle swarm optimization*. (London: ISTE, 2006).

98. A. Moraglio, C. Di Chio, and R. Poli. *Geometric particle swarm optimization*, In ed. M. e. a. Ebner, *Lecture notes in computer science: Proceedings of the European conference on genetic programming (EuroGP)*, Vol. 4445, pp. 125–136. Berlin: Springer, (2007).

99. M. Loovbjerg, T. K. Rasmussen, and T. Krink. Hybrid particle swarm optimiser with breeding and subpopulations. In *The Third Genetic and Evolutionary Computation Conference (GECCO)*, San Francisco: *Kaufmann*, pp. 469–476, (2001).

100. C. Wei, Z. He, Y. Zhang, and W. Pei. Swarm directions embedded in fast evolutionary programming. In *The IEEE Congress on Evolutionary Computation (CEC), Honolulu, HI. Piscataway: IEEE*, pp. 1278–1283, (2002).

101. T. Krink and M. Loovbjerg. The lifecycle model: combining particle swarm optimization, genetic algorithms and hillclimbers. In *Lecture Notes in Computer Science. Proceedings of Parallel Problem Solving from Nature (PPSN), Granada, Spain. Berlin: Springer*, pp. 621–630, (2002).

102. R. Poli and C. R. Stephens. *Constrained molecular dynamics as a search and optimization tool*, In ed. M. e. a. Keijzer, *Lecture notes in computer science: Proceedings of the 7th European conference on genetic programming (EuroGP)*, Vol. 3003, pp. 150–161. Berlin: Springer, (2004).

103. J. S. Vesterstrom, J. Riget, and T. Krink. Division of labor in particle swarm optimization. In *The IEEE Congress on Evolutionary Computation (CEC), Honolulu, HI. Piscataway: IEEE*, pp. 1570–1575, (2002).

104. N. Holden and A. A. Freitas. A hybrid particle swarm/ant colony algorithm for the classification of hierarchical biological data. In *IEEE Swarm Intelligence Symposium (SIS), Piscataway: IEEE*, pp. 100–107, (2005).

105. T. Hendtlass. *A combined swarm differential evolution algorithm for optimization problems.* In eds. L. Monostori, J. Váncza, and M. Ali, *Lecture Notes in Computer Science: Proceedings of the 14th International Conference on Industrial and Engineering Applications of Artificial Intelligence and Expert Systems (IEA/AIE)*, Vol. 2070, pp. 11–18. Berlin: Springer, (2001).

106. W.-J. Zhang and X.-F. Xie. Depso: hybrid particle swarm with differential evolution operator. In *The IEEE International Conference on Systems, Man and Cybernetics (SMCC), Washington, DC. Piscataway: IEEE*, pp. 3816–3821, (2003).

107. R. Poli, W. B. Langdon, and O. Holland. *Extending particle swarm optimization via genetic programming*, In ed. M. K. et al., *Lecture Notes in Computer Science: Proceedings of the 8th Eu*, Vol. 3447. (2005).

108. R. Poli, C. Di Chio, and W. B. Langdon. *Exploring extended particle swarms: A genetic programming approach*, In ed. e. a. H.-G. Beyer, *The Conference on Genetic and Evolutionary Computation, Washington, DC. New York*, pp. 169–176. ACM, (2005).

109. M. Lovbjerg and T. Krink. Extending particle swarms with self-organized criticality. In *The IEEE Congress on Evolutionary Computation (CEC-2002), Piscataway: IEEE*, pp. 1588–1593, (2002).

110. T. Blackwell and P. J. Bentley. Don't push me! Collision-avoiding swarms. In *The IEEE Congress on Evolutionary Computation (CEC), Honolulu, HI. Piscataway: IEEE*, pp. 1691–1696, (2002).

111. T. Krink, J. S. Vesterstrom, and J. Riget. Particle swarm optimization with spatial particle extension. In *The IEEE Congress on Evolutionary Computation (CEC-2002), Piscataway: IEEE*, pp. 1474–1479, (2002).

112. X. Xie, W. Zhang, and Z. Yang. Dissipative particle swarm optimization. In *The IEEE Congress on Evolutionary Computation (CEC), Honolulu, HI. Piscataway: IEEE*, pp. 1456–1461, (2002).

113. J. Kennedy. Bare bones particle swarms. In *The IEEE Swarm Intelligence Symposium (SIS), Indianapolis, IN. Piscataway: IEEE*, pp. 80–87, (2003).

114. T. Richer and T. M. Blackwell. The lévy particle swarm. In *IEEE Congress on Evolutionary Computation, Vancouver. Piscataway: IEEE*, pp. 3150–3157, (2006).

115. Y. P. Yurachkovsky. Convergence of multilayer algorithms of the group method of data handling, *Soviet Automatic Control.* **14**, 29–35, (1981).

116. Y. Yurachkovsky. Restoration of polynomial dependencies using self-organization, *Soviet Automatic Control.* **14**, 17–22, (1981).

117. G. Ivahenko. The group method of data handling: a rival of method of stochastic approximation, *Soviet Auto. Contr.* **13**(3), 43–55, (1968).

118. A. G. Ivakhnenko and H. R. Madala. *Inductive Learning Algorithm for Complex Systems Modelling.* (CRC Inc, 1994).

119. A. Ivahnenko. Polynomial theory of complex systems, *IEEE Trans. Systems Man Cybernet.* **12**, 364–378, (1971).

120. S. J. Farlow. *The GMDH algorithm.* In ed. S. Farlow, *Self-Organizating Methods in Modelling: GMDH Type Algorithm*, pp. 1–24. Marcel Dekker, (1984).

121. A. J. Muller, F. Lemke, and A. G. Ivakhnenko. Gmdh algorithms for complex systems modeling, *Math and Computer Modeling of Dynamical Systems.* **4**, 275–315, (1998).

122. B. B. Misra, S. C. Satapathy, B. N. Biswal, P. K. Dash, and G. Panda. Pattern classification using polynomial neural networks. In *IEEE Int. Conf. on Cybernetics and Intelligent Systems (CIS)*, (2006).

123. B. B. Misra, S. C. Satapathy, N. Hanoon, and P. K. Dash. Particle swarm optimized polynomials for data classification. In *IEEE Int. Conf. on Intelligent Systems Design and Application*, (2006).

124. S. Oh, W. Pedrycz, and B. Park. Polynomial neural networks architecture: analysis and design, *Comput. Electr. Eng.* **29**(6), 703–725, (2003).

125. S. K. Oh, T. C. Ahn, and W. Pedrycz. A study on the self-organizing polynomial neural networks. In *Joint Nineth IFSA World Congr.*, pp. 1690–1695, (2001).

126. D. Huang. A constructive approach for finding arbitrary roots of polynomials by neural networks, *IEEE Transactions on Neural Networks.* **15**(2), 477–491, (2004).

127. T. I. Aksyonova, V. V. Volkovich, and I. V. T. Tetko. Robust polynomial neural networks in quantative-structure activity relationship studies, *Systems Analysis Modelling Simulation.* **43**(10), 1331–1339, (2003).

128. I. V. Tetko, T. I. Aksenova, V. V. Volkovich, T. N. Kasheva, D. V. Filipov, W. J. Welsh, D. J. Livingstone, and A. E. P. Villa. Polynomial neural network for linear and non-linear model selection in quantitative-structure activity relationship studies on the internet, *SAR QSAR Environ. Res.* **11**, 263–280, (2000).

129. J. A. Muller and F. Lemke. *Self-Organizing Data Mining Extracting Knowledge from Data.* (Trafford Publishing, 2003).

130. V. Schetinin and J. Schult. The combined technique for detection of artifacts in clinical electroencephalograms of sleeping newborn, *IEEE Trans. on Information Technologies in Biomedicine.* **8**(1), 28–35, (2004).

131. N. L. Nikolaev and H. Iba. *Automated discovery of polynomials by inductive genetic programming,* In eds. J. Zutkow and J. Ranch, *Principles of Data Mining and Knowledge Discovery (PKDD'99),* pp. 456–462. Springer, Berlin, (1999).

132. B. B. Misra, B. N. Biswal, P. K. Dash, and G. Panda. Simplified polynomial neural network for classification task in data mining. In *IEEE Congress on Evolutionary Computation (CEC),* pp. 721–728, (2007).

133. B. B. Misra, S. Dehuiri, G. Panda, and P. Dash. A reduced comprehensible polynomial neural network for classification in data mining, *Pattern Recognition Letters.* **29**(12), 1705–1712, (2008).

134. B. B. Misra, S. Dehuri, P. K. Dash, and G. Panda. Reduced polynomial neural swarm net for classification task in data mining. In *IEEE World Congress on Computational Intelligence,* (2008).

135. C. L. Blake and C. Merz. Uci repository of machine learning databases, (2009). http://www.ics.uci.edu/~mlearn/MLRepository.html.

136. B. B. Misra, S. Dehuri, and S.-B. Cho. A notable swarm approach to evolve neural network for classification in data mining. In *ICONIP 2008–15th International Conference on Neural Information Processing of the Asia-Pacific Neural Network Assembly, Auckland, New Zealand,* (2008).

Chapter 10

SOFTWARE TESTING USING GENETIC ALGORITHMS

M. RAY* and D. P. MOHAPATRA[†]

Department of Computer Science & Engineering,
National Institute of Technology, Rourkela, India 769008
**mitabindar@nitrkl.ac.in*
[†]*durga@nitrkl.ac.in*

Traditional software testing methods involve large amounts of manual tasks which are expensive in nature. Software testing effort can be significantly reduced by automating the testing process. A key component in any automatic software testing environment is the test data generator. As test data generation is treated as an optimization problem, Genetic Algorithm has been used successfully to generate automatically an optimal set of test cases for the software under test. This chapter describes a framework that automatically generates an optimal set of test cases to achieve path coverage of an arbitrary program.

10.1. Introduction

Testing software is a very important and challenging activity. Nearly half of the software production development cost is spent on software testing.[1] The basic objective of software testing is to eliminate as many errors as possible to ensure that the tested software meets an acceptable level of quality. The tests have to be performed within budgetary and schedule limitations. Since testing is a time consuming and expensive activity, an important problem is to decide when to stop testing the software. An important activity in testing is test case design. In the software testing process, each *test case* has an identity and is associated with a set of inputs and a list of expected outputs.[2] As the software industry always faces time and cost pressures, test cost minimization has become an important research problem. This cost could be reduced by making the testing process automatic. One of

---

[†]Corresponding author. Tel.: 0661-2462356
[†]Website: www.nitrkl.ac.in

the most important components in a testing environment is test data generator. Manually generating test data is too costly as it takes maximum time in testing phase. So, the solution to reduce the high cost of manual software testing is to make the test data generator automatic. It is found that automatic test data generation has achieved some success by using evolutionary computation algorithms such as genetic algorithms. Basically, a test data generator system consists of three parts: *program analyzer, path selector* and *test data generator*. The source code is run through a program analyzer, which produces the necessary data used by the path selector and the test data generator. The job of path selector is to inspect the program data and find the paths leading to high code coverage. For the test data generator, the input is a path and outputs are the test data that exercise the given path. In this chapter, we focus on *path selectors* and *test data generators*. Some test data are more proficient at finding errors than others. So, testers have to choose the tests carefully to generate a good test suite. A proficient test case is one that has a high probability of detecting an as-yet undiscovered error.

One test case is not sufficient to satisfy all the test requirements. Usually, a suite of test cases is required to satisfy all known possible requirements. In every step of testing, a new test case may be generated and added to the test suit. Thus, a test suite may undergo a process of expansion in practice. Most of the times, it is found that a test suite contains more than enough test cases for satisfying the target test requirements. So, some test cases in a test suite are redundant. If those redundant test cases are removed from the test suite, the resultant test suite may still satisfy all the test requirements that can be satisfied by the original test suite. A good test suite is one which contains no redundant test cases. Therefore, finding a sub-suite of an existing test suite that can satisfy the same test requirements as the original test suite becomes a research problem. This problem is usually referred to as test suite reduction and the acquired sub-suite of test cases is called the representative set. If no subset of a representative set can satisfy all the requirements, the representative set is called optimal representative set or minimum representative set. As the aim of test suite reduction is to minimize the test suite, it is also referred to as test suite minimization. An optimal testing strategy selects the best test cases each time during testing. Since a large number of test cases can be designed, and an effective test suite needs to choose out of these, test case design can be considered as a typical search problem. A search algorithm must decide where the best values (test data) lie and concentrate its search there. Test suite reduction is a multi-objective optimization problem, which is NP complete in nature.[3]

A test case is a property or a case to be tested; on the other hand, test data for a test case are actual values of input necessary to test the case. This is explained by an example. Consider a triangle verification program. For a triangle to be valid, it must satisfy two conditions: length of all sides must be greater than zero and each side must be shorter than the sum of all sides divided by 2. In other words, if a, b, c are the three sides of a triangle and $s = (a + b + c)/2$, then $s > a$; $s > b$; $s > c$ and $a; b; c > 0$ must hold. There are four cases of a triangle: (i) invalid triangle; either $s < a$ or $s < b$ or $s < c$ or any of a, b, c is zero (ii) valid triangle, equilateral; $s > a$; $s > b$; $s > c$, a=b=c, and $a; b; c > 0$ (iii) valid triangle, isosceles; $s > a$; $s > b$; $s > c$; $a = b \neq c$, and $a; b; c > 0$ (iv) valid triangle, scalene; $s > a$; $s > b$; $s > c$, $a \neq b \neq c$, and $a; b; c > 0$. These four cases (properties) are actually the four test cases of a triangle verification program. On the other hand, possible test data (values of input a, b, c) for the case (i), which is the test case for invalid triangle, are ([0,0,0], [0,0,1], [0,1,0], [1,0,0], ..., [1,5,15], [2,5,15], [3,5,15], ...). It is evident that for a test case, in general, there is a large number of test data (which corresponds to the same test case).

Genetic Algorithm (GA) provides a general-purpose search methodology, which uses principles of natural evolution.[4] GA has been used successfully to optimize the generated test data. The overall objective of this chapter is to automatically generate test data using GA.

10.2. Overview of Test Case Design

The main objective of software testing is how to select test cases with the aim of uncovering as many defects as possible. Basically, testing is broadly categorized as structural testing (white box) and functional (black box) testing. The basic goal of functional (black box) testing is to test a given program's behavior against its specification. No prior knowledge of internal structures of the program is necessary for this. At the time of structural testing, test data are derived from the program's structure with the intension of covering each branch of software. A test suite is run on the software under test, and the outputs are examined by the tester. He decides whether it is correct, by comparing the actual output with the expected output. If the output is incorrect, then an error has been discovered. So the program must be changed and testing must start again.

The basic white box testing method uses coverage criteria as a measurement of the test data.[5] In this method, first the source code is transformed to a control flow graph.[1] A simple program with its control flow graph is shown in Fig. 10.2. The path of the graph which is covered by test data is considered as the coverage criteria. There are three types of test data generators for coverage criteria such as *Path wise data generator, Data specification generator and Random test data generator.* Our discussion is based on *Path wise data generator.*

10.2.1. *Path wise test data generators*

Path wise test data generator is a system that tests software using a testing criterion which can be path coverage, statement coverage, branch coverage, etc.[5] The system automatically generates test data to the chosen requirements. The aim of this test data generator is to generate test data to the chosen requirements. A path wise test data generator generally consists of tools for Control Flow Graph (CFG) construction, path selection and test data generation.

Once a set of test paths is defined, then for every path in this set the test generator derives input data that results in the execution of the selected path. In path testing, basically we have to generate test data for a boolean expression. A Boolean expression has two branches with a *true* and a *false* node as shown in Fig. 10.1. A reference to the sibling node means, the other node, corresponding to the current executed node. For example the sibling node of *True branch* is *False branch.*

Each path belongs to a certain sub domain, which consists of those inputs which are necessary to traverse that path. For generating test cases

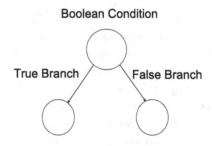

Fig. 10.1.   Sibling nodes.

for each path, it is helpful to apply global optimization rather than local search technique. It is because in local search technique, only local minima for the branch function value may be found which might not be good enough to traverse the desired branch. This problem can be solved by Genetic Algorithms because it is a global optimization process.

In this chapter, partition testing is used to test each path. In partition testing, a program's input domain is divided into a number of sub domains. At the time of testing, the tester selects one or more elements from each sub domain for analysis. The basic idea of partition testing is that each path of the software belongs to certain sub domain, which consists of those inputs which are necessary to traverse that path.

The domain is the set of all valid test sets. It is divided into sub domains such that all members of a sub domain cause a particular branch to be exercised. The domain notation may be based upon which branch (*true* or *false*) has been taken. The domain for the variables A and B of the program in Fig. 10.2(a) is shown in Fig. 10.3. A character code shown in Fig. 10.3 specifies the branch (here also path), e.g., TT (True True), TF (True False), F (False), etc. In addition, the respective node is also mentioned. In Fig. 10.3, the sub domain of node 5 is the dark grey area, the sub domain of node 3 is the diagonal line, the sub domain of node 4 is the light grey area whereas the sub domain of node 2 includes the light grey area (node 2) plus the diagonal line (node 3). Domain testing tries to check whether the border segments of the sub domains are correctly located by

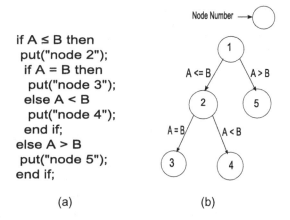

(a)   (b)

Fig. 10.2. (a) A sample program. (b) It's control flow graph.

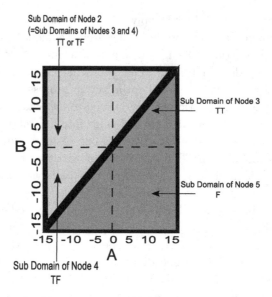

Fig. 10.3.   Example of input space partitioning structure in the range of −15 to 15.

the execution of the software with test data to find errors in the flow of
the control through the software. These test data belong to an input space
which is partitioned into a set of sub domains which belong to a certain
path in the software. The boundary of these domains is obtained by the
predicates in the path condition where a border segment is a section of the
boundary created by a single path condition. Two types of boundary test
points are necessary; *on* and *off* test points. The *on* test points are on the
border within the domain under test, and the *off* test points are outside the
border within an adjacent domain. If the software generates correct results
for all these points then it can be considered that the border locations are
correct.

Domain testing, therefore, is an example of partition testing. In this
testing, first a partition $P = \{D_1 \cup D_2 \cup \cdots \cup D_n\}$ of the input domain
D is produced. It divides the input space into equivalent domains and it is
assumed that all test data from one domain are expected to be correct
if a selected test data from that domain is shown to be correct. This
form of assumption is called *uniform hypothesis* of partition testing. Each
sub-domain may be affected by two types of faults such as *computation
faults*, which may affect a sub-domain and *domain faults*, which may affect

the boundary of a sub-domain. The tester detects computation *faults* by choosing randomly one or more test cases from each sub-domain. One or more test cases are selected from the boundaries to detect *Domain faults*.

Automatic generation of test data for a given path in a program is one of the elementary problem in software testing, hence the difficulty lies in the fact that how to solve nonlinear constraint, which is unsolvable in theory. As GA has the property of solving non linear constraints, this chapter mainly focuses on generating test data by applying GA, to check each path in a control flow graph of a problem.

In the next section, we discuss the basic concepts of GA. Then, the application of GA to test data generation for each path is explained in the sub sequent section.

10.3. Genetic Algorithm

Optimization problems arise in almost every field, especially in the engineering world. As a consequence many different optimization techniques have been developed. However, these techniques quite often have problems with functions which are not continuous or differentiable everywhere, multi-modal (multiple peaks) and noisy.[6] Therefore, more robust optimization techniques are under development which may be capable of handling such problems. Many computational problems require searching through a huge number of possible solutions. For these types of problems, heuristic methods play a key role in selecting an appropriate solution.

10.3.1. *Introduction to genetic algorithms*

Genetic algorithms (GA) represent a class of adaptive search techniques and procedures based on the processes of natural genetics and Darwin's principle of the survival of the fittest.[6] There is a randomized exchange of structured information among a population of artificial cromosomes. GA is a computer model of biological evolution. When GA is used to solve optimization problems, good results are obtained surprisingly as well as quickly. In the context of software testing, the basic idea is to search the domain for input variables which satisfy the goal of testing. Evolution avoids one of the most difficult obstacles which the software designer is confronted with: the need to know in advance what to do for every situation which may confront a program. The advantage of GA is that it is adaptive. Evolution is under the influence of two fundamental processes: *Natural selection* and *Recombination*.[6]

The former determines which individual member of a population is selected, survives and reproduces, the latter ensures that the genes (or entire cromosomes) will be mixed to form a new one.

10.3.2. *Overview of genetic algorithms*

GA offer a robust non-linear search technique that is particularly suited to problems involving large numbers of variables. GA converges to the optimum solution by the random exchange of information between increasingly fit samples and the introduction of a probability of independent random change. Compared to other search methods, there is a need for a strategy which is global, efficient and robust over a broad spectrum of problems. The strength of GAs is derived from their ability to exploit in a highly efficient manner, information about a large number of individuals. An important characteristic of genetic algorithms is the fact that they are very effective when searching or optimizing spaces that is not smooth or continuous. These are very difficult or impossible to search using calculus based methods such as hill climbing. Genetic algorithms may be differentiated from more conventional techniques by the following characteristics:

(1) A representation for the sample population must be derived;
(2) GAs manipulate directly the encoded representation of variables, rather than manipulation of the variables themselves;
(3) GAs use stochastic rather than deterministic operators;
(4) GAs search blindly by sampling and ignoring all information except the outcome of the sample;
(5) GAs search from a population of points rather than from a single point, thus reducing the probability of being stuck at a local optimum which make them suitable for parallel processing.

The block diagram of GA is shown in Fig. 10.4(a) and the pseudo code of GA is shown in Fig. 10.4(b). As shown in Fig. 10.4(a), GA is an iterative procedure that produces new populations at each step. A new population is created from an existing population by means of performance evaluation, selection procedures, recombination and survival. These processes repeat themselves until the population locates an optimum solution or some other

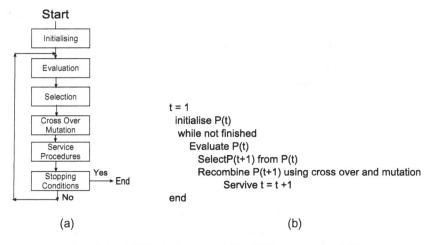

Fig. 10.4. (a) Block diagram of GA. (b) Pseudo code of GA.

stopping condition is reached, e.g., number of generation or time. The terms such as selection, cross over, mutation used in both Figs. 10.4(a) and (b) are discussed comprhensively in Mitchell.[6] However, we briefly present them here for completeness and ready reference.

- Selection: The selection operator is used to choose cromosomes from a population for mating. This mechanism defines how these cromosomes will be selected, and how many offsprings each will create. The expectation is that, like in the natural process, cromosomes with higher fitness will produce better offsprings. The selection has to be balanced: too strong selection means that best cromosome will take over the population reducing its diversity needed for exploration; too weak selection will result in a slow evolution. Some of the classic selection methods are Roulette-wheel, Rank based, Tournament, Uniform, and Elitism.[6]

- Crossover: The crossover operator is practically a method for sharing information between two cromosomes; it defines the procedure for generating an offspring from two parents. The crossover operator is considered the most important feature in GA, especially where building blocks exchange is necessary. One of the most common crossover operator is Single-point crossover: a single crossover position is chosen at random and the elements of the two parents before and after the crossover position are exchanged.

- Mutation: The mutation operator alters one or more values of the allele in the cromosome in order to increase the structural variability. This operator is the major instrument of any particular area of the entire search space. Survival step is required to choose the cromosomes for next generation. Unlike selection and crossover phase, it is not always mandatory to work out this phase. This phase is needed for selecting the cromosomes from parent population as well as children population by fitting some random numbers.

GA can solve optimization problems having a lot of constraints because there is a very few chance of falling in local optima. An optimization problem is a problem, where we have to maximize/minimize a function of the kind $f(x_1, x_2, \ldots, x_m)$ where $(x_1, x_2, \ldots, x_m)$ are variables, which have to be adjusted towards a global optimum. The bit strings of the variables are then concatenated together to produce a single bit string (cromosome) which represents the whole vector of the variables of the problem. In biological terminology, each bit position represents a gene of the cromosome, and each gene may take on some number of values called alleles.

The search begins with an initial population comprising of a fixed number of chromosomes. On the initial population, genetic operations are carried out large number of times. The stopping criterion can be based on considerations such as number of iterations, quality of the solution front namely convergence, diversity etc. At the end of iteration, inferior solutions are discarded and superior solutions are selected for reproduction [4].

10.4. Path Wise Test Data Generation Based on GA

Automatic test data generation strategy based on GA is explained in this section through an example. For better understanding of the procedure, test data are generated for the control flow graph given in Fig. 10.2(b). This example along with the experimental results are taken from Sthamer.[7]

The most important parameters of GA(for this case) are given below:

- Selection of parents for recombination is *random*.
- The mutated genes (Bits) are marked bold in off spring population.
- Fitness is calculated according to reciprocal fitness function.

Table 10.1. First generation.

P_i	A	B	Look	Path	Cromosome	Fitness	$f_{i,norm}$	$f_{i,accu}$
P_1	4	10	2	(1,2,4)	00100 01010	0.0278	0.365	0.365
P_2	−7	−15	2	(1,5)	11101 11111	0.0156	0.205	0.570
P_3	8	15	2	(1,2,4)	00010 11110	0.0204	0.268	0.838
P_4	3	−6	2	(1,5)	11000 01101	0.0123	0.162	1.0
								$F_t = 0.076$

- Single crossover.
- Survival Probability $P_s = 0.5$.
- Mutation Probability $P_m = 0.1$.

Table 10.1 shows the first generation which is randomly generated by the testing tool. Each row in the table represents a member of the population whose size is four. The columns in Table 10.1 have the following meanings:

- P_i indicates a member of the parent population;
- A and B are the values of the identifiers representing the input variables;
- look (short for looking) gives the node number to be traversed;
- *Path* indicates which nodes have been traversed by this current test data of A and B;
- *Cromosome* displays the bit pattern of the test data in binary-plus-sign bit format;
- *Fitness* gives the fitness value calculated according to the test data and the node required to be traversed;
- $f_{i,norm}$ is the normalized fitness;
- $f_{i,accu}$ is the accumulated normalized fitness value;
- F_t indicates the population total fitness value.

In Table 10.1, a 5 bit representation per input test data has been chosen. Therefore, the cromosome size is 10 bits where the first five bits represents the input data A and the rest five bits represents input data B. The least significant bit is stored on the left hand side and the most significant bit (sign bit) on the right hand side of the two substrings within the cromosome. A large $f_{i,norm}$ value indicates that these population members have a high fitness value and hence have a higher probability of surviving into the next generation.

The fitness function f, which calculates the test data performance based on the condition $A \leq B$ (in the code) is given by $f = 1/(|A - B| + 0.01).^2$

As the boundary condition to traverse the node $A \leq B$ (node 2) is $A = B$, this fitness function guides to generate test data to test on the boundary and off the boundary for the node $A \leq B$ (node 2). The test sets in the first generation execute nodes 1, 2, 4, and 5 leaving only node 3 untraversed. This fitness function ensures that test data where A and B are numerical, close to each other have a higher fitness value. When a *looking* node is executed with a test data (e.g. in this case node 2, first test data set in the first generation), the fitness values of the remaining test data (here second, third and fourth test data sets in the first generation) will be still calculated for the *looking* node and no offspring population will be generated in this case. Therefore, the first generation now becomes the starting point in the search for test data which will execute node 3 (see Table 10.2). The predicate controlling access to node 3 is the same as that for node 2, and hence the test data and the fitness values shown in Table 10.2 for the second generation are the same as those in Table 10.1.

Since the looking node (node 3) has not been traversed within the second generation, GA now generates an offspring population using crossover and mutation as shown in Table 10.3.

In Table 10.3 the new offspring test data are indicated by O_i and the parents which have been used for reproduction are indicated by P_i. These parents are chosen randomly. Two parent members generate two

Table 10.2.   Second generation.

P_i	A	B	Look	Path	Cromosome	Fitness	$f_{i,norm}$	$f_{i,accu}$
P_1	4	10	3	(1,2,4)	00100 01010	0.0278	0.365	0.365
P_2	−7	−15	3	(1,5)	11101 11111	0.0156	0.205	0.570
P_3	8	15	3	(1,2,4)	00010 11110	0.0204	0.268	0.838
P_4	3	−6	3	(1,5)	11000 01101	0.0123	0.162	1.0

$F_t = 0.076$

Table 10.3.   Offspring population generated by GA.

O_i	P_i	P_i	Look	Path	Cromosome	fitness	$f_{i,norm}$	$f_{i,accu}$	A	B	K
O_1	P_2	P_4	3	(1,5)	11101 01111	0.0204	0.289	0.289	−7	−14	5
O_2			3	(1,5)	11100 11111	0.0021	0.029	0.318	7	−15	
O_3	P_1	P_4	3	(1,5)	00000 01101	0.0278	0.393	0.711	0	−6	3
O_4			3	(1,2,4)	11000 01010	0.0204	0.289	1.0	3	10	

$F_t = 0.071$

offspring members during the recombination phase. The columns *look*, *Path*, *cromosome*, *fitness*, $f_{i,norm}$, and $f_{i,accu}$ have the same meaning as for the parent population. A and B represent the new test data values and K indicates the single crossover point. The genes displayed in bold and italics are the result of mutation.

The mating process has resulted in an offspring population which includes the member O_3 which is the same distance of 6 from node 3 as P_1 in the parent population. This is manifested by both these members having the same fitness value (0.0278). Additionally, O_3 has the highest fitness value among the offspring population and is rewarded with a high value for $f_{i,norm}$ which in turn results in a high probability of this member surviving into the next parent generation. However, the total fitness value F_t of the offspring population is less than that of the parent population indicating that an overall improvement from one population to the next is not guaranteed.

We now have two populations (parent and offspring) each containing 4 members which will provide the members of the next generation. Because the probability of survival (i.e. P_s Value) is 0.5, on average the next generation will be made up from two members of each population. Table 10.4 shows how the members M1–M4 of the next generation are selected. For each member of the new population a random number is generated. This is shown in the *parent vs. offspring* row in Table 10.4. If the random number is >0.5 (>P_s) the parent population is selected; otherwise the offspring population is used. Once the population has been selected, another random number in the range 0.0 to 1.0 is generated to select which member of the chosen population survives to the next generation.

For example, when selecting member M1 for the next generation, the *parent vs. offspring* random number generated is 0.678 which means the parent population is selected. The next random number generated is 0.257 which selects member P_1 using the $f_{i,accu}$ column of Table 10.2. This process

Table 10.4.   Survival of offspring members.

	M1	M1	M2	M2	M3	M3	M4	M4
Parent vs. Offspring	0.678	—	0.298	—	0.987	—	0.457	—
Survived Parents	0.257	$P1$	—	—	0.71	$P3$	—	—
Survived Offspring	—	—	0.026	$O1$	—	—	0.609	$O3$

Table 10.5. Third generation.

P_i	A	B	Look	Path	Cromosome	Fitness	$f_{i,norm}$	$f_{i,accu}$
P_1	4	10	3	(1,2,4)	00100 01010	0.0277	0.288	0.288
P_2	-7	-14	3	(1,5)	11101 01111	0.0204	0.212	0.500
P_3	8	15	3	(1,2,4)	00010 11110	0.0204	0.212	0.712
P_4	0	-6	3	(1,5)	00000 01101	0.02278	0.288	1.0
								$F_t = 0.096$

O_i	P_i	P_i	—	—	—	—	—	—	A	B	K
O_1	P_3	P_1	3	(1,2,4)	00010 11010	0.1111	0.689	0.689	8	11	7
O_2			3	(1,2,4)	10100 11110	0.0099	0.062	0.751	5	15	
O_3	P_2	P_4	3	(1,2,4)	11000 01101	0.0123	0.077	0.828	3	-6	4
O_4			3	(1,5)	00011 01111	0.0278	0.172	1.0	-8	-14	
											$F_t = 0.161$

	M1	M1	M2	M2	M3	M3	M4	M4
Parent vs. Offspring	0.034	—	0.295	—	0.785	—	0.546	—
Survived Parents	—	—	—	—	0.540	$P3$	0.952	$P4$
Survived Offspring	0.158	$O1$	0.331	$O1$	—	—	—	—

is repeated for each member of the new population. The new generation is shown in the top part of Table 10.5.

The whole process repeats itself again, until all nodes are traversed. Table 10.5 presents the third generation of the test run. The third generation of the parent population has a total fitness increase over the second generation which can be seen in F_t. The offspring population, produced by crossover and mutation, generated a test data O_1 which is only three integer units $(11 - 8 = 3)$ away from the global optimum according to node 3. A high fitness value is calculated for this member and is chosen to survive twice into the next generation. Table 10.6 presents the fourth generation.

In the offspring population, two test sets (O_1 and O_4) have been generated which are close to satisfying the goal. O_4 is actually closer to the *global optimum* and, therefore, has a higher fitness value. The total fitness F_t has improved by 280 from the third to the fourth generation. Table 10.7 presents the fifth generation.

In general the total fitness value F_t increases over several generations. Node 3 has been traversed in the fifth generation with the test data set of

Table 10.6. Fourth generation.

P_i	A	B	Look	Path	Cromosome	Fitness	$f_{i,norm}$	$f_{i,accu}$
P_1	8	11	3	(1,2,4)	00010 11010	0.1111	0.411	0.411
P_2	8	11	3	(1,2,4)	00010 11010	0.1111	0.411	0.822
P_3	8	15	3	(1,2,4)	00010 11110	0.0204	0.075	0.897
P_4	0	−6	3	(1,5)	00000 01101	0.0278	0.103	1.0
								$F_t = 0.27$

O_i	P_i	P_i	—	—	—	—	—	—	A	B	K
O_1	P_1	P_2	3	(1,2,4)	10010 11010	0.2499	0.199	0.199	9	11	2
O_2			3	(1,5)	00010 11011	0.0028	0.002	0.201	8	−11	
O_3	P_4	P_3	3	(1,2,4)	00000 01110	0.0051	0.004	0.205	0	14	8
O_4			3	(1,2,4)	00011 11101	0.9990	0.795	1.0	−8	−7	
											$F_t = 1.26$

	M1	M1	M2	M2	M3	M3	M4	M4
Parent vs. Offspring	0.691	—	0.124	—	0.753	—	0.498	—
Survived Parents	0.356	$P1$	—	—	0.861	$P3$	—	—
Survived Offspring	—	—	0.551	$O4$	—	—	0.050	$O1$

Table 10.7. Fifth generation.

P_i	A	B	Look	Path	Cromosome	Fitness	$f_{i,norm}$	$f_{i,accu}$
P_1	8	11	3	(1,2,4)	00010 11010	0.1111	0.081	0.081
P_2	−8	−7	3	(1,2,4)	00011 11101	0.9990	0.724	0.805
P_3	8	15	3	(1,5)	00010 11110	0.0204	0.015	0.820
P_4	9	11	3	(1,2,4)	10010 11010	0.2499	0.180	1.0
								$F_t = 1.38$

O_i	P_i	P_i	—	—	—	—	—	$f_{i,accu}$	A	B	K
O_1	P_4	P_1	3	(1,2,3)	11010 11010	100.0			11	11	9
O_2					00010 11011				8	−11	
O_3	P_3	P_4			00010 10010				8	9	6
O_4					10110 11110				13	15	

O_1 with A = B = 11. As soon as the last node has been traversed the test run finishes.

Figure 10.5 shows the test data in each parent population which were generated using GA in the different sub domains. It can be seen that the test data get closer to the domain of the path (1, 2, 3) (the diagonal). The

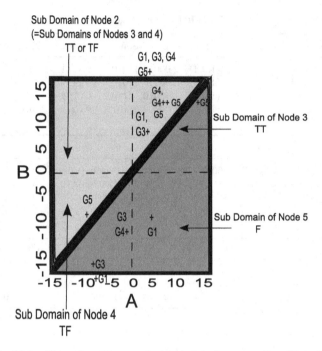

Fig. 10.5.   Example with generated test data for generation G1 to G5.

test data which traversed node 3 is the point (11, 11), as shown in Fig. 10.5. No test points are drawn for the second generation G2, because they are identical to the first generation G1. The limitation with the discussed test data generator is that, it cannot generate boolean or enumerated type test data. Miller *et al.* [8] have solved this problem. They [8] have proposed a method for test data generation using *Program Dependence Graph* and GA.

10.5. Summary

Automatic test case generation is an important and challenging activity in software testing. Again to get good test data is a NP–Complete problem. In this chapter, we have discussed issues relating to the path wise test data generator. We have also discussed the basic concepts of Genetic Algorithm. The chapter concludes with a discussion of path wise test data generation using GA with an example. It is observed that non redundant test data for a test suite can be generated automatically using GA.

References

1. R. Mall. *Fundamentals of Software Engineering*, (Prentice-Hall, 2005), second edition.
2. P. C. Jorgensen. *Software Testing: A Crafts man's Approach*, (CRC Press, 2002), second edition.
3. M. H. S. Yoo. Pareto efficient multi-objective test case selection. In *Proceedings of the International Symposium on Software Testing and Analysis*, pp. 140–150, (2007).
4. D. E. Goldberg. *Genetic Algorithms in Search, Optimization and Machine Learning*, (Addison-Wesley, 1989).
5. R. S. Pressman. *Software Engineering: A Practitioner's Approach*, (McGraw-Hill, Inc., 2000).
6. M. Mitchell. *An Introduction to Genetic Algorithms*, (First MIT Press paperback edition, 1998).
7. H. H. Sthamer. *The Automatic Generation of Software Test Data Using Genetic Algorithms*. PhD thesis, University of Glamorgan, (November, 1995).
8. J. Miller, M. Reformat, and H. Zhang, Automatic test data generation using genetic algorithm and program dependence graphs, *Information and Software Technology.* **48**, 586–605, (2006).